The Changing Face of Football

The Changing Face of Football

Racism, Identity and Multiculture in the English Game

Les Back, Tim Crabbe and John Solomos

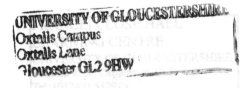

BERG

Oxford • New York

First published in 2001 by
Berg
Editorial offices:
150 Cowley Road, Oxford, OX4 1JJ, UK
838 Broadway, Third Floor, New York, NY 10003-4812, USA

Berg is an imprint of Oxford International Publishers Ltd.

Library of Congress Cataloging-in-Publication Data
A catalogue record for this book is available from the Library of Congress.

British Library Cataloguing-in-Publication Data
A catalogue record for this book is available from the British Library.

ISBN 1 85973 478 2 (Cloth)
1 85973 483 9 (Paper)

Typeset by JS Typesetting, Wellingborough, Northants.
Printed in the United Kingdom by Biddles Ltd, Guildford and King's Lynn.

For Charlie, Louis and Daniel

Contents

Preface   ix

Introduction   1

Part 1 Fan Cultures and Local Cultures of Racism

1   Mapping Race and Racism in Football Cultures   21

2   'Playing at Home': Community, Ritual and Race   39

3   Wearing the Shirt: Exclusion and Dialogue in Football Fan Cultures   75

4   Faces of Racists, Sounds of Hate: Football Fans, Abuse and
       Structures of Antipathy   103

Part 2 Racism Inside the Game

5   'One of the Lads': Accommodation and Resistance within
       Football-playing Cultures   139

6   'There is No Racism in Football': Football Institutions and the
       Politics of Race   161

7   'Let's Kick Racism Out of Football': Anti-Racism and
       Multiculturalism in English Football   185

Part 3 Race, Nation and Diaspora

8   'Keep St George in My Heart': England Fans, Race, Nation and
       Identity   221

9   Gringos, Reggae Gyals and 'Le Francais de la Souche Recente':
       Diaspora, Identity and Cosmopolitanism   253

Conclusion   277

Bibliography   289

Index   303

Preface

The primal scene for the genesis of this book was a grey Saturday afternoon at the Hawthorns. By an accident of fate the three of us found ourselves in the West Bromwich Albion ground as the Baggies prepared to face the south London side Crystal Palace on 12 September 1993. It will come as no surprise to anyone who has followed John Solomos' publishing career to find out that he is a dedicated West Bromwich Albion fan. This fact is celebrated in each of his many books whose acknowledgements sections read like a season-by-season record of the Baggies' fortunes. As is customary at English football, fans are often stopped and searched on their way into the ground. This afternoon was no exception. A very surprised West Midlands policeman was confused to find on frisking one of the most prominent professors of British sociology, a copy of the *Guardian* newspaper, a packet of Thornton's sweets, and a heavy philosophical tome by Friedrich Nietzsche. Although John lives in London he was a season ticket holder. He had followed West Brom since his childhood in Cyprus and continued his infatuation with football when his family came to London in the 1960s like so many Greek Cypriots.

John sometimes used his many trips to Birmingham to catch up with Les Back with whom he'd collaborated on a piece of research into race and local politics in the second city. Afterwards, they would often go on to the game together. This game was particularly special because Les Back was born in Croydon, the London borough from which Crystal Palace draws most of its following. Although not a Palace fan himself, favouring instead south London rivals Millwall, the game was still something of an 'academic derby'. Tim Crabbe, himself an equally dedicated football fan, was standing in the visitors end supporting his beloved Crystal Palace. He stood opposite his future colleagues and watched his team trounce the Baggies 4–1 in front of a crowd of 13,000 people. As West Brom's fate was sealed in the second half the atmosphere in the ground became sour and laced with racism. The project had begun but we didn't quite know it yet.

The Hawthorns is on the edge of the Handsworth district of Birmingham. The bus from the city centre of Birmingham takes fans along the Soho Road. The sari shops, Hindi film outlets and west Indian food stalls register the diversity of people from India, Pakistan, Jamaica and the rest of the Caribbean who, along with their children, have made this place their home. It is striking that going to football at West Brom one is reminded in stark terms that there is an absence of traffic between the fact of multiculture in Handsworth and the almost exclusive whiteness of the Hawthorns. It is as if these two worlds pass each other without ever touching; they coexist temporarily on the streets with limited social intimacy.

Inside the ground that day there was almost no presence that reflected the cultural dowry of Handsworth. This was quite another kind of place. It was the home of what was left of the Black Country's white working class, drawn from the former industrial towns of Smethwick, Oldbury and Sandwell. The departure of its factories and heavy industry left the Black Country a derelict landscape haunted by the ghost of work. West Brom had also been a historic place where black players had established themselves. In the late 1970s and early 1980s West Brom boasted three top-class black footballers in Laurie Cunningham, Cyrille Regis and Brendon Batson. The 'Three Degrees', as manager Ron Atkinson dubbed them, made a historic impact on English football because it was the first time that such a significant proportion of an English side was comprised of black players. They encountered torrents of abuse, hate letters and threats as they ran the gauntlet every Saturday at places such as West Ham, Liverpool and Manchester United.

On this autumn day in 1993 the situation was very different. West Brom fielded an all-white team. The Crystal Palace side registered the acceleration in the rise of black professionals since the days of Cunningham, Batson and Regis. Six black players started for Palace in a side that included John Salako, Chris Armstrong, Eric Young, Paul Williams, Richard Shaw and Bobby Bowry, with two black players on the subs bench (Dean Gordon and David Whyte). The game started well for West Brom and they led one nil at half time, but with the second half things went all the Londoners' way. This Palace team captained by Gareth Southgate – himself destined for international notoriety while playing for England – were at the beginning of a momentous season that would eventually see them promoted to the top flight as First Division champions. Palace overwhelmed the Baggies in the second half and were simply too strong for them. As the goals by Chris Coleman, Gareth Southgate, Chris Armstrong and David Whyte flew in, the atmosphere turned to poison in the home end. A young white man in his twenties repeatedly spat racist abuse at the Palace players – 'Fuck off you nigger cunt.' One of the white Palace players, Chris Coleman, who showed on his skin the signs of a summer Ibiza sun tan, was also targeted for racial abuse. 'You fucking dirty Paki' screamed the same man. The force of his words stained the air and seemed to propel him forward knocking into a group of supporters that included Les Back and John Solomos. The intensity of the racism was prodigious, yet the people bringing it to voice were seemingly 'respectable' fans. Down the isle of the stand still in earshot of this bile was a single Asian man wearing a blue and white scarf.

C. Wright Mills wrote in 1959 that often our private lives feel like a series of traps while societal forces bear down on us so that 'in other milieu [we] remain spectators' (Mills 1959: 3). For Les and John there was a sense of being trapped and unable to counter the voice of hate found here in the most public of private obsessions. It felt as if it was impossible to do anything but be a bystander and spectator because to speak out was to run the risk of being trapped in a crowd of recriminators. This was exacerbated by the fact that both were committed to countering racism in their work. Les Back – from a white English background – had written about youth and popular racism, and John – from a Greek Cypriot migrant background – had by this point been writing on and researching racism for over ten years. The frustration and culpability felt in that moment was to have an enduring and spectral effect. Its haunting quality provided one of the intellectual and ethical drives behind this project. This punitive silence, policed by a worry about the consequences of speaking out, meant that in that unnerving moment we were cast in what Primo Levi called 'the zone of grey consciences' (Levi 1987: 171). We have been stirred to write so much because here we said so little.

At the Smethwick End the air was sweeter, though the open stand meant that the jubilant Palace fans were exposed to the elements. They didn't seem to care. Tim Crabbe was amongst the celebrating horde of south Londoners, already thinking that this might be their year. Tim, a white activist, had become a prominent member of the Football Supporters Association and was becoming involved in the nascent Let's Kick Racism Out of Football campaign. Tim was also working at the University of Birmingham as a sociologist.

We had all witnessed the profound tensions evident in English football. In the major cities like Birmingham football grounds had remained a bastion of whiteness in which racism could be expressed openly to such a degree that even those who opposed it felt helpless to say anything in response. Yet, a new generation of young black footballers was coming through into the professional ranks. The line separating the field from stadium had become a contact zone separating two faces of England. On the pitch the fact of cultural diversity was only too evident. Nevertheless, the social composition of the stands pointed to the ways in which white Englishness remained unaffected by the cultural diversity that increasingly defined what it meant to live in England.

The three of us came to this research from quite different directions. We met in part through the fact that Tim and Les worked together at the time in the Department of Cultural Studies, University of Birmingham. The game at the Hawthorns gave us a common point of reference to anchor our idea for investigating the political, cultural and theoretical consequences of the drama we had witnessed unfolding on that Saturday afternoon. To a large extent the intellectual problems posed by the combination of change and continuity in football were set against Tim's immediate political priority of finding ways of thinking critically about what was happening inside the anti-racist football campaigns. The research project entitled the Cultures of Racism in Football Project (R000 23 5639) was funded by the

Economic and Social Research Council (ESRC) and enabled Tim Crabbe and Les Back to work on the project full time. We are grateful to the ESRC for their support.

We all shared a common interest and love for football, so this book has been a labour of love. However, on many occasions it has been less than comfortable having to associate with convicted racists and witness them in action. The book is the product of three different people with a shared goal. This should not be read as an attempt to reflect a single extant reality. The stories we record in the pages that follow and the things we have observed are as particular observers at specific times. These are not views through some omniscient eye that is placeless yet sees all. As Clifford Geertz has commented:

> The renunciation of the authority that comes from 'views from nowhere' ('I've seen reality and it's real') is not a loss, it's a gain, and the stance of 'well, I, a middle-class, mid-twentieth-century American, more or less standard, male, went out to this place, talked to some people I could get to talk to me, and think things are sort of rather this way with them there' is not a retreat, it's an advance. It's unthrilling perhaps, but it has (something in short supply in the human sciences) a certain candour. (Geertz 2000: 137)

Rather, the account that we offer in this book is from the vantage point of positioned or situated observers (Rosaldo 1989), or what George Marcus terms the move from the omniscient 'ethnographic eye' to the personal 'I' who see at a particular moment (Marcus 1994: 41). In large part the field research was conducted by Tim and Les, both white, male ethnographers in their thirties.

> It seems to me that the whole question of where one is when writing has to do with this – it's that phrase used by Robert Capa who said something like 'agh you know, when the picture's not good enough – go closer.' And it seems to me what I've tried to do in maybe all the books I've written is to get in very close and then to try and bring something back from a starting point outside. How much I succeed, and what I am bringing back, I often don't know [. . .] maybe the actual way I work implies this displacement, this displacement of going in as close as you dare, and then finding, sometimes with difficulty, a way back. (John Berger, from an interview with Jeremy Isaacs – *Face to Face* BBC 1995)

We wanted to capture and record, as far as possible, the dynamics that we had witnessed at the Hawthorns: to come as close as we could to the ways in which racism featured in football culture, while trying to understand what it was like inside football itself. This involved a detailed ethnography of what was going on either side of the 'white line'. Following Paul Willis and Mats Trondman we aspire to the 'development of reflexive forms of social theorizing, allowing some kind of voice to those who live their conditions of existence' (Willis and Trondman

2000: 7). All three of us had participated in the cultures of football support, played football – to different levels – and were committed to presenting a critical yet fair portrayal of football fandom and the institutions of the game.

Since starting the project properly in 1995 we have tried to combine academic work with writing for popular journals, newspapers and football fanzines. We have approached the writing of this book with the aim of making it accessible to the general reader while not compromising the complexity of the subject matter. Each of the main chapters of the book begins with a particular context that sets the scene for the issues we want to examine. Our intention here is to situate the reader in the social reality in which the issues we want to discuss are most intensely at play. Our intention is to provide as vivid a picture of football culture as possible while unsettling conventional wisdom and common-sense.

We have attempted to combine the process of writing this book and conducting the research with making a contribution, however modest, to anti-racist campaigns and local strategies for countering racism in football. Tim Crabbe, as part of his role as Chair of the Football Supporters Association, was integral to the United Colours of Football fan initiative and the first stages of the Let's Kick Racism Out of Football campaign. Tim also served on the multi-agency Advisory Group Against Racism and Intimidation. Collectively the three of us conducted an evaluation of the 1995/96 Let's Kick Racism Out of Football campaign, which culminated in the publication of '*Alive and Still Kicking': An Overview Evaluation of Anti-Racist Campaigning in Football* (1996). In the aftermath of this report we have – collectively and individually – been involved in the evaluation of the anti-racist theatre productions put on by Arc Theatre Ensemble. In addition, since 1998 Les Back served at chair of the Kick It Out – South London Initiative a localized strategy of the Kick It Out Campaign. He is also an active member of Millwall Football Club's Anti-Racism Committee.

The three of us have chosen to write the book in a single voice. The reason for this is in part to avoid the clutter of personal pronouns and individual claims to responsibility and culpability for what is on the page. One of the dangers of this strategy is that some of the nuances of the dialogues with each of us contained within the material may be obscured. As Pierre Bourdieu has rightly stated, writing ethnography involves reconciling the complications and nuances in the research data and in the research process with the desire to produce a readable narrative accessible to its potential readers (Bourdieu 1999b: 622).

It has taken us five years to complete this study. We could have chosen a more traditional line of academic investigation in this book and kept out of the messy world of politics and policy. If we had, the book would certainly have been written sooner. However, we would have learned much less and probably this would have been a less interesting study. We certainly gained much from our direct involvement in the campaigns but there have been times when we have become part of the story we try to tell in these pages. Where relevant we've tried to discuss our position within football culture and integrate it into the analysis.

There are many people that we need to thank. First, there have been people involved in the world of football who helped us with access, insight and feedback. In particular we'd like to thank Ken Chapman, David Dean, Laurie Dhal, Graham Ennis, Asquith Gibbes, Mark Gilman, Howard Holmes, Piara Powar, Ben Tegg and John Tottman. Second, there are several colleagues and writers who have helped us sharpen our ideas and we would like to thank Alice Bloch, Adam Brown, Ben Carrington, Stephen Dobson, Paul Gilroy, Syd Jeffers, Michael Keith, Colin King, John Masouri, Karim Murji, Pat Slaughter, Fran Tonkiss, Garry Robson, Flemming Røgilds and Neil Watson. Third many friends have contributed to the completion of this book; in particular we would like to thank Dom Bercelli, John Curran, Ben Gidley, Mark and Debbie Glynn, Paul Goodwin, Roxy Harris, Lez Henry, Kevin Jones, Pete Jones, Paul Moody, Ash Newall, John and Irene Welsh, Ron Warshow and Nigel Woodcock. Our respective institutions helped to give us the space and time to conclude the writing of this book. Also, special thanks to Sebastian Lexer who provided the football song transcriptions in Chapter 2 and Mark Edmondson who helped with the preparation of the photographs contained in the book. Last, but not least, we would like to thank Kathryn Earle for having faith in the project and for being a rightfully impatient editor in order to expedite the book's completion.

Of course none of the above should be held responsible for the lines of argument developed in what follows. We would also like to thank all the fans, players, managers and the people involved in football who gave us their time to discuss the issue of racism and multiculturalism in football. We have tried to protect the identities of those people who wanted their views to remain confidential. While respecting these wishes we hope that they recognize themselves in this portrait of the changing face of football. Our initial impulse was to break out of the confinement of being a mere 'spectator' named so eloquently by C. Wright Mills and turn private troubles into public issues. At the very least we hope this book is compelling and transcends the comfortable stereotypes that have pervaded the public debate about racism in football.

Les Back
Tim Crabbe
John Solomos

London and Manchester

Introduction

The rituals of Englishness are on display as the nation settles to watch the biggest event in the sporting calendar. Wembley, drenched in sunshine, prepared to bring the 1997 football season to a close with the denouement of the FA Cup competition. The military band leads Cliff Richard and the capacity crowd through *Abide with Me* and the national anthem; but this final between Chelsea and Middlesbrough seemed different. Chelsea, managed by the black Dutchman and former international player, Ruud Gullit, eventually triumph 2–0 over a cosmopolitan Middlesbrough side that included the Italian Fabrizio Ravanelli and the famed Brazilians Juninho and Emerson. The Middlesbrough fans' performance of the unlikely phenomenon of a 'Teeside Samba' at Wembley seemed to signal that local football culture, even in England's North East, has assimilated new rhythms and textures. The match marked something more than a new beginning for the victorious West London club. It captured in microcosm the changing face of English football.

As Chelsea's 'cheeky cockney' Denis Wise lifted the cup for his club for the first time in 26 years the television coverage cut to the jubilant Chelsea fans. Two young black men appear in club colours singing 'Chelsea, Chelsea – Chelsea, Chelsea' as Suggs' Cup Final anthem *Blue Day* rang out of Wembley's PA system. One row behind them a white fan wearing a wig of dreadlocks with blue and white beads added his voice to the celebrations. The victory was billed as an opportunity to begin a new era and put to rest the ghost of Chelsea's 1970s success, when the club won major domestic and European titles. The game also promised another kind of break with the past, when Chelsea was a club closely associated with bigotry and racism.

When Chelsea's first black English player, striker Paul Cannoville, took to the Selhurst Park field to face Crystal Palace at the end of the 1981–2 football season he was met by monkey grunts and racist abuse from his *own* fans (see Williams et al., 1989: 83). Indeed one of us bore witness to this spectacle, which is remembered vividly by Crystal Palace and Chelsea fans alike. Equally, Pat Nevin, who is white and played alongside Cannoville in that Chelsea team, recalled the shock he felt. When interviewed after the game he made his feelings plain:

> I just told the journalists that I was disgusted with the Chelsea fans for the way in which they were treating one of our players. Before the next game, David Speedie,

Kerry Dixon and myself all walked out on to the pitch alongside Cannoville in a show of support. Normally, the fans would always sing my name, or the names of Speedie or Dixon, first. But this time they started to sing Paul's name first. It was one of the most moving moments of my footballing career. A group of players had said something and it had an effect on the fans. It wasn't just my comments. It was also the actions of David and Kerry, in showing solidarity, that helped to turn the tables on racist chanting. I'm not saying that we eliminated it. But it was a lovely moment and it helped to point the way forward. It was an important turning point. It gave the whole team, not just the black players, a genuine lift. (quoted in Thrills 1998: 67)

Could the scene at Wembley be read as a realization of the anti-racist statement made by Nevin and his associates? The team's fortunes had been rejuvenated by foreign imports like Roberto Di Matteo, Gianfranco Zola and Frank Leboeuf combined with a legion of black English players including Eddie Newton and Frank Sinclair. All of these images are signs of changing times, certainly in relation to the role of race and ethnicity in English football culture. But what do they tell us? Do they signify that English football is becoming more multicultural? Is racism a thing of the past in popular football cultures? In the recent past, after all, football grounds provided one of the largest public arenas in which racism could be openly expressed. Does the transformation of clubs like Chelsea from an apparent bastion of overt fan racism to an international trendsetter mean that the form and quality of football racism has shifted radically? It is precisely these questions that we have addressed in the course of our research on cultures of racism in English football, and they form the background to this study of the changing dynamics of racism in football cultures.

A key concern that shaped our initial thinking about this project was the need to go beyond the convenient and simplistic stereotypes that shape much popular discussion about racism in football or other spheres of life. As we have tried to show in our previous work, racism is inherently a complex and changing ideology that needs to be situated in specific social and political environments (Solomos and Back 1996, Back and Solomos 2000). Thus in practice the rejection of overt racism in one moment can co-exist with exclusion and discrimination in other times and places. The point we want to stress here is that the first question to wrestle with is the fact that there are contradictions and ambivalence within the culture of racism in football that have been largely glossed over in the way the issue has been dealt with publicly. It is feasible for the same crowds of fans, in this case Chelsea, to have – at different times – vilified black players as subhumans and eulogized them as sporting heroes. We want to try and make sense of these ambivalences and take them seriously.

It is with such images and questions that we began our research on the cultures of racism in football. Before moving on to the substantive parts of the book we want to situate our research within the context of the key empirical and theoretical issues that provided us with the starting point for our own project. We then move on to examine some of the limitations of these frameworks and draw on the findings of our research project in order to suggest an alternative way of framing questions about racism and multiculturalism in football. Our starting point is that the transformations that have occurred within English football in recent years mean that it is necessary to revise radically the way in which we understand racism in football and other popular cultural arenas.

Unfinished Legacy of Racism in Sport

In recent years the emergence and prominence of black sporting figures has precipitated comment from a range of commentators and critics. For example St Lucian poet and Nobel prize winner Derek Walcott told the *Observer* newspaper in the summer of 2000: 'I'm still amazed and thrilled that the captain of the English cricket team is of Indian descent and when I see black footballers playing for England' (The *Observer*, 2 September 2000). For intellectuals like Walcott, who spent their youth under colonial rule, the fact that the icons of English national pride include amongst their ranks children from the former colonies is a profound twist of history. Here black sportsmen and women display both a promise of multicultural change and the paradox of neo-colonial racism. Similarly Stuart Hall has been moved to write:

> Nothing is closer to the heart of the average Englishman – as opposed to the fields where classically blacks have been outstanding, such as cricket and boxing – than the heartland of soccer . . . There isn't an occasion when you can pick up a decent Sunday paper, with its photos of Saturday's matches, and not see black faces. Are blacks in the boardrooms of the clubs? Of course not. Are they relatively powerless in the institutions which organise the game? Of course. The question is whether they have any currency, any visibility in the culture of sport where the nation's myths and meanings are fabricated. The answer must be 'yes', and to say this is to note the significant degree to which the culture has turned in the past fifteen or so years. (Hall 1998: 43)

It shouldn't be a surprise that post-colonial intellectuals like Walcott and Hall should see the significance of sport, particularly as it relates to debates about race, nation and belonging. In many respects they have inherited the legacy of C. L. R. James, who tried to tell the story of empire from the vantagepoint of the imperial game's crease. James' classic book *Beyond a Boundary*, first published in 1963, showed how an analysis of the game of cricket can reveal social and political forces that lay beyond the boundary rope. 'West Indians crowding to Tests bring with them the whole past history and future hopes of the islands' writes James. He continues:

English people, for example, have a conception of themselves breathed from birth. Drake and mighty Nelson, Shakespeare, Waterloo, the Charge of the Light Brigade, the few who did so much for so many, the success of parliamentary democracy, those and such as those constitute a national tradition. We of the West Indies have none at all, none that we know of. To such people the three W's, Ram and Val wrecking English batting, help to fill a huge gap in their consciousness and in their need. (James 1983: 233)

For James sport was a place in which blows could be struck in the nascent struggles for independence and post-colonial autonomy. A place in which a sense of identity and pride could be garnered for those colonial subjects for whom history was a luxury denied to them by the colonizers. Reading this alongside Stuart Hall's analysis shows quite how far the debate about sport, culture and identity has come since the early days of independence. In the context of Britain today it is not just that sport provides a means for people of West Indian and other colonial backgrounds to establish a proud alternative identity to the nationalism of the imperial power. Rather, sport becomes a place in which national myths are reconfigured and the relationship between race and nation, at the heart of how Englishness has been traditionally constructed, redefined.

This is not to say that there has been a complete transformation of the mores of racial stereotyping and exclusion. Hall perceptively warns that the assimilation of black people within the national imagination as sporting heroes need not in any way be congruent with access to the centres of decision making and institutional power. This is a point that has been picked up recently by Paul Gilroy who has argued that sport has played a central role in both fetishizing racialized bodies and perpetuating ideas that 'reify race through icons of black physicality' (Gilroy 2000b: 258). More than this, Gilroy identifies the ways in which the economic success of black sportsmen also masks the enduring legacy of white supremacy. In particular, he cites the Brazilian football star Ronaldo. Gilroy writes about the circumscribed nature of black superstardom and the commercial forces that resulted in Ronaldo appearing in the World Cup Final against France in 1998, despite the fact that he had experienced what seemed like an epileptic seizure prior to the game. Gilroy argues: 'The Brazilian team's commercial sponsorship by the Nike Corporation, to which his iconic presence was deemed central, required him in sickness and health to assume his place in front of the cameras. For that descendant of slaves, the future suddenly began to look a lot like the past' (Gilroy 2000b: 348).

The point here is not that black sports stars are somehow equivalent to highly paid athletic chattel. No, there is something subtler at play. Whilst the sports arena may provide access to hero status, material wealth and personal liberation the stars that reap these rewards, both black and white, are performers reliant upon the patronage of, predominantly Western, white-dominated institutions and consumers. Within this medium of contemporary commercial sport, ideas about racial difference become exemplified and projected onto the bodies of black athletes. In this sense, sport can become the modality through which racial difference is made 'self evident' and is reproduced by stealth. This is not somehow the same as past moments of racial domination and white supremacy. But, rather the history of racial thinking is being piled up in the present. They are like continual aftershocks. The experience of Ronaldo, and other sportsmen who have found themselves in a similar position, cannot be understood simply as a remnant from the past. Equally the racism they experience is not solely created in the turbulence of the present. To borrow Walter Benjamin's famous phrase, the past 'flashes up at a moment of danger' (Benjamin 1992: 247). As Ronaldo's corporate masters order his appearance the legacy of racial domination erupts in the present. While at the same time, Ronaldo's prominence as one of the highest paid global sporting superstars vectors towards new twists and mutations in the condition of a select few within the African diaspora. In such circumstances there can be no innocent notion of linear progress, improvement or change.

One of our key interests in this study is to develop a sensitivity to precisely the ways in which new conditions are producing ruptures and changes, while at the same time recognising how racism can endure, be it in nascent or antecedent guises. So when reports are made that things are 'getting better' and that racism on the terraces is 'in decline' we should be sceptical and mindful that the future of the past, in this case the legacy of imperialism and slavery, is incomplete.

Equally, we want to suggest that the history of racism in sport is not already predetermined. In the rituals of sporting life the relationship between race, nation and inclusion is repeatedly stated and defined, through the 'us' that is manifest between teams and their devoted supporters. Here, 'race' and 'nation' function not as given entities but social forms that are staged through 'big games' and repeated sporting dramas. Their form and quality are defined through the perf-ormance itself and continuities are established through repetition. So, here 'race' is not a given but the process in which 'racial difference' in invoked and connected with issues of identity, entitlement and belonging (Miles 1989). Through focusing on the repeated or cyclical nature of these processes in sport, it is possible to identify moments in which ruptures occur that may challenge the tenets of racial exclusion.

It is within the everydayness of sport that we can find the micro enactment of inclusion/exclusion, group definition and identity. Interestingly, in their recent and much debated report, the Commission for the Future of Multi Ethnic Britain commented:

Sport is part of a place's cultural fabric. Among other things, it provides (at least for men, and particularly young men) a huge reservoir of talking points, and of shared memories, jokes and allusions, which transcend the rivalries that are an inherent part of sport. For there are shared values – the rules of the game, admiration for skill and teamwork, the concept of 'foe-honoring.' Sport is an essential element in the daily business of 'putting the world in order' through continuous chat and social interaction. (Parekh 2000 : 173)

Even in the definition of rivalries within sport there is recognition. The issue that we want to focus on is the degree to which the ways in which sporting cultures 'put the world together' implicitly constructs limits on the levels of participation from Britain's diverse minority communities.

We also want to argue that within these seemingly trivial pastimes there is real significance. Salman Rushdie has written that politics and sport – like art – are 'inextricably mixed, and that that mixture has consequences' (Rushdie 1991: 100). It is the consequences of the admixture of sport and politics, of sport, identity and belonging that we want to unravel in this book. This also involves facing the vexed question about how to define and conceptualize racism. The forms of racism that we want to highlight here are cast through either the racialized body (the notion that racial difference can be connected with athletic prowess, and by implication also cerebral function) and ossified notions of culture that are defined in the relationship between particular 'cultural groupings' and their relationship to sport and sporting cultures.

A recurring theme in the chapters that follow are the ways in which sporting racism operates through the logic of absolute biological or cultural difference. By exploring the articulation of this theme in various contexts we want to understand racism as a multiply inflected and changing discourse that organizes and defines human attributes along racial lines that code in an exclusive way the definition of identity, entitlement and belonging. In this sense, we want to suggest that the explicit presence of overt racist language is only one among an array of elements within what might be called the culture of racism. This involves understanding how forms of inclusion and exclusion operate through the interplay of overt racist practice and implicit racialized codings. So, our notion of a culture of racism also includes the normalizing whiteness that is at the centre of English football culture and the implicit connotations of what it means to belong and identify as a fan or what is defined inside the game as a 'football person'. Equally, we want to suggest that the culture of racism is unevenly developed and that it is important to resist 'blanket definitions' of racism, be it in relation to popular or institutional forms. One of the things that we want to guard against is the easy, some might say slothful, ways in which particular football clubs have been demonized as permanent bastions of racial hatred.

'Don't Go Down There, That's a Racist Club': Ritual, Identity and Football Culture

The issue of racism in football culture is either spoken of too much or too little. Football clubs are either designated as being entirely and thoroughly racist, or the issue is dismissed by fans, chairmen and administrators alike as having no relevance, through the assertion that 'we don't have a problem with racism in our club'. Particularly damaging in this regard is the tendency to define particular teams as 'racist clubs'. Football culture is by its very nature – two sides contesting a result – about constructing oppositions. These are always relational in that the definition of 'us' is always implicated in the form that its opposite – 'the them' – takes. In this respect the labelling of particular clubs as uniformly racist can provide a false comfort in that it designates the problem of racism as relevant to a few 'bad apple' clubs. Two of the clubs we chose to focus on ethnographically have been routinely defined in this way, namely Millwall and Everton. Yet, both of these clubs have complicated histories with regard to racism. It is true that racism is evident in both of these clubs, both historically and today, but they are certainly not monumental dens of racial bigotry and proto-fascism, as some popular images of them would have it.

Perhaps unsurprisingly during the course of our research we found that one of the characteristics of racism amongst supporters is its uneven nature. It is because of this unevenness that we found the circulation of a caricatured image of xenophobic football thugs ultimately unhelpful because it seems to us that it helps to mask the complexity and nuances within fan racism. It may be true that fan cultures of particular clubs embody different impulses with regard to the expression and performance of racism, but they do not necessarily explain in a mechanistic way the likelihood or frequency of racist abuse or action. It does, however, affect the way such actions are either inhibited or legitimized. One of the over-arching findings of our research is that racism amongst fans is both *relational* and *nested* within a particular milieu – it is situated in a specific ritual setting, within histories of cultural practice and local culture. It is for this reason that we chose to focus our ethnography on four English clubs in order to elicit contextual nuances.

In some respects this approach is similar to that found in the work of Christian Bromberger and his associates. We want to pause here to summarize some of the key insights that we are drawing from this work, in particular the issue of how to integrate such an appreciation of football ritual and questions of social identity and locality. Central to Bromberger's approach is the idea that football provides a means through which 'public' identities can be performed and embodied. It argues that the ostensibly secular culture of football 'is washed through by the sacred' (O'Connor 1993), so that it provides a means to express collective emblems of belonging that are lived rather than stated explicitly. This work focuses primarily on continental football and draws on anthropological analytical frameworks quite different from those found in British sociology or cultural studies. Bromberger argues, employing a Durkheimian sensitivity towards cultural representations, that the style of a particular club is part of a 'collective imaginary' in which fans 'narrate their team's game and their lives. For a young fan, progressively discovering the nature of local style is a kind of sentimental education in the values which model the city's and the region's imaginary' (Bromberger et al. 1993a: 91). Within the stadium and through match day rituals public identities are defined and whilst these may be inflected with class meaning and association they cannot be simplistically reduced to them. So, the football encounter results in what Bromberger refers to as a 'spectacularisation of social relations' (Bromberger et al. 1993a: 100). The football ground is transformed during the fixture as the fans turn the stadium into a theatre in which collective identities are mobilized and commemorated.

The importance of Bromberger's analysis for this discussion is that he points us towards the significance that these spectacular representations of identity have for the relative balance between cultural openness and exclusivity. In his discussion of L'Olympique de Marseille he points out that foreign players in Marseille more often than not possess a 'superior aura' when compared to French players of equal talent. This he suggests is the result of the complex and ambiguous quality that the representation of the foreigner possesses in the context of this Mediterranean city-port. Here:

> The foreigner has a double image. On the one hand, devalued, that of the poor immigrant, arriving on masse to earn a livelihood in the port, in industry or in commerce. On the other hand, there is the image of the foreigner coming from the sea, founding the city [Marseille was founded by a Phoenician sailor, who married Gyptis, the daughter of a local kind. The Medallion that some L'Olympique de Marseille supporters wear has a picture of this couple on the emblem]. A pioneer, bearer of material and symbolic riches, bringer of glory and prosperity for the city, he is capable of hoisting high the image of the 'golden city unjustly despised.' It is in this second register that the figure of the foreign star plays on the imagination of Marseille, a symbol of an ideal cosmopolitanism of the city, where the presence of the Other is to be a source of wealth and honour, not conflict and stigmatisation. (Bromberger et al. 1993b: 123)

Bromberger's attention to the interplay between the 'collective imaginary' of L'Olympique de Marseille, and Marseille more generally, and the emergence of foreign players and patterns of immigration and ethnic minority settlement suggests that adulation of 'foreign stars' can go hand in hand with social exclusion. While the foreign star players are lionized as 'contemporary Phoenicians,' local Arab youth bear the stigma of the unwanted 'immigrant'. It is precisely the variegation in the culture of racism that we are concerned to identify. Bromberger's approach offers a useful way into these questions because of its attention to the relationship between locality, history, myth and collective memory.

The ritual practices, or 'master symbols' (Mills 1957) of football fans cannot be simply seen as either reactionary and conservative or alternatively anti-hegemonic forms of popular resistance. They open up alternative public spheres. In this sense clubs are 'owned' by their fans within the realm of symbolism and ritual, regardless of the corporate shareholders who hold legal claim to ownership within the structures of the contemporary professional game. At the same time, fan cultures possess an often implicit normative structure that is coded in terms of race, class and gender. These variegations in how the 'norm' is defined (what a 'normal fan' connotes, looks like and where s/he comes from) police and limit those who can belong to and legitimately wear the teams colours through the ever present normalizing gaze of the fan collective. This normative structure is embodied in the recursive patterns of fan culture defined in match day rituals, the social networks of sporting gossip and rumour, the definition and reproduction of collective memory and the ecology of particular urban settings. This process of defining collective representations works at both a local and a national level.

The composition of fan cultures might be best described as what John Berger refers to as a 'screen of clichés'. Berger writes: 'Every culture produces such a screen, partly to facilitate its own practices (to establish habits) and partly to consolidate its own power' (Berger 1991: 72–3). In this sense we want to see the ways in which particular fan cultures consolidate the power of tradition and identity through informal means. As a fan buys an entry ticket to a game he or she is also trying to gain access to a symbolic collectivity. Such passports to inclusion are issued through informal means and involve the internal assimilation of skills, dispositions, attitudes and identities. We will return throughout the book to this notion of the 'entry ticket' as a metaphor for thinking about the position of ethnic minorities in football. For now, we want to signal that the exclusion or inclusion of ethnic minority fans needs to be understood in relation to the normative structure of fan cultures. More than this, the price of an 'entry ticket' to English football for an ethnic minority fan often involves leaving alternative traditions of football support and their cultural mores at the turnstiles.

Researching Race and Racism in Football

The main focus of our research has been to use detailed qualitative research amongst football fans and institutions of football clubs to establish a picture of the contemporary forms of racism within football culture. This is why we stress the importance of understanding the expressions of racism in football within particular institutional, regional or national settings, while at the same time developing an awareness of the broader patterns in racist action. In order to get to these different levels of analysis we decided to focus on a series of professional local clubs, the English national team's support and the support engendered within the diaspora of the Jamaican and Indian national teams. The local clubs we chose to focus on included two in the north of England (Manchester City and Everton) and two in the south of England (Crystal Palace and Millwall). We chose these clubs because each in different ways had become associated with manifestations of racism and/or the changes we were interested in examining.

Initially only one of the clubs (Crystal Palace) agreed to be involved in the research. This meant we were faced with a considerable dilemma of how to approach the issue of racism inside the institutions of football given the resistance that existed to outside interventions. We decided to keep the case studies and continue with the research without official collaboration. Eventually, our second London club (Millwall) agreed to co-operate with the research. However, with a few exceptions the higher levels of management and administration within the two northern clubs (Everton and Manchester City) remained closed to the research.

In order to compensate for the lack of access to the northern clubs we decided to broaden our focus and interview a wide variety of people within the institutions of football. As a result we have had only limited success with regard to the institutional dimension of the case-study research. However, we feel confident that broadening our focus to other clubs has produced a unique and interesting insight into the forms of racism that haunt the institutions of professional football both on and off the pitch more broadly. In a similar fashion to the approach discussed in relation to fans previously, we wanted to look at the ways in which the professional cultures of English football define the 'norm' and the ways in which the normative forms within player cultures and the footballing institutions inhibit or enable change and cultural diversity.

The central concern of the research was to collect data relating to the qualitative nature of racism within football culture. The methods we deployed were specifically tailored to particular aspects of football culture and the sample groupings. These are best summarized under the following headings.

Fan Ethnography

This part of the ethnography focused on

1 participant observation in football stadia and the related leisure spaces of fan culture including public houses, clubs and fan organizations;
2 semi-structured and informal unstructured interviews with football fans;
3 life story audio diaries kept by fans.

Audio tape recordings were made of each of the games we attended. The participant observation started during the 1995–6 season and continued to the end of the research period in 2000. We carried a tape recorder so that an aural record was made from which reliable data could be gathered on the frequency and form of racist interjections from football fans. As the research developed it became particularly important to be able to make accurate observations of the precise timing of fan song cycles. Retrospective ethnographic reporting was simply not detailed enough to be sure of the validity of the timing of particular observations. Through using audio tapes, retrospective reports and video material it was possible to develop an understanding of the relationship between fan responses within the stands and the action on the pitch.

The frequency and quality of racist activity varied between particular sections of the ground and even within stands. As a result we conducted observational work in all of the main seating sections of the stadia under study. In total we observed and recorded crowd behaviour at over 100 matches between January 1995 and December 2000. These also included participant observation at the Euro 96 tournament, during the 1998 World Cup and Euro 2000 qualifying and final tournaments and extensive field research with England fans both home and away.

In addition we conducted semi-structured interviews with over 100 fans. The club, gender and ethnic breakdown of this sample is outlined in Appendix 1. These interviews were organized around a series of common themes including: fan biography, locality and regional identity, particular fan culture, the emergence of black players, fan racism, football and the activities of the far Right, campaigns against racism, nationalism and support for the England team. We also asked 12 supporters to keep an audio diary during the 1995–6 football season. We prepared the diarists by providing information with regard to our core interests but then encouraged them to set their own agenda. Seven of the participants completed their diaries.

Players, Clubs and Football Institutions

One of the things we found in conducting interviews, particularly with players, managers and administrators, was the way in which these encounters were affected by the forms of talk associated with the public face of the game, which in most cases are directed at the news and sports media. We frequently encountered highly managed and defensive patterns of informant response. Accordingly it was important to remain sensitive to the particular contexts in which accounts were offered and their conventions. In this sense we have tried to analyse this data through an appreciation of the moral and cultural forms deployed by informants drawing on critical perspectives developed within sociology on the status of qualitative interview data (Silverman 1993).

Given the difficulties we encountered with access, we decided to approach a wide range of players, coaches and managers. In total we conducted semi-structured interviews with 34 professional and ex-professional footballers (12 white and 22 black). Where possible we spoke to players within our chosen case studies and beyond this we managed to secure interviews with some of the most prominent players in the English game along with players from lower divisions and those at the beginning of their careers. Additionally, we interviewed 11 managers and coaches (six white and five black). To complement the interview material we also conducted observational work in and around training grounds in an attempt to gain insight in to the daily routines of professional sport. We triangulated this data with the interview material to establish a sense of how the issues of race and racism featured in everyday interactions on the training ground, dressing room and players' lounge.

Observational work was also conducted inside football stadia on match days and included shadowing ground safety officers, stadium managers and stewards. This enabled us to collect data on the organizational management of fixtures and the internal workings of football clubs. We interviewed 17 people involved in football administration and marketing, ground safety and the 'football in the community' initiatives. In addition to this we interviewed 8 club chairmen and board members.

Anti-Racist Campaigns, Football Authorities and the Police

We felt it important to establish the ways in which the football bodies themselves were framing the issue of racism. For this reason we interviewed members of the Football Association, the Professional Footballers' Association and a number of referees and match officials. In addition to this we also interviewed small numbers of football agents, journalists and writers. Given our interest in the development of anti-racist initiatives we also conducted extensive work on the Let's Kick Racism/Respect All Fans initiative during the 1995/6 season. This included participant observation at meetings, campaign events and interviews with key actors involved in the initiative. In addition we evaluated Arc Theatre Ensemble's production entitled Kicking Out which was sponsored by the Advisory Group Against Racism and Intimidation (AGARI), the steering group for the Let's Kick Racism Out of Football Campaign. This work involved interviewing teachers, students and members of the production company (Back, Crabbe and Solomos 1996) and resulted in a total of thirty-six interviews. We have also worked with the company evaluating two subsequent football-related anti-racist plays. Finally, we interviewed eleven police officers who had responsibility for football related policing. These included Football Intelligence Officers, Match Commanders and members of Scotland Yard's Football Intelligence Unit.

A total of 222 interviews were completed for the research. Most of these interviews were tape recorded. The sensitive nature of the research matter meant that a number of informants were unwilling to be recorded and here interviews were reconstructed through field notes. In addition to this material an extensive collection of newspaper cuttings, campaign documents, fanzines and other related printed material was also collected.

One of our key aims was to present as faithful a picture as possible of the changing face of racism in football. We wanted, on the one hand, to attempt to construct a sympathetic picture of the experience of fans while at the same time remaining critical of the presence of racism amongst groups of supporters. This meant that we were placed in a sometimes ambiguous ethical position in relation to the people we were working with and the kinds of dialogues we were entering into.

As white researchers the ethical stakes were different when interviewing white or black and minority fans, players and people inside the game itself. Often black people were having to operate in white-dominated worlds and we wanted to avoid the research ending up in another kind of white scrutiny. Our intention was to listen faithfully and examine the ways in which they experienced English football culture and be alert and respectful to the range and variety of responses offered. Perhaps, our desire to transcend the sense of scrutiny can never be fully achieved. Equally, and as we have written elsewhere (Back 1996: 24), it is foolish to think that these relationships were not free from the effects of racism, which are perhaps always a matter of degree. Our aim was to open up the conditions for what Bourdieu calls 'non-violent communication' (Bourdieu 1999: 610) to listen actively with respect and to ask questions with humility.

The discussion of Jamaican fan cultures discussed in Chapter 9 was the only context where we tried to research a football context in which black fans were the hosts. This part of our ethnographic work was done by Les Back. It posed different kinds of issues and problems. On the one hand, there was a desire to record and describe the emergence of a form of spectator culture that had black fans at its centre. At the same time there was the danger of slipping into the forms of ethnographic scrutiny that have often had damaging consequences for Britain's black communities. As Bourdieu has further commented the challenge of presenting accurate portrayals of excluded groups is to avoid 'seeming either to crush them or exalt them' (Bourdieu 2000: 234). What we tried to do here is an attempt at grasping, however partially, the quality of football support amongst Jamaican fans through forms of 'realist construction' (Bourdieu 1999b: 618), that is to say a version of ethnographic realism that incorporates a self-conscious appreciation of its own partial and situated vantage point. In short, these accounts are not omniscient views from nowhere; their lines of sight are apprehended through the eyes of a white researcher at a particular moment in time.

The fact that our focus was, in large part, on white racism and white people did not make our ethical relationship unproblematic because the study was conducted by white researchers. On the contrary, it was precisely experience of, and proximity to, the transmission of racism that posed difficult and urgent dilemmas. On some occasions we witnessed racial crimes being committed. In this situation there was a stark choice between remaining a sociological bystander or bearing witness to racism. The choices were never straightforward.

On one occasion plans were revealed by one of our ethnographic sources to visit the Nazi concentration camp at Auschwitz in Poland during a visit to the country for an England World Cup qualifying game, which we were invited to join. Tim Crabbe had himself recently visited this site with his partner, who is Jewish, and had found it hard to come to terms with what they had witnessed there. In the context of our informant's relation of stories of friends having previously taken pictures of one another outside the camp whilst performing Nazi salutes, the obvious attraction of such a trip within the framework of our research could not be divorced from the personal trauma and anger that might be associated with having to bear witness to such a scene. Domestic and professional responsibilities are not easily reconciled in such moments but are themselves often taken over by the course of events since ultimately this group did not make the trip to Auschwitz. Furthermore, others in Poland for the game did visit the concentration camp but were more inclined to express their shock at what they had seen than to engage in displays of racist symbolism, disrupting the casual assumptions that might be associated with the notion of England fans visiting a Nazi concentration camp.

More instrumentally, on a number of occasions we were approached and asked to give information to help police initiatives aimed at prosecuting racism in football grounds. We did give information of a general nature relating to the forms and location of racist behaviour. This was out of a commitment to use the research to intervene in countering racism and it did contribute to arrests, although not of people that we had prior knowledge of or who we had interviewed before the prosecution. Yet, at the same time it was clear that the impetus on the part of the police to prosecute racists was connected with an attempt to ameliorate the wider crisis of legitimacy that the police faced in the aftermath of the publication of the Macpherson Report into the murder of Stephen Lawrence which revealed grave shortcomings in the treatment of black victims and institutional racism in the Metropolitan Police.

We also wanted to represent those people who articulate racism in a non-stereotypical way. Much of the writing about football fans is picaresque and we felt it important to try to represent the banality and prosaic nature of the people who articulate racism. This destabilizes some of the comfortable ways in which racists are portrayed as demonic archetypes who, as a result, can be viewed as 'extreme' and thus positioned as outside of 'respectable society'. We felt it was necessary to undermine the ways in which the debate about racism in football has been managed through such means. We also wanted to analyse the ways in which we found racism being articulated by respected figures inside the game and its institutions. This was the result of a wider aim to broaden the debate about racism in football. This also produced another series of difficulties, particularly a tension between presenting the prosaic and uneven nature of racism and judging the content of racist acts. Stressing the complexity of the lives of racists does not absolve them and make them less culpable. However, we recognize that there is a danger that some of the portraits we present in this book might be read as such. Rather, we want to insist on the importance of trying to adduce as accurate a picture of contemporary racism as possible, while at the same time remaining resolute about judging its contents ethically and politically.

This process was further complicated when initial reports about our research entered the public domain. We became the target of hate mail and telephone harassment and were denounced in the British National Party's magazine (Thurgood 1998: 17). The tension between a commitment to both critique and dialogue placed us in a very difficult and vulnerable position. The same kinds of people who we had interviewed, socialized with in pubs and informal social spaces, were then making violent threats and vituperative abuse by phone and letter. Equally, some of the incidents of racism that we had collected inside the game were also reported in the newspapers. A prominent newspaper tried to link in print one case of racism inside football that had been reported to us to a high-profile football club chairman. The chairman in question threatened libel action against the newspaper, which would have meant that our research would have become embroiled in a legal case. A concerned editor telephoned us asking for corroboration for the link he had made between the incident and the football club chairman, but to provide this would have meant revealing our ethnographic source to whom we had promised confidentiality. The case was settled out of court.

The space in which this book has been produced blurred the relationship between intellectual and political concerns precisely because of the way we approached the research. In the end we were left with the dilemma of trying to make strategic choices and balancing ethical concerns with public interventions. The aspiration of the project was to try and shift the terms in which racism in football was discussed. It was also necessary to think through what kinds of strategies for combating racism we preferred. As Paul Gilroy has written recently 'however noble, the idea of anti-racism does not communicate any positive affirmative notes. What after all, are antiracists in favour of? What are we committed to and how does it connect with the necessary moment of negativity that defines our political hopes?' (Gilroy 2000: 52-3). We have tried to embrace this problem in both the way we have conducted this research and also the types of interventions we have made through the research itself. In short, we want to move beyond the conventions of moral anti-racism that try to achieve social transformation through edict. This involves a close examination of the social processes that inhibit or enable the open expression of overt racism. Equally, it begs an understanding of the ways in which social exclusion operates through implicit means in both informal cultures of support and the institutions of the sport itself at all levels.

The book is divided into three parts. The first, entitled 'Fan Cultures and the Local Cultures of Racism' examines the relationship between specific clubs and the local contexts and the prevalence and forms of racism. We begin with a review and critique of the ways in which the relationship between football culture and racism has been understood. An argument is developed concerning the limits of simply conflating the problem of racism with other forms of anti-social behaviour and in particular the debate about football hooliganism. We argue for a widening of the critical imagination to link racist practice and implicit forms of racial exclusion. From here there are three chapters that examine particular local contexts of footballing cultures. The first of these chapters focuses on the ways in which forms of identity, entitlement and belonging are written into the rituals of football support. Here we try to establish how in particular contexts normative models of identity are enshrined in football songs and fan culture more broadly. This leads on to a discussion of how black and ethnic minority fans are positioned in relation to the culture of particular clubs, which both police and define the terms of belonging. The final chapter in this part of the book foregrounds both the styles of racism we have recorded amongst fans and the social profiles of the perpetrators of racism. The aim here is to both identify patterns within the culture of racism in football while portraying the often complex and contradictory social backgrounds of racists.

The second part of the book is entitled 'Racism Inside the Game'. This consists of three further chapters that attempt to widen the debate on racism in football by looking at the institutions of football itself. First, we look at the experience of professional players and the forms of racism evident on the pitch and within the professional cultures of football. In particular we examine the ambiguities of dialogue and division within these cultures. From here we broaden out the discussion to examine the ways in which the issue of racism is managed inside football itself and also the forms of racial stereotyping that still pervade the institutions. Finally, we review the ways in which racism in football has been countered within fan responses and also the high profile campaigns organized by football's institutions.

The last part of the book is entitled 'Race, Nation and Diaspora'. Here we shift attention from the domestic to the international and examine how issues of race and racism connect with the national and international context. This section consists of two chapters. The first is an ethnography of England fans. Here we raise issues about how the discussion of racism in the local context might be contrasted with the discussion at a national level. This leads on to a wider discussion of contrasting national and diasporic footballing traditions. In particular, we focus on the kinds of fan culture organized around the Jamaican national team during the 1998 World Cup in France. Jamaica's support was largely drawn from black communities based within the diaspora, many of whom were attending football matches for the first time.

Before getting into the main empirical section of the book we now want to develop a critique of the ways in which racism in football have been understood. It is to this issue that we now turn.

Table 0.1. Cultures of Racism in Football Project: Sample Categories and Total

Fans:	White	Black and Asian	
Millwall FC	16 (13 male, 3 female)	4 (3 male, 1 female)	
Crystal Palace FC	14 (13 male, 1 female)	1 (male)	
Everton FC	15 (all male)	2 (all male)	
Manchester City FC	17 (15 male, 2 female)	3 (all male)	
Other fans:	10 (7 male, 3 female)	13 (8 male, 5 female)	
Diarists:	6 (5 male, 1 female)	1 (male)	
			Total = 102
Players:	12 (all male)	22 (all male)	**Total = 34**
Managers, coaches and directors of football:	6	5	**Total = 11**
Chairmen, shareholders and board members:	8 (all male)		**Total = 8**
Football administration, ground safety and community schemes:	17 (14 male, 2 female)		**Total = 17**
Media, journalists and writers:	5 (3 male, 2 female)		**Total = 5**
Agents:	1 (male)		**Total = 1**
Referees and officials:	4 (all male)		**Total = 4**
Community schemes and anti-racist organizations:	41 (21 male, 20 female)		**Total = 41**
			SAMPLE TOTAL = 222

Part 1
Fan Cultures and Local Cultures
of Racism

Mapping Race and Racism in Football Cultures

The phenomenon of racism in football first became a subject of widespread concern in the late 1970s and 1980s. This was a time when there was increasing evidence of racist behaviour related to football and attempts by extreme right-wing movements to use football as a basis for recruitment (Buford 1991, CCS 1981, Fradley, 1983, Robins 1984, Williams et al. 1984, Leeds Trades Council 1988, Waters 1988, Turner 1990). Groups such as the National Front were regularly seen selling their newspapers and magazines outside football grounds. But interest in the issue was also partly related to the increasing presence of black players amongst the ranks of professional footballers during the period since the 1970s. With the emergence of black players at all levels of football, phenomena such as racist chanting and abuse directed at them became common at many football grounds.

The pervasiveness of such displays of racism during this period in English football is by now well established both by recent research and by anecdotal evidence in popular publications and books. Interestingly enough, just after the start of our own research on cultures of racism in football two specific events highlighted the variety of expressions which racism can take in the game. The first was the public furore around the confrontation between the Manchester United player Eric Cantona and Mathew Simmons, a Crystal Palace supporter, in January 1995. Simmons was accused of shouting xenophobic insults and other abuse at Cantona, and the incident led to a wide-ranging public discussion, among other things, about the extent of xenophobia and nationalism among football supporters in England. The second incident was the behaviour of sections of the England supporters in the match between the Republic of Ireland and England in Dublin in February 1995, which led to the eventual abandonment of the game, in the midst of scenes of violence on the terraces. The events in Dublin focused attention once again on the supposed influence of extreme racist groups, including the paramilitary Combat 18, among sections of football supporters, particularly those that follow the England team (Greenfield and Osborn 1996).

As one of the England supporters interviewed after the Dublin events commented:

Figure 1.1 The 'Racist Hooligan,' Dublin 1995. Published with permission of the Sun.

You've got to show pride in your team. It's fucking pride. It's Eng-erland we follow. I mean, I know two blokes who are in Combat 18 because they believe in the English, no black in the Union Jack and all that. I mean I'm really there for the football, but I do agree with them. (*Guardian* 17 February 1995)

Dramatic incidents like these focused the public's attention, and attracted widespread debate in the media about the role of racism among certain groups of supporters and about violence and hooliganism. It is perhaps not surprising, therefore, that most studies of racism in football tend to concentrate either on the nature and extent of racist abuse in and around football stadiums (Holland, 1992a, 1992b, 1994), or are preoccupied with the recruitment activities of extreme right-wing movements (CCS 1981, Leeds Trades Council 1988, Waters 1988). In addition a number of writers have analysed the phenomenon of the growing presence of black players in football, notably Cashmore (1982, 1990), Woolnough (1983), Hill (1989), Orakwue (1998) and Vasili (1994, 1998, 2000). Phil Vasili concluded in his research for the BBC's *Black Britain* programme that between 1985/6 and

1997/8 there was an increase of 200 per cent in the numbers of black players in the Football League (Vasili 2000: 190). He estimated that black players make up approximately fifteen percent of the profession as a whole.

Most studies of racism in football have focused on the issue of fan behaviour. Given the public concern about the issue this is to some extent understandable, but we have tried to show in this study that racism is apparent at other levels. At an institutional level, for example, the growing presence of black players in professional football over the past two decades has not had a significant impact on management and coaching or in the boardrooms. Indeed one prominent football club chairman appeared on television as late as the early 1990s to play down the abilities of black players and their capacity to make the transition to football club management (*Critical Eye* 1991). This raises serious issues about the institutional framework of British football and the attitudes towards racism and ethnicity of key actors such as managers, owners and directors.

A whole series of incidents from the mid 1990s onwards have posed questions about the extent of everyday racism inside football. The public debate in the aftermath of complaints by the black Welsh International Nathan Blake regarding alleged racist comments made by the team manager Bobby Gould is but one example of a broader set of issues. Blake's complaints related to comments made by Gould in the wake of dressing-room discussions after the home World Cup qualifier against Holland in and during preparations for the following match against Belgium. The incident and the controversy it provoked led to vehement denials from Bobby Gould that he was in any way racist as well as to Blake's decision, for a time at least, to withdraw himself from the Welsh national squad. Following an inquiry the Welsh FA decided to take no further action. Incidents such as these have helped to highlight the tensions around the question of race that seem to be present in the game and that remain little understood.

Football Culture, Racism and the 'Hooligan'

Part of the explanation for the absence of a serious analysis of race and racism in football cultures can be found in the discourse of fan 'hooliganism' that has tended to establish the parameters of debate about virtually every aspect of football culture. The following quote from Holt's (1989) study *Sport and the British* illustrates this perspective perfectly:

> Chauvinism, local and national, lies at the heart of hooliganism and England fans seem to find in foreigners a convenient target for a vague resentment at Britain's diminished place in the world. Football has become a substitute for patriotism amongst disaffected, half-educated white working-class youth of a nation which only a generation ago was respected and feared throughout the world. (Holt 1989: 343)

This emphasis is not surprising because it is clear that the emergence of football as a field of academic study in the 1960s and early 1970s was from the outset related to an interest in manifestations of violence within the game, and more particularly (and peculiarly) with the violent tendencies of English football supporters. But the question that needs to be addressed is the adequacy of focusing on violence among fans as an adequate model for analysing phenomena such as racism in football culture.

The question that we want to pose here is the adequacy of seeing the issue of racism as merely a constituent element of the broader cluster of 'anti-social' forms of behaviour which form the basis for the concern around football 'hooliganism'. Some of the early studies of football disorder touched on the relationship between racism and football in the context of wider research into aspects of football culture and 'hooliganism' (Dunning Williams and Murphy 1986 and 1988, Williams 1986, Robins 1984, Turner 1990). These studies, however, tended to be largely descriptive and document rather than *explain* the extent of racist activity in football grounds (Melnick 1988, Waters 1988, Holland 1992 and 1993). The result is that these studies provide important evidence of football racism but only a partial insight into its relationship to the culture of football supporters. Journalism and auto-biographical writing have provided interesting accounts, yet they only result in glimpses of the relationship we seek to explore (Allan 1989, Buford 1991, Critical Eye 1991, Hornby 1993).

Some qualitative research on football supporters, such as Robins (1984), Dunning, Murphy and Williams (1986, 1988), and Williams, Murphy and Dunning (1989) has achieved many valuable insights into the popular culture around football. The ethnographic work of Armstrong and Harris (1991 and 1993) has led to a useful debate about the key issues facing researchers when analysing the social context and everyday practices of 'football hooligans' (Dunning et al. 1991, Hobbs and Robins 1991) but these studies do not provide a rounded analysis of the development and role of racist cultures in football. In fairness to these authors this issue was not central to their research focus. However, comments about fan racism are appended to wider concerns and seen as an extension of the problem of football violence and disorder. The result is that racism among football supporters is portrayed as representing all that is wrong with British society, whereas little attention is actually given to the wider context of racism and racialized social processes.

Without being drawn into the prolonged and at times personalized debate over the 'hooligan issue', it is useful to reflect on how the question of racism in football has been mapped onto this field of enquiry. Among the first academic interventions in this field were a number of articles by the late Ian Taylor. Taylor attempted to relate the development of 'football hooliganism' to a Marxist analysis of changes in the game of football itself and, more particularly, changes that were occurring in the relationship between the (male) working-class supporter and his home team (Taylor 1971). The 'football hooligan' was thus initially defined in romanticized terms as a defender of football's traditional working-class communitarianism against a growing embourgoisement of the game. This perspective gained support from others writing about football culture in the 1970s (Cohen 1972, Hall and Jefferson 1976, Clarke, 1978) and those concerned about the new right's use of a media-led 'moral panic' in generating populist attitudes towards dealing with crime (Hall 1978, Hall et al. 1978).

References to the racist attitudes of 'hooligans' and the activities of the far right were made in the early football literature. Indeed a report by the Centre for Contemporary Studies in the early 1980s on *Football and the Fascists* (CCS 1981) made the correlation explicit. This stated that as a result of racist activity at football matches 'the arbitrary and random violence of the skinhead becomes the political and organized violence of the Nazis'. It was in this context that Taylor (1982) reassessed his original perspective, with support from Robins (1984), after considering the emergence of the skinheads (see Clarke 1973) and other 'fighting gangs' associated with 'racist-populist politics'. Taylor argued that 'the repertoire of some of these ["hooligan"] groups now extended far beyond the "taking of ends" and the property vandalism of the 1960s to involvement in National Front-inspired attacks on blacks' (1982: 158) and other violent activities. The 'hooligan' was now depicted as a member of a lumpen 'underclass', ripe for manipulation by fascist elements. Whilst this kind of Marxist inspired analysis remained sympathetic to members of this class, whose lived experience is described as one of 'material and psychic frustration', the 'hooligan' was no longer held up in the same romanticized 'class fighter' terms. Rather, the popular fear of 'hooligans' was now seen as a rational response to their actual behaviour.

Perhaps the most influential body of research on football violence over the past few decades comes from researchers at the University of Leicester (Williams et al. 1984, Dunning et al. 1988, Murphy et al. 1990). These studies combine statistical and ethnographic material to produce a theory of 'football hooliganism' grounded in Eliasian sociology and Suttles's (1968) concept of ordered segment-ation (Dunning et al. 1992). The approach suggested that 'football hooligans' since the mid-1960s have come predominantly from the lower working classes. This is the group who have been less influenced by the 'civilizing processes' that Eliasian theory (Elias 1978, 1982) suggests have historically moderated aggressive violent behaviour.

The centrality of this theoretical approach to the Leicester teams' work led their analysis of racism in football to become something of an extension to their broader analysis of 'hooliganism' and the social processes underpinning it. Considerations of the relationship between the culture of football supporters and racist behaviour are focused on the attraction of groups of 'football hooligans' to neo-fascist groups, despite the recognition of 'the frequent expression of racist sentiments . . . by far larger sections of British crowds' (Murphy et al. 1991: 12). The life experience and values of the lower working classes are seen to generate racist behaviour in the football context:

> Probably only a handful of football fans support or even understand the political aims of movements like the National Front and the British Movement in their entirety. Many more, however, perhaps especially those from the lower working class, the ones we have identified as most centrally involved in football hooliganism, appear to be attracted by the pro-white, anti-immigrant stance . . . of these organisations. (Williams et al. 1989: 150)

Racism in football from this perspective is an element of the 'hooligan' problem such that 'demonstrations by England fans against black players in their country's Under-21 side were added to their repertoire of hooligan behaviour abroad' (Murphy et al. 1991: 144). Thus no distinction is made between the social processes underpinning patterns of racist and 'hooligan' behaviour and no attempt is made to signify the differences between those patterns.

While a number of these studies of football hooliganism have much of value to say about the culture of football supporters they have also tended to fix our understanding of the nature of football racism within fairly narrow terms of reference. The portrait of racism offered in most studies is limited to the behaviour of young working-class men, often connected closely with support for the national team. This way of framing the issue transcended the academic arena and has had far-reaching influence on the way football authorities have tackled this issue. It is to this issue that we now turn.

Social Policy, Racism and the Racist/Hooligan Couplet

Up until quite recently the conflation of the issue of hooliganism and racism has dominated the debate around social policy and anti-racism in football. It is for this reason that it is particularly important to examine this relationship and its history. In the aftermath of three major hooligan incidents at Luton, Birmingham and Heysel during 1985 attention was placed on the role of racism within these spectacular moments of disorder and anti-social behaviour (Home Office 1986, 1990, 1991).

The growing concern with football related racism culminated in Lord Justice Popplewell's request that the environmental psychologist David Canter and his colleagues provide evidence for his Committee of Inquiry into Crowd Safety and Control at Sports Grounds. Canter's investigation (Canter et al. 1989) gave specific consideration to the question of racism in football by including relevant questions in a survey of football supporters. Whilst recognizing that 'there is a danger that the effects of racism and the influence of political groups may be confused' (Canter et al. 1989: 119) the authors concentrated on the relationship between the activities of far-right political groups and 'hooliganism'. Their findings led the Popplewell inquiry to conclude that 'the majority of those involved [in far-right political activities] were distributing literature, chanting or making gestures or displaying or wearing signs or symbols' (Home Office 1986: 59) rather than instigating acts of 'football hooliganism'. Nevertheless one of the provisional recommendations of Popplewell's Interim Report was that 'consideration should be given to creating a specific offence of chanting obscene or *racialist* abuse at a sports ground' (authors' emphasis).

This recognition of racism in football by Popplewell is significant in that it flows directly on from the more fundamental interest in dealing with 'football hooliganism'. It is not informed by a broader concern with how the cultural context of football provides a platform on which racism can be expressed and celebrated. Neither is it concerned with the social processes that underpin that racism. Rather there is an association between racism in football and the general 'unacceptable' and 'rowdy' behaviour of football fans involved in 'hooligan' activities.

The theme was continued in Lord Justice Taylor's report into the Hillsborough stadium disaster where it is stated that 'if there is a . . . specific offence of chanting obscene or racial abuse . . . *hooligans* [authors' emphasis] will know precisely what is prohibited and that they do those things at their peril' (Home Office 1990: 51). These comments were taken on board when the Football (Offences) Act 1991 made it 'an offence to take part at a designated football match in chanting of an indecent or racialist nature' (HMSO 1991).

Popplewell's Final Report also makes reference to shifts in the makeup of 'hooligan' groups (which had in actual fact been widely evident a number of years earlier), suggesting that many 'hooligans' no longer belonged to 'the so-called "rough" working class category' (1986: 56) which had previously been associated with racist practice on the terraces. At this time there was wide academic recognition of the new 'fighting crews' (Dunning et al. 1986) and football 'casual' movement (Redhead and McLaughlin 1985) if less agreement about changes in the social makeup of these groups. But this did not lead to any re-assessment of the role of racism in football culture. Instead an intensification of the relationship between racism and the 'new hooligans' was identified.

More recently a general recognition of the narrowness of 'hooligan' discussions has been combined with a greater awareness of important changes in fan culture (Turner 1990, Duke 1991, Jary, Horne and Bucke 1991, Haynes, 1995, Giulianotti 1999) and the emergence of a new wave of football writers. These writers have helped to broaden the focus of attention during the last few years, both academically (Williams and Wagg 1991; Taylor 1992, Giulianotti and Williams 1994, Sugden and Tomlinson 1994, Wagg 1994, Haynes 1995), journalistically and biographically

(Davies 1990, Lansdown and Spillius 1990, Bull 1992 and 1994, Hornby 1992 and 1993, Fynn and Guest 1994, Kuper 1994, Horton 1995, Taylor et al. 1995). Yet whilst 'these publications carry or are imbued with a far more sanguine view of football in the 1990s' (Haynes 1995: 4) the 'hooligan debate' has left a seemingly indelible mark on the approaches and considerations associated with the new football writing.

This is not to say that there have been no changes. Richard Turner's description of football culture in the late 1980s, for example, deals with racism in football in the context of far-right politics and 'organized' violence but does at least offer an insight into the contradictory processes at work within the game, stating that 'the majority of supporters accept black players in their own team because they are "one of our boys"' (Turner 1990: 31). He also talks of the ways in which football creates an atmosphere where chanting and abuse goes almost totally unchallenged so that many, particularly young, supporters see nothing wrong in using terms such as 'Nigger', 'Paki', 'coon' and so forth.

These claims have wider significance than merely identifying specific acts of fan racism. What has emerged is the formation of a sporting person, namely the 'racist hooligan', as the effect of a certain kind of knowledge (Wickham 1992). Here, following Foucault (1979) we might usefully connect this process of person formation with a project of governmentality in which fan populations are subjected to strategies of maintaining order and establishing new codes of behaviour. The *racist/hooligan couplet* makes it possible to both establish a moral pariah, and then in contrast to this image of deviance promote new codes of propriety and 'acceptable behaviour' inside football stadia. The point here is that 'anti-racist' responses of this kind are the result of a very particular set of discourses that, in order to perform their work, conceal the complexity and variety of expressive racism at all levels of football.

This is best illustrated by the experience of anti-racist campaigns in football. At the beginning of the 1993–4 football season the Commission for Racial Equality and the Professional Footballers Association launched the Let's Kick Racism Out of Football campaign, in recognition of the fact that football provided a useful platform for anti-racist strategies:

> The first campaign we did was a football campaign, *Let's Kick Racism Out of Football*, because we looked at the whole area of young people and how to get to them, what medium we could use which would hold a message against racism and for equal opportunity and would also speak very clearly and directly to all people. (Interview with CRE Campaigns Unit, Quoted in Carver, Garland and Rowe 1995: 19)

Whilst this policy angle was very much in the CRE's mind it is also clear that their understanding of the issue of racism in football was still dominated by the concept of the 'racist hooligan'. This was made explicit in the CRE's press release which accompanied the campaign launch on 12 August 1991, which spoke of the emergence of a 'new generation of football hooligans using the game as a front for a mixture of serious crime and far right politics [involving] the leafleting of racist material at matches' (CRE 1991).

Elsewhere we have stressed that this is not necessarily a bad political strategy (Back, Crabbe and Solomos 1996). Such an approach has clearly had the effect of galvanizing a range of football authorities, the CRE, fan organizations and other professional bodies who otherwise share little by way of a common political or organizational agenda. However, the participants in this alliance may well be around the same table for starkly different reasons. For some, it seems clear that the campaign against racism is merely a convenient way to promote greater constraints on fan behaviour. A related consequence of this is that racism in football is defined in a very narrow and unrepresentative way. Thus, politically, the advantage of representing racism in this way ultimately becomes a constraint. The dependence on the 'racist/hooligan couplet' means that fans do not recognize this image of racism. Rather what is more familiar, and in some ways more challenging, are the intermittent and often banal forms of racism practiced by strikingly ordinary fans.

Ambiguous and contradictory expressions of racist practice get ignored because their perpetrators don't accept them as racism. A man in his seventies who shouts abusive racial epithets at a black player doesn't comply with the image of what a racist fan is supposed to look like. Thus such name calling can be explained away and rationalized: 'Well everyone gets abused – if you've got ginger hair, or fat you'll get grief as well. It's not racism – they are only winding them up.' For racism to 'count' within this logic the exponent has to fit the category of person we have identified as the 'racist hooligan.' In order to widen our understanding of the issue of racism in football it is imperative to (1) recognize how these regimes of knowledge work; and (2) to transcend their terms of reference. With this in mind we want to look at ways in which the agenda might be shifting within recent football research and writing.

Re-thinking Racism in Football

The period since the early 1990s has witnessed the publication of a series of reports aimed at informing policy makers about the nature and extent of racism in football (Holland 1992a, 1992b, 1993; HMSO 1994). These reports have offered a mixture of practical policy measures based on research (West Midlands Sports Council 1991; Holland 1993a 1993b; Carver, Garland and Rowe 1995), observation and policy practice (Stirling District Council 1992). What was interesting and important about this work was its attempt to marry research and policy intervention. Whilst some of the above cited studies do touch on the social basis of racism, few sustained attempts have been made within the policy arena to ground policy interventions in an understanding of manifestations of football racism and its forms of legit-imation.

This problem has been recognized by some of those writers who have chosen to focus on specific aspects of the problem such as the 'political racism' of extremist groups. Holland et al. (1996) in their consideration of the influence of racism and the far right at Leeds United's Elland Road stadium and the counter strategies of the club and a group of supporters, recognize 'that it is impossible to identify uniform patterns of racism or prejudice or race relations' (Holland et al. 1996: 169), and rationalize their own choice of focus on the basis that 'terms such as race, ethnicity and sport have to be specifically "unpacked" in terms of content, time and place' (Holland et al. 1996: 183). This emphasis on carefully situating the expression of racism is a particularly useful development, for it challenged us to identify the specific ritual and cultural mechanism through which football culture is racialized. The language of race works differently at local and national levels; what holds in the context of the national team and its fan base may not be the case in particular local settings. It is perhaps only then that we can fully grasp the complex changes that are occurring at the moment.

Redhead (1991a, 1991b, 1993) and Williams (1991) have re-evaluated the centrality of 'hooliganism' to football culture in the aftermath of the Heysel stadium disaster, by focusing on the emergence of the explicitly anti-violent and non-racist 'alternative football network' of fanzines and independent supporter groups. In the case of Williams, this reappraisal was extended into an exploration of the relationship between popular music cultures and football:

> A new popular agenda has been established by football fans in England which, in some ways, mirrors the anti-racist campaigns around music and football of the late 1970s. (Williams 1992: 24)

Williams has also developed a more nuanced notion of the politics of racism within English football. Interestingly he used Phil Cohen's (1988) use of Hannah Arendt's notion of 'nationalism of the neighbourhood' to discuss the ways in which minorities can win contingent inclusion within local working-class collectivities. Equally, intense working-class localism, often organized around allegiance to particular football clubs, can also provide a strong obstacle to entryism from right-wing political groupings:

> This is a key reason why racist organisations have had relatively little success in achieving support for their ambitions which cut across local club allegiances. (Williams 1991: 170)

However the contingent, and sometimes total, inclusion, of young black men in a racially heteroglot form of 'neighbourhood nationalism' (Back 1996) need not pre-empt the expression of racist abuse against opposing black players and fans.

Equally, Williams (1992) pointed towards the way issues of racism are being played out inside the institutions of the game itself. Here he describes the 'naturalness' of racist assumptions and how football 'simply, "has a way of saying things", an accommodative code or a form of (racist) "banter" which incorporates rather than alienates the growing number of black players in League football' (1992: 2). It is within this context that he recognizes that 'racism on the football terraces and in the stands is rather more overt and, for most people, easier to identify than the semi-institutional forms that tend to characterize professional football culture.' The paper does not explore these issues inside the professional structures of football, returning instead to the influence of the far right and the relationships between hooliganism and terrace racism. However, Williams points the way to another research agenda that transcends the traditional preoccupation with annexing the issue of racism within broader discussions of crowd violence.

Williams also reflects more deeply on the institutionalized basis of racism in football in an account of the history and experiences of the playing members of a local amateur black football club in Leicester (1994). This contribution marks a definite move beyond the restrictive parameters to the debate discussed earlier, but the concentration on a rather untypical amateur league club leaves us short of an understanding of the broad based legitimization of racist practice in the wider football culture. However, Williams does raise a number of important questions with regard to the attitudes of football institutions as a whole to the position of black clubs and players.

An important feature of the current situation is the growth in the number of black professional players, largely from African-Caribbean and African back-grounds, which some estimates claim represent close to 20% of all players in the English game. This has been accompanied by a small but no less important increase in black representation in management and coaching. Black players and managers have made important advances at the occupational level but this has not been the case for south Asians and other ethnic minority communities. This leads to a related question about the variety of forms of racism that affect particular minority groups. Jas Bains and Raj Patel in their path-breaking work *Asians Can't Play Football* (1995) pose this issue strikingly and provide one of the few discussions of the multi-accented forms of racism that are generated inside football. This diversity of Asian football experiences was given full treatment in Jas Bains and Sanjiev Johal's excellent *Corner Flags and Corner Shops* (Bains and Johal 1998). The book explodes the myth that there is no interest in football in south Asian communities in Britain and provides a unique insight into these passions through the personal testimonies of Asian fans themselves.

Some recent texts have attempted to provide a more rigorous analysis of contemporary forms of racism in football culture. Fleming and Tomlinson (1995), for example, seek quite consciously to provide a fuller analysis of the processes of normalization of racism in football culture and provide an insight into the wide variety of forms of instrumental racism in the game. They recognize that:

> Football can embody a popular aesthetic of collective endeavour, but it can also encourage prejudice, discrimination, stereotyping and ethnocentrism. It can bring different cultures together in common celebration, but it can also provide the basis for extreme, and very public, forms of xenophobia and racism. (Fleming and Tomlinson 1995: 2)

Refreshingly, their understanding is built around a much broader conceptualization of the processes at work in the generation and normalization of racist behaviour. The activities of the far right and hooligans are highlighted but they are recognized alongside the equally important vernacular cultures of football as expressed by supporters, players, managers, administrators, directors and elsewhere and the relationship between popular racism and the social institutions of the football industry. This point is also made by Chas Critcher (1991) and leads to a broader sense of the context in which racism features within football.

New Research Agendas

Despite such arguments, until the mid-1990s the debate about racism in football focused almost exclusively on the problem of fan behaviour. Focusing on fan behaviour became the key way in which the football authorities both addressed the issue and diverted attention away from the forms of racist practice and racial inequality manifest inside the professional game itself. But the way in which these issues have been traditionally discussed has been overtaken by shifts within the politics of racism in football culture, as reflected in a number of high-profile campaigns against racism in football. It is striking that the growth in public attention to this issue and the increase in anti-racist campaigning has taken place at a time when there is a decline of the overt mass racial abuse that preoccupied earlier writers. Cyrille Regis, a now-retired black player who experienced some of the worst kinds of racist expression in the late 1970s and early 1980s, argues:

> I welcome the fact that anti-racism in football is getting its stamp [of approval], it's a great idea in theory [but] it's like twenty years too late. Authorities didn't do nothing about it in the seventies. All right it's fine now, it's fine now when you can get one or two and chuck 'em out, but when there was five thousand – how do we deal with it? Do we chuck them all out? It's like – now it's manageable – now it's manageable, now you can turn round and put all these . . . things into motion. (Interview, 4 December 1996)

We review the policy and campaigning developments more fully in Chapter 7. The Kick It Out Campaign, which is an extension of the Let's Kick Racism Out of Football initiative, has attempted to develop a new agenda for tackling racism in football (Back, Crabbe and Solomos 1996). Kick It Out currently operates independently but major organisations in football and outside have backed it financially, including the Commission for Racial Equality, the Professional Footballer's Association, the FA Premier League and the Football Trust. The current campaign has embraced the critique of the conflation of racism and hooliganism, focusing on localized strategies that bring the aspirations of the campaign closer to local activitists and pratitioners within particular regions. Currently, Kick it Out is addressing issues of minority under-representation in coaching and administration, racism inside the sport and the importance of anti-racist codes of practice within local authorities which serve the amateur game (Powar and Tegg 1998).

While a reframing of the campaigning priorities has occurred in this field, the academic analysis of racism and sport remains within a limited analytic framework and isolated from wider debates about race and racism. There is a real gap between contemporary social theory relating to questions of race, social theory and the politics of difference and the literature on the sociology of sport. This has been identified elsewhere (Carrington 1997, Jarvie and Reid 1997). A case in point is the controversy about John Hoberman's (1997) *Darwin's Athletes*. Hoberman's book has caused a considerable uproar in the US and elsewhere (see Allison 1998, International Review for the Sociology of Sport 1998). Writing as a cultural historian Hoberman sees racism as a historical legacy whose echoes are replayed constantly within American life. An example of this is his observation about the lineage between military segregation and the profound lack of black athletes in the cerebral spheres of sports coaching and management. His central contention is that sport is implicated in the perpetuation of the myth of race which binds black and white Americans in a racialized straightjacket of stereotypes. More than this, multi-racial sport becomes:

a Darwinian theater, which has preserved like no other public forum the evolutionary drama that transformed the human image during the nineteenth century. (Hoberman 1997: 13)

There is much of interest in these observations and the points made by Harry Edwards (1969) much earlier, but the problem with this account of racism is that it doesn't adequately deal with the possible ruptures and transformations within the culture of racism(s). The recognition of the plural and multifarious nature of racial power is one of the key contributions of recent theorizing in this field (Goldberg 1993; Solomos and Back 1995). Such nuances are missed when racism is reduced theoretically to a Darwinian inspired discourse of racial biology. Equally, there is a growing consensus that suggests it is necessary to carefully situate the processes of racialization with specific national, class and gendered contexts. Yet such issues have yet to be seriously taken up in empirical or theoretical work about the sociology of football and other sporting arenas.

In the course of our own research we found that the 'racist/hooligan couplet' was not an adequate way of framing the complex forms of racist expression that are part of football culture. In order to understand more fully the culture of racism in football we found it necessary to identify the range of *sporting contexts in which processes of racialization occur*. In this sense racism can be seen as a mutable and changing phenomenon in which notions of biological or pseudo biological cultural difference are used to explain and legitimate hierarchies of racial dominance and exclusion (Solomos and Back 1996). The processes of racialization are both fluid and changing, yet it is also clear that they can play an important part in maintaining patterns of privilege, domination and white supremacy. This perspective sees patterns of racist discourse as changing in line with the dynamics of a particular social formation. For example, the intense fan racism directed at black players in the late 1970s and early 1980s provides a key episode in the racialization of English football. Yet, racism and racist discourses are by their very nature volatile and adapt to new circumstances. So, the disappearance of this particular form or style of racism in the 1990s need not necessarily be a measure of greater tolerance or unambiguous 'progress'. This is precisely one of the key themes that runs through the analysis in the substantive chapters of this study.

It is possible to appreciate that real changes have occurred in English football in relation to questions about race but, equally, that continuities remain with past styles of racism which may well combine with neoteric forms of racial discourse. Some of the stereotypes relating to the attributes and playing skills of black players have been exploded by the variety of black players in the professional game. These were classically articulated through suggestions that 'black players couldn't play in the cold', 'while skilful they lacked the grit and determination of their white counterparts', and lastly that 'black players had attitude problems, were lazy and with insufficient application to the game.' The sheer presence of black players has shifted some of the ideological terms of these stereotypes and muted their expression. In the wake of this displacement, however, other forms of racial discourse are being generated.

This is not merely the return of pseudo-biological racism that codes athletic prowess 'black' and mental acuity 'white' (Hoberman 1997). Rather, older strands of racial ideology are invoked and applied alongside new variants contrived to suit present circumstances. In particular, prospective black managers have to face preconceptions about their assumed incapacity to manage multi-racial teams evenhandedly, or cope with the organizational load of football management and its associated responsibilities. As we show in Chapter 6 black players who were in the vanguard of change in the 1970s and 1980s are now facing new and masked forms of racial stereotyping as they make the transition into management and coaching. At the same time, the blackness of figures like Ruud Gullit can be dissolved by the media who represent him as an exceptional superstar figure. It was telling that the media coverage hardly mentioned that he was the first black person to lead a team to victory in the 1997 FA Cup Final but rather represented him as a 'foreign manager'.

In order to establish an overall sense of how the processes of racialization work within the broader structure of football culture we need to distinguish between specific arenas in which racism may feature. We have identified four inter-related fields within football culture that are summarized in Table 1.1. These are distinct but inter-related sectors providing specific contexts in which particular forms of racialization can be analysed. For example, the cultural industries provide a distinct set of issues, in the main concentrating on how difference is represented in a range of media from advertising to news and electronic media. Here we have in mind the ways in which different sporting bodies are represented and racialized. Sportive racism provides the device through which black and white bodies are given specific meanings. Hoberman comments that the fetish for racially integrated sport in the US promotes both a mollifying spectacle and a means by which invidious pseudo-biological stereotypes flourish (Hoberman 1997: 28–51). Another related question here is the degree to which the racial difference of these sporting figures is marketed as a resource to be exploited economically (Jarvie and Maguire 1994: 101) and the saccharin forms of corporate multiculturalism that often result (Back and Solomos 1996). Multinational corporations use black sporting heroes as exemplary 'super organisms', reinforcing the aesthetics of racialized sporting prowess, while allowing black athletes to coalesce synonymously with the company's brand identity (Katz 1994, Barber 1996).

Media discourses are an important context in which ideas about the relationship between race, nation and entitlement are articulated. This point is developed by Hugh O'Donnell in his discussion of national stereotypes within sports journalism (O'Donnell 1994). O'Donnell argues that a macro-discourse exists that codes European, South American and African nations within paired sets of attributes. Brazilians can thus be acclaimed for their flair, skill and physical grace. Lurking beneath this discourse is a scepticism about flaws in the mercurial Latin American temperament, sexual impropriety and absence of discipline. These kinds of formulations were articulated by journalists and pundits during the 1998 World Cup. On 11 July Tony Francis, presenter of London Weekend's Television's World Cup 98 Encore programme, suggested to former England Manager Terry Venables that the volatile nature of the Croatian team could be explained by their 'gypsy nature'. Venables replied cautiously, but his co-panellist and Manchester United manager Alex Ferguson embraced and repeated the suggestion. Ferguson concluded that Croatia's performance during the competition had ultimately been inhibited by the 'Gypsy thing'. These kinds of prosaic stereotypes flourish within football, in part because they can be articulated less self-consciously than ideas about colour-coded racial attributes. However, they share the elemental absolutism of racist ideas and equally fix and ossify the diversity of humankind within a gallery of national archetypes.

Table 1.1. Racialization in Football: A Framework for Analysis

Arena	Context	Forms of racialization
Culture Industry:	Advertising and marketing	Imaging racial difference
	Sponsorship	Racialized patterns of commercial endorsement
	Print media and journalism Electronic media	Elite racist discourses concerning race and nation
Institutional:	Administration and ruling bodies and decision making	Racial inequality in terms of access to decision making forums
	Players organizations, club ownership and boardroom control	Racial discourses of exclusion
Occupational:	Scouting and patterns of recruitment	Connection between racialized attributes and sporting capacity and professional competence
	Players' occupational culture	Racialized rumours and decision making Racist abuse within the playing/coaching arena
	Transfer market Management and coaching Administration and Marketing	Conceptions of the market and internal culture of football clubs.
Vernacular culture:	Race and nation within the context of the national side	The racialization of entitlement and belonging' and racialization of the national body politic
	Club, region and identity Geography of support and patronage	Racialized hierarchies and 'neighbourhood nationalism'
	Player symbols History and club rivalries	Positioning of black players and the club collective identity
	Expressive rituals of support	Racialized forms of abuse The relationship between right-wing politics and fan cultures.

The second arena we have identified is the institutional domain of football's governing bodies. The administration and management of football has remained predominantly white in its composition. This stands in stark contrast to the changes in the racial and ethnic makeup of the players. Networks of patronage operate within the sport that need investigation and, like other contexts in which black and ethnic representation has emerged in recent years, sophisticated forms of racial discourse are tailored to resisting institutional change (Solomos and Back 1995). This is associated closely with the third arena – the occupational cultures of the sport, including all aspects of the professional structure from scouting, player cultures, the dynamics of the transfer market, management and coaching and the under representation of black people in marketing and administration of the clubs. Processes of racialization here include the forms of stereotyping that fix the attributes and skills of black and white players respectively and the prevalence of racialized forms of rumouring regarding the characteristics of black players. These discourses may act informally as networks of 'white knowledge' that are rarely explicit. Equally, racist behaviour in this context would also include explicit forms of abuse from white coaches and players against their black counterparts.

Lastly, the vernacular culture of fans, as we have already seen, constitutes an arena in which these issues are managed. This works differently within supporter cultures at a local and national level. Indeed, there are overlaps here with the elite discourses of race/nation discussed in relation to sports journalism (see also Carrington 1998). Here we are proposing that the relationship between fan culture and racism be conceptualized at a number of levels, namely the ways in which ideas of race are worked through the language of nation, locality, club identity and the geography of local fan networks. One of the features of many clubs located in inner city areas is that every Saturday afternoon ethnically diverse neigh-bourhoods are 'invaded' by white fans from outer city and suburban areas who reverse the patterns of residential 'white flight' to support their team. As we argued earlier, complex negotiations may also take place between fans around the construction of club identities and their forms of collective belonging. This includes what we referred to as 'neighbourhood nationalism', which can establish patterns of inclusion and exclusion, whereby some black fans are admitted as contingent insiders while other minority groups and opposing black fans and players are vilified and cast as outsiders. The success or otherwise of right-wing political organization might also be discussed in relation to the local patterns of territory and identity organized around specific football clubs. Overt racist abuse and their ritual structure would also be included within this arena. In order to understand the range of racist activity one needs to examine the relationship between processes of racialization and the collective ritual and symbolic practices that give any particular fan culture meaning. In this sense differences with regard to the level and intensity of racism need to be understood in terms of the way racist practices are nested within the ritual and collective symbolism of each fan culture.

The framework outlined above offers one means of broadening the analysis of racism in football. Patterns of racialization within this sporting context demonstrate a complex combination of continuity and change that challenges the adequacy of the conventional means of understanding them. While the public debate and academic writing has constructed a vivid portrait of what a 'racist football fan' looks like, little attempt has been made to define precisely what racism constitutes in specific sporting arenas. As a result this discussion of racism in football takes on a kind of everything and nothing quality, a catchall notion that is rarely explained and defined theoretically. What we have attempted to do in this chapter is to designate the specific processes of sportive racialization and how these are situated in institutional and demotic arenas.

Viewing racism as merely a constituent element of the wider problem of 'anti-social' behaviour has resulted in some issues being organized onto the political and intellectual agenda while others have been ruled out. It is possible to talk about racism inside football grounds but it is more or less taboo to ask about this issue on the training ground, the field of play and in the board room. The crude labelling of racists as 'moral degenerates' within what we have described as the racist/hooligan couplet will do little to identify and tackle these broader problems. Indeed, the continued preoccupation with crowd behaviour has become part of the problem itself. The pervasive image of the right-wing 'hooligan' both feeds and gives legitimacy to a broader project of regulating fan behaviour regardless of whether or not these rituals are connected with racist practice. There is an urgent need to widen the terms of the sociological imagination with regard to under-standing racism in football, and it is with this task in mind that we move to the substantive chapters of this book. We shall return to some of the conceptual debates touched upon in this chapter in the substantive empirical chapters that follow and in the conclusion.

–2–

'Playing At Home': Community, Ritual and Race

'On Victory Street' Saturday 21 October 1995, Moss Side, Manchester

Another match day: Manchester City versus Leeds United. It's around 1.40 p.m. City Fans are walking up Winnicombe Street, just behind the new Kippax stand, looking around for somewhere to have a drink before going to the match. Walking through the labyrinth of back to back terraced houses is to encounter worlds colliding. On one side of the street white football fans make their way to Maine Road, the destination of their Saturday afternoon pilgrimage. On the other, the multicultural community of Moss Side tries to go about its business as normal.

Four groups of casually dressed young black guys hang out on doorsteps or beside their cars. A string of Asian men in small groups make their way to the Shahjalal Mosque just off Victory Street. Black and white young kids are playing in the street, several of whom are wearing City shirts. They are warming up for a match too but they are not going anywhere. In contrast, groups of white young men, many of whom are wearing City colours, demonstrate all the signs of pre-match excitement. Some are heading for the ground, others making their way between pubs. They appear to be comfortable with their surroundings but still look strangely out of place amidst the prosaic multiculture of this weekend scene. Two City fans stand urinating against the wall of a house just behind the pubs on Victory Street.

Moss Side is an area with many street corner shops and businesses. Outside several shops groups of black men in their later years are passing time over a chat. There was a very convivial air about it all but one that was totally divorced from the white football supporters making their way to the ground and occasionally entering shops for a drink, cigarettes or snack. Along Wilmslow Road the pattern continues, with an ever-increasing throng of supporters arriving in the area from buses and on foot. They are moving in the direction of the ground or local pubs whilst local people, many black and Asian, get on with their own priorities. Inside the Withington pub friendly banter is flying around, with the City fans good naturedly pessimistic about their chances for the afternoon and the season. One of the lads, Russ, asked with a mixture of curiosity and humour 'So are we going to be in your book then?' Russ then began to provide a typology of the Maine Road supporters. He stated that most of the 'headcases' and 'nutters' went in the North Stand, 'the old romantics go in the Umbro Stand, the Main Stand is like any Main Stand I suppose, and the Kippax . . . well . . . is the Kippax. But in the North Stand they're all nutters.' The chat is about football, the night before, sexual exploits, mutual friends and the evening to come. All of it was good humoured and self-deprecating, the self image typical of City supporters everywhere. They are fans who revel on the fact that they are prepared to have a laugh at their own expense and not to take the football too seriously. Always determined to enjoy themselves and, in the context of City's start to this particular season, they are acutely aware that an over reliance on the football was not the best way of gaining any satisfaction.

2:40pm. Time to get to the ground. Outside fans rush to get their cars parked. The weekend co-existence of the local community and the increasingly frenetic fans is more uneasy. Two groups of around half-a-dozen black youths aged between eleven and sixteen, several of them on mountain bikes, are selling their services as car minders to any driver attempting to park in the area. A group of four white men in their thirties with closely cropped haircuts and wearing City shirts walk past. One commented audibly 'fucking black kids, telling you where you can park, I don't know what's goin' on, they're as bad as fucking scousers.' Rather than laugh at this association the others in the group merely tutted in a kind of resigned acknowledgement. As kick off time approaches these two worlds – that of the football fans and the residents – appear separated and alien to each other.

* * *

We start this chapter with this all-too-common scene in order to ask the question 'who is "playing at home" at fixtures like this one?' In many respects this scenario is replicated at other clubs that, like Manchester City, are located in English inner cities. These encounters reverse the usual association between migration and race. It is generally the racial other that is cast as an alien interloper. In these Saturday afternoon urban 'contact zones' it is the white travellers – the fans – who interrupt the ebb and flow of multicultural urban communities in Manchester, Birmingham and London. Many return to these urban areas to commune with the rituals of fandom and an association that may have long since past. Put another way, we might ask in whose home is the Saturday afternoon match day drama being played out?

It is, of course, more complicated than making a simple distinction between the local 'insiders' and the invading football supporting 'outsiders'. Support for City is found among the residents of places like Moss Side and Rusholme and other neighbourhoods surrounding the ground. But, like other clubs, this is not uniform and some sections of the local community do not identify with the club. Even if they do, poverty and economic deprivation militate against local residents participating as spectators. While, the supporters of City are predominantly white, in the 1991 census 50% of the Rusholme population was drawn from ethnic minorities and in Moss Side that proportion was even higher at 53.64%. Even more starkly these areas exhibit high levels of unemployment (Moss Side 58.41% and Rusholme 44.12%) and overcrowding. This is not to suggest that the associations and identities that are articulated around football support should be seen as disconnected from the question of localism and regional identity. Quite the opposite is in fact the case. Football clubs provide a key ritual and cultural mannequin onto which the clothes of identity, locality and regionalism are tailored and paraded. The fact that City fans may no longer live close to their ritual home does not make their identification with its nuances any less significant. The simple point that we want to make here is that it is important to distinguish between the ways in which identity, belonging and entitlement are defined in the rituals of football support and the changing cultural ecologies of their locations.

Football stadiums can operate as sacred ground for their devotees. Much is often made of the parallels between the liturgy of football and religion. There are many examples of the distress and controversy caused when teams are forced to move grounds either temporarily or permanently. John Bale has described this issue through his discussion of Charlton Athletic's temporary move from the Valley (Bale 1994) and Garry Robson has discussed similar issues in relation to Millwall's move from their Coldblow Lane ground to the New Den (Robson 2000). As Bale has pointed out the ground itself can serve as the key site that holds the history of the club, and all it stands for, *in place*. In his book he referred to correspondence he had with a Manchester City fan:

> I have been a supporter since birth, well, since my parents first took me when I was around two years old. Since that time my interest has revolved more around the stadium than the team. Of course, I support the team through and through, but to me the club is Maine Road as that is the only part that rarely changes. Managers, players, directors, and even supporters come and go but the stadium never disappears. (cited in Bale 1994: 133)

This sense of football ground as sustaining historical continuity is underscored by the request often made by fans to have their ashes scattered on the pitch itself after their death. The playing surface provides a connection to past and future heroes who perform on it but it also serves literally and metaphorically as an altar of memory and commemoration. The physical structure of the ground is associated with a sense of geopiety (Tuan 1976) because it is a home that 'incarnates the past' (Tuan 1974: 247). It is a place to both play and be at home.

It is our contention that one can only fully understand the degree to which particular football clubs are open to black and ethnic minority fans and players by understanding the often implicit and embodied normative structures at the heart of particular local football cultures. The key questions we want to ask in this chapter are 'how do football clubs provide a means to ritualize community and represent locality and how do these issues connect with questions of ethnicity and race?'

It is for this reason that we chose to focus on the four case study clubs, Manchester City, Everton, Crystal Palace and Millwall mentioned earlier. We want to establish a nuanced picture of how identity and belonging are written into football rituals and the ways in which football grounds provide the theatre of memory, comemorialization and identity. We want to suggest, in line with other recent work (Robson 1999, 2000; Giulianotti 1993; 1996; Armstrong 1998; Armstrong and Giulianotti 1997), that the triumph and despair of the club's fortunes encode the broader traces of social identity and cultural history. In this sense, we want to suggest that football can offer a context in which urban cultural change and uncertainty are diluted through the renewal of the sense of place and belonging that is captured as fans move towards and through the turnstiles on matchdays.

These introductory points will be expanded through a detailed discussion of the quality of this local process within our case study clubs. Our broad aim is to show why it is important to situate the growth in numbers of black players discussed in the previous chapter within the cultural ecologies and histories of particular clubs. This will include a detailed discussion of football rituals, songs and chants as a means for embodying and representing particular versions of local identity and history.

'South London is Wonderful': Locality, Football Culture and 'Symbolic Homes'

Given the encounters and disjunction described outside Maine Road, we might ask what is 'local' about a football club like Manchester City playing at home. In a sense the stadium provides one sphere in which the theatre of locality, to use Christian Bromberger's (1993) terms, is produced, made and renewed, while the young black men offering their services to 'mind' cars are producing another version of locality. The key here is to see how locality is produced through patterns of ritual and cultural life, rather than constituting an underlying ethological essence (Appadurai 1995).

In cultural theory 'the local' is invariably coded as the parochial antithesis of our current globalizing world. Bruce Robbins has appealed recently that 'we cannot be content to set against [globalization] the childish reassurance of belonging to "a" place' (Robbins 1998: 3). The churlishness about localism on the part of left intellectuals has a long history. Garry Robson in his excellent recent study of football culture suggests that this ambivalence to the embodied culture of football and it's attendant rhetoric of locality amounts to a 'leftist-intellectualist opprobrium' (Robson 2000: 6). In the case of clubs like Millwall, he argues, urban myths ultimately reduce the club and its supporters to the breeding ground of proto-fascism. Taken together these positions mean that football fans that construct themselves as 'local patriots' are viewed as either 'infantile' or 'fascistic'. In order to avoid these shortcomings, local identity should be viewed as a product that is achieved through the practice of culture and commemorative rituals. This is not to suggest that the *symbolic home* that a stadium provides to its fans is a phantasm or a mirage. Rather, it is the arena for the embodiment of particular forms of social life, that have their own routines and cultural modes of expression. In short the football stadium provides one context in which local identity can be ritually defined, regardless of the changes taking place in its immediate environment and patterns of migration. For example, a City fan coming to Maine Road may be returning to an ancestral home, place of former residence or family association. The process of attending the match is a communion with the affective community that is embodied in supporting Manchester City. The quality and nature of this affective community and how it connects with issues of racism and ethnicity is for us the crucial issue.

The frequency, and to some extent the form, of the racism we encountered in football grounds varied greatly between clubs. The fan cultures of particular clubs often share common ritual elements. For example, football songs are largely drawn from a relatively limited repertoire of melodies. With slight modifications the tunes for Rod Stewart's *Sailin*, or *When the Saints Go Marching In* or versions of Brit pop hits by Blur or Oasis can be heard in most of England's stadia. At the same time each fan culture exhibits distinct forms of prescribed formal ritual behaviour and symbolism. In order to understand the range of racist activity one needs to examine the relationship between processes of racialization and the collective ritual and symbolic practices that give any particular fan culture meaning. In this sense differences with regard to the level and intensity of racism need to be understood in terms of the way racist practices are nested within the ritual and collective symbolism of each fan culture. This is a very different type of argument to that which suggests that the fan cultures of particular clubs are wholly racist. Rather, we would suggest it is a matter of identifying the points where racialization takes place and equally those aspects of fan cultures that are more open to cultural difference and diversity.

Within our London case studies we found a stark contrast between the high frequency of racism observed amongst some sections of Millwall's support when compared to neighbouring Crystal Palace, where racial abuse from fans was almost non existent. There are some common features within the ritual forms of expression used at these clubs. For example, both clubs sing a song entitled 'South London is Wonderful.' Here is the Crystal Palace version:

Interestingly, in Millwall's rendition of the song there is a second verse which contrasts south London with a racist image of East London where Millwall's main rivals West Ham play:

We will return to this song in more detail later. The two clubs share many of the same melodies in their football songs. For example, the Eagles' collective song *We are Palace* and Millwall's hymn *No-one Likes Us* are both sung to the Melody of Rod Stewart's *Sailin*:

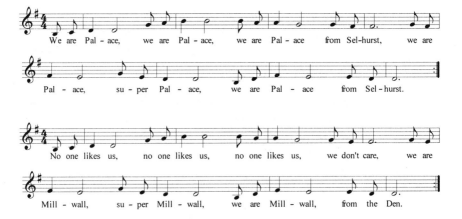

Despite these shared elements the difference between the two clubs with regard to the frequency of racism can to some degree be explained through an understanding of the contrasting nature of these fan cultures. As Garry Robson has pointed out, Millwall's collective imagery and symbolism is tightly bound up with the reproduction of a local, class-inflected masculine culture that bears the traces of the white working-class communities that worked in the docks and that have in large part disappeared (Robson 2000). Traditionally, the club's support is drawn from the areas of Bermondsey and inner South East London. The irony of this situation is that today the club's support is drawn from the outer London suburbs, from where fans migrate every Saturday to New Cross, reversing – albeit temporarily – the patterns of residential 'white flight'. According to the 1991 census 40% of the population in the Marlowe ward in which the New Den is located is drawn from the ethnic minority communities. However, the culturally heterogeneous nature of South London life is not evident in the collective symbolism of Millwall. Rather, as Robson suggests, Millwall's collective imaginary is embodied and sustained through ritual and recursive means.

This concern with the pageantry and symbolism of the working class past is enshrined in the club's theme song *Let 'Em Come* performed by Roy Green and played before every home game. The tune has also been taken up amongst the fans as one of the collective rallying crys. The lyrics of the verses represent a pre-war Cockney idyll, complete with jellied eels, beer and reference to Millwall's ancestral home, The Old Den in Coldblow Lane:

> It's Saturday a Coldblow Lane and we've all come down to cheer
> We've got our jellied eels and our glass of beer
> Come rain or shine all the time our families we'll bring
> And as the Lions run on the pitch everyone will sing
> Let em come, Let 'em come, Let 'em come . . .

The version sung in the ground also culminates with an altering of the melody like a pub singer giving a rendition of a popular song on the Old Kent Road. The sung version sounds like this:

At the core of Millwall culture is a form of 'neighbourhood nationalism' that is defined through local and class-specific terms of inclusion and exclusion. As we shall see in the next chapter, black participation is determined by the degree of shared experience of region, class and masculinity. In this sense Millwall represents a largely white enclave in an increasingly multi-racial environment.

In contrast Crystal Palace, located just five miles away, is less intensely connected with a white working-class past and the forms of localism that follow from this in the case of Millwall. Palace fandom is more mixed in terms of its class composition. It reflects the diverse quality of the South London suburbs of Croydon, Bromley and Merton. This to some extent comes through in the symbolism and ritual of Palace fandom. The Club's nickname was changed in the 1970s from 'The Glaziers' to 'The Eagles'. The main rallying cry for fans is a two note melodic dirge that intones the word 'Eagles':

For Palace, the Dave Clark Five's 1960s hit *Glad All Over* is the equivalent to Millwall's *Let 'em Come*. The melody of this tune is altered slightly in the fan's rendition. The song resounds with the enduring traces of postwar social change in this part of suburban London. In this sense *Glad All Over* resonates with the experience of class mobility, improvements in council housing and 1960s affluence which affected this district and the families from which Palace fans are drawn.

Glad All Over – fan version

Alongside Palace's middle-class fans the club draws support from white working-class enclaves like New Addington and other suburban council estates and the contemporary forms of multiculture evident in districts like Thornton Heath, Norbury, Streatham and Forest Hill. Selhurst Park is located at the boundary of three wards, namely South Norwood, Thornton Heath and Whitehorse Manor and at the 1991 census the ethnic minority proportion of the total population was 20%, 31% and 30% respectively. The association between Palace with black London was amplified during the 1980s by the string of black Londoners who played for the team including Vince Hillaire, Andy Gray, Ian Wright, John Salako and Mark Bright.

We want to stress the importance of understanding the relationship between the two different contexts and the frequency and propensity for racist action. Put simply, we want to suggest that the different experience of these two clubs can only be understood by appreciating the ways in which the various fan cultures either inhibit or facilitate the expression of particular styles of racism. This, as we will argue, does not necessarily mean that one club is simply more racist than another. Rather, we suggest that there are different styles of expression in each case, be it the crude explicit racism of Millwall fans or the rather mute forms of racial stereotyping exhibited by Palace fans.

There is an overwhelming tendency for people involved in both the recreational and professional cultures of the game to play down the significance of racism in football and to speak, in very general terms, about the 'improvements' witnessed since the 1970s and 1980s. This approach, at once, ignores the uneven development of racism within the game and the complex means by which racialized notions can be expressed in contemporary fan culture. We would point to the twin processes of continuity and change that have historically characterized the development of racism within the game.

'Sounds of the Crowd': John Barnes, Merseyside and Difference

Experiencing football as a fan was always as much about the sounds of the stadium as the visual spectacle of the game itself. Danny Blanchflower, former Spurs captain, once said that 'The noise of the crowd, the singing and chanting, is the oxygen we players breathe' (quoted in Thrills 1998). It is for this reason that we argue that there is a need to try and represent the corporeal nature of the fan culture in all its sensory dimensions. Particularly important here is the culture of sound, the songs that are sung and the acoustic quality of the noises in the crowd. It is primarily through songs and banter that a structure of feeling is produced in football stadia. John Bale has argued that the 'sound of sport is a major medium for the enhancement of the sport landscape experience' (Bale 1994: 141). It is this auditory aspect, the formless noise and the spontaneous plainsong of football that we want to focus on in the remaining parts of this chapter.

The mass crowds of the years immediately after World War Two must have garnered an awesome sound. These voices were not disciplined in song, rather they were a mass of the sharp-witted workplace wind-ups. Keith, a Millwall fan remembers what it was like to go to the Old Den in those days:

My first memories I suppose have got to be the atmosphere. Obviously at that time which was when I first started to go on a regular basis was the early 1960s and I mean obviously all the docks was thriving then and we all had an average gate of 17, 18 to 22 thousand. And obviously that's where Millwall I think got their reputation for their noise and for their crowd getting behind them and everything else. And yeah I suppose it was the atmosphere down there and that's what I fell in love with the Club was the atmosphere and of course the wit the dockland wit I suppose. It used to be four bob to get in then and I always used to say two bob for the football and two bob for the wit. (Interview, 8 November 1995)

As the boom of British pop music emerged in the sixties, so to did a culture of singing – what we want to refer to as football plainsong – emerged in the grounds themselves.

Merseyside played a central role in the development of football fan song in England. Keith reflected: 'I think basically I suppose the Beatles came from Liverpool and I think they all thought they were a bit of songwriters themselves and a lot of them came from them' (Interview, 8th November 1995). Catherine Long has pointed out there was little direct connection between local pop musicians and the city's football culture (see Williams, Long and Hopkins 2000). Nevertheless, the noise generated by the mass terrace of the Kop became the standard against which fans measured their vocal power. The Liverpool home end, named after a bloody battle during the South African Boer war, was at one time the largest single span structure in English football. Connections between empire and slavery are written into the cityscape of Merseyside through street names and monuments like the Kop. Similarly, Everton F.C. was founded by Will Charles Cuff, who lived in the then affluent suburb of Everton. Cuff attended the Congressional Church of St Domingo that was named after two Merseyside Streets that derived their names from slave trade connections with St Domingo (Hodgson 1985). In 1878 St Domingo F.C. was founded and later renamed Everton.

However, these imperial traces were overshadowed as Anfield and Goodison Park emerged as two of the iconic grounds in football culture. Adrian Thrills wrote of the unique quality of the Kop:

Inspired partly by the pugnacious humour that is part of the city's character and partly by the strains of the beat boom that was sweeping the port's nightclubs, the 28,000 souls who stood on the Kop started to express themselves with passionate versions of pop hits such as 'She Loves You' by the Beatles, 'I Like It' by Freddie and The Dreamers' and 'Anyone Who Had a Heart' by Cilla Black. 'You'll Never Walk Alone,' the song that was to become their anthem was written by Rodgers and Hammerstein for the musical *Carousel*, but adopted by the Kop after Gerry and the Pacemakers charted with the track in 1963. (Thrills 1998: 31)

Mass singing of club anthems possessed a phatic quality, it revealed shared feelings and established an atmosphere of sociability rather than communication. The songs were always addressed to an audience but they were not about conversation, rather they were about being affective – raising the home team's game, or stifling the opposition. Nowhere was this more evident than at Liverpool.

While the crowd noises are the player's oxygen, as Danny Blanchflower said, football songs are also about suffocation and intimidation. Vince Hillaire, one of the first black players to play for Crystal Palace, remembers visiting Anfield:

> Terry Venables liked players to go out for a warm-up before the games. I'm putting the boots on and that and I'm thinking: 'Well, Anfield, first time I've ever played here'. Anyway I was putting the boots on and it must be about quarter-past/half-past two, the ground's filling up, I mean it was a full house so it must be 20,000 people in the ground already, and I've run out and I can hear the buzz out there, and I've run out the tunnel and all of a sudden – well, it seemed all of a sudden I think – it just, the ground was silent, completely silent, kicking balls around, and all of a sudden I heard this lone voice in the Kop go: 'Dayo – we say dayo, we say dayo, we say dayo', and then the rest of the Kop started. Looking back on it was quite funny, very humorous – it wasn't nasty, but it did intimidate me for a bit, until the game started and we got, we got into the game. The stick – well, it makes me laugh, you know, when I hear about if you – it's a public order offence now to do something like that. If that was the case in the mid-70s and up to the mid-80s there'd probably be no-one left watching football, they'd all be in like prison or banned from the grounds for life and that. It was a bit, it was unmerciful and a lot of the, the black players that played then, that's the only debt of gratitude I think that the players playing now owe them a bit because they did take some merciless stick and that and it was malicious and nasty and, you know, no need for it, but yet – and you had to turn a deaf'un, you know, you copped the deaf'un and – but, you know, it'd be a lie if you said it didn't get to you a bit, you know, it worried you. (Interview, 27 January 1997).

The 'Dayo' chant is sung in the form of a Calypso parody. It has no explicit racist content but its associations are clear – minstrelsy blackness of a primitive lazy bones.

Da - yo,   d - d - da -   yo,—   day -light come and we wan- na go home.

Another staple form of racist abuse is the making of 'Monkey noises.' This crude form of mistreatment and aping attempted to reduce black players to subhumans.

ou ou ou ou

The primary purpose of the forms of abuse, most common during the 1970s and 1980s, was to suffocate black players on the field of play. The paradox in the performance of this chant is that it is the white abuser who 'apes' the monkey while no doubt is left over the intention as to who is taken to be closer to the beast.

The transfer of John Barnes to Liverpool brought the issue of race, locality and team loyalties into sharp focus on Merseyside. By the middle of the 1980s Liverpool F.C. was established as a global footballing force. Garth Crooks summed up the fans effusive singing and Anfield's reputation as one of the most difficult places to play. The humour of the Liverpool fans was a 'satirical sword . . . Before you even got to the generals of Anfield, you had to deal with the infantry [of the Kop]'. (Quoted in Nawrat and Hutchings 1995)

During the postwar era, Everton has largely been in the shadow of its Merseyside rivals. This wasn't always the case. In the 1920s and 1930s it enjoyed success led by the legendary striker William Ralph Dean known to the fans as 'Dixie'. He established goal scoring records during his career at Everton that are still standing today. 'Dixie' Dean became the Club's pre-eminent player symbol, a historic figure of legendary status. In the 1927–8 season he scored a mammoth sixty goals and during his time at Everton between 1924–38 he notched up some 349 league goals.

Part of 'Dixie' Dean's story also reveals the complex legacy of imperialism and race on Merseyside. He was born in 1907. His father was an engineer from Chester and his mother was from Birkenhead and like so many working-class girls during the period was 'in service' – she worked as a domestic servant of the local upper middle-classes. Dean had a dark complexion and a mop of wavy black hair. While playing for Tranmere Rovers – his first club – the supporters gave him the nickname 'Dixie'. Dean resented the title at first and insisted on being called 'Bill' by acquaintances and friends. His biographer Nick Walsh wrote about his resistance to embrace the name:

> The reason perhaps was that at that time he felt 'Dixie' had connections with colour problems connected with the southern states of America, and therefore contained an inference that he was of that origin, or halfcaste. (Walsh 1977: 51)

It may also have been that the reference invoked the image of the 'black-faced minstrel' also popular at the time. Whatever its source 'Dixie' inferred some reference to race that was projected onto Dean's body.

'Dixie' Dean was also renowned for his fondness for humorous stories. Often these would be at his own expense or self-deprecating stories about Everton. A story that he told repeatedly again referred to race and racism. The story began as follows:

> An Everton director was one day strolling along Upper Parliament Street in Liverpool when he came across a coloured boy playing football. The boy was on his own kicking and heading the ball with remarkable skill against a large brick wall. The Everton director watched with utter amazement and fascination, and was so impressed with the boy's evident talent he approached him and said, 'How would you like to play for Everton, my boy? I am a director of the club and I could easily arrange for you to sign up to play for the first team.'
>
> 'Not bloody likely,' the boy replied. 'It's bad enough being black in this City.' (Walsh 1977: 62)

The story is funny precisely because it plays with Everton's status as a poor footballing relation on Merseyside. Equally, it acknowledges the profound racism and racial segregation that exist in Liverpool.

In contrast to their Mersyside rivals, Everton fans construct their club as a proudly traditional, even aristocratic, local team, devoid of the trappings of glamour, international fame and effusiveness. Everton fans pride themselves on what Garry Robson has called an anti-charisma, a contrariness and an increasingly open hostility to everything that Liverpool F.C. stands for. From the point of view of Everton fans Merseyside's two clubs are represented in terms of a series of binary oppositions, or what Robson refers to as taxonomic sets (Robson 2000: 87). These are coded symbolically in very different ways, we have attempted to summarize this process in the Table 2.1.

Table 2.1. Taxonomic sets: Everton/Liverpool

Everton F.C.	Liverpool F.C.
Local	Global
Anti-charisma	Fashionable
Laconic	Loquacious
Footballing artisans	Money grabbing stars
Contrary	Ostentatious
Loyal	Ephemeral
Aristocratic	Nouveau riche

The ways in which Anfield and Goodison Park are constructed as *symbolic homes* through such images provide the crucial backdrop to the controversy that surrounded John Barnes' first Merseyside derby in 1987.

At the end of October and beginning of November 1987 Everton played Liverpool at Anfield on two occasions within the space of four days, firstly in the Coca-Cola Cup and then, in the then Barclays League Division One. The first of these games in particular has gone down in the folklore of Merseyside football (Hill 1989) and marked John Barnes' first appearance for Liverpool in a Merseyside derby. His appearance for Liverpool prompted some of the most widespread racialized chanting and barracking, by Everton supporters, ever witnessed in an English football ground. However, when we look more closely, even this notorious example reveals a complex range of social processes.

The patterns of chanting reveal the weakness of attempts to label particular clubs and groups of fans as monolithically racist. In the aftermath of this game much media attention was focused on the behaviour of Everton's fans and their displays of racism and BBC2's *Newsnight* even produced a special feature on the racial abuse directed at John Barnes. The subsequent failure of Everton to sign any black players until Daniel Amokachi in 1994, whilst Liverpool went on to sign several other black players, including Michael Thomas, Mark Walters and David James, led to a whole series of accusations that Everton was a 'racist club'. It was suggested that the attitude in the boardroom reflected that identified on the terraces during the derby match with Liverpool and that there was a policy of not signing black players. This was contrasted with the way Liverpool fans embraced John Barnes and the succession of black players who were later signed by the club.

However, it is clear from video recordings of both of the matches from 1987 that although John Barnes was the target in each of the key chants, 'Everton are White' and 'Niggerpool', their audience was the predominantly white Liverpool supporters. Everton fans were making a statement about the perceived normative identity and racial preferences of Merseyside, which could only work if the Liverpool supporters shared those preferences. This came through in the form of the chants themselves. Alongside the famous *You'll Never Walk Alone* the key anthem of Liverpool support is the repeated singing of the name of the club.

Liv - er - pool

As we have seen previously these kinds of dirge are common within the context of football culture. These songs act as a kind of summoning of collective identity. It is equally common that opposing teams take the opposition's prized mantra and parody it. The parody thus becomes a means to both insult and respond. This is precisely what Everton fans did in the context of this match where they subverted Liverpool's rallying call and turned it into a crude racist parody.

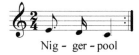

Nig - ger - pool

In contrast the Everton fans and their team declared themselves to be the true upholders of white Scouse identity:

Ev - er - ton are white.

It is worth stating that today Liverpool shows high levels of racial segregation with its black communities focused around the Toxteth area. While the overall population of Liverpool in 1991 was 96% white, the county ward of the city in which Goodison Park is located was 99.2% white and the Anfield ward where Liverpool play 98.5% white. The complete whiteness of the Everton team was being celebrated whilst the name of Liverpool was denigrated by reference to the introduction of a black player into the side. The intention was to 'wind up' the Liverpool supporters on the premise of a *shared* antipathy towards 'niggers', which is located within a common understanding of the racial characteristics associated with the Scouse identity. As Jimmy, an Everton fan in his forties, put it to us:

> I think it was an attack at the player and an attack at the football club and an attack at the fans. Suddenly Liverpool supporters who had been making racist comments about other players stop making racist comments because they . . . have John Barnes playing for Liverpool. (Interview, 20 December 1995)

Vince Hillaire's experience, quoted earlier, supports this claim. Brian, an Everton fan of a similar age who was at both the Anfield games, argued that:

> They were no different from us, and as soon as Liverpool's black players went they'd be right back to where they were. You know, Liverpool fans did seem to have a holier than thou attitude because they had black players, therefore they weren't racist anymore, but that wasn't true. (Interview, 26 January 1996)

Graham Ennis, editor of the Everton fanzine *When Skies Are Grey* developed the point:

> It's one of these things Liverpool fans will now sort of never admit to, but John Barnes, when it was widely reported that he was gonna come to Liverpool, one of his last games for Watford was at Anfield, and he was booed for 90 minutes. It's a fact. It happened. The same as the famous banana-throwing incident at Highbury (Liverpool fans were

reported to have thrown bananas on the pitch during this match, which was Barnes' debut for Liverpool), it happened. I'm not saying it was representative of all Liverpool fans, but it happened. (Interview, 26 January 1996)

We will show how these same normative racial preferences are used in the contemporary context by fans from outside of Liverpool to express a regional antipathy towards Merseyside. Before we move on, however, it is important that we understand the instability of the supporters' expressive traditions. Whilst the racialized chanting at both games was clearly audible, on the second occasion, following much media criticism of the Everton fans' behaviour during the match the previous Wednesday, it was played down by the television commentators. The atmosphere was specifically compared favourably to the reception that Barnes had received during the first derby match, when dozens of bananas had been thrown at the player on the pitch and a monkey was stolen from a local zoo, which was later found sitting happily on top of a piano in the Clarence pub, with the intention that it would be let loose on the pitch. Jimmy Hill commented on BBC 1 after the game:

> What we should be grateful for I think is that this was a real local derby with none of the nastiness really of last Wednesday night. It was just what it should be.
> (*Match of the Day*, 3 November 1987)

From our perspective this seems to say more about the significance of the event, local identity and club rivalry than the significance of particular historical periods in mapping the development of racism in football. For the first 25 minutes of the second game the Everton supporters, referring to John Barnes, took up the racial taunting where they had left off the previous Wednesday night, but after this point the taunts were not invoked again throughout the remainder of the match, despite Barnes' continued presence on the field.

It seems unlikely that the changing pattern of Everton supporters' interventions during this match was due to any recognition that their previous actions were not those of true 'Evertonians' (as was suggested by the Club Chairman in the local newspapers) or due to some newly found enlightenment into the benefits of a multi-cultural society. It is more likely that the arrival of John Barnes at Liverpool (the first black player to play for one of the city's professional clubs in fifteen years) and the particular occasion of a Merseyside derby provided a unique platform for the celebration of an exclusively white Scouse identity through an association with Everton FC which could be played out at the expense of the Liverpool supporters.

The gradual winding down of the taunts was a reflection of their declining originality in the context of a second derby game in the space of four days. Changes in behaviour then can be the product of a host of different factors which may change from minute to minute just as readily as decade to decade. It was precisely the fact that John Barnes was making his *first* appearance in a Merseyside derby that encouraged the response he received in the initial game. At any moment the potential was there for the abuse to resurface during the second game but the universal, communal statement was no longer necessary, as 'a marker' had already been laid.

I'd rather be a Paki than a Scouse: Regionalism and Racialized Formulations

Alongside this very sudden change in behaviour, a decade later, we have found forms of racialized expression which are generically mobilized against fans from Merseyside with the intention of offending the Scouse regional identity and its associated perceived racial preferences. The chant of *I'd rather be a Paki than a Scouse* and regional variations is used by fans of a number of clubs and reinforces the sense that we need to move beyond seeing the fan culture of individual clubs as merely the product of particular local conditions, to considering patterns of cultural interchange and syncretism within fan culture nationally. Indeed, its use during the Euro 96 and Euro 2000 games against the Scottish team and fans emphasises the degree to which such songs can be adapted and elements substituted in different contexts while retaining the same racialized structure.

We observed the song *I'd rather be a Paki than a Scouse* being sung frequently during Millwall games in the 1995/96 season where the opposition was from Merseyside but also by Manchester City fans in games against Liverpool. In contrast to the chanting of *Everton are White*, where the notion of race is central to the celebration of the Scouse identity, this song is racialized only in the sense that it involves a racialized category – 'Paki' – as a means to express contempt for that same emblematic regional identity. But in both cases the efficacy of the insults is premised on the notion of a shared abhorrence of the racialized categories 'Paki' and 'Nigger'.

In order for these insults to work it is necessary for there to be an implicit ideal or normative structure of collective identity. In the case of the chant 'Everton are White' this normative structure is confined to two main components – reference to the club and a notion of race. However, in the case of *I'd rather be a Paki*, the central component becomes region. It is this shift that allows the song to be freely expressed despite the general decline in racialized chanting and the introduction of legislation under the Football Offences Act (1991) aimed at curbing this type of fan song.

In this formulation the club and regional components are quite straightforward but the third component is only racialized by a discourse of whiteness that structures the terms of these identities whilst the content remains absent. Here, white ethnicity is implicitly present but explicitly absent. The result is that whiteness is equated with normality and as such it is not in need of definition. Thus 'being normal' is colonized by the idea of 'being white' (Dyer 1988, 1997). The result is that two parallel sets of identity hierarchies are invoked as the norm.

I'd rather be a Paki as a particular form of racialization within fan culture also poses a series of difficult practical and theoretical problems with regard to how racism is defined within the context of football. The complexity of this pattern of culture cannot be easily understood either within policy frameworks or for that matter the academic literature. Is *I'd rather be a Paki* a racist chant? If it is a racist chant why is it principally directed at white supporters? In order to grapple with these complexities we need to develop an understanding of how particular aspects of fan culture are racialized. It is precisely these nuances that are lost when clubs like Millwall are crudely defined as racist. In order to develop a more accurate picture of these processes of racialization it is necessary to first uncover the semiotic structure of these texts and the normative models of collective identity to which they implicitly or explicitly refer and, second, develop an understanding of the precise nature of their performance which situates them within the fan culture as a whole and types of incident which trigger their invocation.

a) Semiotic Form and Normative Structure

I'd rather be a Paki than a Scouse is sung to the tune of *She'll be Coming around the Mountains*:

It was sung frequently during Millwall games during the 1995/6 season where the opposition was from Merseyside. It was also sung at the Tranmere Rovers home fixture. It continues to be sung today although our general sense is that the appeal of this insult is starting to wane. The song is racialized in the sense that it involves a racialized category – Paki – as a means to express contempt for an emblematic regional identity, the Scouser.

In order for this insult to work it is necessary for their to be an implicit ideal or normative structure of collective identity. This normative structure includes three main components: reference to the club, regional identity and a notion of race.

The club and regional components are quite straightforward. The third component is racialized by a discourse of whiteness that structures the terms of these identities without making them explicit. The result is that two parallel sets of identity hierarchies are invoked as the norm. The normative structure of this identity takes the form of an identity triplet – club, region and race.

Table 2.2. Normative Structure of Club/Race Identity

Everton/Scouser/White	Millwall/Londoner/White
'Paki'	'Paki'

Whiteness is the defining principle of this collective identity but it is not exclusively white. In keeping with the kinds of negotiation that take place between black and white young people within football culture it becomes possible for 'black cockneys' to be included as 'contingent insiders' (Back 1991). This inclusion is always established from the position where 'white' is defined as normal. In circumstances where anti-black racism is absent the normative structure outlined previously needs to be altered as in Table 2.3.

Table 2.3. Contingent Assimilation of Black Cockney/Scouser

Everton/Scouser/White Scouser	Millwall/Londoner/White
Black Scouser	Black Cockney
'Paki'	'Paki'

Black cockneys can be legitimately included within the local dimension of this structure. Such forms of inclusion are always contingent upon the absence of a specifically anti-black racism within the fan culture. The black/white notion of regional inclusion not only changes the racial patina of the 'US' category, but it also widens the scope of the insulted 'THEM' to include black and white Scousers alike. These fraught inclusions mirror the same processes that operate with regard to black players. In both cases racism stands on the 'sidelines' as a potential resource to be used strategically to exclude or undermine the belonging and legitimacy of black fans and players. 'Black cockneys' can be assimilated within the Millwall collective but depending on circumstances and context they can be transformed into vilified 'black bastards'. Both of these versions of collective identity are socially active.

What is established is a racialized hierarchy. In order to understand this process it is important to cross the analysis of racialized identities with an understanding of how these intersect with gender relations and masculinity. It may be that commensurable, class-inflected conceptions of black and white masculinity provide a common ground for black-white alliances in fan culture as we will see in the next chapter. The internal configurations and contradictions found in white working-class masculinities police the determinants of racial inclusion and exclusion. Here 'Pakis' are constructed as generally weak and feeble. Within these white constructions black men are both *feared and desired,* while 'Pakis' are vilified as soft and effeminate.

It is only by understanding these underlying structures that the venom of the *I'd rather be a Paki than a Scouse* chant can be understood. The chant works as an insult because this normative structure is parodied within play. Its status as a 'play insult' is crucial. Bateson (1978) outlines the processes by which meaning is transformed by metacommunication in play. He uses material gathered from animal behaviour to show how an act of aggression – like a bite – can have its meaning emptied in the course of play. So much so that this act of aggression becomes invested with a new meaning to the extent that it constitutes a kind of 'fiction' (Bateson 1978: 155). Verbal comments, practices and actions, which are invested with non-play meanings, are subverted and inverted by the shared performance. Through playing, a negotiated alteration of meaning takes place that dislocates practice from what it 'stands for' in wider usage. The context of the football stadium is precisely an arena where the temporary suspension of conventional patterns of communication produces this kind of 'play.'

Through singing *I'd rather be a Paki than a Scouse* Millwall fans are playfully re-ordering the racialized hierarchy outlined above as in Table 2.4.

Table 2.4. Normative and Play Structures

Identity Hierarchy – Normative	Identity Hierarchy – Play
Millwall/Londoner/White	Millwall/Londoner/White
Black Cockneys	Black Cockneys
Everton/Scouser/White	'Paki'
Black Scousers	
'Paki'	Everton/Scouser/White
	Black Scousers

The venom of the insult is in the way the hierarchy of most desirable identities is reordered. While the insult indexes a whole range of socially available identity categories and social formulations, the particular meaning and fit of these formulations only make sense within this play context. They are certainly not literal 'identity desires' or preferences. In this sense the preference for the category 'Paki' over 'Scouse' is as much about the choice of an effective insult within the fictional play context. The song is directed at the white Everton fans that have a history, or an association, with racist practices both in terms of the fan culture and the organization. To profess a desire 'to be' a despised minority over the alternative prospect of being an Everton fan – who is by implication white, or at best black and white – takes on added malice. However, this is all taking place within the context where racial meanings do not 'stand for' what they would outside the context of the game and the stands. What is important here is that racialized meanings are referenced through the implicit discourse of whiteness and explicit means through invoking racist epithets. This process of activating racist semiotics occurs alongside parody and meaning altered by metacommunication. The key to understanding the cultural politics of *I'd rather be a Paki* with regard to racism lies in its normative structure that is replete with stigmatized racist categories and a racially exclusive notion of who a 'normal' fan is and what s\he looks like. What is worrying here is the banality, the taken for granted nature, of this form of implicit collective identity. What *I'd rather be a Paki* shows very clearly is the way in which these types of racialized hierarchy and exclusion are normalized within fan culture. We want to suggest that it is important to make a distinction between crude racist performances and songs like the ones discussed here that work through implicit and explicit racial codings. This latter category we want to refer to as racialized songs.

b) *Performance, Song Cycles and Racialization*

While the semiotic form of this song tells us a great deal about how racialized meanings are made normal, it is also important to situate the performance of these songs within the particular context of the football match as a ritual event. Here we want to look at the ways in which this song was performed during the Everton versus Millwall Coca-Cola Cup replay at Goodison Park on 4 October, 1995.

I'd Rather Be A Paki Than A Scouse was sung by the Millwall away fans five times during the game: four times in the first half (1.40, 6.42, 12.00, 39.00), and once in the second half (51.39). The tie went into extra time but this song was not sung at all during this period. During this game it was apparent that the song also needs to be understood within particular cycles or song sequences. These song cycles often operate as a means to mobilize collective identities, throw down a gauntlet and to insult the opposition. This cyclical element within the fan culture was particularly in evidence at the beginning of the game. It seems important that we try and develop a series of concepts that will enable us to describe and analyse these song cycles. Songs are combined in a supplementary fashion calling into play a range of available elements within fan culture. These sequences do not have formulaic patterns. They respond to both the dramas on the pitch and the expression of collective identities through songs in the stands.

The initial deployment of *I'd Rather Be A Paki* was part of a five-song cycle, which lasted 1 minute 51 seconds. The sequence begins with two of Millwall's rallying cries i.e. *No One Likes Us* and the *Lions Roar*. Garry Robson refers to these songs in his study of Millwallism as 'doing songs,' meaning these songs bring about a form of embodied social identity through their illocutionary force (Robson 2000: 177). *No One Likes Us* is sung to the tune of Rod Stewart's hit *Sailin*. It is perhaps, the ultimate rallying cry for the Millwall fraternity. It gained popularity in the 1980s in the aftermath of the civil unrest that took place during an FA Cup fixture against Luton. It is sung at the beginning of a game, after a player has been challenged, or if either team scores a goal. It is a key tool in the summoning of Millwall's identity.

Similarly, the *Lions Roar* is one of the truly unique aspects of Millwall fan culture. It possess a drone like quality that is impossible to represent in words. We have notated it here musically in an attempt to describe its tonal quality. It begins with the first syllable of Millwall but the word is never fully formed in the song, unlike the Crystal Palace's dirge *Eagles* discussed previously. It is sung through staggered breathing so that as one fan starts to sing the song another catches a breath so the sound produced is like a huge single voice that appears ceaseless needing neither inhalation or pause. It is, curiously, both the most musical of all the examples of football plainsong discussed here, but at the same time it has no words and no melody.

The Lions Roar

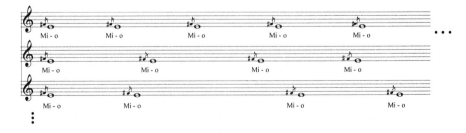

Robson's description of the *Lions Roar* is worth quoting at length:

Being effectively wordless, and lacking any harmonic resolution, this merging of the resonating individual voice with sustained collective performance produces an atmosphere of extraordinary intensity, a kind of sonic field in which time stands still and being itself hangs, static unelaborated in the air. As the roar of one singer dies another begins, crashing into and rolling over another against the sustained aural backdrop of thousands of open throats and resonating chests . . . This is collective mnemonic immersion of the most extraordinary kind, and represents – despite being seen from without as savage, inchoate and moronic – an exemplary ritualising practice which draws upon a deeply rooted and anthropologically widespread musical technique: the sonic constitution and activation of a group's implicit sense of the world. (Robson 2000: 183)

These songs are exodic in the sense that they are about expression of a collective presence within the stadium. They are addressed to the opposition fans but they also have an endo/autophonic quality in that they are about the fans building an internal highly symbolic sense of themselves. Here, being and voice are fused as the sound of fan identity resonates in terms of both its identity and its collective quality. They are classified as equivocal within Table 2.5 because they possess both an endo and exodic quality.

These songs are then followed by the staple fare of oppositional insults in football culture *You're supposed to be at Home* (to the tune of *Bread of Heaven*), *Shit and Crap* (to the tune of *Bread of Heaven*). Then a tailored challenge *Where were you at the Den* (to the tune of *Bread of Heaven*) and then finally *I'd Rather be a Paki Than A Scouse*. This sequence is directed at both the opposition fans and the team. Here there is a sequence of three songs, which relate to behaviour and performance. The first ridicules the Everton fans for not singing in their own ground. The second reacts to poor play by Everton players. The third questions the commitment of the Everton fans because few of them travelled to the away leg in London in the way that the Millwall fans had for this game. The invocation of *I'd rather be a Paki* returns the sequence to the symbolic and collective realm.

The point to stress here is that the racialized song emerges out of an accumulated process of social action that is highly symbolic. In this sense, we need to understand racialized songs in this context as a moment when racism is invoked in a broader rhetorical process where singing is the means to define the collective in opposition to the rival fans. This cycle of songs is represented here in the following table:

Table 2.5. Cycle 1: First Use of *I'd Rather Be A Paki*

Song Sequence	Address/ Function
No One Like Us . . .	Club collective identity – equivocal
Lions Roar	Club collective identity – equivocal
Your Supposed to be at Home	Opposition fan insult – exodic
Shit and Crap	Opposition team insult – exodic
Where were you at The Den	Opposition fan insult – exodic
I'd Rather Be A Paki	Opposition fan insult – equivocal
Pause – silence 24 secs	

In this sense the sequence follows a pattern of:

Symbolic/expression of club identity	Oppositional insults: Everton players and fans	Symbolic/collective insult

The take up of *I'd rather be a Paki* was pronounced when it was harnessed to a period when the collective identity of the Millwall fans was expressed most vocally. As a rallying call this racialized chant was relatively weak and unsuccessful. Unlike, *Let 'Em Come, No One Likes Us* and the *Lions Roar* this racialized chant did not produce a strong collective response from the fans outside of song cycles. In order for it to be effective it needed to be connected to a period of heightened passion and intensity within the crowd. There was one exception to this pattern.

The final time that it appeared during the game was in the second half after Everton had been awarded a penalty and they took a 1–0 lead. In the aftermath of this incident the fans mobilised and turned their venom against the Everton fans in a period of vituperative chanting that lasted almost ten minutes. During this period *I'd rather be a Paki* was more effective at raising Millwall's collective voice than the *Lions Roar*. This suggests that racialized chants are more effective at mobilizing fans in such moments when there is intense animosity and conflict. In this type of context racialized chants may not need the fuel of collective/symbolic song cycles in order to amplify their volume and take up.

Cycle 2. South London is Wonderful – East London is Like Bengal

This song sequence follows soon after the Cycle 1. The first fifteen minutes of the game was particularly intense in terms of the expression of the collective and symbolic repertoire of Millwall fan culture. In the aftermath of the first rendering of *I'd rather be a Paki* a series of songs from the Millwall repertoire were sung including the *Lions Roar, No One Likes Us* and *Millwall, Millwall, Millwall* (to the Match of the Day TV theme). However, the next cycle included another racialized song. But this time it worked through the relationship between South London and East London.

Before describing the song cycle we just want to look at the content of this song in more detail. The *South London is Wonderful, East London is Like Bengal* chant is made up of two parts. The song is sung to the tune of *When the Saints go Marching In*. The first part of the song is a eulogy to South London:

> Oh South London [caller] Oh South London [response]
> is wonderful [caller] is wonderful [response]
> [together] Oh South London is Wonderful
> It full of tits, fanny and Millwall
> Oh South London is wonderful

This song can be sung on its own in its own terms but it can also be coupled with a contrasting rendering of the character of East London.

> [caller] Oh East London [response] Oh East London
> [caller] is like Bengal [response] is like Bengal
> Oh East London is like Bengal
> It's like the back streets of Bombay
> Oh East London is like Bengal

Taken together the song sounds like this:

What seems important is the way in which the songs invoke notions of Asianness by way of stigmatizing and vilifying east London. Like the *I'd rather be a Paki* chant it is primarily directed at white East London racists – those who would be alarmed about the fact that their beloved area was like a foreign, alien country.

This form of region/race song also has important characteristics of its own that are different from the *I'd rather be a Paki* genre. It does not necessarily invoke play meanings in the way that *I'd rather be a Paki* does. There is no playful suggestion here that Millwall fans would rather be 'Pakis' than Eastenders! Rather what is offered are a series of stark contrasts between Self and Other. The first part of the song is a celebration of the self, which is expressed through the region. South London is also desired because of it's women folk – or more correctly particular sexualized anatomical objects – and the Club's home location. Thus, South London is a place full of sex and football! The absent racial presence here is the implicit understanding that South London is white or at best a place where black and white cockneys stand proudly side by side within a culture normalized by 'whiteness'.

East London is coded through a contrasting language of racial and Oriental Otherness. Race is transcoded through all of these references from the 'foreign back street' to the 'oriental city' so that the racialized subject of 'the Paki' can be invoked without actually being referred to directly. These images are all the product of a particular racialized imagination. Bombay is neither in Bengal nor Pakistan! The inconsistency and inaccuracies here show the notion of the 'Paki' provides a cipher to denote all aspects of a foreign subcontinent Otherness.

The introduction of this song during the Everton game fell into the same sequence as in Cycle 1. This sequence lasted 1 minute and 24 seconds and only contained songs that were self-referenced to the Millwall collectivity. They were equivocal in the sense that they were establishing the fan presence within the soundscape of the football ground but at no time in this sequence were the Everton fans or players addressed directly. The songs reference the club/region and its 'others' initially in terms of hated clubs. The 'fuck em all' chant cites 'United, West Ham and Liverpool' as the important 'out-group' of loathed fans and clubs. However, when this process of defining self and other takes a racialized turn the response peters out. This is in part to do with the fact that the dynamic on the terraces is disrupted by the action on the field of play – the calling of 'East London is like Bengal' coincides with an Everton attack and an eventual shot on goal by Paul Rideout. However, this is not the only reason. It felt at the time that this chant was immediately inappropriate in the context of this particular game. There may be a whole range of things going on here. The use of this racialized chant had no direct instrumental purpose because the opposition would not be hurt by its use.

Singing songs about hated other clubs takes on the form of revelry and carnivalesque enjoyment within the fan collectivity. These songs are being addressed to the Millwall fans themselves. Now, it may follow that similar types of enjoyment might be experienced by Millwall fans' expression of a kind of racialized geography.

The point of such chants is to offend a white audience, which might also include associated black Eastenders. The absence of such an audience in this context meant that the chant itself had no efficacy apart from a gleeful localism and a certain transgressive pleasure enjoyed in articulating racist sentiments that are otherwise subject to legal and moral prohibition.

The point that emerges from this is that racialized meaning and forms of discourse in football are not irrational and gratuitous but rather they operate within

Table 2.6. Songs Cycles and Racialized Geography

Song Sequence	Address/Function
Millwall, Milwall, Millwall (Match of the Day Theme)	Club collective identity – equivocal
Fuck em all . . .	Club collective identity – equivocal
Lions Roar	Regional collective identity – equivocal
South London La La La	Regional collective identity – equivocal
Oh South London is wonderful	Regional self-identity – equivocal
Oh East London is like Bengal	Regional other identity

conventions of appropriateness and instrumentality. Put another way, we need to develop an understanding of the way racialized meanings are used against particular audiences and the desired effect that is intended. Whether it is to ridicule the opposing fans and their imagined communities, or if the intention is to intimidate an opposing black player these chants possess an instrumental logic. In this sense the racialized chants are defined by their exodic nature. Where these chants are self-reference (the 'I' part of the *I'd rather be a Paki*) it is conducted with the suspended and altered meanings that are generated in play. While these racialized chants are directed outwards – summed up in the concept of exodic chants – they are often underpinned by a normative structure which defines who Millwall fans are and what they stand for.

All football fans and football clubs want to know about how they measure up when compared to their rivals. Competitive comparison is pervasive in all areas from how many goals the team concedes to variations in the frequency of racist abuse. Questions like 'How do we compare with . . .?' or 'What racism did you find at . . .?' recurred in our interviews frequently and particularly with white fans, administrators and professionals. It seemed that evidence of racism at other clubs provided some consolation, particularly to clubs who had been labelled as 'racist.' This syndrome has been exacerbated through press reporting. The *Guardian* newspaper ran a story on the 7 January 2000 with the headline 'Everton fans top racist "League of Shame"'. The story was based on an academic paper given by Dr Sean Perkins who had referred to a supporters survey conducted by the Sir Norman Chester Centre for Foorball Research at Leicester University at a conference in Brighton. The survey had asked fans: 'Have you witnessed racism aimed at players this season 1998–9?' In response 38 per cent of Everton fans concurred. On the basis of this form of self reporting, itself a rather flimsey indicator, because it could refer to both home or away fans, the *Guardian* dubbed Everton 'notorious' reproducing the famous picture of John Barnes 'back-heeling' a banana during the Merseyside derby in 1988. The survey which was wide ranging and not focused around racism was miss-reported much to the frustration of the academics concerned. It was also picked up by the *Daily Telegraph*, *The Times*, the *Sun* and the *Liverpool Echo* all of whom published stories on the 7 January that reproduced to lesser or greater extent the 'league of shame' story line.

This approach to reporting racism in football simply erases the complex nuances discussed earlier in this chapter and merely reinforces the image of certain racist clubs whom fans, the media and people in the institutions of football can comfortably condemn without having to scrutinize themselves. The argument that we want to forward here is that in order to understand the patterns of racist expression and exclusion amongst fans it is first necessary to appreciate the ways in which identities and association accrete to particular clubs. We want to stress the importance of resisting the impulse to define or rank football clubs in some perfidious 'table of racial bigotry'. Rather, we want to suggest that racial exclusions operates in multiple and complicated ways. Overt racist abuse is only one feature of what we want to call a culture of racism in football.

Back on Victory Street: 'Blue Moon,' Englishness and the Whiteness of the Crowd

Finally, we want to return to Victory Street and Manchester City, where we began this chapter. We have discussed in some detail the cultures associated with three out of the four clubs that formed our research case studies. We now want to focus on Manchester City. Within football culture, City fans are held in an almost universally positive light. To some degree this is due to the fact that their neighbours Manchester United are loathed in equal measure. The club and its supporters are viewed as an underdog that prides itself on coming from Manchester. Mark, a lifelong City fan now in his mid thirties, accounting for the anti-charasima at the heart of City's appeal, argued that support for the club was never about the pursuit of glory:

> You've got to remember there's a lot of glory-hunting bastards that surround you at school and wot-not, and when I was fairly young – about 8, 9 – I went to school in Ashton, and there was a lot of people that supported Leeds then, in our class, and all those Leeds fans, without exception, 3 years later they all support United. And I'd supported City all the way through. And all the time they're giving me jip about City not being this and not being that, and you sort of develop this hatred of glory-hunters, and that progresses to hating United fans, and just the fact that I feel that I've got righteousness on my side. (Interview, 12 January 1996)

The allure of clubs like City is precisely the joy in being associated with under achievement. Failure is recast as evidence of a true, authentic and unvarnished love of the game. This appeal is also about the pleasure in disappointment and self-deprecation. Part of the popularity of City can be explained in the way that they touch something that is universal within English football: the joy of inconsistency and the inevitable disappointment that follows from the fact that victory for your team is never certain. This kind of ethos was presented in many of our interviews with City fans, as Mark went on:

> Yeah, it's part of the fun of being a football fan, I think, and that's one of the reasons that I don't like United, cos I don't think they've got any of that self-irony. If they've got a shit player, if we've got a shit player we sort of moan about him and want him out of the team, but we have a laugh in the meantime, and lots of people will tell you that he was their favourite player, and Rick Holden and Gary Megson spring to mind, but United don't have any of that irony at all. I think it's not living in the shadow, it's more that we've been unsuccessful, that allows you to be ironic. We've had some pretty big lows. (Interview, 12 January 1996)

Whilst acknowledging the derogatory nature of much of the humour found amongst City supporters, an 'English' sense of 'fairness' and compassion was seen to be embodied within the City fan culture which for some of our respondents extended to a rejection of the display of overt forms of racism. Dave, a white City fan in his fifties argued that:

> It is part of the Manchester humour to ridicule people for whatever reason, and I don't think you can hide behind that about racism; it is a very insulting type of humour. I don't know if you have noticed this since you have been up here, but I have never been conscious of the monkey chant and I remember a game at Old Trafford when United played West Brom and it was on telly, the United fans were giving the monkey chants to Regis and Batson and the other lad, Laurie Cunningham, and they were beaten 5–3 and it was brilliant, it was the best answer they could get. I know I am biased but I have never noticed that at City games, but you know you can be in one part of the ground, it can happen in another part of the ground and you can't hear it. I have never been conscious of it. I have always genuinely found City supporters to be – unless it is a very, very tense game – I have always found them to be reasonable supporters – they have always applauded the opposition for a good move, or a good goal even, even to the extent of people round about shouting people down for applauding and they have said no, that was a bloody good move and a good goal and I am applauding it and you can naff off.

Making the extension to a notion of 'national' characteristics, he continued:

> I think the City crowd . . . can be very very very very critical but if they realise it is destroying somebody they will turn it the other way because they think that because that is the way we are, like the Oasis lads, they are just typical Mancs really, you know, and they will give each other tremendous stick but if they thought it was really getting

through they would put their arm round each other probably wouldn't they? It is that sort of thing, it is probably the same, in other areas, but it might be the sort of English way, it is certainly not the foreign way. I spent some time in Canada and they couldn't understand it, there were three of us there in the office and we called each other rotten, and they said hey listen guys if you go out to clubs and say things like that you are going to get into fights and things like that. They couldn't understand this sort of self-deprecating sense of humour that we have. (Interview, 10 February 1997)

The revelling in inconsistency, self deprecation and eccentric celebration of the underdog is indeed deeply ingrained in English nostalgia and culture. This is often manifested in a fascination with 'the bizarre' and nowhere is this more apparent than in the context of football. In the late 1980s the trend of carrying inflatable bananas to matches started at Manchester City (Bale 1994). For the critic and writer Paul Morley this was the acme of oddity associated with being a City fan, something that was incomprehensible outside of football culture:

The New Statesman once commissioned me to write an article about inflatables in football. Why people held bananas. And I delivered an article and they were very disappointed with it, because they wanted me to read into this banana situation some kind of racist connotation – that people were holding up bananas as some kind of declaration on the nature of Johnny Barnes or Clyde Best, I think. No it didn't go that far back, but anyway – it was meant to be a comment on black footballers because these 'people' like *The New Statesman*, the Lefties, claim that bananas are being flung, bananas are being held up as some kind of connotation. But my reading of the situation was that a very smashed supporter, one day – mid 80s wandered along, probably won an inflatable banana in a competition or something, and for a long time he was on his own standing on the terraces with this banana. Very slowly a few smashed Manchester City supporters sort of joined in, so a few bananas happened and there is no good reason for it, and I couldn't explain to the *The New Statesman* that it was a representation of the eccentricity of supporting Manchester City . . . The bananas, the songs that happen. They just happen. I remember the first time I ever heard City fans sing 'Blue Moon'. It was a wonderful moment. A very moving moment. Because again Manchester City fans are comedians and they like nothing better than when they're 4-1 down to sing 'We only sing when we're' losing'. There's never much there except the fact that it happens. (Quoted in Redhead 1997: 77–9)

The song *Blue Moon* is however equivocal in that it brings to life the fans collective sense of themselves. In this respect it serves the same function as the *Lions Roar* in the case of Millwall and *Glad All Over* at Crystal Palace.

A second version of *Blue Moon* is sung to raise the fortunes of the team or to encourage the fans to get involved with the game. This is sung in double time and is accompanied by hand clapping as follows:

City fans have also integrated a series of songs by the contemporary rock band Oasis who are themselves devoted fans of the club. Most significant of these was a version of *Wonderwall* sung during the 1996/97 season:

> And all the runs that Kinky makes are winding,
> And all the goals that Uwe scores are blinding'
> 'Cause maybe, you're gonna be the one that saves me,
> And after all, we've got Alan Ball

Steve Redhead has argued that the musicalization of football is closely tied with the game's commercial domestication producing docile 'post-fans' (Redhead

1997). Without wishing to get drawn into a long debate about the notion of the 'post-fan', we want to suggest that focusing only on football music that is recorded and sold ignores, or at best only makes fleeting reference to, the 'music of the stadia' and the soundscapes of the football crowd. As Adam Brown has pointed out:

> The notion of 'the crowd' is important in that it both heightens the pleasure of the consumption of popular music and football and plays a crucial role in its production – indeed, it is difficult to imagine either existing at all without that mass audience (although both can be, and often are, consumed in various ways 'individually'). Here, the consumer in football culture and popular music culture is also very much the producer. (Brown 1997: 86)

As such, sacred collective songs like *Blue Moon* are also open to parody and subversion by opposing fans. In 1993 during a derby match, Manchester United fans appropriated *Blue Moon* and sung an altered version back to the Maine Road faithful. This was in the aftermath of the departure of Howard Kendall the most successful Manchester City manager of recent times. The United fans also taunted their rivals referring to the previous game where United had recovered a two goal deficit to draw 3–3:

> Blue Moon
> You started singing too soon,
> You thought you'd beat us three-one,
> And now Howard Kendall has gone

The City fans responded, invoking the memory of a 5–1 victory over United in 1989:

> Blue Moon
> United singing our tune
> They won't be singing for long
> 'Cause we beat them 5–1
> 5–1 we beat United 5–1

The fact that the fans are both the consumers and producers of these songs gives them a dynamic and call and response or antiphonic quality. In the stadium itself they are performed both for the opposing fans and for the home team. The songs themselves can provide a means to do battle as the voices of opposing fans wrestle in mid air for acoustic prominence.

Equally, claims are also laid to the affiliations of commercial music producers as a means to further contest the authenticity and credibility of club identities. As

Tony, a City fan whose Manchester United supporting friend Mark plays in a band, acknowledged:

> Oh yes, we always get that one in, I mean certainly to someone you know, Mark, we always have a great laugh at how unfashionable United are – I mean the sort of people that are associated with City are people like Mike Pickering out of M People, Johnny Marr from the Smiths, and Electronic, and Oasis, and who have they got – they did that awful song with Status Quo didn't they and Simply Red – so yes we like to have pop at them about that. (Interview, 20 December 1995)

The 'cheerful Englishness', banter and popular musical preferences referred to here all seem to resonate with a nostalgic notion of working class community. Nowhere is this better illustrated than in the 'City Chippy' on Claremont Road. This is a very 'traditional' chip shop, which is extremely popular on match days when long queues form outside amongst supporters embracing traditional symbols of the English working-class 'day out' – fish and chips, football and beer.

The chip shop, located amongst the tightly packed, Coronation Street style, terraced houses of Moss Side, clearly plays up to these sensibilities and is decked out in City's sky blue livery, has fixture lists on the wall and various other artefacts indicating the proprietor's support for the club. It is not just a fast food outlet exploiting its proximity to a major 'leisure facility': it is an integral part of the communal experience being sought by a large section of supporters. On match day, the chat in the queues is typically about family and friends, spoken through the context of support for the club and the community networks that the club helps to sustain.

What concerns us is the extent to which these identifications are characterized by a normalized whiteness at the heart of the club's support which acts to exclude black and Asian supporters in more subtle and hidden ways than might previously have been considered. Steve, a black Huddersfield fan who lives in the vicinity of City's ground and now goes to City games observed that:

> It is really weird because in Manchester, as in Huddersfield, all the best football teams in the district, they are black, their best players, you know loads of black kids playing soccer, but they are not watching it . . . Even from a lot of the City lads I knew they were from mad areas like Eccles and Moston . . . So I don't really see it being a big Moss Side crowd inside the ground, I don't think there is at all, you know. City supporters are pretty much all round the area. I don't think Moss Side really is represented inside the ground, especially with black people. I think it was more in the 80s there, but now it is virtually none. (Interview, 31 October 1996)

When asked about the lack of local minority presence at Maine Road, a black fan and community worker struggled to find a way of talking about these subtle forms of exclusion:

There used to be a myth around [about black supporters] well when you get cold the black kids don't want to know, you know just, oh it's too cold you know what I mean and oh you should go back to where you come from, crap like that I used to put up with it when we were Kids, you know. But um, getting back to the point of going to matches I don't know how you can get em involved, maybe the club ought to do something about it, you know like you said they're in the heart of the community you know, I don't know. (Interview, 29 November 1995)

Perhaps, it is the close tie between Manchester City fan culture and a particular version of Englishness that is at the heart of why there is so little appeal outside of its white fans. For whilst there may be little evidence of overt racist chanting or abuse many of those who connect with Manchester City on match day may well identify with the implicit if unspoken whiteness of the crowd. As Steve continued, reflecting on his own experiences of racism at Maine Road:

What has kept racism away from Maine Road a lot of the time as far as I see is that obviously a lot of City supporters come from all round, you know you play somebody like Rochdale and Bury and on your outskirts, and a lot of them, I have heard them in the pub, and they are a bit dodgy. I think what has kept them in check is that they may, your lads or whatever . . . they are all interlinked with a lot of black guys anyway in the culture of going to clubs and everything. So I think if the main sort of lot of lads at Man City were racist, those other fellows from around the areas would have loved it because then they could have just cut it there with them and just shouted monkey chants for 90 minutes, but because the main City lads don't bother with any of that all the others can't shout it or else they will get a slap. Yes, I have seen some guys obviously get a bit frustrated . . . and they are dying to give it one, but they know that is not really part of City, it won't wash, so they keep quiet and just save it for England games, there is always that dodgy Man City flag at the England games, so they just save it for that, the rantings and ravings of a few of them, nutters from wherever. (interview, 31 October 1996)

Indeed we have found connections with support for the England national team and Ulster Loyalism amongst a small section of City supporters from outlying areas of Greater Manchester. However, the point we want to emphasise in relation to Manchester City is that these processes of normalization and exclusion can take cheerful and nostalgic forms as well as being expressed through violent chauvinism.

Conclusion

Finally, we want to return to the question that we posed at the beginning of this chapter, namely, in whose home is the Saturday afternoon match day drama being played out? How does football culture define the contours of inclusion and exclusion? John Berger has pointed out in his wonderful little book *And our Faces, my Heart, Brief as Photos* that the term 'home' has been taken over by two kinds of moralists. He writes that it 'became the keystone for a code of domestic morality, safeguarding the property (which included women) of the family. Simultaneously, the notion of homeland supplied the first article of faith for patriotism, 'persuading men to die in wars which often served no interest except that of a minority of their ruling class' (Berger 1984: 55). This second form of moralism can be connected to the racially exclusive notions of local patriotism that we suggest are manifest in the rituals of football support.

A key mechanism through which racism is manifest within the rituals of football culture is through racialising the normative structure of collective identities. As a result it is necessary to establish a distinction between the expression of *denotative racism* which is explicit (the Dayo chants, monkey chanting, racist epithets) and *connotative racism* (racialized collective identities) which maintain the hegemony of the 'white norm'. An examination of football plainsong is particularly revealing. Like the work songs of the early industrial period they represent social life 'connotatively rather than denotatively, figuratively rather than functionally' (Porter 1992: 152). Put another way, the songs and rituals of football support provide a means to represent locality and social life in the realm of metaphor and symbolism.

These songs can also combine explicit or denotative elements while implicitly invoking connotations about identity, regionalism and belonging. In this way the *I'd rather be a Paki* chant combines both denotations (the use of the term 'Paki') and connotations relating to racially exclusive notions of identity and belonging. This particular example is important because it focuses on these processes of racial normalization within football culture. The fact that this particular ritual insult relies on the assumption that both the perpetrators and the audience is white – albeit with a few assimilated black peers – show, how and to what extent football fan culture continues to be defined as a white preserve. There is, however, a tension here because two kinds of conclusion can follow from our discussion of chants like 'I'd rather be a Paki than a Scouse.' Either, it can be read as the tip of a prodigious iceberg like whiteness that lies at the heart of English football culture, or, it can be viewed as a specific moment in the racialisation of particular patterns of culture and embodied social identities. We would suggest the best course is to pursue the latter strategy.

It is important here to stress that we are not suggesting that these processes of white normalization are necessarily stable, or functional in the sense that they are based on some autochthonic social foundation. The anthropologist Maurice Bloch has suggested that a ritual type of authority works precisely because it inhibits communication. Here, ritual speech acts – like songs – provide a mechanism to formalize or standardize social life. As a result dissent, dialogue or even con-versation is impossible: 'in a song, therefore, no argument or reasoning can be communicated, no adaption to the reality of the situation is possible. '*You cannot argue with a song*' (Bloch 1974: 71). This may be so. As we've shown fans certainly trade insults through singing but the form of the songs and the collective identities expressed within them remain. However, while one cannot argue with a song, *one can stop singing it*. In recent years, the numbers of fans who are willing to give full voice to *I'd rather be a Paki than a Scouse* or *South London is Wonderful, East London is like Bengal* has ebbed at Millwall. It is noticeable that voices simply fall away when the *East London is like Bengal* second verse is called. This may well be a sign of the lack of willingness to participate in the revelry of racism. Might this also be a sign of a greater sense of openness to black and ethnic minority fans within the culture of football support itself? This question, along with other issues, form the basis of the next chapter.

We want to end by stressing that the notion of home need not necessarily always involve exclusions. John Berger has argued that beneath the patriarchal and nationalistic conceptions of 'home' that are current today there is another meaning. Here, the notion of 'home' means simply the centre of one's world, not in a geographical but an ontological sense, a place to be found, a place of Being. Bob, a Millwall fan in his seventies, articulated precisely this sense of 'home'. He lives in Croydon in a neighbouring borough to his beloved team. Each Saturday of every home game Bob makes the short train ride from East Croydon to New Cross Gate. As he passed through New Cross in August 1995 to see the Lions play Southend he mentioned with sadness the recent death of his friend and companion 'Black George'. He looked out of the train window into the streets where he spent his youth: 'Of course the area has really gone downhill since then, it used to be that people could leave their doors open and everything but that's all changed now. All that's left of me from that time is my family and Millwall.' The rituals of football culture provide a context to summon notions of self and being that cannot necessarily be articulated in any other way.

In this sense 'home' is produced not simply through a particular address or residence but through the interconnection of habitation, memory and ritual. The centre of Bob's world, the places where he feels at home, is in his family and Millwall. As Berger concludes 'without a home at the centre of the real, one was not only shelterless, but also lost in non-being, in unreality. Without home everything was fragmentation' (Berger 1984: 56). The key problem that we want to pose in the next chapter is the degree to which black and ethnic minority fans can gain access to an inclusive sense of belonging when their team is playing at 'home'.

—3—

Wearing the Shirt: Exclusion and Dialogue in Football Fan Cultures

Love and Hate in South East London – 2 May 1998, The New Den

The sun is shining on South London's industrial wasteland as Millwall Football Club prepares for its last home game. It's been another bad season, the club, verging on bankruptcy, has languished at the bottom half of the English Nationwide League Division 2. Millwall, although never really a successful club on the pitch, has occupied a central and iconic place in English football. The lack of on-field success has been more than made up for by its tradition of passion, sometimes violently expressed, and pride. The club's symbol is the rampant blue Lion and its stadium is referred to ominously as The New Den. Located in the former dockland areas of London, in the 1970s and 1980s the club and its supporters became branded the quintessential manifestation of football hooliganism, xenophobia and racism. Everyone in football it is said, from the highest ranking Football Association official to the lowliest opposition fan, loves to hate Millwall.

For fans particularly, the lure of Millwall is part of why it is loathed. The visitor's aversion to straying into this corner of South East London is more than compensated for by the cache of bar-room folklore engendered by those male adventurers who made the journey into this metropolitan heart of darkness and lived to tell the tale. The grudging respect offered to Millwall fans is garnered because they have proved so resistant to the wider changes in English football, including the move to all-seater stadiums, the growing numbers of middle-class fans and the decline in football-related violence. For many – friend and foe alike – Millwall is one of the last vestiges of unfettered white working-class male culture. Having said this, the Millwall fan community is not only a male bastion. Throughout the club are numerous working-class women of all ages who share the men's passion for Millwall and all it stands for. On Coldblow Lane where the famous old Den stood, fans gather around a burger bar for a pre-match cup of tea. Amid the smell of fried onions and the traffic of burgers and hot dogs over the counter, a silver-haired woman called Dorothy offers predictions and insightful commentary on the state of the Millwall team. The spectacular male rituals of football violence and disorder have often eclipsed the presence of women like Dorothy and their contribution to football culture.

Approaching the walkway to the entrance of the South Stand a T-shirt seller is displaying his wares on the wall of a warehouse. One shirt sponsors a lion backed by the red cross of St George and the Millwall supporter's anthem, *No-one Likes Us We Don't Care* is emblazoned across the top. Another shirt shows the American cartoon characters Beavis and Butthead in Millwall strip, their shorts dropped and their hairy behinds are 'mooning. 'West Ham can kiss my Arse!' reads the shirt's caption directed at their hated east London rival West Ham United.

Today's game in the South London sunshine marks something more than just the end of the season though: it is Tony Witter's last game for Millwall. In his five-year tenure at the club, Tony Witter, a little known black centre half and a journeyman footballer in every sense, has become something of a cult figure amongst Millwall's fans. He started his professional career relatively late in life, he first qualified as an electrical engineer before spending short periods at Crystal Palace and Queen's Park Rangers and then finally signing for Millwall. What he lacked in skill he made up for in passion, commitment and speed. In recent times Tony Witter had fallen foul of successive managers and lost his regular first team place.

Emerging from the stairs of the South Stand the verdure of the sacred turf seems more vivid under the brilliant May sun. The fans are on their feet giving a spontaneous ovation. Tony Witter stands in the centre circle and receives an award for making 100 appearances for the club. The crowd strike up with Witter's own personalized song, an honour only bestowed on the most revered of players. Witter's theme tune was coined during a particularly bleak winter in 1995 and it is sung, bizarrely, to the lyrics of Bing Crosby's *Winter Wonderland*: 'There's only one Tony Witter, one Tony Witter. Walking along, singing a song, walking in a Witter wonderland.' The chant is repeated over and over again. The voices of 6,000 mainly white fans swirl around the stadium in tribute to the passing of their black hero. Witter's apparent complete acceptance now and perhaps forever in this alleged den of intolerance, complicates the image of racial prejudice associated with Millwall and its status as the exemplary face of English bigotry.

* * *

What we want to argue is that the acceptance of black players like Tony Witter is actually very conditional. As Kobena Mercer has pointed out such conditional acceptance is not necessarily an indication of less racism: 'turn to the back pages, the sports pages, and the black man's body is heroized and lionized; any hint of antagonism is contained by the paternalistic infantilisation of Frank Bruno and Daley Thompson to the status of national mascots and adopted pets – they're not Other, they're OK because they're "our boys"'(Mercer 1994: 178–9). Further than this we want to suggest that these processes of accommodation may have particular local, gendered and class-inflected qualities. In order to understand how the

Figure 3.1 Tony Witter. Reproduced with permission of Millwall Football Club.

boundaries of acceptance, and for that matter vilification, work, it is necessary to develop an appreciation of how the rules of entitlement and belonging operate within particular football fan cultures. Purchasing an 'entry ticket' to a football match is always much more than a financial transaction. Gaining entry to the interpretive community of football fans is a matter of being able to articulate and master the implicit cultural codes that police the boundaries of acceptance.

Zygmunt Bauman has argued in the context of the experience of European Jewry that the emancipation of migrants was haunted by a perverse paradox. In order to gain entry to any sense of universal humankind, Jews had to renounce Jewish particularity. Bauman concludes that: 'Exit visas were a collective matter, whereas entry tickets had to be obtained individually' (Bauman 1988: 51). This points to the ways in which boundaries of inclusion and exclusion are mediated through cultural terms. What follows is divided into two broad areas. The first part of this chapter will examine the means through which black players and fans have been assimilated into English football fan cultures. In short, this part of the chapter will look at the cultural price of their 'entry ticket' and focus on what remains implicit with regard to gaining acceptance as they pass through the turnstiles of a football ground. Secondly, we focus on the patterns of racist abuse practised by fans. Our starting point is simple, that the patterns of popular racism are complex and the portrait of those who perpetrate these acts does not fit with the commonly held image of what the face of racism in football looks like. In particular, an argument is developed for the importance of examining how boundaries of inclusion and exclusion operate at the level of the local body politic. In order to illustrate this we want to focus on Tony Witter and the experience of black Millwall fans.

'Witter-wonderland': Racism, Locality and Masculinity

Tony Witter was not the first black player to wear the Millwall shirt. The first player of colour to appear for Millwall was Hussein Hegazi. He was born in Cairo, Egypt on 14 September 1891. We don't know how he came to London but he made two appearances for Millwall and posed in the 1912/13 team photograph. He also played for Fulham and Dulwich Hamlet and went on to attend Cambridge University. He gained a 'blue' for football through representing Cambridge in a 2–1 victory over their rivals Oxford University in 1914. It was another fifty years until another minority player represented Millwall. On the 21 December 1968 Frank Peterson made his debut as centre forward in a match at Fratton Park versus Portsmouth in front of 21,868 spectators. It wasn't a winning debut, the Lions going down 3–0. In fact, Frank never appeared on a winning Millwall side (Back and Chapman 2000, Chapman 1998).

Peterson never really made an impact, but two black players who followed him did, namely Phil Walker and Trevor Lee. Walker and Lee made their debuts on 4 December 1975 and throughout the late 1970s – when the association between Millwall, hooliganism and right-wing politics were at their height – they were very popular players. Walker was a midfielder with speed, skill and application. More than anything Millwall fans admired his unflinching commitment and passion echoing the wider uncompromising male cultures of working-class dockland. During this time the archetypal representation of this was Harry Cripps, a blonde-haired Londoner who came to personify the values of Millwall. Walker and Cripps, while 'racial opposites', were galvanized from the same footballing mould and loved with passion by the Millwall faithful.

away fixture earlier in the season, some disquiet was registered by an older white man about a new signing who was black. His son immediately checked him: 'I don't care what colour he is as long as he wears that shirt.' Tony Witter always played for Millwall with pride, passion and authority. This was his 'entry ticket' to inclusion within the Millwall pantheon. What is telling, however, is that such an incorporation need not unsettle the wider culture of racism within these specifically working-class and often male cultural settings.

Tony commented on the discussion he had with Ian Wright in the bar after the game that ended in a 0–0 draw.

> After the game Ian says to me: 'Witts, man, how can you play here, man?' I said to him: 'Ian, they're as good as gold *to me*.' That's the whole thing, I am playing *for them* [with emphasis]. (Interview, 21 May 1998)

The inclusion of players like Tony Witter is engendered through the embodiment of a set of highly localized working-class values and cultural capital. The shared experiences of class and masculinity offer a terrain in which contingent forms of inclusiveness can be established across the line of colour.

Other black players wearing the team's colours can be excluded because they are not seen to possess the correct kind of cultural passport. Bobby Bowry a black Millwall player who was a contemporary of Tony Witter was never really accepted by the Millwall faithful. Bobby Bowry transferred to Millwall from rivals Crystal Palace in July 1995. Over five years he made 143 full appearance and a further 14 as a substitute. Only Phil Walker has appeared in a Millwall shirt more times than Bobby. Yet, the relationship between Bowry and the Millwall fans was always ambiguous. Early in his career at Millwall Bobby Bowry received regular racist abuse from his own fans. Although a busy, hard-working player, he possessed a slight build and a wiry physique. Fans would regularly sing in the pre-match build up at home games – *Bobby Bowry's an Ethiopian*. This song activated associations with a plethora of racist jokes popular during the 1970s and 1980s that focused on famine in Africa. Thus, Bowry's blackness and body type is folded jokingly into the image of a 'starving primitive'.

In order to understand why particular players are assimilated and others are excluded it is necessary to understand how these players become interpreted as emblems with distinct characteristics. The problem is then how to understand the intersection between the symbolic attributes associated with a particular player – in the case of Bobby Bowry as a symbolic entity – and the normative structure of fan culture as a whole. The outline of this relationship was revealed during a conversation that we recorded at a home game in the south stands of the New Den on the 20 September, 1995. The fixture was a cup tie against Everton. Bobby Bowry had played badly and towards the end of the game he was pushed off the ball a couple of times and had given possession away through careless passes. The following exchange took place between three men George, Bobby and Stephen. George and Bobby are both white men in their fifties, they are season ticket holders and lifelong Millwall fans. Stephen is George's son and is in his mid twenties. This conversation was triggered by an event on the pitch involving Bobby Bowry who was jostled off the ball by an opposition player during open play.

Stephen: [turns to George and Bobby] See Bowry – he's too light weight.
George: Bring back Graham [former Millwall midfield player].
Stephen: You see he's got everything going against him. He's short, light-weight . . .
Bobby: [interrupting Stephen] Palace!
George: [following straight after Bobby before Stephen has a chance to add anything] Black!
[*Bobby and George laughing*] (Fieldnotes, 20 September, 1995)

Looking beneath the surface of this conversation one can establish a series of oppositions that define both the normative centre of Millwall fan culture and criteria by which Bobby Bowry is excluded.

There are at least three lines of distinction being made in this short exchange. Firstly, the accusation that Bobby Bowry is a 'lightweight' player is contrasted implicitly with the types of playing style that are valued at Millwall: players that are 'heavy weight' – fierce, physical, uncompromising. Secondly, Bobby Bowry is associated with being local South London team Crystal Palace. Garry Robson has pointed out in his study of Millwall fan culture that the symbolic relationship between Millwall and Crystal Palace is characterized, at least in the eyes of Millwall fans, through opposing, ideal-type, taxonomic sets:

Millwall as	**Crystal Palace** as
Inner-urban	Suburban
Working-class	Middle-class
Strong	Weak
Virile	Effete
Passionate	Dispassionate
Volatile	Pacified
Dangerous	Harmless (after Robson 2000: 87)

Thus, when Bobby Bowry dons a Millwall shirt he is faced with the symbolic residue of his association with Crystal Palace who are dismissed with contempt by Millwall fans. It is important to state that other ex-Palace players like Tony Witter and Andy Gray have not faced this problem. However, their inclusion was established at the first order of association: they *became* Millwall players because they possessed the requisite types of playing style, and through their passion and speed (in Witter's case) and skill (in Gray's case) they were assimilated. Lastly, Bobby Bowry's blackness is invoked. This is made in contrast to an implicit association between Millwall and whiteness. What is significant here is that colour contrast is invoked as a final and concluding point in this chain of distinction making ('light weight, Palace, black'), pointing to the ways in which this process of racialization is articulated to other lines of social division. In this sense the undoubted racism directed at Bobby Bowry is fed by the matrix of social definitions that define what it means to be included.

It is only through an appreciation of these processes that one can gain any purchase on why a figure like Tony Witter is lionized while Bobby Bowry is vilified. In Witter's case his style of play and mastery of the cultural codes privileged by Millwall fans provide him with a cultural passport that occludes his blackness. He can wear the shirt symbolically and to such a degree that he is almost playing with 'it over his head'. Bowry, on the other hand, possesses little of this cultural capital and as a result is vilified and open to abuse. The inclusion of Tony Witter is not in any sense at odds with expression of racism and the exclusion of Bobby Bowry. Rather, these complex processes point to how racism is articulated and its social bases. Put simply the expression of racism is nested within particular local contexts that both define identity, entitlement and belonging and their antonyms.

Showing Your Colours: Black Football Fans, Dialogue and Football Violence

These patterns of assimilation and exclusion are reflected in the stadium as well as on the pitch. We found that small but significant numbers of black men have always followed local teams and gained access to these fan cultures. Garry Robson has suggested that black fans need to both occlude any sense of ethnicity while displaying a mastery of the forms of white masculine culture that form the centre of football fan cultures (Robson 1999: 230). We want to develop the idea that the 'entry ticket' in to football fan culture involves a 'cultural passport'. This we define as the proficiency in the vernacular forms of fan culture and their regional, gendered and class inflected knowledges and embodied culture.

In the course of our research we found a number of men who gained access to particular fan cultures through such means. This was particularly true in our Manchester City and Millwall case studies. In both areas we found examples of small numbers of black men from within the local communities who were assimilated within these fan cultures. In each case they were largely from neighbouring multicultural areas: Brockley in South London and Moss Side in

Manchester. Some of the most prestigious figures in the 'hooligan firms' in both places have been black. Indeed one of the most interesting paradoxes in both of these examples is that the so-called 'hooligan networks' were often much more multicultural than comparable groups of 'respectable fans'.

As we argued in Chapter 2. Manchester City's fan culture is vitiated with English nostalgia, yet a small but significant group of black young men from Moss Side attended Maine Road from the mid-1970s onwards. Their story is recounted in Mickey Francis' memoir *Guvnors*. In the book he includes extensive interviews with Donald Farrer, a black City fan who saw a psychiatrist to treat his compulsion to go to football matches. Farrer was key in the formation of the Cool Cats firm which started in 1974. He recounted how the respect and acknowledgement from other City fans had to be literally fought for.

> The Cool Cats was a black thing to start with. A lot of the young black and half-caste lads from the area gradually joined together. City wasn't known as a hooligan club but there were a few mobs, like the Beer Monsters and the Beano Boys from Gorton. There was also a big National Front following, Scotty and Co. Although there was a certain amount of mutual respect between us and them, they didn't like us. It was skin deep and there was friction. In the end it spilled over. Our first organised battle as the Cool Cats was against our own supporters. At a home game, our Chris went to the toilets and got done by five or six NF geezers. We had had enough, so after the match we waited for them to leave the ground and as they came out we did them . . . There was a fear factor of fifty coloured and half-caste guys. It is a psychological game. Being half-caste, you are neither white or black, you get it from both sides, so it makes you tough. (quoted in Francis and Walsh 1997: 32–3)

The Cool Cats modelled their identity on the mutual opposition to both their local rivals Manchester United and the National Front. Led by Donald Farrer the group grew to close to 100 fans and like the National Front-allied City crews they travelled on a coach together for away games. To their opponents the sight of an integrated group of fans was incomprehensible. While acts of racism would be tackled physically and directly members were dismissive of overt racism in the form of abuse. Mickey Francis commented:

> Racism never bothered me and I didn't hold any grudges [. . .] At the time, not many black guys went to football matches. With City being in Moss Side, we had a big percentage and when you went away you didn't have to wear a scarf; your skin was your scarf. Rival fans knew that if you were black, you were from Moss Side and Man City. If you went somewhere like Liverpool, where blacks didn't go to football, you stood out a mile. (Francis and Walsh 1997: 36)

This sense of wearing their colours on their skin is something that black fans of this generation return to repeatedly. They were literally more visible and equally this meant that black fans were also targets. Donald Farrer recounted another story of a confrontation with Birmingham City fans who also had a reputation for having small numbers of black fans.

> Like us, Birmingham had a lot of blacks. They were always the first people we went for. If the white guys saw us giving it to their black guys, they'd often get on their toes, because a lot of whites are scared of black guys. When I was outside the ground, with Mike stood next to me, this black geezer game up and, in a broad Brummie accent, said, 'Have you seen the Man City lads?'
> And I said, 'Yes, we're here,' and whacked him
> They used to call me Bullethead because I could butt three or four times in succession. I butted this half-caste at Stoke and pulled out an afro comb and slashed him across the face. The police handcuffed me to a fence and I got kicked to fuck by the Stoke. I got a suspended sentence for that. (Francis and Walsh 1997: 41)

The intensity of the violence reported here precludes any sentimental romantic interpretation of these kinds of dialogue. While these peer groups were multi-racial they could equally be implicated in targeting opposing black fans as special targets. The shape of these paradoxes is worth explicating. Black men could be assimilated within these worlds because of fears and anxiety that white peers could feel about black masculinity. In this sense the image of black masculinity as invulnerable, 'hard' and 'terrace tough' is alarmingly similar to racist notions of dangerous/violent 'black muggers'. Black fans like Donald understood intuitively the ways white fans both venerated and feared their black peers and identified them as key figures to be taken out. In a perverse twist this kind of violence becomes racialized because of the particular nature of the ways in which black men are assimilated within their respective fan cultures and as a result they become prized targets for their adversaries both black and white. This point was illustrated during a fixture between Everton and Millwall at Goodison Park on 4 October 1995 discussed in Chapter 2.

Tony, a black Millwall fan, travelled with two white friends John and Phil to the night game on a club-organized coach. Tony was the only black person on the coach but he was at ease with his two life long friends. The three men had gone to school together in Bermondsey. Tony possessed the same demeanour of laconic restraint as his two friends, few words were passed between them but their bodies showed that they were comfortable and at ease with each other. Tony smoked slim panatela, which he held between his thumb and index finger so that the smouldering tip of the cigar was close to the palm of his hand. When he took a drag it looked like he was throwing a dart from his lips. We arrived at the ground late, it was dark and as the Millwall fans left the coaches the police herded the fans into a channel bordered by policemen on each side. It was a quarter of a mile walk from the coaches to the ground. As, the procession of Millwall fans approached the ground and the hundreds of Everton fans gathered on the street corners the police disappeared.

Tony was in the middle of the ranks of Millwall fans filing through the crowd. As a gap opened up in the cortege of away fans, a white Evertonian walked in amongst the Millwall fans with the purposeful stride of an assassin. He targeted Tony, paused briefly at his shoulder and whispered in his ear 'You're dead.' Tony turned around quickly. The bold Evertonian vanished as quickly as he had appeared. As Tony turned the faces of hundreds of Everton fans pass bye, his shoulders pushed back, his neck craning and moving from side to side in readiness for another incursion. His two white friends mobilized around him at his shoulder and watching his back. It was like watching a ballet of masculinity. No one followed the lone Scouser who stole into the Millwall ranks. It was telling that Tony was targeted in this way. This supports the idea that while the configurations of black hyper-masculinity covers the price of entry into these fan cultures it also means that the cost for black men is that they are targeted precisely because they are feared. They carry the equivalent to a price 'on their head' because the perverted coupling of race and masculinity attracts an extra cache for their adversaries who try to take them down.

The position of black fans in these gendered and classed milieu needs to be carefully evaluated. Like their white counterparts some black men are equally vituperative in their abuse of opposition players and fans, some of whom also happen to be black. During a particularly acrimonious fixture against Birmingham City on 10 March, 1996 at the New Den the mirror opposite of what is described above occurred. Birmingham City brought a small number of fans to the game, barely 300. Birmingham, as was mentioned earlier have also developed a reputation as having a small but significant black following. A group of Millwall fans, including Tony taunted the Birmingham fans singing 'Where are your famous Zulu boys?' A lone white voice shouts 'Where's your fucking Rastafarians. Where's your fucking Rastafarians.' He starts singing again 'Where's your famous Zulu boys' and twenty or so fans join in.

On the last row of the away supporters end was one solitary black face. The black Birmingham fan who was wearing a Puma top was immediately picked out for special treatment and a torrent of abuse was hurled his way – not least from Tony himself. Some of this abuse included racist invective. A white fan stood up and shouted 'Sit down you sooty bastard.' This was followed by his friend who shouted 'Who's that Sooty at the back.' This was received with laughs around. This was followed with a chorus of 'We laugh at the Birmingham, we laugh at the Birmingham' to the tune of 'Go West.' A young white man shouted "specially that Coon at the back'. His friend followed: 'Sit down you big black cunt.'

The position of black fans like Tony is very complicated. On the one hand they can be proximate with crude racism of the kind describe above, yet at the same time their road into football culture is paved by shared experiences. Ron, a black Millwall fan who grew up in Lambeth described how he was drawn to the club:

> Now to be honest with you Millwall had a reputation and it was very big then to show off your machoism, right, so we would be quite often met with a confrontation, and it certainly dawned on me the sort of respect you had by supporting Millwall, you know, and I say that now in schools that if you support Charlton, you support Millwall, you are going to get more respect being a Millwall supporter, because of all what Millwall stand for. (Interview, 27 September 1995)

The nuances of this involvement can't be understood within the dominant narratives of 'football hooliganism'. Within the context of shared class location Millwall symbolized masculine mastery and respect. But the entry points of these fans almost always involved peer networks that provided the first introduction. Ron was initially drawn to Chelsea 'a Champagne club' and then he attended some Crystal Palace games, sometimes secretly. In what follows Ron describes the contrast between the two fan cultures:

> A kid who actually went to my primary school and secondary school and we had known each other so long, his parents used to take us to Palace in the car, so Palace was my first team. Getting on the bus at the age of ten or eleven was an adventure. I used to say to my mum I am going to my mate's house, he used to say he was coming to my house and we would disappear for the afternoon. A best mate of mine . . . supported Millwall and we used to show each other programmes after the game and compare the game and talk about it blah blah blah, and he said are you coming to Millwall and I went never heard of them sort of thing, you know. He goes like 'My dad will give us a lift.' I couldn't believe it in ten minutes I was there from Camberwell. I thought oh it has got to be a lot easier. What struck me about Millwall, what I really enjoyed about Millwall was that you could almost write your name in Tippex where you stood and come back and stand in the same place. You would know the person to the right, to the left, in front of you. You know the immediate family – very very family orientated. A really nice feeling. Very strange because it wasn't about winning, it was this group of guys who met, or these groups of people who met and win lose or draw it was having a piss up, having a drink, because they sold drink on the terraces then. I remember going and they used to say to me, they used to call us the boys, and giving us a half of lager, and I was fifteen/sixteen sort of thing. So that was very apparent, that was the big difference between the two. Millwall also had Phil Walker and Trevor Lee playing at the time in the 70s and I would say probably the only two black players in the country, two black players in one team in the country at the time. (interview, 27 September 1995)

Ron was attracted to the specific type of white working-class culture and sociability mobilized around Millwall. Equally, young black kids could identify with the teams in a period when it was very rare for two black players to be playing in the same team. For Ron there was never any threat of racism:

> There was never any racism involved or anything like that. No, none at all. Millwall has actually had black leaders as far as their football – Tiny has been the guy leading Millwall for years and now they have got a guy called Salman, and another guy who died recently, Lenny. There has always been a handful of black supporters who have gone. What has happened is that these guys don't see us as being black. Do you understand that? I will give you the great example right. John Fashanu was playing for us and I was standing there on the terraces and they were shouting 'you black bastard, get off your arse and do something you fucking nigger.' Then they turn round and say 'sorry mate, no offence, I am talking to that black bastard on the pitch!' That really hit home how racism can be misinterpreted, exaggerated or whatever. (Interview, 27 September 1995)

Superficially this seems curious. Why would a black guy defend the mitigating circumstances of white racism articulated by his peers. Ron is in no way a dupe. He has a very sophisticated understanding of the ways in which racism structures British society. When pushed on the issue of racism at Millwall he replied:

> Yes, you would hear sometimes but [racism] never affected me personally, me personally it didn't affect. You could be giving out stick to the away team and then every now and then you would hear racist chants and things like that. But it wasn't, at Millwall, it wasn't the whole end, it was certain quarters that would do it, and when you go for a drink in the pub you would hear certain racist things, but again I repeat that I think a lot of the guys didn't see us as black. I remember going to a party in Welling and being the only black guy there out of 300 people, and a guy said something, he asked him to do something and he said 'What do you think I am black?' He looked at me and he knew he had said something wrong but his company, who I knew a couple of them. They said 'Don't worry about him, forget him, he didn't mean what he said and he wasn't being racist.' I think a lot of them actually don't think it is being racist. (Interview 27 September 1995)

Accounts like these ought not to be dismissed too quickly as some ethnic equivalent to false consciousness. The sense of inclusion and involvement articulated by Ron and other black fans is deeply felt. Perhaps, this is best understood through appreciating the common points of reference he shares with his peers. Gary, a black Millwall fan who grew up in Plumstead, recalled:

> We was completely accepted by the people we went with, but whether we was completely accepted by the majority or the rest of the crowd I couldn't, I wouldn't like to say really you know, you know I wouldn't like to be in a situation where Millwall fans were upset you know would they take it out on me you know, as an individual you know not as

another Millwall fan but as an individual as a 'black cunt' as a wanker like, it never happened cos we all used to go down there firm handed you know and we would stick together through thick and thin you know that's the bonding we had and there was I suppose there was about 30 or 40 of us at our strength and a good fifteen or sixteen were black, half-caste or Indian. (Interview 16 January 1997)

When asked if the presence of racism in the ground deterred him, Gary was unequivocal:

It hasn't really, didn't really deter me from going though you know, that was part and parcel of it , yeah you know it was gonna be happen, you know, sometimes the opposite side used to run out you can see a black player go, oh fucking hell yeah he's gonna get it.

Yet, for Gary the racism in the ground also made him uneasy:

As he got the ball 'o-o-h-h o-o-h-h.' You'd think 'Oh shut up you lot.' You'd turn round like that and all these faces have been looking at ya for not saying anything. You'd turn back 'o-o-h-h!' you know. Every now and again no-one you know. That's where it comes in the crowd's got no head or no brain, they're just going along, they're rolling along with the flow like it's like a bit of tumbleweed you know what I mean, like snow rolling down hill: one does it they all do it. (Interview, 16 January 1997)

For black people in these environments apprehension is produced by the expectation or anticipation of racism. Sharon Davidson and Colin King have pointed out that for black fans in this context part of the sense of vulnerability is that racism is 'just waiting to happen' (Davidson and King 1998). This is summed up when Gary concluded 'Oh yeah he's gonna get it' as a black player runs out of the tunnel on the opposition team. So, even when overt racist abuse is absent the sense of apprehension in the minds of black fans is a latent presence. The safety of people like Gary could be protected through having some association with the key black figures in the 'hooligan firms':

Yeah, the thing is some of the geezers we used to go with they're big reps anyway, big reputations anyway you know, I knew Tiny you know, I could say it meant sort of just to show some strength I could go up and say a few words to Tiny during the day, other people see that think, oh he knows Tiny, Tiny knows Walford, Tiny knows all the top boys and all that you know, so it'll be like a knock-on effect so my face'd get noticed do you know what I mean thinking well he knows all the top boys and that you know so there'd be a place for me? (Interview, 16 January 1997).

Paradoxically, when access to these networks was gained they were amongst the safest places for black men to be involved in the culture of football. Fans like

Gary and Ron were vulnerable and conspicuous, particularly when travelling away, yet at the same time the networks of which they were a part also protected them.

Another issue here is the status of the 'race talk' that is expressed in the footballing context. As we argued earlier, within the ritual arena of the football ground verbal abuse can take on an altered meaning (Bateson 1978: 155). Whilst this does not necessarily dislocate the efficacy of racist language within the stadium it certainly changes its status. A white Lions fan wrote into the Millwall fanzine of an incident that illustrated this altered quality:

> There was an 80s match at the Den (can't remember who we was playing) with a group of thumbheads [skinheads] at the front of the terracing shouting out some racist stuff while about eight rows back, three youngish black guys were rolling their eyes in mock terror and pissing themselves laughing. [This incident] always comes to mind when I hear shit in the news about the 'fascists' at Millwall – yeah it's always there but it's a bit of a bad joke. (*The Lion Roars* Issue 51: 29)

The mistake that is all too often made is that such 'race talk' is either read as 'meaningless play' or taken as 'consequential race hate' and the expression of deeply felt racial animus. Rather, its true significance is found in the ambivalence between these two positions – within a mode of expression that oscillates between the ludic and the literal. In order to be able to read and ridicule racism as described in the above quotation, it is necessary to be able to explicate these taunts in their context. Such acts of subversion involve participation and proficiency in this highly class-coded and gendered oral culture. A black person who did not share these experiences or anyone else not familiar with this highly specific milieu would not see a 'bad joke' but a grotesque performance of racial zealotry.

This would not, however, protect them in other sorts of social spaces like pubs and clubs. Gary illustrated this point with a story:

> We used to go down Bexleyheath to a pub down there called the Jolly Draymen. There used to be some pretty girls down there you know, it was like a magnet like a meeting point for the young you know, meet up in the Draymen have a few drinks and then go out. About ten or fifteen of us used to go down there might be five or six blacks you know and I knew the landlord quite well you know. He'd come up to me and go why are the blacks down there guv? He used to say to me, who are you looking for and that, I'm just out for a drink you cunt what's the matter with ya. You know but it'd always draw attention. 'Why all the black geezers, man? What's happening? What's going wrong?' They always thought we was down there for more of the reason than we were, we always had a game of pool and chat to girls you know, doing normal things like you know, but they always thought there's someit more to it. (Interview, 16 January 1997)

In this respect the conditions of belonging are related to his participation in a working-class male cultural matrix. In this sense the inclusion of black fans is determined by their competence with embodied forms of masculine culture that operate through implicit class-coded means.

This raises important questions about the contingent forms of inclusion that black fans and players experience within football. In many respects the boundaries of this incorporation are circumscribed by the degree of fit or compatibility with the hegemonic white working-class masculinities that form the normative centre of football culture. In keeping with the kinds of negotiation that take place between black and white young people within football culture it becomes possible for 'black cockneys' or 'blackskins' to be included as *contingent insiders* (Back 1996). These fraught inclusions mirror the same processes that operate with regard to black players. In both cases racism stands on the 'sidelines' as a potential resource to be used strategically to exclude or undermine the belonging and legitimacy of black fans and players. 'Blackskins' can be assimilated within the Millwall fan collective, but depending on circumstances and context they can be transformed into vilified 'black bastards'.

From the perspective of Millwall's white fans, high-profile black figures became almost totally assimilated, gaining notoriety and unquestioned respect. They became majestic figures within the symbolic dominion of the white fan collective and when they attended games this respect would be embodied through highly ritualized patterns of acknowledgement in the form of verbal and non-verbal greetings. This, however, does not preclude the same figures being targeted by opposing fans in a racialized fashion. Equally, white peers and even friends can indulge in the mirror opposite forms of racialization when directed towards black fans that support Millwall's rivals. While other groups, most strikingly Britain's south Asian communities, are completely excluded and reviled through a whole range of anti-Asian songs as discussed in Chapter 2.

What is established is a racialized hierarchy. In order to understand this process it is important to cross the analysis of racialized identities with an understanding of how these intersect with gender relations and masculinity. Commensurable class-inflected ideals about black and white masculinity provide a common ground within black-white peer groups. Where young white men are forming alliances and friendships with black peers it is important to question the constructions of blackness they may be finding attractive. For young white men this may be located around racialized definitions of masculinity. At the moment when racist ideas are most vulnerable, in situations where there is intimate contact between black and white men, stereotypical ideas can sometimes be reproduced as positive characteristics to be emulated. This equally can operate in the sphere of sexuality revealed here in a story of interracial fraternity offered by a white Millwall fan. This incident took place in the aftermath of a game at Chelsea in the 1980s:

Coming out of that game some black bloke fainted in the crush getting through the poxy stupid gate. Immediately a group of other (white) Millwall supporters shouted for order while they tried to lift the unconscious geezer to his feet. He could have literally been trampled to death in half a minute. Even so it was hard to get him upright, he seemed to weigh more than Ken Bates' head [the Chelsea Chairman]. Then I heard one of the other lifters offer an explanation – 'it's his bloody knob [penis] innit?' (*The Lion Roars* Issue 51: 29)

This example of terrace humour shows that racialized constructions around black men's sexuality may underpin the affiliations established between black and white fans. The point here that these stereotypical ideas like black men have 'big dicks' and a 'penchant for violence' may be undisturbed while black peers are integrated within the fan culture. These formulations may even be reinforced through interracial banter and friendship. The parameters of black inclusion in this class-defined cultural milieu are relatively narrow. It excludes black women or black men who adopt other versions of black masculinity more centrally placed within the rituals of the black alternative public sphere.

Wozzy, a black women born in South London, who was involved in the setting up of an Anti-racist Committee at Millwall reflected:

Well most cultural people, most ethnic minorities will never go to Millwall, I think. I don't know whether that perception will ever change – my sister runs a modeling agency and she felt what on earth are you doing getting involved with Millwall – she knows that a lot of the stuff I do will always have a community aspect and I won't get involved in anything that I don't think that is worth trying to fight for. We had great discussions about Millwall and for me, because I am from Lewisham Borough, I went to school here, and knew a lot of Millwall fans who were at school with me and one of whom went away for murder. It was that stabbing that took place in the early '80s at Millwall at the old Millwall ground. He's out of prison now and his life is messed up in many different ways. He was a mixed-race young man who got caught up in that whole movement because at my school there was a lot of Millwall fans. It's that little group thing, men more than women need all that male-bonding stuff, they need that group thing. (Interview, 4 August, 2000)

The 'passport to inclusion' within this version of local patriotism is issued through shared participation in class-inflected and masculine notions of local identity. While this admits black fans like Ron, Gary and Donald it does so on quite specific and racially scripted terms.

We want to argue two things: firstly, it is important not to over-politicize these involvements beyond a kind of prosaic coming to terms around localized forms of legitimate entitlement and belonging; secondly, that the nature of these ambiguous dialogues have been ignored within the wider attempts to address racism within football, precisely because they are not easily rendered comprehensible within the established frameworks for anti-racist campaigning that viewed racism as a component part of a broader definition of unwanted anti-social behaviour. It is telling that the emphasis of the Kick Racism Out of Football Campaign was shifted in large part because of the insistence of the Football League who wanted a focus a intimidatory behaviour in the broadest sense. This contributed to the decision of the Advisory Group Against Racism and Intimidation – the campaign's steering group – decision to adopt the twin themes of 'Lets Kick Racism' and 'Respect All Fans' during the 1995/6 football season. Our argument put simply is that the complex and ambiguous nature of black entry into class-based football cultures needs to be taken seriously, particularly in the context of local footballing rituals.

Equally, we want to stress that the nature of these football fan cultures police the lines of inclusion and exclusion. Being 'a real football fan' has a normative structure organised around key principles. These might be summarised as: 1) developing an unbreakable affiliation to a single club; 2) the performance of authentic fandom through attending games; 3) assimilation of the masculinist/class inflected argot of consumption (involvement in the spheres of football fandom: pre-match drinking, familiarity with networks of rumour, gossip and football folklore). All these practices involve manifestations of distinction and are the equivalent of Pierre Bourdieu's notion of cultural capital (Bourdieu 1986).

The majority of black and ethnic minority football fans are excluded from these very specific ways of 'being a football fan'. As a result they articulate quite different patterns of support and affiliation. As one black fan put it: 'This whole thing about having one team never made any sense to me. It was never an option for me to support the "local" team because I knew it was a place that black people weren't welcome. So I followed two teams – Tottenham and Palace' (Interview, 23 September 2000). The fact that football grounds were seen to be racially exclusive places precluded the kind of attachments that have been normalized within English football culture. Black fans who wanted to gain entry into those worlds had to do so through norms that were not only implicitly coded white but also both gendered and inflected with class associations. Yet, this sidelines and obscures the variety of ways in which black people have followed football in England and elsewhere. For example, Ginna, a 35-year-old Manchester United fan from Nigeria, has never attended a football match in her life. She has not even visited the city of Manchester. Yet, she has followed the fortunes of the team since she was a child. Ten years ago she moved to London. Each week she religiously follows the form and news of the team through the safe vantage point of satellite television. We will return to this issue in later chapters, for now we want to emphasize that the experience of black fans points to alternative ways of being a football fan.

Locality, Fan Culture and Racism

The frequency, and to some extent the form, of racism in football grounds varies greatly between clubs. Shared codes of ritual behaviour hold true for all clubs but as we've argued each fan culture exhibits distinct forms of prescribed formal behaviour and symbolism (Bromberger et al. 1993). In order to understand the range of racist activity one needs to examine the relationship between processes of racialization and the collective ritual and symbolic practices that give any particular fan culture meaning. In this sense differences with regard to the level and intensity of racism need to be understood in terms of the way racist practices are nested within the ritual and collective symbolism of each fan culture. These issues will be picked up in greater detail in the next chapter.

Within our London case studies we found a stark contrast between the high frequency of racism observed amongst some sections of Millwall's support, when compared to neighbouring Crystal Palace where racial abuse from fans was almost non-existent. This difference can be explained in part by the contrasting nature of these fan cultures. Millwall's collective imagery and symbolism is tightly bound up with an extreme localism and traces of the white working-class communities that worked in the docks and that have in large part disappeared. As we suggested earlier there is some irony in the fact that despite these affiliations the club's support is now largely drawn from the outer London suburbs where fans migrate every Saturday to New Cross. The culturally heterogeneous nature of South London life is resisted or refused within the collective symbolism of Millwall, which represents a white enclave in an increasingly multi-racial environment.

In contrast Crystal Palace, located just five miles away, is less intensely connected with a white working-class past and the vehement forms of localism that follow from this in the case of Millwall. Palace fandom at a superficial level at least is more affected by the contemporary forms of multiculture evident in this part of London (Hewitt 1986). In large part this has been amplified by the string of local black south Londoners who have played for the team. As one white Palace fan put it:

> We had our little quartet of black players [in the 1980s who] . . . took Palace to the highest heights they'd ever been. I remember really liking that because whether or not they were from South London, it seemed to me to somehow symbolize something about the area and I was able to identify with them. I mean we're talking about Ian Wright, Mark Bright, Andy Gray particularly and then later John Salako . . . I liked the fact that, you know, these were lads that probably could have been on the streets of Tulse Hill (an area of South London). I could have gone to school with them and that was good, that was good. (Interview, 8 November 1996)

Numerically Crystal Palace had approximately the same levels of support from black London communities as Millwall. What is most significant is the impact of the multi-racial character of the team on white fans. The Palace fan base is largely drawn from the immediate locality and the predominantly white areas of south Croydon and beyond. The face-to-face negotiations that have muted popular racism in the surrounding, highly diverse South London neighbourhoods have been carried over into the stands. Ian Wright was a symbol of this change for many. John, a Palace fan, commented:

> Wright was this kind of figurehead, you know, he had the gold tooth and the extreme, you know – I remember once Wright was injured and we were standing on the Arthur Wait stand before it was all seater, and you know, we just, everyone's head was turning, and Wright was in the crowd with us, you know, he was in the crowd with his, you know, dressed up really stylish watching the game with us. And he was going: 'Oy, lads!' and we're going oh, this is the coolest player around, like hanging out with us, this is an honour . . . There's clips of Wright and Bright up in the air grabbing [after scoring goals] – or Gray and Wright – grabbing each other's hands, you know, which you would never see, so it was bringing . . . style to Palace. You know, we had all these things, you know. I felt always proud of the fact that we had these six great players, or you know, six black players for Palace, you know, and black's cool as well, you know. I remember like one time when players were training – you know, the deejay, you know, you always had music, was: 'Oh, and Ian Wright's kind of requested this one', and it was a reggae tune, and you saw Ian Wright dancing and you think oh, that's wicked. And, you know, there were times at Palace you'd get a ragga tune being played over [the PA], a soul tune or – you know, out of the charts. [You] felt actually this is a little bit different, it's almost like a kind of, you know, a kind of a different kind of feeling here. (Interview, 7 February 1996)

In contrast to the Millwall context where black involvement in the fan culture was predicated on the idea that black fans occluded any sense of difference, the white Palace fans we interviewed spoke explicitly about the legacy of multi-ethnic London and black popular culture. If the 'blackness' of black Milwall was 'not seen', at Palace the shadow that black players and fans cast on the fan culture was embraced as a prize possession that bolstered its authenticity. In contrast to the Millwall case, the presence of black fans, particularly men, was explicitly about the presence of difference. This process is nevertheless ambiguous and by no means complete, these kinds of dialogues co-existed with middle-class forms of racism that were outside of the kinds of dialogue referred to in John's account.

It was telling that in our interviews Palace fans that came from outside of these ethnically mixed urban contexts spoke a very different language. Middle-class fans from places like Purley and those who travelled to games from beyond the surrounding area referred to Palace's 'coloured players' in less prestigious terms occasionally alongside quibbles about them having 'attitude problems' and 'chips on their shoulder'. Through the fame of black players like Wright and Bright, black London had a lasting impact on the culture of Palace fandom. It is perhaps the class mixture of the fans and their association with being passionless and effete by rivals like Millwall (Robson 2000) that enabled this shift to take place. Put simply the defining centre of Palace fandom is not so tightly scripted by white working-class masculinities.

During the late 1980s and early 1990s Crystal Palace regularly fielded teams half of which were composed of black players. In this period noticeably larger numbers of black fans started to attend games. Dominic recounted a particularly vivid memory of a game where the presence of black fans at Palace was manifested dramatically. It was the final fixture of the 1989 season against Birmingham City at Selhurst Park. Palace had already secured a play-off place and Birmingham had more or less been condemned to relegation. Dominic picks up the story:

> Driving to the ground we'd seen that a lot of the Birmingham fans had put on fancy dress. They were all wearing Mickey Mouse outfits and all that. A lot of them seemed to have been on the beer all day. When we got in the ground we was in the Arthur Wait, when it used to be standing down the front. We was right next to the Birmingham fans who were in the corner of the Holmesdale. We were stood quite near and their end was absolutely packed. There must have been three or four thousand in that little corner. It was really choca. (Interview, 4 January, 2000)

He continued:

> Think we won the game quite easy. Wrighty got a few goals and it was quite near the end of the game. All the Birmingham fans seemed to go piling down to the front. We didn't have a clue what was going on. We were just stood there watching 'em. They all started getting over the fence and falling on the floor and it looked to us at first like it was a crush and they were trying to get out of it by jumping over the fence and onto the pitch. There were very few policemen in the ground at the time. Then their famous Zulu warrior cry went up. Everyone looked over an' thought – what's that all about? Then all the Birmingham got up all wearing fancy dress and they started taking their masks and hats off and produced a load of weapons out of their gear that they were wearing. They came piling into our end. I was about halfway up. I was scared but I was also riveted by what was going on. (Interview, 4 January 2000)

The result was a bizarre spectacle of men dressed in cartoon costumes fighting with the Palace fans. Dominic continued:

> So a load of our lot from the Arthur Wait went piling down as well and it was just a big scrap in the middle of the pitch. It was going on and on and people was waiting for the

Old Bill to come but they didn't come. So it was just kicking off. They had metal bars, bits of wood all sorts. They were really taking the Palace fans to pieces. Then after about, probably only a minute or two but it seemed like a long time. I saw from the Palace about six big black lads walk down, as calm as you like. Walk down the side and got onto the pitch. I think they must have been security guards or something. They were all just massive geezers. They just got on the pitch stood in a line and just started taking out all the Birmingham fans that came towards 'em. They were all pretty 'andy. They just formed this little line and it was only about ten yards long and no one got past 'em. Every fan that came towards them they just laid 'em out. Eventually stewards and police came along and it all calmed down a bit. There was a lot of people got hurt. But we went through the play offs and went up and they went down. (Interview, 4 January 2000)

What is interesting in these stories is the ways in which a black presence and black popular culture are seen as prestigious. Some white Palace fans referred to these black men, both fans and players, as 'the brothers'. However, following the point raised earlier, the images of blackness, particularly black masculinity, is dangerously vitiated with ideas of hyper-masculinity that reinforce racial stereotypes.

The presence of black fans at Palace was not enduring. When the high-profile black players like Wright, Gray and Salako left the club black supporters largely left with them. Wallis, a black football fan and community worker commented:

This is automatic because [black football fans] don't feel like it is their ship, it is not part of their culture. English people, people like myself who grew up and were born here, take everything for what it is, but then you go there and you know it is like a recognition thing – oh hi! – because that black person was there last week. Oh hi! I saw you in the players lounge, so there is like an acknowledgement of the few [black people] that are in football. Some people go to the games because their sons play, or their cousins play. They will go and watch a game because their cousin got them a ticket or because they have got the time to go to that particular game. But [clubs's like Palace] won't actually get a black audience similar to what their white audiences, no way. (Interview, 26 September 1997)

For all of their associations with black players and the effects of black popular cultures on white fans, for black fans Crystal Palace remains a foreign place.

Nevertheless, it is true to say that the levels of overt racism at Palace were almost non-existent. Irene, a season ticket holder at Palace, recounted a particularly telling experience:

I did hear one guy once up from us, it was an evening game there was a really rough, rough tackle by a black opposition player on a Palace player. He went, 'You black . . .'

and then he stopped. Then he just said, 'You bastard . . .' He checked himself straight away you know it was kind of like he would have said it normally had he not been at Palace or if he'd been at home in front of the TV but [in the ground] he checked himself. I thought that was interesting. That's the only time I've ever heard that so hopefully it's that you know most people do fully accept it's not just black players really it's black people isn't it it's um, their attitude to black people full stop you know cos I think accepting black players is an easy thing to do because they're your players. (Interview, 7 November 1996)

Irene had some reservations on the degree to which the acceptance of black people off the pitch followed from the adulation heaped on the black Palace players. It was certainly the case that public expressions of racism are frowned upon. This is despite the fact, as we will point out later, that the club had been the centre of a controversy over racism in the boardroom (see Chapter 7).

The absence of racism at Palace was also supported in the accounts offered by black fans that attended Palace games. Wallis, quoted earlier, told of a particularly interesting experience. Wallis is a tall man and he wears large peaked caps of the kind that are very common in the black community. This kind of head gear is a marker of black style and culture. Wallis begins by stating that he has never heard racism during games:

I have never heard it, never heard it in all the time I have been to Palace, I can definitely say I have never heard racist chanting. I mean even to this hat, and you know walk up through the tunnel, I don't like sitting down straight away. I take my time, because I am me, that is me, nothing to do with anyone else, but my hat gets in the way of people sitting behind me and this geezer is going 'Oy you, get out the way!' When I turned round there was about 30 geezers sitting down and I looked round, that is how I am, I just looked round. He said 'You, your bloody hat's in the way, get it out the way!' and he could have easily said 'you black cunt, get out the way.' He could have easily said that if he wanted to, do you know what I mean, because there was 30 of them! But he just said that, there is just a geezer standing in my way, what is he doing, is he mad? He was going 'hey you, with the hat, get out the way!' So I turned round and then just sat down. You know, I have got to tell you the God's truth, I have never heard it [racist chanting]. There is a blonde guy up there who, I don't think he does anything else, I think he just goes to football – an original football hooligan – and I haven't heard him say one word about race. (Interview, 26 September 1997)

There remains a perplexing fact. Despite the almost complete lack of overt racism at Crystal Palace the level of black and ethnic minority participation at Crystal Palace is little more than their South London neighbours even though, at Millwall, the frequency of overt racism was much higher. The answer to this lay in the fact that despite Palace fan culture being more benign with regard to explicit racism, it's normative centre is still very much defined as a white preserve. Wallis captures this vividly when he says that black people simply don't think of the club as having anything to do with them – it simply isn't 'their ship.'

Conclusion

Throughout this chapter we have looked at the ways in which the defining centre of football culture at a local level defines the terms of legitimate inclusion for black football fans. One of the things we argue is that it is important to understand these processes because they show how the intersection of class and gender produce complex combinations of racial dialogue and exclusion. In this sense, we are arguing that the conflation within the policy arena of racism with other sorts of violence and intimidation misses the nuances that we've tried to explicate. More than this, some of the strictures of moral anti-racism make it impossible to render the complex forms of contingent inclusion won by black fans. The result is that these histories are made at once both incomprehensible and invisible. This is not to say that the cultural entry tickets to inclusion offered here are unambiguously progressive in terms of some latent class romanticism that has elsewhere dogged the debate about football violence (see discussion of this debate in Armstrong 1998; Giulianotti, Bonney and Hepworth 1994; Murphy, Williams and Dunning 1990). The point we want to make emphatically here is that these dialogues are profoundly partial and limited.

We have explored the intersections between gender and class that police the boundaries of acceptance in football culture. The game provides a key context in which racial exclusions and negotiations are manifest within the local body politic. We have developed an argument about the scope of black inclusion in football fan culture and its limitations, be it by the defining centre of English football fan culture or the variegations of local patriotism and its normative structure. The nationalisms of the neighbourhood and the circumscriptions of Englishness we outlined here offer black fans passports to entry that are always issued with specific terms and conditions. These circumstances are largely restricted to black males who perform and participate in class-inflected forms of hegemonic masculinity, which may at the same time exclude people who don't conform to these versions of masculinity – gay black men, or women, and Asian fans both male and female. This line of argument holds in a number of our case studies (Millwall, Everton and to a lesser extent Manchester City), but the loosening of the hegemony of these class inflected masculinities need not automatically lead to a more racially inclusive fan culture.

At Crystal Palace the fan culture was less orientated around gendered and class based norms and fan racism was almost non-existent. Despite the impact of high-profile black players like Vince Hillaire, Ian Wright, Mark Bright and Andy Gray the connection between the club and local black and ethnic minority communities remained weak. The affiliation of black fans to the club lasted only as long as they saw themselves represented in the black players who donned the Palace shirt. When the black players left they no longer felt a part of the club. The key point we want to emphasize here is that at a collective and symbolic level a team like Crystal Palace does not belong to black London. When black people look into the colours of a Palace shirt they do not yet see something that represents them. Perhaps, the significance of football as a form of popular culture is that it allows the politics of these identifications and definitions to be laid bare. In the next chapter we want to focus more directly on the styles and patterns of racism that we encountered amongst football fans while at the same time attempting to portray 'the racists' in all their complexity.

−4−

Faces of Racists, Sounds of Hate: Football Fans, Abuse and Structures of Antipathy

Woolwich Crown Court 17 October, 1996

The prison van carrying two football fans convicted of racial violence is delayed. The sentencing is due to take place at 9.30am but it has been put back until after lunch. The night before we had all agreed that tomorrow was going to be a good day: we would be able to record the successful prosecution of two perpetrators of football-related racial violence. The families of the two convicted racists waited in the cafeteria for the fate of their loved ones to be sealed. They consoled themselves with cups of tea. We had observed the trial at its various stages and, over a period of months, we gained some insight into the type of families the assailants had come from. The two young men – Paul Jackson and Ken Southwell – had quite different histories. Paul had been involved in petty crime and had a series of convictions for violence. Ken, on the other hand, had no prior convictions. He was from a working-class family, and, at the time of his arrest, was in full-time employment and had a girlfriend whom he planned to marry. Neither of the two men had been involved in organised racist politics or associated with racist youth cultures. Their racism was of the everyday or quotidian variety.

They sat in the cafeteria and Ken's barrister came over to give some information about what was going to happen during the sentencing. His mother, step father and grandfather – a retired policeman – hung on every word. As the barrister uttered the phrase 'Custody is inevitable' their faces seemed visibly shaken. It was as if a secret hope had shattered inside them. The two men had been convicted of the violent crime of wounding. The prosecutor told us that:

> My impression of Southwell was that he got drunk and got carried away and that had this not happened he would have otherwise been able to support himself in society and make a decent living. He was part of the crowd and got caught up with what was happening about him. Jackson I think is another thing altogether. I think he is a vicious and violent young man. The strange thing is that they both seem to come from respectable and loving families. (Interview 18 October, 1996)

On being refused entry to a match the two fans had gone to a local pub with a group of other friends. They followed the fortunes of their team on the teletext and started to drink heavily. Their team lost 2–0 and, disgruntled, they left the pub, itself just a short walk from the stadium. They were looking for opposition fans to confront as a way of compensating for the collective loss of honour engendered by the humiliating defeat by a local rival team. After a few abortive skirmishes they came upon a young black man waiting for a bus. They attacked him. But the lone black man fought the group off, to the extent that the white group started to walk away. The black man picked up a brick and followed his assailants up the street, since he wanted to make sure that they were going to leave him be. The police arrived and arrested all the young men including the black person who had been attacked. At the time a policeman told us that the 'victim was no angel'. This expectation itself seemed to be informed by the stereotypical images of black masculinity held by the white policeman.

After a few days the police dropped their inquiries into the behaviour of the black man and focused attention on the group of white men. Of a group of six to eight youths only two were prosecuted. The role of racism in the attack took up a good deal of the trial. Ken's barrister made much of the fact that his sister was black; his family had adopted her at a young age and they had grown up together. Ken's sister appeared in court as a character witness and denied the accusation that Ken was a racist. The prosecution lawyer produced a policewoman as a witness. She had sat in the back of the police van with Ken after his arrest and read out what he had said, a mixture of drunken rant and resentful racism. The black victim of the assault also came and gave evidence, describing the racist epithets and insults directed at him during the incident. He told us in a subsequent interview that both young men had been key instigators in the attack.

> They were calling me black bastard, I mean they were trying to intimidate me. But it was from when he Paul Jackson spat on me – like there was something – I just knew I was going to be fighting these guys . . . And what was going through my mind was the Stephen Lawrence thing, you know. This is a good day for them. They'll have a drink and then beat somebody up. I was thinking . . . it's not going to happen to me. (Interview, 6 March 1997)

As they waited for the minutes to pass Ken's family prepared for the inevitable. His mother turned to the family, 'When that boy who'd been attacked gave his evidence he just sat there smiling, didn't he?' she said. There was no attempt to dismiss what Ken had done or explain it away. Ken's stepfather replied 'Well, there's no getting around it – what they did to that boy was wrong and Ken's going to have to face that. There's nothing we can do about it, what's done is done' (Fieldnotes, 17 October 1996). This was not a family of committed racists.

They displayed no more racism and no less tolerance than is typical amongst white working-class families. What was striking was how ordinary they were.

Word was passed that the two men had arrived at the court. The families, journalists and the rest filed into the court room. The barristers joked with each other and passed inane pleasantries across their respective benches. It was just another case for them; they seemed to conduct themselves with a disregard for the fact that the gallery was full of people scrutinising their every word and gesture. Each of the barristers representing the two convicted men stood to give mitigating comments to the judge prior to sentencing. As they stood up to hear the judgement, Paul's face was expressionless as if this was almost routine. Ken was visibly shaken. He stood with his hands clasped together in front of him; he looked at them and held his head down. The judge said that the seriousness of the offence meant that it would be a custodial sentence: 'I will be taking the racial character of your crimes into consideration.' He sentenced Paul first to imprisonment for two years. Then, turning to Ken, he told him that he would be sentenced to 18 months in prison. As Ken heard the news, his bottom lip started to quiver. There was a terrible fear written on his face. Dazed, he looked back desperately at his parents and his girlfriend for a brief moment. His was the face of complete dread. This very ordinary young man would have the distinction of a criminal record for violent racism. The court guard led him away to the cells to begin his sentence.

* * *

We start this chapter with this scene for two reasons. Firstly, we want to argue that the portraits of racism that are implicit within much of the public discourse have resulted in an all to easy conflation of racism with people who possess deviant, evil, personal pathologies. We want to stress that it is important to position racism within very ordinary lives and develop a more nuanced idea of how racism can co-exist with respectability and the banal routines of football fandom. Here Ken and Paul represent two very different social constituencies: the first, an aspirant and respectable working class male; the second, a working-class man involved in petty criminal behaviour. Each of them articulates popular racism but neither is derived from organized racist politics. The portrait of racism and racists that we want to paint here is one that tries to capture the complexities of the experiences of the people who perpetrate these acts. Equally, we want to take seriously the suggestion that we made earlier that it is important to understand fan racism as a form of ritual.

In Chapter 1, we showed how the emergence of black players at all levels of football was met by crude and mass racist chanting and abuse directed at them. What was striking about the fan racism of this period was the premeditated quality it possessed. Fans would prepare to perform their racism by taking bananas to throw at black players or writing hate mail letters. Cyrille Regis played alongside two other black players – Laurie Cunningham and Brendon Batson – for West Bromwich Albion in the early 1980s. He remembered: 'We used to get letters all the time, you know . . . When I was called up for England for the first time there was a letter, an anonymous letter saying "If you go to Wembley and put on an England shirt you'll get one of these through your knees". There was a bullet in the envelope' (Interview, 4 December 1996). This was not just perpetrated by a 'hooligan minority'. In fact, the types of racist practice that we found confounded the easy association of fan racism with wider concerns about football-related violence.

'Hooligan' groupings adopt a style of self-presentation during games that signals a demeanour of restraint, readiness and calm. These sit in stark contrast to the highly expressive and overt forms of behaviour commonly associated with racist practices at football grounds. The reasons for this are quite clear and straight-forward. These groups are aware that they are being closely surveyed by the police through electronic means and by football intelligence officers. As well as embody-ing the stoicism associated with some versions of working-class masculinity then these supporters are reluctant to draw attention to themselves within the ground and as a result are extraordinarily quiet and inexpressive. Beyond this very practical response, in a variety of metropolitan contexts we found that these networks often include high profile and often-prestigious black members as we've already shown. Indeed, in places like London and Manchester the networks associated with 'hoolig-anism' are often far more multi-racial than the wider population of 'respectable fans'. As we have demonstrated the presence of black peers need not pre-empt the expression of racism. Equally, the reluctance to indulge in racism in the ground need not preclude involvement in racial bigotry outside and harassment of local minority shopkeepers and residents.

In some circumstances we did find an articulation between the culture of football hooliganism and racial bigotry. In the Manchester City case study we found connections between British National Party support, Ulster Unionism and casual racism within some fan groupings. These groups were closely associated with the hinterlands of Manchester City support in towns like Bury and Rochdale and included committed England supporters whom we conducted extensive ethno-graphic work with during the 1998 World Cup qualifying campaign (see Chapter 8). The important point here is that the subcultural formations and networks associated with football hooliganism can foster both multi-racial groupings and exclusively white mobs exhibiting high levels of racial chauvinism. In some circumstances, particularly where there is a common opponent, contradictory alliances are established between these incommensurable groupings, which unite around a shared loathing of another national or ethnic group.

Our research suggests that the involvement of right-wing political groupings in football culture is limited. We did find small numbers of fans with far-right political associations and allegiances who were also involved in the social networks associated with football hooliganism and later in this chapter we will offer a detailed portrait of one such fan. However, more broadly, the relationship between the far-right and football culture is instrumental rather than organic. Small groups of activists, who may be football fans, map their political agendas onto certain clubs and their social constituencies. There is little political leafleting in or around grounds as was previously the case. However, right-wing activists use graffiti, fly posting and political stickers in an opportunistic fashion in the wider vicinity of football grounds. These campaigns are highly organized. Neo-fascist activists descend on the localities in which football stadia are located and plaster stickers on lamp posts, put up posters and spray graffiti in local train stations and bus stops. These materials often include contact addresses and recruiting propaganda. Anti-fascist activists counter these activities by removing neo-fascist materials and replacing them with their own. This battle occurs, in large part, independently of the fan culture. The result is that relatively small numbers of far-right activists can have quite an extensive visual impact on a stadium and its surrounding urban environment. We found that the people most commonly indulging in racist name-calling and abuse were often remarkably 'respectable'.

Forms of Racial Abuse Amongst Fans

All of the informants we interviewed for this study reported that the general frequency of racism from fans is in decline. This decline has been particularly noted in relation to the Premier League, where recent initiatives and trends are seen as having a direct impact on the extent of popular expressions of racism. However, we observed and recorded racist abuse being directed at opposition black players in all of the clubs under study. These activities ranged from individual abuse and verbal insults, usually directed at black players, black stewards and fans and occasionally black policemen, to sporadic monkey chants and songs that invoke references to racial difference. What we want to do in what follows is summarize the general trends in fan racism that were encountered in our research. These are best summarized in six main areas with regard to the nature of fan racism.

a) Racist Verbal Abuse in Grounds Occurs in Intermittent Outbursts

It is inaccurate to represent racist activity in football grounds as consistent and organised. Racist epithets and slogans are invoked in specific contexts and serve particular functions. This activity is often, although not always, connected with high profile games or charged confrontations with rivals. It is within these intense situations that racist slogans and interventions are most likely. As a result a series of fixtures may pass without any racist activity and then a fixture with a heightened atmosphere can produce an explosion of racist name calling. We want to suggest that racist abuse should be best understood as part of a much wider context of abuse and what we want to refer to as a 'structure of antipathy' that may vary according to local conditions, personalities and events while sharing some key themes. These forms of abuse are structural in the sense that they are produced through the interplay between the normative ideals held to personify a particular collection of fans, as previously discussed in Chapter 2 and aversive characteristics projected onto opposition players and fans.

b) *Racist Activity is Unevenly Developed within the Ground*

Overt expressions of racism are localized within the ground as a whole. Whilst racism can occur in any part of a stadium particular sections of a ground may be the place in which racist verbal abuse has been established as permissible and legitimate through informal or implicit agreement amongst fans. This is not to say that all fans within these areas agree with these sentiments; rather it is a matter of collusion through silence or non-opposition. It is important to see football grounds as consisting of a series of 'moral landscapes' that have different features with regard to the propensity for racist activity to flourish. While racism can go uncontested in some places it is viewed as illegitimate in others. The implicit and explicit moral prohibitions against racist abuse are weakest within the context of the away supporter's areas. Fans often speak about the contrast between the vitality of going to away games and the sterile and highly policed experience of seeing their club at home. The lessening of the moral prohibitions on fan behaviour away from home also allows for the freer expression of racist abuse. For example, the two incidents of racist behaviour we observed amongst Crystal Palace supporters were in the context of away fixtures.

c) *Racist Verbal Abuse Takes a Variety of Expressive Forms or Ritual Styles*

We have identified a range of forms of racist abuse within football grounds. These can be characterized as:

- Individual racial slurs directed at black players in response to incidents on the field of play. These forms of football racism usually combine a racial or national epithet with an insult. Common examples include: 'you black bastard', 'black cunt', 'nigger bastard', 'fucking jiggerboo', 'fucking wog'. Usually, directed at opposing players these forms of abuse can also be used against black players from the perpetrator's own team when that player is playing badly or makes a mistake.

- Proactive racial abuse aimed at intimidating black players and affecting their performance on the field of play. Here forms of verbal abuse are intended to actually affect play and not merely to punish the black players. Examples of this behaviour include 'monkey chanting' often elided with booing, 'dayo chanting' (see Chapter 3) sometimes combined with fans scratching under their arms in ape fashion. These forms of abuse are performed as opposing black players receive the ball, when tackling an opponent and when on the ball.

- Collective songs and chants use racial meanings to express club identities and are combined with racist epithets producing complex racially exclusive representations of group identity. We discussed this form of racism at length in Chapter 3. Here collective identities are embodied through invoking racial meanings both explicitly and implicitly. We found other examples where the use of racist constructions of south Asian communities were deployed within these rituals. On some occasions when away fans visited towns with large south Asian populations they would often sing less sophisticated songs suggesting that Leicester or Bradford was simply 'full of Pakis'. What is significant about the use of racist constructions here is that they are not necessarily targeted at south Asians. Rather they are directed at a white audience, which by implication would be embarrassed by being confronted with the facts of regional multi-culture. We have also observed some white players who had dark complexions being referred to as 'fucking Pakis'.

In similar vein, although with a slightly more ambiguous target in mind, a variety of songs and noises are sometimes invoked, particularly (although not exclusively) in the context of matches where Tottenham Hotspur provide the opposition, which express anti-Semitic sentiment. Tottenham, with the club's location in north-east London, have long been associated with having a large Jewish following. As Dave, a middle-aged Manchester City fan put it to us:

> Yes, I mean Tottenham do flaunt this Jewish thing, don't they, they have flags don't they with the Star of David and stuff like that. This thing, the Yiddo Army and all that sort of thing. (Interview, 10 February 1997)

In contrast then to other fan groups Tottenham fans are seen to embrace and celebrate this ethnic minority identity label even if only in a playful reaction to opposition taunts which have taken on some of the most sinister forms. Perhaps the most troubling of these is the sound of hissing from opposing fans which is intended to invoke the sound of gas entering the chambers at a Nazi concentration camp. Whilst aware of the fans' intentions in producing this sound, Paul, a black Spurs fan illustrated the impact that it can have when he recalled:

I mean I'm always contending that the two scariest chants that I've ever heard in a football match ever have been the sound of monkey grunts, which you don't hear at all now, and a gassing sound when fans make, you know, a fake gassing sound, which you do hear all the time, and it's just incredibly frightening. I think that's when – I think that's when you take things over the line, but I understand why they do it – especially Arsenal fans – Arsenal fans always do it. You know, and I just guess football fans'll see it what's the difference between making gassing sounds and singing songs about Munich, the Munich air disaster, you know, there's no difference and I admit I sing songs about, you know, the Munich air disaster, so I guess I'm just as bad as the fans who make the gassing sounds. But I feel the fans who make the gassing sound – I don't know – I was gonna say I don't think there's no racial intent, but there obviously is some – I just think, I just think they're just doing it because they wind the Tottenham fans up even more. Because that is the one thing that always makes the Tottenham fans flip – you know, they're always like: 'Oh, fucking let's go, let's have 'em!' you know, the moment that happens, yeah . . . Yeah, just total wind-ups, total, total wind-ups – you know, you find a team's Achilles' heel and you sing about it non-stop, you wind the fans up. (Interview, 30 October 1996)

Equally other opposition fans have shown a willingness to invoke these identity labels in a more inventive, opportunistic fashion as we observed during a fixture between Manchester City and Tottenham at Maine Road at the start of the 1995/96 football season. During this match an isolated group of fans sitting directly in front of us in the Main Stand who were in their early to mid twenties and wearing replica City tops began singing 'Spurs are on their way to Belsen, Hitler's gonna gas 'em again' to the tune of the 1981 'Chas and Dave' cup final song *Ozzies Dream*. Reflecting on the origins of this song and its place within Manchester City fan culture Dave went on:

I think that came from that Wembley song that started 'Ozzies Dream', and there is no doubt about it that City, they might even have done it at Wembley [The Cup Final in question was between Tottenham and Manchester City] I can't really remember, but certainly I remember City fans singing that the next game, I thought what are they singing, and they were singing about 'Spurs are on their way to Belsen . . .' a dreadful thing, and then the hissing which we have always put down in the Fanzine . . . But yes, City fans have certainly sang that song and certainly done the hissing at corners at both Maine Road and Whitehart Lane.

Whilst these songs are implicitly targeted at an audience of Tottenham fans who are identified as Jewish and associated with a 'Jewish club' the ability to 'wind up' those fans is premised on the location of this ethnic identity outside of the defining centre of the broader English football culture. As such it is the clubs affiliation with a Jewish identity that is perceived, at least externally, as the principal means of demonization.

d) *Racism is Often Expressed Rhetorically through Humour and Play*

Racism is not always couched within abusive forms of 'hate speech' or harassment. There is a creative and playful dimension to the expression of racist sentiments. This enables racist assertions and stereotypes to be normalised. A white fan, who is a clergyman in his fifties, commented:

> Sometimes, you see, I think when they're [racial comments] thoroughly acceptable then they're humorous . . . Some years ago at the [ground] there was a Pakistani linesman, and he was standing on the corner, and someone shouted 'Get him off that corner, he'll open a shop!' . . . To some people that was racist. To some people that was funny. As long as there's humour in it [then it's OK]. I think these Pakistani and Indian corner shops offer a tremendous service to the community. (Interview, 28 February 1996)

Humour works with insidious racial stereotypes yet enables their expression in a legitimate way. A common claim made by the defenders of racialized fan banter was that such commentaries are meaningless play as opposed to meaningful abuse. The nature of such abuse needs to be carefully situated within the everyday conventions associated with working-class male subcultures in which verbal play and 'wind ups' form a central role in conveying social status (Willis 1977). As we commented earlier this type of racist performance is a product of a particular stage: the altered meanings that are produced in the ground itself. This type of racist humour is directed across the white line at players but it is also importantly directed at peers and fans within earshot.

In some contexts young men's expression of explicit racist language was closely associated with vying for individual status within the peer group. To be racist in the football ground was to dare to say the unspeakable. Racist abuse in this context was as much about conferring status on particular members of the group as it was about racial chauvinism. In this sense racism and racist practice became part of the alternative commentaries that are so much a part of English football culture. These are narrated amongst peers who are jockeying to have their voices heard and opinions accepted. We reported an earlier example of this with regard to the commentary about Bobby Bowry offered by George, Bobby and Stephen in Chapter 3.

These expressions of racism also demonstrated an inventive quality that was sometimes coded. Here fans adapted songs to refer to contemporary events. The O.J. Simpson trial in particular was invoked in this way during the 1995/6 season. In one of the case study clubs a small but vocal section of its support chanted 'O.J., OJ.' whenever a black steward appeared regardless of whether this was at home or away. Equally, white fans shouted at black stewards 'Oi, OJ, where's your gloves?' A song sung to the tune of *Old Macdonald* followed this:

O.J. Simpson had a knife
Ee Ey Ee Ey Oh
And with that knife he stabbed his wife
Ee Ey Ee Ey Oh
With a stab stab here and a stab stab there
Here a stab, there a stab
Everywhere a stab stab
O.J. Simpson had a knife
Ee Ey Ee Ey Oh

The steward would at the beginning laugh along with the playfulness of the joke. After being subjected to this repeatedly there would be no doubt that this abuse was meant maliciously with the intent to undermine, disturb and separate him from the fan collective. What is interesting about these types of abuse is that they don't have to explicitly refer to race. They operate through metonymic associations. Everyone knew that O.J. Simpson is a black American – a black American on trial for murdering his wife. The song marks out the steward through a metonymic trigger which invokes the idea of black criminality. The expressions on the faces of those singing these songs revealed that the joke was meant to hurt.

There is also another dimension to this form of racialized abuse. From the late 1990s there was a growing sense amongst fans of the prohibitions against open and crudely expressed racism at football. A response to this shift in public consciousness is that the encoded forms of racism that work through metonyms and connotation have also increased. In the same way that the reference to OJ triggers an association between race and criminality, this operates through a process of metonymic elaboration: the reference to 'O.J. connotes ideas about black criminality that also resonate with associations between black masculinity and criminal violence. As a result racist effects can be achieved without the presence of crude racist language. For example, in London we have recorded cases where football fans have shouted 'Cab, Cab, Cab' at black players on the field. The minicab sector is a place in the economy where minority communities have established themselves, particularly recent migrants from West Africa. Here, reference to the blackness of the player is made without any direct reference to race. Yet, there is no ambiguity as to the effect of this abuse. The intention is to target the player's blackness (the association with black cab drivers and the black livery of metropolitan taxis) and also to undermine the status of that player (to identify them with a marginalized low-status occupation). Equally, we found similar processes on Merseyside.

In 1995 Daniel Amokachi was the first black player to have been signed by Everton for many years and whilst, tough, hard working and unpretentious in appearance, he brought a new set of characteristics to the club. Amokachi is Nigerian, a nationality with a quite different cultural heritage from that of Liverpool,

Britain or indeed Sweden (from where Everton's other 'foreign' player at the time, Anders Limpar, hails). During his time at Everton Daniel's embracement by the supporters cannot be understood purely in terms of his status as 'their black player'. Whilst he embodies many of the characteristics for which Everton supporters have illustrated a preference he could be wasteful, over elaborate and indeed expressive in a highly individualistic manner in the aftermath of scoring. Earl Barrett, a black British player, matched the preferences of the Everton supporters more completely, although he was almost universally seen as ineffective and lacking in ability and was accordingly freely abused, albeit rarely in a racial sense.

By contrast the Everton supporters that celebrated his distinctiveness embraced Amokachi. He was not seen as threatening in the same way that a distinctive, unknown black foreign opposition player might be. Nor was he seen as threatening to the white male identities at the centre of Everton's collective fan culture, because he was African and would return to Africa once his time with the club was finished. As Mark, an Everton fan in his thirties reflected 'he actually is a personality. He's slightly . . . he's an African international, which is something which is unusual, and I think people have taken him to their hearts.' (Interview, 26 January 1996).

However, in the context of the contrariness amongst Everton fans that was raised in Chapter 2, Graham suggested that rather than embracing his distinctiveness and talent, the signing of Amokachi provided the fans with a platform upon which they could counter the popular discourse which constructs Everton as 'a racist club':

> They [Everton fans] don't know the game they just want players to win the ball. But they are also a contrary bunch. They don't do as they're expected. People expected them to hound Walker but they didn't, they expect us to back Royle but everyone's having a go at him, and they expected Amokachi to get a hard time. I think the Everton fans just got behind him to prove everyone else wrong. (Interview, 26 January 1996)

Yet, at the same time there was evidence of ambivalence. Everton fans gave him the nickname 'Amo-taxi' which, through humour, invoked a less crude racial reference than the previous association with 'black mini cab drivers'. The name providing the punch line to the joke 'What's big, black and carries five passengers?' – 'Amotaxi'. Whilst in some senses celebratory the joke still marks out the player's difference through his blackness and the invocation of stereotypical notions of black physicality.

e) Racist Abuse can Take on 'Player-specific' Forms

This occurs where high profile foreign and black players constitute a threat to the teams and a symbolic aversion to the normative identity of the fan culture.

In the course of the research it became clear that high profile players are targeted for specific forms of abuse that take on both the individual biographies of these players as well as mobilizing racists or national xenophobic elements. This type of abuse is to some degree detached or 'segregated' from both the course of the game and the other abuse strategies deployed during the match. We found that high-profile black players like Ruud Gullit and Ian Wright and white 'foreigners' like David Ginola and Ronald Koeman became particularly targeted. This antagonism is the product of a history of grievances that produce within opposing fans a weight of conflict and expectation of threat. This form of abuse was particularly prevalent at Everton.

An ethnographic account of the fixture between Everton and Newcastle United held on 1 October 1996 provided a good example of this process of player specific strategies. David Ginola is a French international winger who had joined Newcastle United during the previous close season. He is a spectacularly talented player who has been lauded by supporters, commentators and reporters throughout his subsequent career for his ball skills and crossing ability. He is also exceedingly good looking, with a chiselled bone structure, blue eyes and long immaculate dark hair. These characteristics have led to his off field employment as a fashion model, the development of something of a 'play boy' image and a presence in some of the most glamorous social circles.

Ginola also has a rather petulant image within the game and left France for Newcastle after having fallen out with the French footballing authorities and been dropped from the national team. Perhaps even more significantly, media representations and particularly television interest in the player have led to the development of a reputation for 'diving' when challenged.

Throughout much of Everton's home match with Newcastle there was sporadic, indiscriminate booing of Ginola amongst the Everton supporters which may have been muted by the general superiority of Newcastle's football. After around 50 minutes of the game however, the player appeared to take a dive outside the Everton penalty area. From all around us were individual cries of 'you cheating French bastard', 'fuck off back to France' and 'you fucking cheat' and group repetitive chanting of the words 'cheat, cheat, cheat'.

After this moment the booing and whistling was far more generic amongst all sections of the Everton support whenever Ginola received the ball. The abuse became even more intense and vitriolic in the sixtieth minute when Ginola appeared to be brought down after running with the ball into the Everton penalty box and was awarded a penalty, which was converted by the white England midfielder Robert Lee. After this incident, which effectively sealed the game in Newcastle's favour, Ginola was systematically and generically booed whenever he received the ball and was abused by individuals, in quite vitriolic fashion, who would freely invoke his Frenchness in a Francophobic way.

Ginola can be situated almost completely outside the norms that structure English football culture. He represents a very particular image of the foreign footballer. His is a game of individualistic skill and artistry rather than 'honest endeavour' and teamwork. His image is flamboyant, 'poncey', even effeminate, rather than unassuming, tough and masculine. His reputation is then situated and vilified within a broader antipathy towards 'foreign' ways which are at odds with a very white working-class 'British' notion of masculinity.

The point we want to stress here is that racist and xenophobic abuse in football is in no sense a simple matter of blind hatred. Rather, it is situated and nuanced. It is part of a larger game taking place between the field of play and the stands where images of character, of normative preference and aversion are constantly being mobilized. Here images of racial otherness and national difference are used against high-profile players as a means to counteract the threat they pose on the field and to respond to and repair histories of conflict.

f) Verbal Racist Abuse in and around Football Grounds Rarely Escalates into Physical Violence

We found examples of verbal harassment from white football fans towards ethnic minority residents within the localities of football grounds. These patterns of abuse were close to what has been established in previous research (Holland 1992a). However, racist verbal abuse rarely makes the transition to racist violence and physical abuse outside grounds. There were two principal exceptions to this general pattern: the black Millwall fan targeted for abuse and physical attack by opposing fans during an away fixture which we discussed in Chapter 3, and the young black man who was standing at a bus stop, described at the beginning of this chapter.

As we have already reported there was much discussion in this trial as to the role that racism had played in the attack. This group had harassed other white fans but it was this young black man's appearance that had marked him out for attack. It was not necessarily that this group had left the public house with the intention of committing a racist attack. They were looking for opposition fans to confront as a way of compensating for the collective loss of honour engendered by their side's defeat by a local rival. However, racism marked out another target – namely a young black man – as commensurable with the masculine culture of football rivalry. These conflicts are structured in terms of how those people are defined as both potential adversaries and allies. In this context male opposition fans are defined as the prime opponent. But, put simply, in this case there were no opposition fans to fight. In their absence the young male perpetrators drew on a wider set of social oppositions provided within the culture of racism that identified a young black man as a target. The perpetrators in both incidents were young white men between 17 and 25 years of age. Incidents such as these were rare and in general the expression of fan racism was confined to the ritual setting of the game itself.

g) Racist Abuse is Perpetrated by Fans of All Ages

We found incidents of racist abuse being perpetrated by people of all age ranges. We have recorded incidents involving very young people between the ages of eight and twelve and some as young as six years of age. During one fixture we observed the intergenerational transmission of these types of ritual abuse. During a match between Millwall and Brentford on 29 November 1996 we saw one instance of a boy of six indulging in racist abuse. His father had racially abused opposition black players on two occasions. One of Brentford's black players – Ijah Anderson – was involved in a couple of tough tackles followed by a confrontation with one of the Millwall players. The ball went out of play just in front of the dugout. Ijah Anderson's football boots came undone, and Brentford had been awarded a free kick. The crowd responded to this with an incredible hostility. There were choruses of 'Oi, oi' and 'Fuck off.' The young boy started to mouth in a moderate voice as if he was almost talking to himself, 'You black' Then he paused full for probably two or three seconds – and shouted 'You black fuck!' Meanwhile his father was screaming and gesticulating at Anderson.

The point to make here is that this boy was learning and rehearsing the styles of racist abuse. An induction into this culture often comes from fathers and peers who pass on these behavioural norms to sons and friends. What is very telling in this particular example is that it is in the football ground that young men learn how to emulate and perform this language. The young boy would not be able to speak in this way in other public contexts. In the football ground there are few prohibitions on his use of 'bad language' or on abusive behaviour. Here he can see and model himself on what his father does, what 'real men' do in that situation. Football then might be seen to provide the social apprenticeship that produces this culture and the styles of racism that are associated with it.

Equally we have recorded incidents with people in their seventies. More orchestrated chanting is most common amongst groups of young men. This behaviour was observed within peer groups between 16–20 and 25–35 years. We did not observe women indulging in this form of abuse although we did observe a small number of women fans demonstrating approval and complicity. An example of this type of racist narrative was recorded during a fixture between Millwall and Sunderland on 23 September 1995. After about 60 minutes Tony Witter skilfully slide-tackled a Sunderland player on the 18 yard box, recovered his footing, dribbled the ball toward the sidelines and cleared to a Millwall player. There was a crackle of applause all around the South Stand. Tony a white fan turned to his friend Kevin and said: 'Witter's having a wonderful time out there.' Kevin replied, 'He's like a completely new player – he could eat at my house breakfast, lunch and dinner the way he's playing.' Pauline – Tony's wife – then commented: 'He's all right out there on the pitch, but I wouldn't want him in my home.' They all laughed. It seemed clear that while Witter was a hero on the pitch, from Pauline's comment it did not necessarily carry beyond this arena.

Again this emphasized the point that racism becomes banal and 'normal'. In many ways it is this banality that makes it disturbing. The everyday casual quality of racism is what is so shocking. Beyond this, the complex combinations of exclusion and inclusion of black players seems really crucial if we are to understand the ways in which racism features in the lives of these people. However, the complex acceptance of black players like Tony Witter within the arena of sport is not necessarily carried over to life beyond the field of play. Following Pauline's comments Tony Witter may be adored on the field of play but not necessarily welcomed into the homes of the people who love him for ninety minutes on a Saturday afternoon.

Women, then, were sometimes involved in a conversational form of racism of the type illustrated above and were sometimes complicit in the face of sustained racial abuse but we did not find any cases of women practising the rituals of racist abuse. Those fans most likely to be involved in this activity were predominantly, although not exclusively, younger men.

Portraits of Racism: Profile of Perpetrators and the Social Backgrounds of Fans Engaged in Racist Behaviour

Having argued that the public debate about racism in football has often been deployed around simplified caricatures of racists, the question remains, what kind of people commit acts of popular racism? As we have argued the image of the racist has been elided with that of the hooligan in much of the public discourse. We want to suggest that it is important to separate racism from the debate over hooliganism so that a more accurate picture can be drawn. In the course of our ethnography we followed a series of court cases where football fans were prosecuted for racism and we interviewed convicted racists. Equally, we talked at length with football fans who articulated crude forms of racism. In what follows, we want to describe three portrayals. The first of these is Kevin Ryan, a Millwall football fan who was convicted for racist abuse. Ryan's conviction was secured through highly sophisticated forms of video surveillance developed by the Metropolitan police at Millwall. We will discuss this initiative and the court case which followed in detail in Chapter 7. Here we want to focus on the social profile of Kevin Ryan.

a) The Kevin Ryan Prosecution

Over a period of eight months Ryan, who was 40 years old at the time, had been video recorded repeatedly using racist abuse. His racism was largely individual verbal taunts. As a result he could not be prosecuted under Section 3 of the Football Offences Act which stipulated at the time that in order to be prosecuted the racist chanting has to include three or more fans. On the 26 April 1997 during a home fixture against Gillingham the police recorded Ryan again, this time group chanting. Confronted with the video evidence Ryan pleaded guilty. His case was heard at Tower Bridge Magistrates Court on the 3 June 1997.

Ryan was recorded on video equipment shouting 'nigger nigger nigger' and, against the opposing fans, shouting 'gippos' and 'pykes'. He was also recorded singing 'There is only one Tony Nigger' in the direction of one of Milwall's own players, the black player Tony Witter. Ryan's racism was of the crudest type. The case was reported widely in the local media (*South London Press*, 6 June 1997; *Lewisham Mercury*, 5 June 1997). The Southwark News reported that the club had supported the conviction with the headline: 'MILLWALL OFFICIALS WELCOME BAN ON RACIST FAN: IDIOT EVEN ABUSED TONY WITTER' (*Southwark News*, 5 June 1997).

In the aftermath of the trial we contacted Kevin Ryan and he granted us an interview at his home. Ryan lived with his girlfriend Cath in St Leonard's on Sea. This is approximately fifty miles from London and a long way from Millwall's home turf. When we interviewed him he was unemployed and lived in a council house in an almost exclusively white area of coastal south east England. The small estate he lived on was typical of the red brick public housing built in abundance in the outer city areas, where working-class communities were resettled, or settled during the 1950s.

On Ryan's front door he'd fixed two stickers that you usually see in cars with Millwall's home and away strip. Ryan welcomed us into his home. The video evidence that the police had recorded showed that Ryan was capable of extreme racism. He not only abused opposition black players and black Millwall players but had also shouted abuse at black Millwall supporters. He had been recorded shouting 'Sing up Sooty' to a black fan sitting close by in the South Stand at the New Den. The video surveillance had also recorded one of his friends as he spat over a black supporter. We had no illusions about the level or intensity of his racism and his intentions.

The internal decoration of his two-bedroom house was something of a shrine to Millwall football club. A blue and white Millwall flag hanging in his front room showed the official club lion in the centre of a white panel, flanked by two blue panels on each side. Underneath was the caption: 'South London'. The local patriotism seemed curiously out of place given that they were in a house some fifty miles from the Club's ancestral home. By the fireplace a stone lion stood painted in blue and white. We were surrounded by these symbols of Millwallism. As Ryan settled in his armchair we noticed that on his finger he was wearing a gold ring in the shape of the rampant Millwall lion. So he was, what is referred to in football parlance – 'Millwall through and through' (see also Robson 2000: 115).

From the beginning of the interview Ryan insisted that he had been treated unfairly and that the police had tricked him into pleading guilty and that there was a double standard with regard to how fans were being banned for using 'bad language' while players and managers could get away with it. On a wall close to where Kevin Ryan was sitting was a framed picture of Tony Witter, Millwall's black defender, whom Ryan had racially abused during the fixture against Gillingham. He responded when we pointed the picture out:

> There you go. If I was that dead against him it wouldn't be up there would he? I accept the fact right, that's the law, that's how it is. Whether I agree that the law's right is a different kettle of fish. Witter I think has been good actually. He can make, you know, really silly mistakes. He gives away too many penalties an' all, but he is fast and there's his saving grace. He's got pace and, you know, he gives a hundred per cent. You've got to give him credit there. Bowry as well. He's not the most gifted player, but he fucking tries. You can't ask for more than that out of a player. I mean we've had black players at Millwall for fucking years. I remember [Trevor] Lee years ago [...]If they're good they're good, if they're crap they're crap. Same as the white players, you know. (Interview, 23 June 1997)

While, Ryan recognized that what he did was against the law, he claimed that his use of racist abuse is simply a matter of using strategically the type of abuse that is effective in the 'heat of the moment'. He claimed that he felt no resentment or bitterness towards black people: 'there's good blacks, there's bad blacks. There's good whites, there's bad whites.' Within Ryan's justification there is an easy equivalence made between racist abuse and other kinds of abusive behaviour.

> And I [will call] 'you [a] fucking black cunt' – it's the same as like if a Scouse scores a goal, 'you Scouse cunt' or you know, Mancunian, whatever. I was colour prejudiced against him because he scored against us. I don't know him personally, so I can't say he was a nice man or a nasty bit [of work]. (Interview, 23 June 1997)

This is a familiar response. It is often claimed that people who have ginger hair get abused or players who have put on weight get abuse. Such justifications gloss the fact that racism and racist ideologies have an ideological weight that is in no way commensurable with ideas surrounding regional associations, hair colour or obesity. No one was ever enslaved for coming from Liverpool, or for being over weight or having ginger hair. But it is important to take Ryan's responses seriously. No doubt he was trying to justify and explain away his racist practices. There was, however, a clear sense of confusion and incomprehension of the severity of the response. For him the use of racist language at football was a normal and legitimate way to vent anger and frustration.

Ryan's social environment is almost exclusively white. In these networks he probably encounters common-sense popular racism. He has little interest in organized racist politics although on one occasion he picked up a leaflet from the racist political party the League of St George at a game. He has one black friend:

> I suppose – you could count the blacks living in Hastings basically and the surrounding areas, probably on two hands, you know what I mean. A fellow called Carl White who's a mate of mine, he's a black fellow. When he heard about the thing on the telly and that, he came in the pub, and he said to me, you know, he was joking, 'you black cunt, you black cunt, you black cunt,' to me. He said, 'You bastard, why didn't you tell them that you was up there with me, and you was calling it to me' you know what I mean. If he can not worry about it, why should someone that didn't even hear it worry about it? (Interview, 23 June 1997)

There is something palpable and genuine about his sense of disbelief. This is in large part the product of the ways in which racism has been normalized within this milieu. Here it becomes legitimate and permissible to use racist abuse against those who threaten or disappoint. Ryan's racism need not be the product of a coherent racist worldview, or a consistently negative orientation to black people. For him the most disturbing aspect of the trial was the suggestion that he was not a 'real' football fan but a thug that exploits football.

> Sitting in the cold light of day, yeah it was a stupid thing to do. It was wrong. I accept that. But I don't think I deserve a five-year ban for it, I really don't, to be honest. I spend a lot of money, you know, following the team and buying nick-nacks and what have you. I mean the magistrate had the arsehole – as I say, he's probably never even been to a football match, but he had the arsehole to turn round and say, 'it's people like you' – what is it – 'put off real football fans'. So he's saying that I'm not a real football fan. (laughs) I travel a hundred and twenty-mile round trip just for a fucking home game. I'm not a real fan. There are people sitting on their arse in Lewisham and fucking Catford and whatever, don't bother. He's trying to tell me that I'm not a real fan! (Interview, 23 June 1997)

Ryan is not a dangerous 'hooligan thug' in the conventional sense of how this notion is used. He has no convictions for football violence. There is some irony in the fact that he expresses resentment about the 'locals' lack of commitment to Millwall while his crass and overt racism has helped to perpetuate the image of the Den as a white space in an increasingly multicultural urban community. It is simply inaccurate to see people like Ryan as alien to football culture, people like him may well be unwelcome in today's game, but his racism is expressed within the context of a football culture that has acted as its stage.

b) *Michael Johnson and the Barnsley Boys*

The second portrait of racism that we want to present here is that of Michael Johnson. During a Coca-Cola Cup-Tie between Arsenal and Barnsley in 1995, Ian Wright had been subject to quite extensive racist chanting from the Barnsley fans. In the aftermath of that incident Michael Johnson was charged. It was some time before Johnson's case came to trial. It was eventually heard on the 15 April 1997 at Barnsley Magistrates Court. The trial was a ramshackle affair. Johnson defended himself and initially planned to call close to seventy witnesses. As a result two days of court time was put aside.

The evidence offered in the trial seemed flimsy to an observer. It was quite clear that the prosecutor took a decision to play down the racist elements of the abuse directed at Ian Wright on this occasion. During the court proceeding we approached the group of friends that Michael Johnson had brought to trial with him. They were all men in their early twenties. During the lunchtime recess we walked to a local bar to talk about the case. Andy, a young man in his early twenties, worked as an office clerk. He was a regular at Barnsley games. As we were walking along he said that everybody gets involved in abuse and claimed it was not a 'big deal'. He was a very open young man, on the one hand obviously siding with his friend the accused, but with a much more complicated attitude toward issues of race. He voiced quite liberal views when he said he didn't agree with the victimization of black people per se, but in the context of football everybody 'gets their names called.' He added: 'You know, everybody is racist in Barnsley and it is because there aren't many black people around 'ere.'

Johnson was the only one amongst the group who wasn't working – all the rest had full-time jobs. Andy had just left the Marines, Paul worked for the mail order catalogue company, Empire, and Scott was working nights at the time as a loading truck driver. What was striking about this peer group as a whole was their ordinariness. They didn't conform to any stereotype of what one might think of with regard to young white working-class men involved in racist chanting. They certainly weren't close to any image of shaven-headed, skinhead thugs. Even though Johnson himself had a crop cut and wore a bomber jacket, neither he nor his friends were interested in far right politics. Their racism was the type that is commonsensical everyday, not the product of a clear set of ideological principles. It was the type of racism that grew out of the sort of place that Barnsley is and what it seeks to preserve in terms of its whiteness, and also its sense of regional peculiarity or distinctiveness. These things came out very clearly during the interview conducted with the group after the trial.

Michael Johnson was found guilty and was fined £100 and directed to pay court costs of £115. He was excluded from watching any football fixture, be it domestic or European or any other such game for five weeks. Although it was not clear at the time, Barnsley were eventually to win automatic promotion to the Premier League. It was curious throughout the trial though, that the issue of race and racism was very much secondary to the prosecution.

As Johnson and his friends walked out of the courtroom onto the steps they seemed stunned and no one talked. Johnson was totally distraught because of the ban whilst the fine and fees seemed of secondary importance. We walked through the centre of Barnsley, and decided to go for another drink and ended up in a pub that was just opposite the pub that we had been in at lunchtime. It was here in the immediate aftermath of the trial that the interview took place. The group spoke very openly and very frankly about the issues of race and racism. What became clear was that Michael Johnson was not the chief perpetrator of racist abuse on this occasion after he admitted that he was completely drunk during the game. He had drunk 12 pints and was almost incapable of standing up. Scott joked and reminded Johnson that he had said in the courtroom that he had only consumed one or two pints. Johnson confessed that on this occasion the person who had been indulging in racial abuse and had spat on David Seaman was another member of the group who had not attended the trial.

Any sense of sympathy over a possible 'miscarriage of justice' evaporated when Michael Johnson admitted to a whole catalogue of incidents of racial abuse both inside and outside of the Barnsley ground in which he had been involved. He boasted about monkey chanting and about throwing bananas. His admission was unselfconscious, unrepentant, and apparently unproblematic. Racism was not something he was ashamed of. He expressed a clear commitment to keeping 'Yorkshire white' and to a racist vision of the local area. He said:

> It is just coons and Pakis isn't it. Everybody round here hates coons and Pakis. Well after a couple of drinks there is a few laughs. If there are some Pakis or some niggers about then they will get some abuse round here.[I am] just the same as everybody else more or less racist round here. It is being natural like, that's how our community is. (Interview, 15 April 1997)

Other members of the group agreed that this type of racism was common. Scott added that the players should also be able to take it, that verbal abuse was part of the game: 'They turn round and stick two finger at us don't they some of them. They should thrive on it anyway.' When it was suggested that the extent of racist abuse would keep black or Asian people from Yorkshire coming to support

Barnsley, Johnson was unequivocal: 'I think it is a white man's sport innit?' Andy disagreed 'No, it is not, there is still blacks in the teams.' Johnson countered with 'All foreign pillocks.' Andy retaliated 'Don't be stupid. Asians, don't see any Asians at all do you, they don't seem to be interested them Asians like.'

At this point Paul tried to mitigate the discussion: 'I think all this racism is dying down in any case – I think it will die out. Do you?' To which Johnson responded 'I don't want it to die out . . . It's a white man's game, but I think it is part of the game that they are going to get stick basically. It is part of the thing, if you play, especially big players, you give them abuse.'

Johnson was not a politically organised racist: like Kevin Ryan he showed no interest in extreme right-wing politics. He did articulate a racism that was consistent and compacted. He wanted Barnsley and Yorkshire to remain white. He articulated a sneering contempt for black people that lived in the vicinity and he admitted to verbally abusing black people in the street. Scott quickly slipped into racist language, using phrases like 'coon' and 'nigger' very easily. The other members of the group were more complicated. Andy, for example, on the one hand had justified the use of verbal abuse against black players but, on the other hand, had also argued against singling out black people or excluding black players from the England team.

While all the members of the group possessed different levels of commitment to popular racism, they all agreed that Barnsley should remain a white bastion, which they compared favourably with multi-ethnic cities like Birmingham and Manchester. They had all perpetrated racist abuse at football. The point we want to stress here is that the culture of football fandom enables young men with varying levels of commitment to popular racism to perpetrate these acts because within the ORA Stand or elsewhere it is seen to be part and parcel of the game.

It was a brilliant sunny day and walking through the streets of Barnsley after leaving the pub it was striking how 'white' it seemed. Popular racism in this part of Britain is prosaic and taken for granted. As the young men had said 'there weren't very many black people so it didn't really matter.' Walking through the market was just one black face in the crowd. A very tall quite thickset white man approached. He had dark hair and was wearing a Barnsley shirt, which seemed a few sizes too big for him. On the man's breast was the blazonry of Barnsley football club stitched against the mass of red cloth. At the centre of the club's badge was the white rose of Yorkshire. The casual racism of Johnson and his friends articulated just a few minutes earlier resonated in the symbolism of the white rose.

c) 'Greigsie' and Connections between Racism and Right-wing Extremism

Largely, the portrait of racism that emerges from our research is a common-sense, demotic, popular racism that revolves around the normalization of racist abuse and the white, exclusive and racially coded claims to local territory and belonging. We have also found, in a few cases, fans that flirted with organized racist politics. In particular we want to describe a Manchester City fan who we refer to as Greigsie, an ardent follower of the English national team.

On the 9 November, 1996 'Griegsie' travelled with England's away fans to Tiblisi in Georgia. Inside the ground 'Greigsie' stood by the perimeter fence, his arm around a Georgian soldier, smiling from ear to ear, thumbs up, posing for a photo to record the moment. He then proceeded to hand out several picture postcards to local supporters, featuring the Georgian talisman, Georgie Kinkladze, in a Manchester City strip. Greigsie made many friends in this former Soviet Republic. The Georgians showed their appreciation and applauded as he and his friend sang the British national anthem at the top of their voices. They did so standing behind Greigsie's giant Union Jack with the words Man City Loyal written either side of a beer mat embroidered into the middle, which depicts a Red Hand of Ulster and the legend Ulster Loyal. Greigsie is in his element, an English ambassador.

Greigsie is a Manchester City and England fan in his thirties who lives and works in his hometown on the outskirts of Greater Manchester. He has served in the British Army and now works as a health service professional but constructs himself almost exclusively through his love of football and support for England, both as a football team and as a nation. His love of the game extends far beyond the loyalty that has seen him travel the length and breadth of Britain and across the globe in support of his club and country. Alongside his paternal image there is an almost childlike innocence to the description of England matches he has attended as 'caps', his diary of travels abroad, collection of mementoes, newspaper clippings and pristine, filed programmes from every England home match since the 1966 World Cup Final.

For Greigsie, who is the organizational force behind a group of up to a dozen young men from his home town who travel to England games, this sense of national identity and pride is similarly reflected in support for the royal family, St George's Day outings to Blackpool and attendance at Remembrance Day services in London. But whilst these nationalist affiliations also find expression in an engagement with and fraternal celebration of foreign cultures they are equally related to a questioning of the commitment and passion that English-born black players share for the national team and, by extension, England as a nation:

> I mean there's been lots of [black players] ... but you've always got to question a player's colour and his passion to the shirt. A lot of them say 'Oh, yeah I'm proud to play for my country' but Tebbit was right as far as I'm concerned ... In the second half of the Moldova game, I was sat with the Under 21s ... and it ended up, all the blacks were sat together behind, personal stereos on, one of 'em's sunbathing, and I walked

round and it were only David James watching the match and Duberry from Chelsea I think, and a couple of others and I thought obviously not appreciating what country they live in, they're not even watching the match. I mean I was the only one that jumped up when Shearer scored. That's what annoyed me. They can't be English, they say they are, they wanna play for England but they don't know what it really means. They even allow blacks in the Army now, they're not serving Queen and country like the white lads are they? (Interview, 20 September 1996)

This perspective was contrasted, shortly after the Euro 96 tournament, with his appreciation of a diverse range of iconic white players:

He's got the right man [for captain], Shearer. Pure old passion, loves his country, he's a tryer without a doubt, and he's a credit to the game. He's a fantastic role model. You could never knock Shearer no matter how bad his goal scoring run got. If you do you're just an arsehole. He's just a genuinely nice bloke. He might come across as being a bit boring, but he's doing alright, a good lad. I've got a lot of respect for him . . . And Adams, unfortunately with his current situation, you can't worry about that though, he's just a boozer, like a lot of people, but again whatever he does, he loves his country. Bellows out the national anthem, stands to attention like Terry Butcher did. Not a lot of people do that, brilliant! Tony Adams, it's like Gascoigne, everyone knocks Gascoigne only 'cos their jealous. He's great, as long as he does it on the pitch couldn't give a fuck what he does in his spare time. (Interview, 20 September 1996)

Whilst there is no doubting the degree to which Greigsie's outlook is influenced by an overtly racist perspective, illustrated in his own reflection that:

I am Fascist, 100% Fascist really but...it's all too far gone now anyway, there's too much, there's too much filth, it's all been poisoned and it's gone too far now, we'll never get it back, there's just too much filth around. (Field note book, 11th November 1996)

Griegsie recognized that his commitment to racism needed to be attenuated in his everyday life:

I've mellowed a lot anyway in recent years, I'm not as far right as I was, like I say, I was a BNP member years ago, came out of it, I've gotta concentrate on me job now, so it's just like keep your head down, I've gotta work with the Asian fraternity. If I wanna job to do, what I'm good doing, I've gotta keep it in line, try not to be too fired up. (Interview, 20 September 1996)

Greigsie has long-standing friendships with black men, people with whom he went to school, grew up with and now socializes. The relationships between these men are entirely fraternal and imbued with the same sort of banter, humour and camaraderie, which characterizes his relationships with other white friends, and fellow England fans. Similarly, isolated black players such as Ian Wright can be respected, as long as they possess the qualities that Greigsie more readily characterizes as being 'white':

> I've got a lot of respect for Ian Wright. He plays the game 120%, loves scoring goals, got loads of commitment, and I think I must admit I have respect for Ian Wright, one of the very few, well, perhaps only black player that I've got respect for, without a doubt. (Interview 20 September 1996)

The point is that however offensive his opinions may be to some, Greigsie can be good company. He is a pleasant, open, sociable, intelligent, generous and entertaining man. However, supporting the England football team brings to the fore his adherence to 'racial purity' that he associates with true English nationalism. Whilst he is willing to work with the Asian community, have friendships with black men from his own background and respect individual black football players, for him they are not ultimately English. They are 'foreigners' unable to represent the country in conflict, whether sporting, military or ceremonial.

In essence Greigsie seems to feel that whilst it may now be pointless pursuing the notion of a 'racially pure' Britain, there is still a need to defend his ideals of 'Englishness' through a racially constructed, if not 'racially pure', England football team. In some senses football provides the discourse through which such extant ideological outlooks can be played out. It becomes the stage where his views can be articulated in an unfettered way. In a football ground he doesn't have to be careful about offending people, or be pragmatic about the consequences of articulating racist views.

* * *

Through these portraits we hope to show the complexities of the people who give voice to crude racism. None of the young men here are unambiguous racists and their racism is not a matter of blind hate. In their everyday lives each of them in different ways and to different degrees modulates his racism. This might be a matter of pragmatism for someone like Griegsie who hides his feelings at work, whilst for Kevin Ryan no differentiation is made between racist abuse and calling people names because they come from a rival town. Regardless of these complexities, football culture provides or facilitates the expression of racism. It is clear that people like the men described import popular racism with them as they pass through the turnstiles of a football ground. But it is equally true that the nature of football culture allows for and amplifies these hateful voices. It is to this question that we now turn.

Structures of Antipathy in Fan Culture

Racial abuse in the context of football culture occurs against a backdrop of what we want to call a 'structure of antipathy'. This provides the underlying criteria against which black or foreign players can be judged and targeted. Our starting point is that racist abuse is not simply a product of ideological hatred of black people. Rather, we want to suggest that the targeting of black and overseas players needs to be understood in terms of how football fans define the values and characteristics that they love as much as the ones that they loathe. In short it is important to understand how football fans establish a matrix of meaning that defines desirability and the positive norms to be celebrated on the one side and repugnance and deviance on the other. What we want to suggest is that it is only possible fully to understand the patterns of racist abuse amongst fans if one develops a nuanced and broader understanding of the structure of fan preference and antipathy. We found repeated examples where particular black players were isolated for racial abuse, while, during the same fixture other black players playing on the same side would not be abused. It is necessary to identify the ways in which particular players become targeted and the criteria on which this is based in order to make sense of this.

Notions of identity, belonging and entitlement are defined implicitly in football fan culture and are literally brought to life in songs and match day rituals. In Chapter 3 we showed how this results in the assertion – at the level of connotation – of norms and values in particular forms of social identity. Abuse targets are produced through the interplay between what are defined as positive attributes associated with the home team and its players and the ways in which 'the opposition' is delimited as contrary to, or a violation of these prised attributes.

We want to illustrate how these broader symbolic preferences can be articulated around the bodies and personas of individual players by looking in detail at a particular example which we recorded that involved Ruud Gullit during a fixture between Everton and Chelsea on 13 January 1996. The incidents of abuse and racism that we recorded were observed from a single vantage point in the Gwladys St End of Everton's Goodison Park ground. From the very earliest moments of this game it was clear that there was going to be widespread booing and jeering of Gullit. Indeed there was booing even before the game began, in response to the announcement of the player's name over the tannoy system. Once the game was underway, Gullit was booed, jeered and whistled at throughout the match whenever he had the ball more than momentarily. However, it was never his blackness alone that led him to be marked out by the Everton fans because Chelsea had three other black players, Duberry, Newton and Phelan, in the side, none of whom received any significant abuse, racialized or otherwise, all match long. The abuse of Gullit was far more generic and sustained than anything we witnessed in previous games as well as being crudely and repeatedly racist.

There were three main categories of abuse directed at Gullit and we have depicted these in Table 4.1.

Table 4.1. Categories of Abuse directed against Ruud Gullit

Category/description	Group dynamics	Action trigger
Generic booing/whistling	Localized groups, stadium wide	Whenever Gullit was a focus for attention, when he had the ball or received treatment
Mocking/jeering	Individuals, stadium wide	Whenever Gullit failed to execute an action as intended
Verbal insults – racialized and non racialized	Individual comments	Prompted by: generic booing/close proximity of player/player complaints or gesticulations

The booing and whistling was wholly generic and was embraced at certain moments by the entire Everton support. It was also indiscriminate in as much as it was invoked by some supporters during even the most passive moments of the game, simply because Gullit had possession of the ball. Yet it was entirely exclusive to Gullit and indeed was all the more noticeable and powerful for that exclusivity.

These collective forms of abuse appeared to provide a backcloth for the more individual verbal insults, which often included crude racist language. As Gullit was being booed, individuals from within the crowd would shout out abusive comments, as the following examples illustrate:

5:16 'Fuck off the pitch ya fuckin' nigger' – shouted by a teenage lad when Gullit received the ball, and backed up by generalized booing and whistling.

29:50 'Snap 'im Unsworth' – shouted in the midst of generic booing whilst Gullit retained the ball.

43:42 'Wog 'ead' – shouted by young boy in context of generic booing and whistling.

71:35 'Knob 'ead' – one of several individual comments with booing as backdrop followed by jeering in aftermath of Gullit losing the ball.

Additionally, individual insults were uttered whenever there was a sense that the abuse might be audible to Gullit, for example, when a corner was being taken in front of the Gwladys St stand with Gullit hovering around the penalty box.

Many of these comments were heavily racialized and vitriolic in their delivery, although they were not racialized in every case of conflict.

Gullit, although at this point moving toward the end of his career, was still a genuine world-class player. Perhaps the most creative European player of his generation, he graced the Dutch national team and formed part of the Dutch triumvirate, with Marco Van Basten and Frank Rijkard, which transformed the AC Milan team of the late 1980s and led to their emergence as the world's premier club side. He had joined Chelsea in the close season and proved to be an outstanding member and inspirational leader of the team. As a player Gullit also had a highly distinctive appearance. Tall, well built, black and with long dreadlocks coming to his collar line. He also presented himself as an articulate, broad-minded person and student of the game who fell out with successive managers, particularly of the Dutch national team, over playing styles. He subsequently took on management positions himself with mixed success. He was also outspoken in his criticisms of racism in football, which culminated in his presence at the launch of the Football Association's *Lets Kick Racism – Respect All Fans* campaign.

To the Everton supporters, a largely white working-class audience, with a reserved, almost conservative demeanour and 'contrary' attitude, this image may have been seen as somewhat pretentious, acceptable in the sophisticated, intellectual environs of Italian football but alien and vulnerable in the context of the English game and Liverpool life. Similarly there was no 'liberal minded' acceptance of his appearance, which sits firmly outside the identity structure of the Everton fan collective. This rejection of Gullit was illustrated in the first half by the cries of 'Fuck off ya hippy' (2:29) 'Wog 'ead' (43:32 , 17:01) and in the second half 'Spider 'ead' (2:58, 5:18); 'Gollywog' (6:26, 29:04) and 'Golly' (26:34). The generic booing of his name at the start of the game pointed to the universality of this perspective. It at once elevated the externally constructed and largely individual attentions of the crowd into a collective expression of intent, by announcing 'That is Ruud Gullit. That is our target.'

This was an important moment. Gullit does not have a reputation for cheating, arguing with the referee or reacting to incidents on the field, beyond his general involvement in the game and so an 'incident' of the type involving David Ginola which we referred to earlier could not have been anticipated. Whilst one did occur (discussed in more detail later) there would have been little strategic point in withholding the array of abusive armoury which was mobilized against Gullit in anticipation of it.

Interviews with Everton fans have cited the eagerness of supporters to react counter to expectations and conventional wisdom within the game. In this sense the reaction of the crowd to Gullit was an indication that his reputation was meaningless at Goodison Park. He was accorded respect in as much as he was identified, but the response was not cordial. It was proactively aimed at disrupting the player's game. In these situations the supporters cannot be viewed as passive individuals merely observing the game. They have a collective presence and seek ways of actively participating in the game and influencing its outcome. Ruud Gullit represented the principal threat to Everton's chances of winning the game and as such attempts were made to influence his performance.

In building a picture of the factors that might lead to the marking out of particular players for abuse we have found that no one factor is sufficient to generate the degree of sustained abuse experienced by Ruud Gullit. Rather, there is a complex package of elements, drawn from the identities and behaviour patterns of the fans, individual player biographies, externally constructed profiles and events on the pitch.

Every football club has a player that defines in the minds of its fans the character of the club. This works the same for Premiership clubs as well as those found at the lower echelons of professional football. For example, in the case of Arsenal, Tony Adams is the exemplar of what it means to wear the Arsenal shirt (see Hornby, 2000 for an, albeit unreflexive, illustration of this process). These iconic images are composed of a series of elements including appearance, style, talent, nation/race and character against which opposition players are judged. It might be useful to consider these factors in terms of a structure of antipathy. As we have already stated players carry with them a symbolic status as emblems of what a particular club stands for. Players and their approach to playing the game embody desirable types of character. Thus, both home and away players are constantly being evaluated in terms of a set of oppositions that are best represented as a series of binary contrasts that define both preference and aversion.

In the context of English football culture generally, the normative, although far from unitary, preference is for players who embody an unpretentious, masculine appearance, whose style of play is hardworking and effective, who possess an uncelebrated and self-effacing talent and demonstrate fair play and honest endeavour. In the case of Everton these characteristics constitute in a condensed form the implicit preference that is embodied in the values demonstrated in the fan culture. We have summarized these below in Table 4.2.

In contrast, to the preferences found in the left-hand column, there are corresponding mirror opposites that identify criteria for antagonism. So players can be marked out for abuse if they are viewed as fancy or pretentious, or flamboyant and attention seeking. Importantly, players can be particularly targeted if they possess spectacular ability that poses a football threat to the home team and its fortunes. Spectacular talent can also pose an additional symbolic threat, particularly if this is an overseas player. It can signal the import or ominous presence of sporting prowess that reveals the shortcomings in domestic – both national and local – footballing ability. This can also contain ideas about character and honesty that cast particular players as 'foreign cheats' of deceitful and suspicious character.

Table 4.2. The Structure of Antipathy

Characteristic	Normative preference	Contrasting aversion
Appearance	Unpretentious, practical, tough Masculine	Effeminate, weak, pretentious or fancy
Style	Hard working and effective team players	Flamboyant attention seeking opponents Self serving and ineffective individualism
Talent	Uncelebrated self-effacing ability	Spectacular ability/a footballing threat
Nationality/colour	White players Black/foreign players as *contingent insiders*	Foreign player, black opposition players *– utter outsiders*
Character	Fair play and honest endeavour	'Foreign' cheats. Reputation for or actual deception

On matters of race and nationality, the normative preference is for white insiders and black or foreign players who become contingent insiders. Their inclusion is contingent because it is predicated on their ability to 'wear the shirt' of the club and the demonstration of the requisite forms of character. In contrast, black players and overseas players representing the opposition often become *utter outsiders.*

It is clear from our research that players are not abused simply because they are black, or because they are foreign. What is more important is their failure to be accommodated into a broader identity structure which can be juxtaposed to the 'structure of antipathy' outlined above. However, we want to stress that each fan culture and each subgroup within it may have its own variations on the 'structure of antipathy' outlined here and that such structures are rarely universally invoked across the fan collective. There need not be a racist element for all fans in order for them to appear to have a single voice. The point we want to stress here is that racist aversions are connected and articulated to a whole range of dislikes.

Furthermore, it is also possible for there to be an aversion to *all* of the individual characteristics presented above and for there still to be no pattern of abuse, in the absence of a 'trigger' incident. The most dramatic and sustained phase of racial abuse directed at Gullit came early in the second half of this game (5:18) when Gullit was challenged in the centre circle and went down heavily. The referee blew up for a foul and the entire Everton support became almost hysterical in their condemnation of the player, believing that he had dived. This booing continued uninterrupted for a full two minutes.

The whole of the central Gwladys began chanting 'cheat, cheat, cheat' before individuals began shouting abuse with a range of racialized epithets, 'Ya fuckin' nigger!' (5:49), 'Fuckin' cheatin', divin' black cunt' (5:52), 'Fuckin' divin' black cunt' (5:55). As Gullit received treatment the racialized abuse continued as more and more fans began to shout racial epithets, 'Fuck off ya fuckin' divin' nigger' (6:08), 'Ya fuckin' black bastard' (6:20), 'Divin' black cunt' (6:24), 'Get off the pitch ya fuckin' Gollywog' (6:26), 'Wog 'ead' (6:29), 'Nigger' (6:41), 'Black bastard' (6:52), 'Nigger' (7:16) and 'Fuck off ya black cunt' (7:20).

What was interesting about this particular phase was the unanimity of the crowd and the universal involvement in the abuse. It was almost as though they had seen an opportunity and unreflexively seized it, without cause to question the validity of their interpretation of the incident. This temporal quality of abuse is always a product of the unfolding drama on the pitch and the reaction to this within the stadium. In similar vein to our identification of song cycles in Chapter 2 it is important to see then how racist abuse is part of what we might refer to as abuse cycles, such that the intensification of abuse following this 'trigger' incident was undoubtedly influenced by the sustained abuse that had followed Gullit around the field all match long. Gullit can be identified with elements that mark him out for abuse (in terms of talent, race/nation, appearance) which allow supporters to isolate particular players from their colleagues. But in this context it was the notion that the player had dived, which was enough to invoke the full invective of the crowd, which in turn readily became racialized by supporters in the central Gwladys St stand.

What we have demonstrated here is how acts that appear to be blind hate possess a rationale and a structure. This enables us to understand how particular black and overseas players are isolated within the logic of what we refer to as a structure of antipathy. Here racism becomes part of a series of other sources of hostility that together culminate in vicious and hateful acts. We would argue that it is necessary to unpick these recondite processes in order to explain how racist abuse is directed at some potential targets and not others. Equally, it enables us to explain how racial abuse of opposing players can co-exist with a professed love and glorification of black players who are wearing the home team's shirt. The other point that we hope we have made conclusively is that popular racism is always nested within the context of particular local contexts and needs to be seen as part of the flow and rhythm of football matches. Here the game and the expression of racism within it is analogous to an unfolding social drama whose plot is always uncertain. This is why it is so difficult to predict when racist responses will occur because they are always a product of the interplay of forces (on the pitch and in the stadium) that cannot be foreseen. Yet at the same time, we suggest that the patterns we have documented here are the product of an underlying knowledge structure that isolates players and targets them for racist abuse.

Conclusion

It is commonplace for those in positions of authority in football to argue that they are facing problems that are not of their making. The logic of this line of argument is that racism is a 'societal problem' that is imported into football. Such positions cast the football authorities as the innocent victims of a society that is divided and unequal. We want to make the argument that racism becomes articulated in the culture of football in very particular ways. While the culture of football doesn't necessarily produce racism – as somehow generic – it cannot be easily understood as a 'foreign import'. The argument we want to make here is that the nature of particular types of football culture provides an arena for the expression of racism through explicit and implicit means.

Racism amongst football fans appears in crude and explicit forms precisely because the arenas in which it is perpetrated facilitate its expression. We have tried to illustrate this through recording and analysing the form that racist talk and abuse takes within the context of the spaces of football fandom. Football grounds as moral landscapes have certainly shifted and the intensity of overt fan racism has certainly waned. The degree to which this will continue is as yet still unclear. What we have suggested in these three chapters is that it is a mistake to view the overt expression of racism as the only issue with regard to issues of racist exclusion. We have tried to show that the implicit normative core of football culture plays a role in determining the degree to which black and minority fans can gain entry. It is precisely these 'implicit cultural passports', to invoke Bauman's suggestive phrase, that put limits on the degree to which a decline in overt racism will lead to a more multicultural fan constituency.

We have argued that the portrait of 'the racist' in the debate about racism in football does not fit well with the football fans we interviewed who perpetrate racist acts. In this sense we need to think much more carefully about the uneven and often ambivalent nature of racism amongst football fans. However, the appreciation of these complexities in football circles – as we shall argue in later chapters – is at best extremely limited. An exception to this general lack of understanding is the Chairman of Millwall Football Club, Theo Paphitis, himself a first generation immigrant who came to Britain from Cyprus as a child of Greek Cypriot parents. Paphitis suggests the future of his club is dependent on understanding the nuances and contradictions of fan racism. He has lived in South London and possesses a first-hand understanding of the complexities of popular racism within the white community.

For him the fact that white fans reach for racist language is to be explained by the way in which racism is normalized as a way to simultaneously target and insult a black player:

It's just easier to say 'black bastard'. They don't mean it it's just identifying who you are talking about. Now, it's not acceptable so we have to deal with it. It's not acceptable to call somebody a 'black bastard'. And you've got to take it stage by stage. But when I sit down to speak to some of the guys and I sit down and have a beer with them, and in fact I have a bit of a laugh with them. And when you've been talking to them about it and then you find that they'll actually admit to you that they just wanted to tell 'im he's shit. 'Well, why didn't you tell him he's shit then? Just tell him he's shit!' [laughs] (Interview, 22 January 2000)

He continued:

You'll have a bit of a chat and then you'll see the ole wags, em and the amount of times they might say 'argh it's all right for you your 'a Bubble' [referring to the cockney rhyming slang phrase 'bubble and squeak', the literal meaning of which is a dish composed of a mixture of mash potato and fried cabbage, but in this context it means 'Greek'] ain't you.' It doesn't bother me and it doesn't worry me and I know what they mean by it. I could take offence but then again I might not but someone else might. So I just think we've got to deal with it in the right way. We've got to deal with it in two stages, there's those people out there who are just out there to cause aggravation and there are those that actually follow 'the sheep' as I call 'em who don't really know why they are following or what they are doing or saying. I think they can be won over quite quickly. Really quick. If you do things right, have a beer and a chat with them they can be won over. And we've done that and I am dead chuffed about that and I dead chuffed with what we've achieved at that level. That's a nice soft one to do and you can do that without getting heavy handed or being silly just by talking to them and having a beer with them and then you find they're very tolerant nice people. (Interview, 22 January 2000)

The image of Millwall fans as 'tolerant nice people' would not be shared by others in the game. However, Paphitis makes a very important point by highlighting the instability of popular racism amongst football fans, many of whom he believes can be won over very quickly. The implications of this view will be picked up in later chapters that address anti-racism in football. Overall, we have tried to portray the voices of hate in football as both pervasive and clearly connected to football culture, while at the same time insisting that they are unstable and ambivalent.

It is at this point that we want to shift our focus. The issue of racism in football has too often exclusively focused on the problem of fan behaviour. One of our key concerns is to broaden this focus in order to examine the ways in which racism features within the professional cultures of football itself. Our discussion in the preceding chapters has hopefully revealed something of the complexity and ambivalent nature of racism within contrasting fan cultures and how players and officials are themselves implicated in the collective identities which football clubs embody. It should now be clear that we cannot read formations of community, identity and expression purely from the stands, and channels of supporter communication. Parallel rituals, dialogue and processes of exclusion feature back on the other side of the white line, amongst players and within the institutions of the game.

In the following three chapters we wish to consider how notions of 'race' feature on the playing field and training pitch and in the boardroom and the complex processes of inclusion and exclusion which permeate the game's player and institutional cultures and indeed the responses to racism within the game. We begin by turning our attention to the players and the discrete, often unspoken, frameworks of exclusion that operate through English football's implicit whiteness.

Part 2
Racism Inside the Game

−5−

'One of the Lads': Accommodation and Resistance within Football-playing Cultures

The Sanam, Rusholme, Manchester, Friday 8 May 1998

It is early Friday evening and a local league amateur football side's end-of-season night out. The club itself has only been running for a few years and is not linked to a particular workplace, pub or district. The players, who come from a range of social and ethnic backgrounds, were introduced to the side through a loose network of friends, colleagues and relatives. As such, there is nothing out of the ordinary about the club or the evening's celebration. It's just an excuse to meet up in a social environment, away from the football field, 'have a laugh' and reinforce the allegiances built up on the field, which often lie at the heart of a team's coherence, style and success.

The general consensus amongst the core group of players in the side was that, as usual, the team would go for something to eat before heading into town to find a few more bars and a nightclub to see us through to the small hours. Andy, the club 'manager', had assured everyone that Mo had made the necessary arrangements for the early evening meal, which was to be a curry in the Rusholme district of Manchester where his family has connections in the restaurant trade.

The venue for the meal was the Sanam, a large, well-presented restaurant on the main Wilmslow Road in Rusholme. As well as being within a few hundred yards of Manchester City's Maine Road ground this district is famed for its south Asian cuisine and culture. Over 100 restaurants and takeaways sit alongside continental food suppliers, Asian clothes and jewellery stores on a half-mile stretch of the road which leads out of the city to the south. 'Having a curry' with a few drinks in Rusholme is a well-established part of Manchester's popular cultural heritage, transcending economic, racial, gender and class distinctions.

However, when the first members of the team arrived at the restaurant and were asked if they would like something to drink it quickly became clear that the waiter did not mean lager. This was a 'dry' curry house. Although contact with alcohol is not permitted according to Islamic faith many of the restaurants in this district, which are mainly run by Muslims of Pakistani heritage, do serve alcohol and the others often allow customers to bring their own in with them. We were just discussing whether one of us might go out to the local off license to take advantage of this cultural 'loophole' when Nick arrived and, upon hearing that there was no bar immediately suggested a change of venue, asking rhetorically 'what kind of football club do is this? I could have had three pints by now. Who's idea was it to come to a curry house anyway?' At that point Mo arrived with Andy and a couple of others and, sensing some discomfort, asked what the problem was. Whilst Nick declared 'There's no fucking beer that's what's wrong', someone asked whether we might bring in our own.

At this moment there was a kind of mutual misrecognition. Mo smiled in an amused fashion, explaining that no alcohol was allowed on the premises and suggested that we might like to have a lasi, a type of milkshake. Some players looked at him incredulously, some laughed out loud as though he was joking, whilst others smiled uncomfortably. Nick continued to suggest that we should go elsewhere and it was clear that several others were less than enthusiastic about beginning the evening and eating a curry without having any alcohol.

Andy, however, was also conscious of Mo's efforts in arranging the venue. Mo works as a barrister in the same chambers where both Andy and Nick work as clerks and whilst not being the most naturally gifted of players he had shown a great deal of commitment to the side. Eventually, as Showaib and Uma arrived, whom Mo had introduced to the side, most of the group jokily accepted the situation and began ordering lasis, other soft drinks and their food. However, there was still an audible, if largely understated and jocular, unease amongst a number of those present with suggestions being made to 'skip the starters, then we can get to the pub quicker' and 'can I organize the annual dinner next year'. In the end we were out of the restaurant and the bulk of the party was down the road in the Clarence pub before 8.00 p.m.

Mo, Showaib and Uma decided not to come for a drink after the meal. Efforts were made to persuade them but, as a practising Muslim, Mo was politely insistent that he did not wish to go to a pub, even for a soft drink. Once the group had split up there was a visible change of atmosphere and behaviour amongst those that headed for the pub where the remaining members of the team began drinking heavily. By now, despite the ethnic diversity in the side as a whole, which at that time embraced three brothers of mixed black and white heritage as well as Mo, Showaib and Uma, those present were exclusively white. In this context, although Mo later reflected to me on the air of discomfort in the Sanam, remarking 'I didn't realize Nick had such a problem with alcohol', the discussions which followed largely constructed 'the Asian lads' as the cultural transgressors. It was Mo who had been 'a bit daft' or 'unthoughtful' in choosing a dry curry house, the 'Asian lads' who had been a bit 'aloof' and 'unsociable' in not coming to the pub for a drink, Syl and his brothers who hadn't shown up at all.

* * *

Associations between professional footballers and alcohol consumption stretch
well back into the game's history, with folklore having it that the legendary Everton
striker Dixie Dean once had a few pints *before* a game between the wars, scored a
hat trick, and then went out for a 'proper drink'. Equally the traditional 3.00 p.m.
Saturday kick off was established in respect of supporters who, after completing a
mornings work would go to the pub in advance of the (pre-liberalization) 3.00
p.m. closing time and then on to the game. The association continued in to the
contemporary era through the sponsorship of the FA Carling Premiership and a
host of top clubs such as Liverpool by major brewers and the promotion of pubs
as venues for viewing games shown live on television.

The point here is that despite the fact that all of these black and Asian players
had socialized with the team on other occasions, it was through their absence from
what is often a key site in the formation of player identities that they became the
subject of a critical 'gaze' and marked out as uniformly 'different'. We introduce
this chapter with this account because it seems clear that throughout the English
game, even within clubs which outwardly display an ethnic diversity and progressive face, there is often a 'core' accommodative culture which is embodied in
many of the features associated with white, working class masculinities –
sociability, camaraderie, conspicuous consumption of alcohol and self deprecation.
To get 'in with the lads' requires an acceptance of, and often an assimilation with,
those norms, or in Bauman's terms, the possession of a valid 'entry ticket' or player
equivalent of the 'cultural passport' discussed in the previous chapter.

The defining feature of this process is the way in which it naturalizes social
formations in terms of a 'racial/cultural logic of belonging' (Back and Solomos
2000: 21). Within these terms, even in the absence of overt forms of racist dialogue,
the 'Asian lads' in this team were perceived to have affronted the [white] norms
of the club and broader football culture, because *they* didn't drink, because *they*
were Asian. It is these totalizing forms of racial discourse and social processes,
often coded in terms of 'difference' and 'culture', which we are primarily concerned
with in the following sections.

*'I've never felt so white': The normalization of whiteness, racial 'banter'
and abuse amongst English professional footballers*

One of the interesting features of the various campaigns against racism in football
organized over the last few years is the extent to which they have focused on the
experiences of black players as victims of overt racial abuse from fans. Far less
attention has been paid to the ways in which processes of inclusion and exclusion
might operate implicitly through routine, normalized practices on the field, the
training ground and social environments surrounding the game as a consequence

of a 'white-centred' player culture. This point was recognized by the then Sunderland striker David Kelly following a regional launch of the Show Racism the Red Card campaign when he was pressed on how he related to the campaign as a white player and responded in humorous fashion by stating that 'I've never felt so white'. (Interview, 17 October 1996)

The comment illustrates the way in which whiteness becomes normalized within football through the silence that surrounds it. As Kelly's remark confirms, the number of occasions on which players have been referred to as white is minimal whereas it has become entirely standard practice to reference the racial appearance of *black* players and cultural heritage of *foreign* players. It is within this context that our informant went on to allude to the everyday nature of racialized 'banter' found in the changing room environment and how it is played out through a discourse which centres and privileges a perceived white, anglo saxon, identity. As John Barnes argues in his autobiography when referring to his white colleagues lack of reaction to negative comments made about *their* racial background:

> Their attitude was that because there is nothing wrong with being white, how could they be insulted by having it brought to their attention that they are white. (Barnes 1999:100)

Following Richard Dyer (1988) then, 'being normal' is colonized by the idea of 'being white'. By extension the implication of Barnes' statement is that there is something *wrong* with being black and yet, as Williams has suggested, the form of 'banter' found in the dressing room often 'incorporates rather than alienates the growing number of black players in League football' (Williams 1992: 2). Indeed, a willingness to tolerate and even engage in racial 'banter', wind ups and the associated cultural norms typically associated with white working class masculinities has, on occasion, become part of the 'character test' applied to aspiring players from ethnic minority backgrounds. As David Hill described in his biography of John Barnes, *Out of His Skin*:

> On his first day at the training ground he sat at a bench with a couple of his new team-mates. Cups of tea were put before the two established players. Barnes looked up at the woman who brought them. He said: 'What am I, black or something?' Everyone fell about.
>
> ... Barnes pre-empted his own initiation. He gave permission for his team-mates to, for better or worse, relate to him in the traditional Liverpool way. I'm black. It's a joke. Everyone relax. 'Barnes has got a brain,' says [a] Liverpool insider. 'But to use it there's got to be someone serious to use it with, and you're not allowed to be serious. If John was on television and he gave a serious interview, he would get some stick. And it's hard to take that sort of stick when you're trying to be part of the team. You've got to act like everyone else does.'

After that, there were lot's of jokes. Jan Molby . . . had earned the nickname 'Rambo' from the Anfield crowd. The dressing room gang soon thought of some more nicknames that rhymed . . . there was Rambo, there was Aldo, Quasimodo and, of course, there was Sambo. (Hill 1989: 129–130)

Barnes himself reflected in his recent autobiography that:

Dressing-rooms are rife with humour and many of the jokes are racist. Newcastle United's players used to say about Shay Given that 'he's Irish, he's thick'. When I inquired 'am I black or something?' it was because I wanted people to understand I am comfortable with it. If other players wanted to make racist jokes, I was fine about that. (Barnes 1999: 97)

What seems to be prevalent within the English game is a reliance on the notion that 'others', whether black, foreign or Asian, should assimilate with the normative, white coded, working class masculine traits of English football – unpretentious, self-deprecating, 'honest', committed, hard working, aggressive. This reveals the racially contingent character of the 'class habitus' and associated cultural capital that Bourdieu has suggested defines the meaning conferred on sporting activity through 'the affinity between the ethical and aesthetic dispositions characteristic of each class or class fraction' (Bourdieu 1978: 836). From this perspective, just as the black boxer 'our Frank' Bruno can be embraced by the [white] nation as his 'class tells us that he is one of the boys' (Gilroy 1993: 91) so have a succession of black footballers been taken into the bosom of player and fan communities.

In some instances, such as the Crystal Palace and Wimbledon teams of the late 1980s and early 1990s the core of the teams were indeed built around the black iconic figures Ian Wright and John Fashanu. Yet it was these players' ability to transcend the stereotypes of inconsistency and lack of 'bottle' or commitment, often applied to black players during the 1970s and 1980s, and embrace a kind of hyper masculine, aggressive, 'street' status that lay at the heart of their attraction, as illustrated by the latter's tabloid nickname 'Fash The Bash'.

Whilst these identity constructions themselves reveal an insidious form of racial stereotyping, on which we reflect further below, the perceived physically dynamic qualities of black men have for some time been readily embraced within the emergent frameworks of interracial sports. For as Hoberman argues 'during the colonial period, the myth of white physical superiority helped to sustain the power of Europeans who viewed physical and emotional toughness as prerequisites for survival. Today, in the age of the global cognitive elite, athletic superiority is, in a Darwinian sense, a vestigial trait that possesses ornamental rather than strategic value' (Hoberman 1997: 119).

Physical and emotional toughness are nevertheless regarded as admirable qualities on an English football field and in this respect the inclusion of black players, like fans, is often related to their competence with embodied forms of masculine culture that operate through implicit class-coded frameworks. It is clear that these processes are far from uniform and can embrace highly visible forms of cultural exchange within the player cultures of those clubs with large concentrations of black players, particularly when located in ethnically diverse neighbourhoods such as those surrounding Crystal Palace. However, although players did suggest that racial abuse now tends to be quite isolated and that it has declined as the presence and status of black players within the game has grown, the contingency of these forms of inclusion ensures that 'race' always remains on the sidelines as a source of division between black players and football's normative core.

The controversy surrounding an attack on Sarfraz Najeib, an Asian student at Leeds Metropolitan University, on 12 January 2000 by a group of white men alleged to include the Leeds United players Jonathon Woodgate and Lee Bowyer also indicates that this potential extends beyond the immediate football context. When the case came to trial in early 2001 the prosecuting barrister in this case stated that the attack was not racially motivated, whilst the victim's family are in no doubt that it was, and the police quickly identified a racial motivation (*The Times*, 27 January 2000). A variety of witnesses and family members have insisted that Nejeib and a group of friends had racist abuse directed at them both prior to and during the attack (*Sunday Times*, 23 January 2000) which resulted in various charges of grievous bodily harm, affray and attempting to pervert the course of justice being brought against seven men including Bowyer and Woodgate and two other Leeds United players. The trial collapsed in a debacle after ten weeks of proceedings when on 8 April 2001 the *Sunday Mirror* newspaper published an article focused on the father of the victims' view of the racism that he felt was an integral factor in the assault. Bowyer and Woodgate's lawyer claimed that the publicity from the story and the 'taint of racism' made a fair trial by jury impossible (*Guardian*, 10 April 2001).

The complexity and disputed nature of the racial dimension of the assault was further complicated by the fact that one of the co-accused was Michael Duberry, Leeds' black centre half, who had given Woodgate and friends a lift home, and was charged with attempting to pervert the course of justice. Furthermore, despite the charges being laid, after some deliberation the club stood steadfastly behind the players, resisting heavy pressure from the family and racial equality camp- aigners to suspend them until any proof of innocence or guilt is established. Indeed the club's manager David O'Leary became increasingly bullish and criticized the FA's decision not to include the players in any of England's representative sides until the case is concluded (*Independent on Sunday*, 19 March 2000).

In this context the reluctance of black professionals as a whole to speak out about racial prejudice and abuse might be related to their having to survive within institutions dominated by white personnel where the instigators of such attitudes are often those who remain in the positions of power. During the trial and in a dramatic turn Michael Duberry revealed in his evidence that he lied in order to protect Woodgate. Then later when he wanted to change his statement, the Leeds United club director and lawyer Peter McCormick advised him to 'stick with his story' (*Guardian*, 22 March 2001) and to lie about what he had seen and heard. Duberry was subsequently cleared of the charges against him. The searching questions remain. Why was there no attempt to charge the assailants with 'racial aggravation' despite the alleged use of racist language during the incident? The tragic irony of the situation was that the trial collapsed because the issue of racism in relation to these players' behaviour entered the public realm. During the whole proceeding Leeds United stood by their valuable assets. The trial seemed to have little affect on Lee Bowyer's form. He hit a goal scoring streak during the trial giving him the dubious celebrity in which the court proceedings featured on front pages of newspapers while photographs of his goal celebrations took up equal column inches on the back pages.

The consequence that we want to discuss is that racism inside football and perpetrated by players themselves is unthinkable for white people inside the game and more or less taboo. One player who was a professional during the 1980s illustrated the perseverance of the problem when reflecting on his own son's more recent short lived career:

> My son went through the same thing [experiencing racial abuse] whilst he was [at Hereford] and he ended up knocking somebody out and they just came with a load of lies and tried to cover it up and tried to say well this, that and the other, so . . . I mean, Brendon [Batson of the PFA] came and . . . when we appealed about him being sacked . . . the decision was overturned in the end . . . I mean if you get sacked for doing things that no footballer is supposed to do, well that's OK but you know, not because he chins somebody who calls him a nigger and then . . . all of a sudden you get the manager saying he doesn't know anything about it and you get the person who it was reported to saying it's a lie . . . things like that, they're especially galling. So it takes place now . . . because the managers today are the same bastards that I was knocking out when I was playing, so why should they change? (Interview, 14 May 1997)

Even for senior professionals such as Mark Bright who, whilst still playing for Crystal Palace, reflected in an interview on the Critical Eye programme *Great Britain United* how the cultural norms within sport can mark out racial distinctions in an exclusionary fashion that are sometimes hard to challenge:

> If you go to a boxing dinner or sportsman's dinner there maybe 4 or 500 men there you know. All ehrm black tie and then, comedian gets up there and you know 'Have we got any of these in tonight, have we got any of them in tonight' and then he aims a black joke and you're one of only a few in there. Some, something happens to you, you go warm round the collar . . . and specially if it's a football dinner or something and he

knows your there and 'here we have Mark Bright at the front' bla bla bla and he says something and you think 'Did he need to say that today, you know is it worth a laugh?' And people at the table laugh and they, they always look at you for your reaction. They look at you and say well 'Oh he's laughing, he's laughing, it's alright'. If you don't laugh then all of a sudden he can't take a joke. (*Critical Eye* 1991)

Taking Care of Business: Player Reactions to Racial Abuse within the Game

Given that racism does not always take on such implicit forms, black players have had to find their own culturally appropriate ways to confront the issue. During our research it was widely held that relatively low levels of racism existed amongst players inside the sport. This view was almost unanimously subscribed to by the white players that we spoke to, whilst a significant proportion of the black professionals we interviewed initially dismissed the issue of verbal racial abuse from their white peers altogether. However, this version of events, often articulated in formal interview settings, stood in contrast to the other reports that racial insults, banter and wind ups were more common on the field of play and in the dressing room.

A succession of incidents involving racial abuse by fellow players have been reported in the press over the last few seasons directed at Darren Beckford, Dave Regis, Ronnie Mauge, Eyal Berkovich, Ian Wright, Stan Collymore and Patrick Vieira in addition to those reported by our informants. We even came across two accounts of former England captains being involved in such activities during games. The first of these was reported as having performed a monkey impression in front of one of our informants who ignored the gesture despite his own team mates' consternation.

What became clear from our extended interviews was that a shared sense of professional propriety was held by players who were unwilling even in the most extreme circumstances to make public accusations against their fellow professionals. It has long been understood amongst footballers, possibly as a result of the short shrift that complaints are given by managers, that grudges are settled within the game and ultimately on the field of play. Jack Charlton, as legend has it, kept a book with the names of the footballing adversaries with whom he had 'outstanding business'. With the authorities turning a blind eye, black players who suffered regular verbal abuse from white opponents learnt to dealt with racism in a similarly direct way. The reflections of one black ex-professional on the strategies that were often employed is worth quoting at length here:

They [white players] would say 'black bastard' or 'fucking nigger' and I always said 'that is what your wife says when I am shagging her', you know stuff like that and then they would go 'arghh' and then the white boy would have a problem with the black man shagging their wives, and I found that always had the desired effect. 'Is it right you have only got a small dick?' and all that sort of stuff, so it was like a banter more . . .

If they got personal on the pitch there was always a nice tackle you could get into – that was just part of it . . . It was always there, every game you get one of them having a pop at you. When you tackled and all that there was a couple who would throw a racial one at you, and I daresay they do nowadays to be fair, but it is not as bad because every team has got black players in it . . . When I played, every one of them, if you booted them that was it . . . 'fuck you stamped me you nigger', so it was just acceptable, well it wasn't acceptable, it was a case of so and so is like NF and he hates all the black players, it was the only way they could hit back and they just hit back with colour rather than football skills, they hit back with colour and that was it. So we had got our one-liners and told them about the size of their dick and their wives and all sorts because there were always a lot more of that. Then we would say if you have got a problem then I will see you in the fucking car park – that was how our attitude was, if you have got a problem then I will see you outside, when the referee can't protect your arse. But after the game, handshakes, job done, have a beer, and that is just what it was like. It was just like it was there and then it was now, bump, after the game, shook hands, it was always like it was part of the game – it shouldn't have been there but it was part of the game, we knew we was going to get it every Saturday. (Interview, 11 February 1997)

There is something of a contradiction at work here. One line of argument which says 'get on with the game, don't let them get to you', whilst at the same time there is a more strategic intervention designed to put opponents off their game in much the same way that those opponents use racial abuse to undermine black players' concentration or performance. What is interesting is that this is often done on the basis of an invocation of much the same racial stereotypes that are mobilized *against* black men in other situations. The notion of the 'black bastard', the illegitimate child, the product of the sexual promiscuity of black men is invoked and turned against the abuser and the sexual insecurities that are intertwined with his racism. 'That's right I'm a black bastard and your wife wants me rather than you.'

This mutual invocation of racial stereotypes is worth considering further in the context of the pervasiveness of these modes of internalization and public denial of racial conflicts, which were dramatically illustrated by the clash between Ian Wright and Peter Schmeichel at Highbury in 1997. The feud went back to the Manchester United versus Arsenal game in November 1996 when Schmeichel was accused of referring to Wright as a 'black bastard'. At the time Wright was reluctant to become involved in a public discussion of the issue, invoking a kind of professional propriety when he told a tabloid newspaper 'I am not in the habit of getting my fellow professionals into trouble'. That there was a case to answer was given added weight, however, when a fan named Junior Lawrence made an official complaint to the FA prompting an investigation by the Crown Prosecution Service. It seems entirely plausible then that the otherwise outspoken Wright's two-footed tackle on Schmeichel during the return match at Highbury represented his own attempt to 'settle the score' in the absence of a willingness to confront the issue through formal channels.

Stan Collymore did make public accusations against his former colleague, Liverpool defender Steve Harkness, after playing for Aston Villa at Villa Park in March 1998 when he claimed:

> I was being wound up all game and was getting racial abuse . . . Harkness called me a coon. There were also other things said that were even worse. It was racial abuse of the worst kind and totally out of order . . . It hurt me very much indeed and I am still considering whether to make an official complaint. I went out of my way to tell the black players at Liverpool what had happened. Harkness has to live with them as well as himself. (*Guardian* 5 March 1998: 3)

Even then the player ultimately still resisted the temptation to make a formal complaint. However, he was sent off the following season for a two-footed challenge on Harkness, which seemed to have more to it than a desire to win the ball. What comes out of these patterns of response to racism in the game, in stark contrast to earlier notions of a 'lack of bottle', is evidence of an embodied masculine self-construction of black players as hard and uncompromising. A prominent black defender during the 1980s who is now involved in the coaching side of the game recalled:

> I remember the PFA called a meeting once to discuss, you know all of these issues and I remember looking at Graham Taylor and saying to him that in football with black players you've either got to be thick skinned or a bad bastard, and there is no two ways about it. Yeah. You've gotta be thick skinned or a bad bastard because if you're bad you can look after it yourself . . . but if your not bad enough you've gotta take it. I mean you've gotta play as if it doesn't trouble you. In the end it's you. You know, you walk away, you're skin's thick enough but it don't trouble you. But that *is* the situation. It really really is. Or, it was when I was playing . . .
>
> And this is, this is the thing in football. Now in football there's lots of fisty cuffs, yeah, and a lot of it is like a manager, if you can't handle yourself he probably doesn't even wanna deal with you anyway. You know if you might fight [and] get you're head kicked in he'll like that 'cos he'll go 'yeahh', you know, shows a bit of bite and things like that and management they can understand it, and then the manager'll look in again and he'll think, well you know if a player's getting like racial stick . . . what they'll be saying is 'if he's getting stick in the changing room and he can't cut it, do I want him in my team?', yeah, and you've got managers, yeah, who you will knock that person out and they will respect you for it, yeah, and then there are other bastards who will sack you for it, yeah, knowing what goes on, right. (Interview, 14 May 1997)

What can be identified here is an example of the oscillation between racial longing and hatred which has previously been revealed in discussions of black sporting and music icons (Wolf [1947/8] 1993, Gilroy 1993, Back and Solomos 1996). In each case black football players are being constructed, sometimes with the complicity of the players themselves, through an implicit reference to stereotypical racist notions of black people as aggressive, tough and violent. Whilst this may in one context generate fear and loathing, in certain circumstances, particularly where players are representing a team in sporting conflicts, these characteristics can be regarded as positive, to be encouraged and emulated. So whilst Ian Wright's uncompromising, 'authentic street attitude' (coded black) could be admired and respected by Arsenal supporters and his manager, it seems he can also be overtly denigrated as a 'dirty black bastard' by Peter Schmeichel, opposing fans and the media. However, as Michael Keith argues in his discussion of the contested nature of claims to authenticity in ethnically mixed urban locales it might not be 'possible to look at such valorised exhibitions of masculine force and then at the criminalising gaze of the mainstream press and say that they are unrelated?' (Keith 2000: 530).

In both cases supporters' and fellow professionals' relationships with the player are being defined according to what Stuart Hall (1981) has called a 'grammar of race'. This is problematic in that whether his actions are perceived as 'good' or 'bad' the frameworks of knowledge rely on a shared perception of the fixed attributes of 'black men' and, as such, reinforce racially constructed stereotypes. Indeed Hoberman suggests that representations of black sportsmen have in fact reinforced broader notions of black criminality 'by merging the black athlete and the black criminal into a single threatening figure in two ways: first, by dramatizing two physically dynamic black male types which are often presumed to be both culturally and biologically deviant; and second, by putting the violent or otherwise deviant behaviour of black athletes on constant public display so as to reinforce the idea of the black male's characterological instability' (Hoberman 1997: 208). If he fails to deal with racial abuse, or 'overreacts' it is the player who is perceived to be at fault, not the institutional structures and cultural norms pervading within the game.

Where the range of responses available to counter racial abuse and prejudice is so restricted there is always the danger that black players will be represented simultaneously as both the victims of racism and the cause of the problem. Accordingly, this situation does not allow any consideration of what happens to players who have not dealt with abuse in the 'conventional' manner, such as Richie Moran who effectively lost his job at two clubs and ultimately left the profession as a consequence of his reaction to what he regarded as racially offensive behaviour. He recounted how when he was playing for Birmingham City, the manager had:

Called me into his office and asked me why I had dreadlocks. And when I explained that it was a reaffirmation of my African heritage it was met with derision, and to me, having explained it was part of my heritage – whatever corner of the globe you come from – he had actually insulted my whole heritage . . . And I told him, with my tongue pretty much in my cheek, that . . . if I should have my hair cut then why couldn't he have elocution lessons to change his Glaswegian accent, which didn't go down too favourably and I didn't play in the first team again strangely enough. (Interview, 11 March 1997)

It is impossible to know how many similar experiences there have been but it is clear that dealing with racial abuse from fellow professionals is sometimes more troubling than dealing with the other wind ups and cultural practices which are part of the game. One leading black player from the late 1970s was sent off three times in his career and on each occasion it was due to his physical reaction to racial abuse that he received from opponents. Twenty years later and despite his current involvement in the administrative side of the game and associated campaigns against racism in sport he continues to be resistant to admitting the connection between his reaction and the racial abuse he received, feeling that he showed weakness by reacting in this way.

Even those players at the highest levels of the game who are regarded as being too valuable to be dismissed or dropped because of their 'sensitivity' or 'attitude' remain reluctant to discuss their experiences. This is partly because nobody likes to talk about their own negative experiences, particularly in a masculine profession like football where there is little tradition of open discussion of complex social problems, but also because there is an unwritten code that states that differences within the game are settled man to man.

'Brothers in Arms': Black Players, Solidarity and Cultural Exchange

Given the tendency to play down issues relating to 'race' and other social problems, there is a suggestion that broader discussions of black footballers' experiences have to some extent been internalized in the context of black friendship networks within the community of professional players. A former black professional and PFA chairman explained that many leading players remain:

unconvinced of the importance of playing a big part in the debate. It's like the whole situation is inverted almost, some black people don't feel as though, they don't *feel* apart or *made* to feel a part of mainstream society . . . and I've not heard one of [the leading black players] speak . . . in a high profile situation er about, about the things that affect them, but I know they do privately. (Interview, 21st May 1997)

Concern about this situation may itself relate to the perception surrounding black footballers, which has more recently been extended to foreign players, that they 'naturally' band together, form friendships and social networks that are sometimes represented as cliques, sitting outside the clubs' normative white centre. The suggestion being that black and foreign players 'stick together' and don't easily 'mix' or 'fit in'. This notion seems to reflect the ethnocentric nature of English professional football culture and its assimilationist approach towards social inclusion.

Friendship groups which are white, black or mixtures of black and white players pervade the dressing rooms of clubs up and down the country but are rarely discussed in public or considered as problematic unless they are exclusively made up of black or foreign members. Indeed the creation of supportive communities of players from ethnic minority backgrounds might be more readily understood than the alternative formulations in the context of the difficulties encountered by black players over the years. As a black player from the 1980s put it to us:

> You see the thing is at the time, because there were so few [black players], it was almost like a clique, you would never pass without saying hello – on the pitch it was like how are you doing and all that because it was all like a kindred spirit, do you know what I mean. Because our team used to have a pop at them and all that, it was terrible, no need for that, it was always with them. It was like a respect there you know, and it is the same now. (Interview, 11 February 1997)

This respect also found expression during a series of testimonial matches and friendlies that were arranged against a black select XI at the time. One of the interesting aspects of these games was the way in which they invoked and made explicit notions of difference, celebrating the presence of black players on the one hand, whilst the authorities implied that there was a problem with black players who constructed an identity outside of the [white] mainstream. As one of the players in these games recalls:

> That was funny because we played at Villa, we played against Albion, Robertson centre half, his testimonial, and at that time it was Cyrille [Regis], Laurie [Cunningham] and Brendon [Batson] were in the Albion team, and me, Bob Hazell and Rickie, a few of them, and he just thought it would be different . . . it was great on the night and pulled a fair crowd to be fair, and it was like the one end was all black and the other end was all white and a lot of people thought it was like black v white and all this sort of thing, but it was a novel thing, do you know what I mean, and when we were playing, there was a bit of an edge to the game, you know, and they had come down to Villa – although it was vicious stuff it was like we won, so it was great, the black team won that night and Handsworth was getting up . . . We had a trip to Trinidad as well, the black team, so it was great, but at the time there was a big political thing, and we were not sure about all

this . . . there was stuff in the papers and stuff and all this and we said sod it, we will just do it anyway . . . We never saw any black journalists having a pop at it, so who has got the problem here? If we haven't got a problem with it and we want to do it – they want us to go and we want to do it – what is wrong with that? (Interview, 11 February 1997)

These events exposed some of the tensions which black players were experiencing at the time and the difficulties associated with acquiring an identity that Paul Gilroy suggests 'is the premise of a thinking 'racial' self that is both socialized and unified by its connection with other kindred souls encountered usually, though not always, within the fortified frontiers of those discrete ethnic cultures that also happen to coincide with the frontiers of a sovereign nation state that guarantees their continuity' (Gilroy 2000: 491). In the context of a football club where interracial human relations are physically embodied on the field of play and training ground and literally stripped naked in the changing room, such discrete notions of difference, marked out on ethnic lines, are hard to sustain.

During his discussion with Garth Crooks on the *Critical Eye* programme, *Great Britain United,* Mark Bright suggested that in the absence of an established black community, players such as Cunningham, Regis and Blissett were in fact pioneers, cautiously creating fractures within the white hegemonic codes of the traditional dressing room and the space for new behavioural norms to emerge:

> For them to pull, to pull out there sort of toilet bags and put on the cream and start putting it on their hands and face and you know the older players must start saying 'what's going on here?' Daren't put it on. But sort of they, like you say they broke the ice and all of a sudden they come through and they're regulars and when the other young players come through and start doing it they just say 'oh, you need to do them things' or you need to use that, so, kind, that type of comb or, you know, well sort of showering together and all this sort of thing and like you're pulling out your own personal soap and 'what are you doing? Isn't our soap good enough for you?' (*Critical Eye* 1991)

During the same interview Ian Wright brought the picture up to date by revealing the more fluid nature of cultural exchange in the Crystal Palace dressing room where he mixed with white players who 'share our stuff. What's that cream for they say, what's that cream for? Let's have some. And we give 'em some you know, so we give em some and that, you know they want some and we're only too happy' (*Critical Eye* 1991). Whilst Ian Wright has experienced a loss of faith amongst some black fans as a consequence of his waving of the Cross of St George during England's 1998 encounter with Argentina, mainstream celebrity status and the award of an MBE in the New Years Honours Lists of 2000 he is also emblematic of the ways in which football's racially coded, fixed archetypes have become more relaxed. Ben Carrington has pointed out, as Ian Wright becomes the object of 'national canonization' he also becomes an emblem of postmodern blackness. Carrington identifies this as a situation in which Wright is 'at one and the same time radical and de-politicised, outspoken but with no agenda, a threat to mono-cultural nationalism, but an uncritical endorser of populist nationalism' (Carrington 2001: p. 114). These new 'inclusive' qualities and postmodern ironies themselves disguise the contingencies and extant stereotypes that continue to situate black players in a negative relation to the games normative discourses and frameworks of power. A prominent referee who is black illustrated this point by referring to the kinds of racialized banter he encounters in the contemporary game and the consequences that his performances might have for other black professionals:

> The comments are like '[it's] one of the brothers', but in general it is normally said when we are coming out of the tunnel, and I know that it is well documented that there is 15% of the players are black in the teams, so there is black players on both sides, so it is done in jest, as a communication, as a sort of breaking the ice type of stuff. But the fact that it is there and the fact that it is said to me and it is not really said to my colleague who is white, means that there is a question in the back of the mind, and I am sure they never meant to do it because there are black players on both sides . . . I don't think they [black players] expect it [to be treated differently], but certainly the comments have been made and I don't take any offence by that because you are in there and people say things and have a jest and have a laugh and I come back to them and say I am not going to be able to control the game and make decisions like that as well, and they accept it. But I do think that most black players give me the impression that they want me to do well because if I do well then they have an easier life in the dressing room because no doubt I do get hammered by or I do get comments made against me by the manager because I am a referee that is not very good, and because I am black, not because I am a black referee. I think that maybe if you were a black player sat in there listening to this then it becomes a bit more personal, so whilst they don't give me any latitude in any way shape or form in terms of their performance because they are professional, I think if you ask most players whether they would want me to do well or not they would say they want me to do well in comparison to other referees and I think that is maybe because of the colour because it makes their life a bit easier. (Interview, 17 January 1997)

Hoberman also talks of a 'widespread and resentful white attitude toward the demonstrative gestures and dancing routines that some professional black athletes have turned into a signature style' (Hoberman 1997: 218) as a way of illustrating continuing ambivalences towards black performers. However these forms of congratulation and celebration, previously constructed as 'black' and given expression on the basketball courts of America, have become ubiquitous within sport, even where the participants are white, as we reflected in relation to the

Crystal Palace team of the early 1990s in Chapter 3. After recalling how Palace's black players had introduced new kinds of celebration and musical styles to the club John, a Palace fan went on to point out how:

> Then you saw white Palace players joining in, so you saw Southgate bogle [a dance associated with dancehall reggae]. You saw Palace white players joining in with the kind of so-called kind of black celebrations of the goal, and being accepted as well – you almost saw that on the pitch, and all the black, white players were also kind of quite local so a lot of them, you know, they'd have gone to schools where, you know, they'd know a bit about black culture. (Interview, 7 February 1996)

Perversely, in this sense the everyday display of increasingly sophisticated, choreographed and often suggestive goal celebrations that are inscribed with racially marked stereotypes of 'black' physicality and sexuality may reflect the pursuit of an 'authentic' sporting identity, by white players. In the midst of a growing focus on the success of black athletes and a speculative search for genetic, cultural and physiological explanations (Entine 2000) black footballers may increasingly find that Bauman's 'entry tickets' are granted in a more collective fashion within the sporting milieu. Yet such terms of inclusion offer a kind of privileged status to the black sporting body which continues to essentialize the notion of racial difference.

Hoberman himself begins his book by stating that 'the modern world is awash in images of black athletes. The airborne black body, its sinewy arms clutching a basketball as it soars high above the arena floor, has become the paramount symbol of athletic dynamism in the media age' (Hoberman 1997: xxiii). The concern with the notion of a distinct black sporting identity then, whether constructed by black athletes themselves or aspirational white sportsmen and interpreters only helps to sustain notions of athletic capacity being related to racially fixed characteristics. We would do better to avoid such signifiers altogether and focus on sports performances and the emergent forms of multiculture within English professional football today.

'They Don't Like it up Em': Globalization, 'Foreign' Players and the Defence of Englishness

Following a close season in which 70 per cent of transfer fees paid by Premiership clubs were spent on foreign players, during the 1999–2000 season Chelsea, led by the Italian manager 'Luca' Vialli, became the first English side to field a team which did not include a single English born player. In recent years concern about the influx of foreign players has become something of a cause celebre within the game and has been reflected in concerted attempts to lobby both the British and

European governments to enable a limit to be placed on the number of foreign players flowing into domestic leagues.

The concern about foreign players has taken on a number of dimensions. Whilst the contribution of players from overseas to the general improvement in standards of play and revitalization of the English game during the 1990s has been recognized, institutional reactions have principally been expressed in terms of the subsequent diminished opportunities for young English/British players. Alongside this structural concern, however, complex patterns of cultural exchange, inclusion and exclusion have been at work, which relate to the normative preferences prevailing within the games' core cultural formations.

Relating back to the structures of antipathy which operate within specific fan cultures which we discussed in the previous Chapter, foreign players and specif-ically foreign black players would seem *more* likely to prompt an aversive reaction amongst those fans and domestic players who share their cultural values. Never-theless it may well be that 'foreign' black players in general have had a different experience of English football as compared to black British players, *due* to their classification as 'foreigners', as one of our informants, then Chairman of a leading English Premiership club reflected:

> We have found here in Leeds that when we got Tony Yeboah . . . he was the player of the year, and apparently he was treated like a God – he doesn't live so far from me – he is Ghanaian, black, African and is here to make money and go back to Ghana, but he is very heavily admired . . . But he is considered to be a Ghanaian, he is not considered to be an Englishman, he is not considered to be a black player. Chris Fairclough I think came from Nottingham, and I think he [had a different experience]. (Interview, 20 November 1996)

This reaction is in line with the patterns of response that we identified in relation to the considerably less effective Everton player, Daniel Amokachi, in Chapter 4. Chelsea's black French international defender Marcel Desailly, who has achieved success in France, Italy and England offered a player's perspective on the ways in which football and its globalized labour market can lead to a suspension of racial stereotypes:

> London is such a cosmopolitan city that the way people look at you is different to the way they do in France. For a black in France, every time you go into a shop you're scrutinised by zealous assistants curious to know what you want, what you're up to, what shoes you're wearing, how you're dressed, as a way of assessing your status. Here, it seems to be better. From the age of around fifteen-seventeen, since I was becoming known as a football player, it helped to cool people off. In truth, I haven't experienced that much racism or sensed people giving me sidelong glances. In football everybody is so used to being with players from different races, from various horizons and countries, that being black doesn't make you feel like an outcast, as is the case in

so many other jobs: its OK. There seems to be less racism in the Premiership than in Italy or France. (*The Observer*, 12 September 1999)

Such perspectives should not, however, be read in a naive liberal fashion. Hoberman, suggests that such reverence may still be located within a racialised framework where the 'presumed instability of the African personality and its related capacity to produce 'soccer magic' are the bipolar stereotypes that confirm the essential abnormality of black potential in a white man's world' (Hoberman 1997: 125). As such, whilst foreign players, both black and white, can be embraced by fans, players and institutions their inclusion remains unstable.

The influx of foreign players into the English game has been associated with increasing 'professionalism' and a shifting of the hegemonic certainties within football's white working-class masculine player cultures. It has been associated with new, more disciplined training regimes, greater attention to diet, more professional medical attention, pre-match exercises and a broadening of social environments, with pasta and wine substituting for chips and beer. Many of these developments have been seen as unproblematic and have been widely welcomed by English players, coaches and the broader networks of commentary and rumour surrounding the game.

Nevertheless, whilst this might suggest there is room for the influx of new ideas and a certain appetite for the exotic embodied in players from overseas, in line with our reflections on football's structures of antipathy in the last chapter, this often remains contingent upon their compliance with certain normative qualities on the football park. Three days into the 2000–1 FA Premiership season Patrick Vieira, France's World Cup and Euro 2000 winning midfield player, was dismissed whilst playing for Arsenal against Liverpool, his second red card in as many matches. With Emmanuel Petit having already moved to Barcelona the British press was quick to speculate that Vieira would now quit Arsenal and the English game, invoking the player's own accusations that he has been subject to racist intimidation and discrimination from players and officials alike.

Vieira was aligned with a succession of French players including Eric Cantona, David Ginola, Emmanuel Petit, Nicolas Anelka and Frank Leboeuf who, it is suggested, have had difficulties coping with the 'demands' of the 'English' game. The previous season Vieira was also sent off during a match with West Ham following alleged provocation from Neil Ruddock who, amongst other things, it was claimed had called him a 'French prat'. After the match, in a television interview, the player joked that 'he could smell the garlic' when Vieira spat at him following his dismissal, which ultimately led to an abortive FA investigation into allegedly racist remarks.

In some senses these events illustrate the ways in which the terms of debate around racism in football have shifted in the context of the growing numbers of overseas players performing for Premiership clubs. Overt forms of racism amongst supporters and racial abuse directed at black players by their fellow professionals have declined steeply in recent years in the face of vociferous public campaigning, but it seems that foreign players have been largely exempt from these moral prohibitions. As West Ham's English manager Harry Redknapp commented in defence of Neil Ruddock:

> What a load of nonsense . . . There is no way he should be punished. What for? For having a joke? If you can't have a bit of a crack and give a funny answer, where is the English sense of humour? The good thing about the English is that we have always been able to laugh at ourselves. (*Guardian*, 30 October 1999)

In this example the abuse that Vieira claimed to have experienced throughout the game becomes marginalized by that which is spoken publicly in the television interview. Its humour renders it harmless within the context of English football's normative cultural formations from which Vieira himself, as a Frenchman, is excluded. A more empowering dimension of this distance is revealed by the emergence of an alternative framework of professional propriety as illustrated by Vieira's willingness to speak out about the abuse he has received from named fellow professionals. This has been particularly pertinent in the context of the increasingly multinational teams playing in pan-European competition where players carry with them a variety of cultural traditions and codes of conduct that may conflict with the restraints currently prevailing within English football. Most recently, during a Champions League game in Rome, Lazio's Yugoslavian defender Sinisa Mihajlovic was alleged to have called Vieira 'a fucking black monkey'. Vieira then freely recounted his experience to the press:

> What is really surprising is it has come from a player who is a foreigner in Italy. It started in the first game at Highbury and I thought maybe it was just because we won the game that he was upset. When a fan does it it's stupid, when a player does it it's unbelievable. It is the worst abuse I have ever heard and it never stopped from the moment the teams were shaking hands at the start. I told him he'd said enough. You could see in his eyes that he was really thinking about what he said. It was very hurtful and difficult to accept when another pro player says things like that. When fans do it, you can do something about it; they can be identified. But when a player says it to you on the pitch it is difficult to prove. I feel I have to speak out about this and do something. You have to tell the truth. (*Guardian*, 19 October 2000)

The English press was largely supportive in this case but their support might also relate to the player's initial conformity with the normative preferences of English football by maintaining a physically uncompromising approach to the game, verbally retaliating to Mihajlovic (allegedly calling him a 'gypsy shit') whilst maintaining his physical discipline. As the *Guardian* reporter put it 'in the past [Vieira] might easily have lost his cool in the face of such provocation'. Where those normative preferences are disturbed through criticism of English players or the 'English' game the reaction is often less sympathetic. The admission by foreign players such as Chelsea's Frank Leboeuf that he finds the English game over aggressive and even frightening was met with scorn and derision by both the player's own union, the PFA, and the popular press. In this respect Leboeuf was merely confirming his adherence to O'Donnell's (1994) national sporting stereotype of the 'soft' Frenchman.

This 'confession' by Leboeuf also coincided with declarations from the then Chelsea manager 'Luca' Vialli and his successor Claudio Ranieri that they wished to employ more English players since there was a 'need' for a core of such players around which to build a team culture suitable to the demands of the English game. This framework of analysis has been invoked in the location of Manchester United's success around the emergence of a crop of home-grown British players including Giggs, Beckham and Scholes and the French Arsenal manager Arsene Wenger's enduring faith in the English defensive quartet of Seaman, Adams, Keown and Dixon.

In some senses the fight for the future of the English game is being fought out on the basis of a cultural logic of belonging that allows the contingent inclusion of both foreign and black players on the basis of their compliance with a set of core cultural norms. However, although the sheer number of black players who have appeared over the course of the last three decades and the broader transformations within the game have helped to shift some of the terms of inclusion and led to less tightly defined cultural expectations, the integration of foreign players remains less complete. Despite the remarkable increase in the number of overseas players in recent years there remains a greater willingness to distinguish between foreign players and British players, to ascribe crude national stereotypes in line with O'Donnell's national typologies (O'Donnell 1994), to talk of a specifically English footballing culture and to point the finger at foreign players when things go wrong.

Conclusion

Conventional understandings of sport often emphasize its cohesive qualities and certainly the demands of team sports such as football require players to form co-operative working relationships if not long-lasting friendships. What we have done in this chapter is to reveal some of the terms of inclusion on which those relationships are established and the ways in which those terms become racially and culturally marked. Unlike the spaces occupied by football fans the football field, training pitch and dressing room do not usually facilitate the expression of crude and explicit forms of racism. What we have tried to suggest is that this does not necessarily lead to the conclusion that football player communities are models of social integration and racial harmony, rather that the forms of racial under-standing within them often operate in implicit ways which normalise certain cultural formations at the expense of others.

Racist language and abuse clearly does feature within football players' profes-sional and social environments but has increasingly been driven out of the game as a consequence of players' physical responses, the multi-racial diversity of the contemporary game and concerted campaigning around the issue. When incidents occur they are readily dismissed as 'heat of the moment' responses, individual mental aberrations that do not conflict with the multi-culturalism that prevails in the majority of English professional clubs.

In this context there is an even greater imperative to move beyond the focus on the overt expression of racism as the only issue with regard to issues of exclusion than there is in relation to fan culture. Rather it is the implicit normative racism located in the everyday embodied practices of football's white core that polices the integration of black and foreign players. The possession of the appropriate 'cultural passport' is not merely reliant upon wearing a particular football shirt but on a conformity with the teams' cultural identity and the white working-class masculinities from which they have emerged as embodied in iconic figures such as Tony Adams, Alan Shearer and Roy Keane.

These implicit forms of racialized exclusion are however disguised from the public's gaze by their very normalcy. In the context of the occasional explosion of overt forms of racist expression the non articulated racialized practices within player cultures do not reveal themselves in the public imagination in the same ways. In turn this enables football to discard the notion that racism exists inside the game's professional structures either at a player or institutional level whilst stating its public opposition to overt forms of racism found amongst the fans and individual players. Colin King (2000) has pointed out in his recent work that black players who are trying to break into coaching and management are confronted with implicit rules and social forces that inhibit and confound their ambitions. More than this, he argues, black players have to both second guess the implicit barriers that affect their fortunes but also find it necessary to mirror whiteness in the way they conduct themselves in order to fit in. He concludes that: 'For black people, "playing the whiteman" means participating in soccer on other people's terms' (King 2000: 26). In the following chapter we wish to look further at the ways in which racism features within the institutions of the game.

– 6 –

'There is No Racism in Football': Football Institutions and the Politics of Race

12 noon, Regent St, London, 15 December 1994

It is approaching Christmas and Regent St is busy with shoppers as I move along keeping an eye out for New Burlington Mews amongst the side streets and passages off the main road. I am due to attend an official gathering of the Carling No. 1 Panel in my capacity as Chair of the Football Supporters' Association, the first of several similar functions I was to attend over the next few years. Finally I find the venue and what appears to be a very modest entrance just to the side of Regent St with a brass name plate reading 'Hedges & Butler Cellars'. Ringing the bell I had no idea what to expect. A formal business meeting? A quick vote on the Carling player and manager of the month? An informal gathering with light refreshments? A full-scale business lunch?

All I did know was that most of those individuals with power and influence within the game had been invited. Rick Parry and Graham Kelly, then chief executives of the Premier League and FA respectively, Gordon Taylor of the Professional Footballers' Association, Vic Wakeling, Head of Sport on BSkyB, the then England manager Terry Venables, Steve Coppell, from the League Managers' Association, representatives from Bass Brewers (owners of Carling), the Football Writers Association, Match of the Day, Radio 5 Live and the Referees Association along with me and a couple of other bit parts from the supporters 'movement'.

The venue had the feel of a private club somewhere hidden away from everyday lives, the low-key single-door entrance accessible from a side street, concealing the opulent surroundings found below. As the doorlock buzzed I made my way in and downstairs to the cellars where the great and the good of English professional football were gathering, seated on luxurious leather sofas. The glasses of vintage champagne and canapés were the first sign of the treatment we were to expect. After a short discussion and predictable agreement on the choice of Alex Ferguson as manager of the month the group were invited into the dining room where the single 25-foot-long table and furnishings revealed a side of our national game which was completely alien to a fan. There seemed to be as much cutlery and glassware at each setting as might normally be found at the average family dinner table at Christmas. Nevertheless there was a convivial, yet unexcited air. These people were all familiar with one another and apparently comfortable with these surroundings and this type of engagement. Unlike me, nobody else was looking around wondering what cutlery to use nor seemed surprised by the opulence of the occasion.

As we made our way through a seven-course meal, the finest wines from one of Bass Brewers' most prestigious cellars served with each course by formally dressed and trained waiters, little insights into the hidden workings and rituals of professional football began to reveal themselves. Whilst the journalists Alex Montgomery, Bob Cass and Jonathon Pearce told a succession of football stories and jokes in the hope that others, windows down, might in turn blurt out the substance of a future article or commentary, football administrators kept a guarded distance and engaged in private discussion with opposite numbers. As the afternoon progressed, brandy, port and cigars circulated whilst the everyday deals between journalists, administrators and sponsors that make football tick were made with a handshake and macho posturing dressed up in false claims to having been 'done'. Despite the atmosphere of suspicious caution, as each of the guests departed they would ritually walk around the table as each 'gentleman' stood up and shook hands in turn, almost as though acting out a Mafiosi scene from *The Godfather* or *Scarface*.

Guests arrived and departed at various points, sometimes with uninvited but readily accommodated celebrity colleagues, as they fitted the meal in around other activities. Despite its unfamiliarity it seems that such functions are as much a part of the everyday landscape of professional football as the stadium and training pitch. However, this is an environment that, in our observations, is almost exclusively occupied by white, middle-aged men who readily adopt many of the bourgeois and even aristocratic codes attached to it, alongside the masculine cultures that are embodied in the posturing, storytelling and piss taking associated with the game.

* * *

Two points seem important here following these observations made by Tim Crabbe. Firstly, the cultural norms within such settings reflect not only these traces of class and masculinity but a white centredness within the institutions of football more generally. As an 'outsider', albeit both white and male, it was difficult to feel entirely at 'home' even though every effort was made to put me at ease. Acceptance into this environment is reliant upon an accommodation with the white, male, bourgeois outlook of its principal occupants, which might prove more difficult for people who normally reside outside these social formations. Furthermore, it is precisely in these kinds of environment where footballing rumours are manu-factured and traded, job opportunities revealed, policy, journalistic and marketing ideas initiated. So whilst Steve Coppell's presence enabled him to reveal his interest in returning to management and to receive tip offs about possible upcoming jobs and the financial position of clubs in the North West, stories were also told about the alleged criminal activities of a black former international, despite his absence from the room.

In this chapter we want to explore this notion of presences and absences further. We wish to seek an understanding of the ways in which the institutional structures of English professional football might normalize the notion of 'whiteness' within the game and militate against the interests of ethnic minority groups in what are often, in the words of Sir William Macpherson, 'unwitting and unconscious' ways. As Macpherson stated:

> Unwitting racism can arise because of lack of understanding, ignorance or mistaken beliefs. It can arise from well intentioned but patronising words or actions. It can arise from unfamiliarity with the behaviour or cultural traditions of people or families from minority ethnic communities. It can arise from racist stereotyping of black people as potential criminals or troublemakers. Often this arises out of uncritical self-understanding born out of an inflexible . . . ethos of the 'traditional' way of doing things. Furthermore such attitudes can thrive in a tightly knit community, so that there can be a collective failure to detect and to outlaw this breed of racism. The . . . canteen [or 'cellar'] can too easily be its breeding ground. (Macpherson 1999: 22–3)

It is our contention that it is precisely these sorts of frameworks, illustrated in the environment described above, which prevail within the institutions of football. However, it is also this normalized, white centredness and the everyday practices of the football industry that leave the institutions of the game with the sense that, rather than being a hotbed of racism, the game actually offers one of the few opportunities for personal development open to young black men. As one Football League club Chief Executive told us:

> At the moment for the black boys there's three ways out of the ghetto: to be sportsmen, to be pop stars or to be drug dealers – that's the three. I'm quite sure that it's better for them being sports stars. (Interview, 12 February 1996)

The very presence of so many black players within the professional arenas of the game is seen as the perfect rebuttal to those who would make allegations of racism. For a number of key spokesmen, quite simply, 'There is no racism in football'. These are in fact the precise words used by Jimmy Hill, the much-maligned and highly opinionated television pundit and football administrator (Fieldnotes, October 1995). Jimmy Hill has often courted controversy with his forthright views on the game, but his credentials as a representative of the football establishment and expert 'interpreter' stand any scrutiny, given his experience as a player, players' representative, club manager, director and chairman, FA councillor, Football League committee member and television presenter and pundit. Despite the maverick image he is a man who is deeply influential in football politics and his reading of race issues within the game is instructive.

What Jimmy Hill was saying, whilst representing the Football League at a meeting with supporters' organizations at the Football Association headquarters in October 1995, was that there is no racism *within* the game. What problems there are come from supporters and people who attach themselves *to* the game. Indeed his views do not appear that dissimilar from many of the club chairmen and football administrators that we encountered during our research. Largely middle-aged or elderly white men, who have made money in private business and commerce, football's power brokers tend to combine a 'common sense', colour-blind approach, when addressing issues of race at an individual level, with a public denial of the existence of any significant problem within the game itself. As the Chairman of one of our case study clubs with a history of employing black players put it:

> There have never been any problems [at this club], certainly not to my knowledge. Never in the history of the club has there ever been any problems and they [black players] are just treated as equally. As I said before I couldn't care less if they come from Mars or bloody Jupiter, as long as they can play football. (Interview, 10 February 1998)

We intend to focus here on the ways in which these approaches have been articulated and constructed around narrow definitions of racism and its relationship to football and an inward looking, highly defensive and strategically managed approach towards public relations.

'Not me Guv': The Racist-hooligan Couplet and Institutional Denial

The typical 'public' response of football clubs and individuals associated with the game to allegations of racism has historically been one of denial: denial that the problem exists at any significant level at individual clubs or amongst players, denial that there is a problem within the game more generally and, on occasion, denial that racism itself exists as a problem in society. Where its presence is acknowledged, incidents are usually located amongst supporters and, more particularly, identified only in their most overt, violent and politically orientated manifestations. There are, however, some important points to stress with regard to the limitations of only locating 'the problem' in the stands and what is left of the terraces.

It has proven easier to talk about racism amongst fans precisely because, for football administrators, the issue of race can be readily added to a range of anti-social fan behaviour. Equally, stressing that racism is an extension of other forms of football violence and abuse means that attention can be deflected from difficult questions relating to the underrepresentation of black people and minority groups within football management and administration. As John Williams has commented, fan racism has been more easily identifiable precisely because of its crass nature, whereas the more subtle forms of racial inequality inside the institutions of professional football have received little attention (Williams 1992).

We suggested earlier that this trend has contributed to the production of a form of discourse characterized as the racist-hooligan couplet. The almost universal adoption of this perspective by academic, media and professional commentators has led to the construction of the 'racist folk demon' as a football supporting archetype. In turn this provides a useful shorthand way of a) understanding what racism in football is and b) locating the problem outside of the institutions of football and into the shady interstices of quasi-criminal subcultures. Where the presence of racism *is* detected it is represented in ways which isolate it from the club and the 'normal', 'respectable' body of fans. It is a problem associated with the 'mindless' minority who 'attach' themselves to football and about whom nothing can be done.

Pronunciations flow from club chairmen and administrators disassociating themselves from this 'evil menace'. Indeed the focus on the more overt forms of fan racism enables football institutions to divert attention from internal tensions surrounding the question of race. Accordingly support can, sometimes reluctantly, be articulated for anti-racist initiatives despite the point that this is often merely a rhetorical gesture. This was illustrated by a community officer at a small football league club who told us how he had taken a letter offering support to the 'Let's kick racism out of football' campaign to the club chairman for his signature. The chairman responded by stating 'I'm not signing that. I'm a racist', to which the community officer replied 'Well, sign it anyway', which he duly did.

Even where such cynicism is not in evidence the pervasiveness of the concern about racism as a cognate of hooliganism has meant that complex and often ambiguous expressions of racism within the institutions of football are largely ignored. Whilst the racist-hooligan is vilified and condemned at all levels from the FA to individual clubs and players, throughout our study, football clubs demonstrated an almost universal resistance towards identifying the issue of racism inside their organizational structures and the game more generally.

The patterns of silencing and denial that characterize institutional responses to racism in football can in some senses be understood in terms of the ways in which the issue is typically understood. With racism being represented in such dramatic terms, it is almost inevitable that clubs will distance themselves from the problem. The nature of racism is simplified and dramatized to such an extent that the more complex and banal forms located within the institutions of the clubs can be ignored and dismissed. The stereotypical representation of racism as the product of demonic, neo-Nazi thuggery creates a situation where the commercial and human resource interests of clubs cannot even embrace the *idea* of the presence of racism.

Within this world view clubs such as Crystal Palace do not have a problem with racism because they do not have more than a handful of expressive and violent racist fans. For such clubs the issue is not broadened to incorporate questions of racial equality within the organization and relationships with the wider community because the problem has not been perceived in that way. So to concede a more general association between racism and football would be to infer that universally abhorrent, sinister influences were at work within the institutions of the game and the clubs. The result is a 'colour-blind' philosophy that fails to prioritize initiatives within clubs which will broaden their appeal to the minority communities, who are so poorly represented amongst supporters and club personnel. In the view of one of our informants, a black 'football in the community' worker, there is a more subtle and 'hidden' variety of racism associated with this process that he encounters in his everyday working life. He concluded:

> What is happening more and more now is that overt racism is actually being driven underground and institutionalised racism is rearing its ugly head. If you are not educated or you are not aware of it, that actually is far more damaging than overt racism. (Interview, 26 September 1995)

These comments resonate within the findings of our research more generally, which have revealed several patterns of institutional discrimination within the game.

Football Institutions and the Normalization of 'Whiteness'

When we talk about the institutions of football we are essentially concerned with the structures and procedural practices through which the game is organized, governed and interpreted. This definition extends beyond the formal bodies and institutions associated with the management of football, such as the Football Association, Premier League, Football League, representative bodies and individual clubs. It is also concerned with the everyday processes, cultures and language through which these bodies and individuals interact and organize the game of football, its social relations and media representations. It extends beyond the football bodies themselves to include schools and scouting networks, the institutional machinery of the transfer market both domestically and internationally, and the commercial activity that has built up around the game over the last decade.

Until very recently the institutions of football in England could be characterized as part of a traditional masculine industry, organized on what appeared to be pseudo feudal lines. Individual clubs were typically owned and controlled by patriarchal local, wealthy business*men* who were 'lords of the manor'. Contracted players were typically drawn from working-class backgrounds and their registrations (without which you cannot play) are still 'held' by their clubs today. Indeed prior to 1963 clubs owned their players' registrations outright, with transfers being negotiated exclusively between clubs without any reference to the player at all. More recently the balance of power has shifted back in the players' favour as a result of the Bosman ruling (see Szymanski 1999) and application of European law. Although their influence is in decline, the Football Association, which is ultimately run by a council of 103 largely elderly and exclusively white men, drawn from the professional and amateur games as well as the armed forces and the old universities, continues to provide overall leadership and guardianship (see Russell 1997, Walvin 1975).

Increasing commercialization, the advent of the Premier League, stock market floatations, globalization flows and growing player power has more recently led to the emergence of a process of 'modernization' (see Conn 1997). However, in keeping with the commercial drive behind this process we would suggest that many of these changes have primarily affected the commercial structure, custodianship and public face of the game rather than necessarily radically altering prevailing 'football' cultures. The institutional and behavioural forms associated with football continue to operate within a normative framework which is essentially 'white', masculine and 'industrial'. Indeed there are currently no black or Asian chief executives and only a handful of individuals from ethnic minority backgrounds sit in the boardrooms of English professional clubs.

In keeping with contemporary understandings of institutionalized racism, football has a way of operating that, without necessarily being overtly racist, is often contingent upon interlopers from ethnic minorities accommodating with the norms of 'white' football cultures. The 'colour-blind' approach and public rhetoric articulated by players, managers and directors and arguably reflected in the numbers of black players employed in the professional game can sometimes disguise a reluctance to embrace notions of cultural diversity. We will try to illustrate this point here by profiling both the 'managed' and less reflexive comments on notions of 'race' and difference of a key figure in the administration of the contemporary game.

Amongst other things Barry Hearn is the Chairman of Leyton Orient Football Club and is the third division's representative on the Football League committee. Since buying the club in 1995 Hearn has made all the usual noises about his connections with the area, his 'fan credentials' and his commitment to the local community:

> I was born in Dagenham, so Leyton Orient is my local side – I was there when I was 10 years old – and I believe that there is a role that supporters like me can play in the game . . . There is a tremendous buzz in working at this level. Developing local talent,

working with the community, and having some fun. It is the greatest challenge that I have ever had in my sporting life – in 25 years of involvement. What is the challenge? The challenge is not Premier League – it is survival, firstly, and, secondly, contributing something to the local community. Premiership football is not the people's game anymore – we are – clubs like Orient are the people's game. (Hicks 1999: 28)

The populist sentiments are fitting for a man who in many ways personifies the new breed of hyped-up, publicity conscious administrators of 'postmodern' sport, his attentions shifting from snooker to boxing to darts to cards and, for now, finding a home at a football club capable of delivering daily media attention. His is the ever-smiling, larger than life personality who 'made' the 'Dark Destroyer' and 'Prince Naz', turned *Simply the Best* into a Chris Eubank theme tune and managed to exploit Steve Davis' dullness so well that he was adopted as a *Spitting Image* puppet. And yet, despite the cast, at a Barry Hearn press conference it is usually Hearn himself that holds centre stage.

However, despite his mastery of the art of publicity Hearn still reflects the white centred, masculine outlook of much of the football establishment, which his natural ebullience and East End cheeky chappy image occasionally reveals. On Wednesday 8 March 2000 Hearn's views on immigration provoked a controversy when they were given a rare public airing during an appearance on Radio 5 Live's *Nicky Campbell Show*, which was wrapping up a phone-in dealing with John Prescott's proposals for building new homes in the south of England. Whilst essentially there to discuss other topics Barry Hearn became involved in the conclusion of the property debate. Prompted by a caller citing immigration as a big factor in the current housing shortage Hearn initially responded in typical jocular fashion before embellishing on the caller's comments:

If you don't let them [immigrants] in you may never get your car windscreen washed again . . . I think it's a huge problem. I agree entirely with the caller. I think it's disgraceful we let all these people in the country. It's about time we started looking after ourself. I wouldn't have one of them in . . . Is there no end to it? It's just that I think that everyone's got opinions. They live in London. That's probably what the mayoral campaign's gonna be about, different people's opinions and er certainly as coming from a London family that moved out into Essex, which seems to be symbolic of most families after the war, we always go back and look at what's happened to where we came from and sometimes what we see, we don't like. And there's a lot of things going on in London that most inner Londoners don't like and need addressing. (BBC Radio 5 Live Broadcast, 8 March 2000)

When asked by Nicky Campbell whether he was 'just trying to fire things up when you said you wouldn't let one of them in?' Hearn went on:

No I wouldn't. I mean I have got a very selfish, but a very strong family attitude to life. You know I think your responsibility is to look after your family and on a national sense I think that family extends to everyone that's born in England. And I think that we are too often the good guys that we do tend to open our doors and even when we don't let them in, we have them in for months and months and years and years while we are queuing up and addressing in the most English way which is totally fair of course – 'cos we are the fairest nation in the world – We let everybody in. (BBC Radio 5 Live Broadcast, 8 March 2000)

Hearn seemed to illustrate in these remarks the way in which the lighthearted, everyday stereotypes referred to earlier can operate at the front end of broader, racially coded reflections, which are rooted in a particular experience of postwar urban transformation. When Hearn constructs and situates himself within this idyllic image of, an implicitly white, East End 'community' who look 'at what's happened to where we came from and sometimes what we see, we don't like' it is not so clear what is meant by his desire to 'contribute something to the local community' and who is being included within this aspiration. Something of the basis of the terms of inclusion was revealed when Nicky Campbell then raised the point that several of Hearn's boxers themselves came from immigrant families and asked 'In your ideal world they wouldn't be here. Prince Naseem and Chris Eubank, Nigel Benn for example?'

No I would have to let those three in because they made me so much money and I would obviously change my principles at that stage being the person that I am. But I'm generalizing when I say that we should tighten our immigration laws we should tighten our laws that allow asylum seekers or so called asylum seekers into this country. (BBC Radio 5 Live Broadcast, 8 March 2000)

Despite his subsequent statement to a local newspaper that 'I am unconditionally opposed to racism . . . My personal commitment against racism is obvious. For the past 25 years I have promoted sport and sports personalities all over the world irrespective of their race, colour or creed. I have never been accused of racism in any manner, shape or form' (*Hackney Gazette*, 16 March 2000: 50) these comments seem to expose something of the nature of more managed public pronunciations on questions of race and equal opportunities. They also illustrate the contingencies associated with football's 'colour blind' approach which, despite Hearn's reflections on immigration policy made it possible for an eighteen-year-old Kosovan refugee to emerge from the youth ranks and appear for the Orient first team shortly after these comments were made.

The point here is not to bring the focus on any one individual but to use this illustration as an exemplar of the more casual, white-centred discourses that prevail within the institutions of the game. One way in which such practices have been institutionalized within the everyday operations of a whole variety of clubs is reflected in the routine hiring of 'old school' comics for club dinners and events. At least two of the clubs which we have studied in detail have hosted 'gentleman's evenings' where Bernard Manning, himself a Manchester City supporter, has been the star guest speaker whose act is widely recognized to include a repertoire of jokes that are rendered at the expense of ethnic minority groups. Indeed black members of the audience often become the butt of such jokes, vividly illustrating a peripheral role within much of the normative dialogue of football culture. A black sports journalist to whom we spoke argued that there is a 'piss-taking' culture that runs right through the very heart of football, which reflects particular conceptualizations of black people's historic position in society:

> Well I think the basic idea, if you can call it an idea, is that you know, black people are people of fun and white people feel, many white people feel they have the right to lampoon them and any sort of aspect of them and if the black person then doesn't like it, they get rather upset, and so of course then they say the black persons' got a chip on their shoulder. (Interview, 23 October 1997)

Indeed such formulations extend beyond the immediate football environment and into the institutions and practices that surround the game and its reporting. This journalist went on to recount an experience he had whilst working at a Fleet Street national newspaper which illustrates the ways in which 'racialized' talk and jokes can be normalized in white dominated environments and how members of ethnic minority groups can be marginalized in such contexts.

One particularly strange and disturbing incident was recounted to us by a black journalist whom we refer to here as Clive. In 1996 this journalist was sitting in front of his computer in the midst of the newsroom on a national newspaper. Clive's white colleagues took it upon themselves to play a 'joke' on him . He was the only black person working on the staff of two or three hundred people at the newspaper. The paper was running a feature on the war hero Douglas Bader. An e-mail circular was sent around the journalists sitting at their computers that poses a series of questions about Bader. Clive was shocked when:

> One of them shouted out across the whole news room 'nigger' and then all the white journalists round me just burst into laughter and they obviously knew what the joke was and I didn't and I'm sitting there thinking what's going on and then someone else shouted out 'nigger' and then someone else said 'oh no no no it was black bastard wasn't it? Wasn't it black bastard?' and I didn't know what was going on.

This profusion of racist language was shocking and undermining. He couldn't understand what had caused it and what it meant. Later he realized that one of the questions on the e-mail asked about the name of Douglas Bader's dog. Bader had named his dog 'Nigger.' All of the people in the newsroom were involved right up to the deputy editor. Clive concluded:

> They all burst into laughter and the deputy editor said 'Oh you're so un PC [politically correct] Gary, you're so un PC.' That was 1996 . . . So that's the typical viewpoint of a Fleet Street journalist. (Interview, 23 October 1997)

The so-called joke gave the white journalist license to indulge in racist language while pre-empting any accusations of racist intent. It made it impossible for this exclusive game to be named as racism but the joke was clearly on the black journalist and aimed to undermine him. Clive has subsequently left the profession.

Within football we have similarly found examples of current Premiership chairmen, whilst away from the media's gaze, freely exchanging references to black players, sometimes on their own side, as 'monkeys', 'niggers' and 'schwarzers' as well as racialized descriptions from a wide range of players and managers. However, there is a non-recognition of such incidents as a problem because racism is seen in monolithic terms from which individual racialized acts can be separated and rationalized. Indeed racialized readings of the game can be mobilized in ways which apparently eulogize the contributions of black players leaving the racist tone of the language apparently 'unproblematic' within the perpetrators' own constructions of what constitutes racism. A leading campaigner against racism in football reported to us how a top Premiership club chairman had been speaking to members of the Arsenal board at half time during a game with their club:

> I think the score was nil-nil or one-all, it was a sort of fairly evenly matched game, and he shouted across 'we'll have you this time because we've got x number of niggers and you've got x number', i.e. we've got sort of more black players than you have so we're going to beat you or whatever. And it's a strange kind of appreciation of black players if you like, you know, because on one hand he's given them a back-handed compliment, on the other hand, you know, that sort of language is still there, quite overtly, from one of the leading figures in the game. (Interview, 26 September 2000)

As we discussed in the previous chapter a small but significant proportion of the black players we interviewed, after some initial reluctance, reported high levels of ethnocentrism and racism within the sport. Equally, they suggested that the reluctance of black professionals as a whole to speak out was the result of them having to survive within institutions that remain white dominated. This tension was well illustrated following a dispute between the Bolton and Wales centre forward, Nathan Blake and the former Welsh national team manager, Bobby Gould.

The dispute followed two incidents involving Bobby Gould, during dressing-room discussions after Wales' home 1998 World Cup qualifier against Holland and during preparations for the next qualifier against Belgium. The manager himself provided a valuable insight into the kinds of racialized language that are common place in dressing room situations when he explained the incidents to the press:

> All I said was, in a situation where we've conceded three goals against Holland, 'why didn't somebody pick the big black bastard up', something like that, something that has been said in many dressing rooms.
>
> And on the training field I said, 'right this is the yellow team, this is the white team in white bibs, and the rest stay in blacks and that includes you Nathan' . . . Perhaps Nathan Blake has finer feelings than other people, I accepted that and apologised to him personally and in front of the players saying no offence was ever intended. (*Guardian*, 2 April 1997)

The incident and the controversy it provoked led to a full investigation by the Football Association of Wales (FAW) and vehement denials from Bobby Gould that he was in any way racist as well as Blake's withdrawal from the squad to face Belgium in the return World Cup qualifier. Blake stated:

> I still want to play football for Wales but I don't want to play for him [Bobby Gould]. I have a total lack of respect for him. Racism is a thing of the past. We're in international football. I am an established striker; I should not have to listen to it from my own people, especially from the manager I play for. (*Daily Mirror*, 2 April 1997)

Nevertheless, following their enquiry the FAW exonerated Bobby Gould and took no disciplinary action against him, apparently due to the committee's sympathy for the manager's understanding of the incident. A former professional and current coach who is black put it to us that the comments made by Bobby Gould are indeed an established feature of the game that have remained largely unchallenged until now:

> You know that thing with, errm, errm, Bobby Gould? Pahh, that makes me laugh so much. You know he would say something like that. I know he would, yeah. But you see the thing is that . . . it's not a problem because he came from like the Old School, you know, and you see, probably when he was there looking at you and shouting 'you little black bastard' and you know and I mean those things, you take those things . . . and I am so glad that these blacks nowadays, right, are taking exception to that. 'Cos before we had to let things like that go . . . It was common place and to him it is common place. He cannot understand what all the fuss is about . . . because what goes through him is, 'fucking hell I can't believe they're making all this fuss about a little thing like that'. (Interview, 14 May 1997)

The everyday, casual forms of racism more readily found within football clubs can then be dismissed as play, wind ups and disciplinary tools – even though this suggests that they are part of the very fabric of the game. The onus is very much on the black players and officials to accommodate these norms rather than for football to change.

'They Don't Like the Cold': Racial Stereotyping and Discrimination inside Football

Racial stereotypes within clubs have increasingly been muted because of wider sensitivities to the issues of race. However, we recorded a series of examples where people at various levels inside football reported overhearing racist formulations. A former England national team manager commented on an incident that occurred in an airport lobby before an international fixture in the mid 1990s, where a councillor of the FA complained to a group of peers that the problem with the national side was that 'There were too many niggers in it.' The problem that seems pervasive within the institutions of football is that these sentiments have been driven underground because of their political inappropriateness and, as a result, racism at this level is relegated to whispers and rumours. This informant continued:

> I have to keep saying to myself all the time, if somebody said to me 'Well, prove it?' It's a very difficult thing to prove isn't it? I still think that there are people who could have possibly got [coaching and managerial] opportunities if they hadn't been black. It's an easy thing to say but I can only base it on what you smell now and again. (Interview, 17 February 1997)

Whilst FA councillors can get off the hook and deny the problem exists by muttering in each others' ears one current Premiership player who we interviewed whilst he was at Crystal Palace believes that:

> There's definitely people that have got a problem with black players or they stereotype black players, but they can't really come out and say anything because there's so many black players now in the game. (Interview, 13 February, 1997)

In fact this point was well illustrated when we first attended the Palace training ground to interview another player and were told by the youth team coach that 'He's gone. You know what those blacks are like. They are up, up and away.' This re-inforces the point that the inclusion of black players within football is not unconditional. Here, a racialized typology of behaviour is invoked to locate the player 'outside' of football's, implicitly white, normative codes. The moment provided a rare insight into the everyday nature of racial understandings in the game, given the 'dual vocabulary', one for the boardroom, bar and training ground and one for the public, which normally prescribes such disclosures. This point was reinforced by our enquiries at Manchester City. The public face of this club is very much concerned with fostering good relations with the ethnically diverse local community in Moss Side. This has been reflected in a number of awards to its Football in the Community Scheme and boardroom support for various anti racist initiatives. The club's former Managing Director, Colin Barlow, articulated this perspective when launching the Manchester performances of 'Kicking Out', a piece of anti-racist educational theatre which completed a national tour of schools in the run up to Euro 96:

> On behalf of the Directors at Manchester City Football Club I'm delighted to host this reception at Maine Road prior to the first provincial performance of Kicking Out . . . Manchester City Football Club has a very strong record in community relations and the work across the whole of the City makes us proud to be associated with Kicking Out. Equal Opportunities is very important to us and I think productions like this do nothing but good and so we're very happy that this has happened for us. You will see in the play the way in which people should be encouraged to react to the overt and the implied racism which extends in many parts of our community and [the] long term benefits for all of us including the football community. (Fieldnotes, 20 November 1996)

Yet the sentiments and racial awareness suggested by this prepared statement sit in stark contrast to the observations of a Manchester City fan who was in close contact with members of the board in the mid 1990s:

> I remember . . . one director made some joke about [local residents] all still being up in the trees round the Platt Lane centre . . . I think [the director] is sexist and racist but without even realising that he is, you know. That is quite a story within that boardroom – that is something we have come across speaking to people in boardrooms, it is kind of a public face and a non-understanding really of what it is that they are saying. They call them 'these blacks' and stuff like that. We have been into all this when it gets cold they don't want to play, we have been through all this with them – just nonsense really, nonsense. (Interview, 10 February 1997)

Stereotypes have classically been articulated through suggestions that: 'black players can't play in the cold'; 'while skilful they lack the grit and determination of their white counterparts'; 'black players have attitude problems, are lazy and give insufficient application to the game'. These sentiments were dramatically illustrated in the Channel 4 documentary, *Great Britain United* (*Critical Eye*, 1991) when the then Crystal Palace Chairman and current Brentford owner, Ron Noades stated that:

The problem with black players is they've great pace, great athletes, love to play with the ball in front of them ... when it's behind them it's – chaos. I don't think too many of them can read the game. When you're getting into the midwinter you need a few of the hard white men to carry the athletic black players through. (*Critical Eye*, 1991).

At this time Crystal Palace had employed more black players than any other club in the football league (Syzmanski, 2000) and was currently experiencing the most successful period in its history after reaching the FA Cup Final and finishing third in the old Division One championship. The side included Ian Wright, Andy Gray, Eric Young and Mark Bright who most observers believed possessed precisely the fighting spirit and resilience that Noades sought. Whilst Noades claimed to have been misrepresented at the time, in a subsequent letter to a football fan, now working as a journalist, who objected to his comments he restates the essence of this argument with the caveat that he was principally referring to the situation as it was a decade earlier (personal communication between Ron Noades and informant, 18 September 1991). Hoberman suggests that the lineage of such sentiments can be traced back to a colonial era when 'the myth of white physical superiority helped to sustain the power of Europeans who viewed physical and emotional toughness as prerequisites for survival' (Hoberman 1997: 119). Within this framework 'compared with whites, dark skinned males can be assumed to be deficient in courage until they prove otherwise' (Hoberman 1997: 111). Research findings relating to racially determined positional segregation in football and sport more generally provide further evidence of this kind of discrimination.

Melnick, whilst stopping short of claiming direct evidence of discriminatory practice on the part of management, found evidence of concentrations of black players in particular positions, specifically identifying 87.5 per cent more black forwards than expected in English first division clubs during the 1985–6 season (1988: 124). Similarly, Maguire (1991) found evidence that black players were 'over' represented in forward positions and 'under' represented in defensive and 'central' positions as well as being more heavily concentrated in the higher divisions of the football league during the 1989–90 season. There is also evidence that black players have, at least until quite recently, suffered market discrimination. Through conducting statistical regression analysis Stefan Szymanski found that: 'Clubs fielding teams with an above average number of black players tended to perform better in the League than clubs which fielded a below average number of black players, even if they spent the same in terms of wages' (Szymanski 1997: 216). The consequence of this is that black players deliver better results for the same wages. This is particularly significant in an increasingly globalized labour market where black players from more deprived countries are particularly susceptible to exploitation. During a personal discussion at a conference on racism in football in Austria, the Dutch former head coach of the Nigerian national football team informed us that young promising players, aged 14 or 15, from African nations have been brought to Western Europe by clubs and agents, only to be left stranded when their African 'genius' did not live up to expectations (Fieldnotes, 10th November 1997). His own interpretation of the problem was revealed in a newspaper interview when, referring to the Nigerian players he stated 'I know them . . . they are immature and easily diverted' (Hoberman 1997: 121).

The reaction to the public articulation of such perspectives and the continuing growth in numbers of black players (see Holland 1997: 271 and Vasili 2000), has shifted some of the ideological terms of these stereotypes and further restrained their articulation by more media-sensitive administrators. In their wake, however, other forms of racial discourse and discrimination are being generated. The importance that is placed on informal networks and patronage, along with the increasing role of agents and the media in generating 'rumour' and gossip continues to ensure that the key institutions and processes concerned with the recruitment of both players and managers are colonised by white personnel. Within such frameworks, 'race' and nationality remain on the sidelines as resources which can be mobilised by managers, agents and journalists in order to reinforce player identifications and team solidarity, invoke discipline or unsettle players in order to engineer transfers.

Much was made of the significance of ethnic make up, as personified by Ian Wright, to the team solidarity and success of the Crystal Palace team of the early 1990s, just as the team's break up was partly attributed to Ron Noades' comments about black players, despite Wright's denials (Wright 1996). Similarly, in an outburst against the role of agents in the game, Alan Smith, manager of a struggling Palace side in 1995, was alleged to have stated in front of eight black players, many of whom he had nurtured through the youth ranks:

> The reason the agents chose you black kids is because you are all naïve. We are the type of club that has to go out and look for players at a young age. Where was your agent when we dragged you black kids off the streets?' (*Sunday Mirror*, 29 January 1995)

Interestingly the article also alleged that the players in question 'tend to stay together in one group'. This point has been made about black players in a number of teams, and most famously in relation to the black and white members of the Dutch national side who it was alleged ate, socialized and celebrated separately during Euro 96 and the 1998 World Cup (*Guardian*, 5 June 1998). The suggestion is that black players don't easily 'mix' or fit in. Reflecting the ethnocentric nature of English and European football cultures, this practice, rather like the gendered nature of attitudes towards promiscuity, never seems to be perceived as a problem when white players socialize together.

The nationality of a number of players has also increasingly been invoked in order to rationalize a perceived inability to 'fit into' the 'English' game. In keeping with O'Donnell's (1994) notion of the 'hot tempered' or 'fiery' 'Latin' player, the press was critical of the Italian Fabrizio Ravenelli and Brazil's Emerson Moises Costa for their inability to settle at Middlesborough in a manner which is rarely applied to English players in similar circumstances. Indeed Emanuel Petit, Arsenal's domestic double and World Cup winning French defender, was continually harassed by the press because of his discomfort with the English weather, despite that particular complaint being almost a British national pastime.

The contemporary forms of British racism, which Gilroy suggests deal in 'cultural difference rather than crude biological hierarchy', align race and nation much more closely and as such we can identify similar concerns about the ability of black players to subscribe 'to the designated standards of acceptable cultural conduct' (Gilroy 1993: 91–2). Within this race-nation matrix, the 'disruptive' behaviour of a succession of black and foreign players, such as Stan Collymore, Nicolas Anelka, Pierre Van Hooijdonk, and Benito Carbone, has been individualized and blamed on their inability to assimilate within the prevailing culture.

However, the increasingly cosmopolitan and multinational nature of English football, which is largely driven by imperatives to seek better, cheaper players may well be creating new conditions in which traditional racial inequalities are broken down as discriminatory practices become 'uneconomic' in the face of competition (Szymanksi 2000). It is hard to assess the extent of any changes at the boardroom but at the highest level the influx of foreign players is changing the approach to the game and the very fabric of the culture of professional players.

These shifts, when placed alongside the institutional denial and silencing around the question of race, have more recently contributed to the emergence of a new focus on the lack of progression of Asian players into the professional game. In the presence of a contextual and discursive vacuum, researchers, campaigners and journalists have been drawn to this issue because of its very obviousness and undeniability. There *are* no Asian professionals currently playing regular first team football at the highest levels. A series of common sense rationales have emerged in response, ranging from pleas to 'give it time', through to stereotypical references to 'cultural' differences such as the perceived emphasis placed by Asian families on education and commerce above sport and the relative physical frailty of Asian players.

Whilst recognizing the complexity of the problem, the groundbreaking report by Jas Bains and Raj Patel, *Asians Can't Play Football* (1996), which addresses the question of racial stereotypes by invoking the irony in the title of the Hollywood film *White Men Can't Jump*, asserts that:

The problems which we have identified in professional football clubs on this issue have stemmed from an ignorance of and a lack of understanding or regard for the Asian population. This constitutes a conventional form of institutionalised racism. We have evidence to support our assertion that such ignorance, such a lack of understanding has perpetuated and reinforced a series of myths held of Asians generally, and of Asian footballers specifically. This is particularly borne out in comments by clubs on levels of interest and participation in football amongst Asians. The fact that so many professional football clubs, quite confidently, assert that interest and participation levels in football amongst British Asians is low is just one example of the way in which false assumptions are made of Asian footballers. The other overriding obsession amongst professional football clubs seems to be that Asians generally do not conform to the physical specifications required of professional footballers in England. (Bains and Patel 1996: 57)

The report goes on to highlight a sense that Asian parents have shown a reluctance to adequately support their children's efforts to pursue careers in professional football. However, it also reveals that what lies behind this perceived lack of support is both a lack of understanding and an unfamiliarity with professional football itself. The notion that Asian parents hold sport and football in low esteem when compared to more traditional professions might have been overstated, but there remains a lack of Asian professional coaches and personnel who might help young players break through and overcome this mutual misrecognition. As one of our informants, a lifelong Bolton supporter and Asian community worker, argues:

I mean the old cliché of parents don't want it is just nonsense now. Maybe so ten years ago but now it is nonsense because they would love to have their son play on Deepdale or Old Trafford or whatever . . . I know loads of fathers who would love their sons to play for Liverpool or Man United or whoever, but they just say it is never going to happen, just a dream . . . I mean you go to any park now, any park, anywhere in the country and you will see Asians with a football playing football . . . The talent is there but it is not being utilised, not being tapped by the footballing authorities . . . The assumption is well, cricket is your game, or no you will not make it, you don't like changing in the same changing rooms, probably we will need to get you separate changing rooms, or prayer times will be 8 o'clock while the match is going on and you don't want to eat meat and it will not build you up – things like that are the normal assumptions which the normal typical scouts have, and some of the PE teachers have . . . [Asian youngsters] need a role model in the coaching sense as well as in the playing sense and I think that is where the problem lies. (Interview, 8 May 1997)

There is a sense in which the 'colour blindness' of clubs obscures a deeper cultural-race matrix, which imposes barriers on the basis of perceptions that Asians do not assimilate into normative 'white' English football cultures. As a West Ham official reported to a national newspaper 'You hear about Asian players stopping practice to say their prayers. They're different from us, have a different culture' (*Independent on Sunday*, 17 September 1995: 9). Indeed 50 per cent of the professional football clubs questioned by Bains and Patel (1996) identified cultural differences such as religion, language and diet as reasons for the lack of progression into the professional game. Part of the problem is that there is a degree to which the stereotypes constructed by white football institutions and society more generally are being consumed and internalized within the Asian community itself, despite the obvious talent on display. As Bains and Patel point out:

> Whilst there may be some evidence to suggest a significant proportion of the Asian population are adopting a more enthusiastic approach to sport, whether it be professional or not, even greater proportions of the Asian population, largely those from the more traditional 'working classes' have not yet embraced sport and leisure in the same way as have their middle class counterparts. Asian working class attitudes towards professional sport and towards football in particular demonstrate levels of awareness and understanding that require a course of intervention, rather than allowing for a process of natural evolution. (Bains and Patel 1996: 31)

The football authorities responded to this call by sponsoring the *Asians Can't Play Football* report and organizing a national conference, 'Asians in Football', in 1996, but their perspective continues to place an emphasis on the need for the Asian community to grasp the opportunity to break into the professional game. Some of the most obvious stereotypes have been recognized and rejected but there remains a sense in which it is the responsibility of Asian players to accommodate to the demands and cultural norms of 'white' professional football clubs, rather than football's responsibility to reach out to the Asian community. There are examples of clubs employing Asian scouts and organizing multi-cultural football events, but the continuing lack of confidence is revealed by the comments of Chris Kamara who, whilst manager of Bradford City, said that 'We've employed an Asian scout and have Asian players on trial regularly, but they seem to think they've no chance even before they've kicked a ball' (*Independent*, 1 November 1997).

This categorization of the Asian population and its associated isolation from the implicitly white or, at best, white and black mainstream of English football runs deep within the institutions of the game as Piara Powar of the campaigning group 'Kick it Out' reflected to us:

> [. . .] there are many many clubs that you go to and they talk about the Asian community for example, because, you know, there are parts of the north where, Lancashire and places like Yorkshire where the kind of dominant minority community is the Asian community, so you're sitting there having a conversation with them and, you know, and one of the things I find personally quite offensive is when they start talking about 'them'. You know, its like 'they' [Asians] are the other. (Interview, 26 September 2000)

'Chiefs and Indians': Race, Power and the Absence of Black Managers

The success of a host of black and foreign players has to some extent exploded the extant myths and stereotypes in football but it seems clear to those inside the game that racism still haunts the life chances of those black professionals who desire to move into coaching, management or other sectors of the sport. With one exception, all of the black players to whom we spoke who are trying to make a break into management and coaching described considerable barriers with regard to winning the support of white club chairmen and their respective boards of directors. The fact is that entrance to coaching and management positions in English football remains as much a consequence of 'personal affiliation with clubs and managers' (Houlston 1982) as the possession of formal qualifications, playing ability and experience. In keeping with Edwards' assertion that the assignment of occupational roles in sport is really 'to do with the degree of relative outcome control or leadership responsibilities' (Edwards 1973: 209), prospective black managers have to face preconceptions about their assumed incapacity to manage multi-racial teams even handedly, or cope with the organizational load of football management and its associated responsibilities. One black coach put it:

> People have got this conception of what black people, black players are like and say: 'No, won't be any good in management.' Nobody knows who's gonna be good at anything for sure until they're given the opportunity . . . they give jobs to lots and lots of white players that come, and a lot of them are crap, useless – never get anything, never achieve anything or whatever, you know, and nothing's ever said: 'Oh no', you know – it's just like: 'Oh, he wasn't good enough', and that's it. Nobody says: 'Oh, he's [white], isn't he?' (Interview, 10 December 1996)

He went on to point out that black players who were in the vanguard of change in the 1970s and 1980s and helped force an adjustment of attitudes, are now facing new and masked forms of racial stereotyping as they make the transition into management and coaching:

> I mean I think it's getting better . . . when we [were] all players they saw black players as fine when it's warm and whatever, yeah, they do a great job, but when it got cold, muddy, the boots were flying and one thing and another they wouldn't wanna know. We had to turn around to show them that we could put the stick around and whatever, if need be. And people now accept that most black players, you know, they're exactly the same as the white players, you know, they've got that in them. And you have to be the same over the course of time at management, 'cause the next step people have to learn to know that you can be as tough as you need to be in any given situation, and you can actually get the team to be playing a certain way and get them to understand and all the

bits and pieces that make up being a football coach or manager, people are gonna be aware that you can do that, you know. So it'll take time for that to be accepted . . . and the people that give them the jobs, they're the ones that have to be persuaded and a lot of those are people that for whatever reason they are maybe quite happy to see black players work and play football for them, but don't want them actually in positions of management.

It makes it more, makes it more difficult. The number of letters I've written to people looking for jobs before and they write back and say to you no, you haven't got the experience. Fine – I haven't got the experience as a manager, but I have got almost twenty years' experience as a player. And I've played in all the different countries, I've played all this, done this, done that and that . . . You know, haven't got the experience – you think to yourself: 'Fine, lovely', you can only go on what they say, but you read into things and you think to yourself: 'Is it because? (Interview, 10 December 1996)

Furthermore, just as the racial stereotypes that feature within the perspectives of some school teachers and club scouting networks might encourage the notion that black children have 'natural athletic ability', leading them to divert their energies into sport (see Carrington 1986: 9–10, Hoberman 1997), those same perceptions can work against the transition into leadership and management positions. As Ron Noades suggested, in the same interview in which he had questioned the tactical awareness of black players, they had failed to progress into management because they were not prepared to sign up for coaching courses or attend games for the purpose of studying tactics (*Critical Eye*, 1991).

As a black former England international and Football League coach explained, without being critical of the situation, such expectations are not always evenly applied:

[Kenny] Dalglish, [Bryan] Robson, you'll transcend any, any barriers. And, the FA have directives and say 'Well for you to do . . . a course, you know, to do certain level of coaching you need badges – Dalglish, behave yourself, do a badge! – I mean Robson, shut up – all right, he just transcends all that. Certain players, certain personalities . . . footballer of the year, you don't tell him to go and get a badge. (Interview, 4 December 1996)

Whilst Chris Kamara and Keith Alexander may provide exceptions (although neither currently has a managerial position at a league club), where black managers and coaches have been appointed it has often been associated with the patronage of former colleagues and jobs with a more peripheral status. John Barnes' appointment as manager of Celtic came as a consequence of the appointment of his former Liverpool colleague and manager Kenny Dalglish as Technical Director of football, whilst Luther Blissett only secured his position as Assistant Manager at Watford following the return of his former manager Graham Taylor. Similarly, after a brief period as a manager in his own right, Viv Anderson worked as assistant to his former Manchester United colleague Bryan Robson at Middlesborough.

Noel Blake has recently progressed from the role of assistant to manager at Exeter City, but the employment of others in the 'number 2' role might suggest the emergence of a pattern whereby black people are beginning to transcend the barrier between playing and coaching but where the step into management may be more blocked off. As one of our informants explained:

> If you're [an] 'Indian' there are certain myths, if you're a 'chief' there's certain myths – As a black person – let me just expand myself – as an 'Indian', you ain't got no power, you're just a player, there's certain myths about that – you can't handle the cold weather, no temperament, blah, blah, blah, such and such – as a chief, you got power, certain myths surrounds that – cannot manage, you know – er – that kind of – good players but they can't manage. And you find that – and it's not so much you can't, no, anyway it's not so much you can't manage, in society as a whole, when it comes to getting power, making decisions, different ball game. When you're making decisions, that's power, buying and playing, buying players, letting players loose, that kind – it's a different ball game, it's power now – partly dealing with millions of pounds and people's emotions and that kind of stuff . . .
>
> But you know, you know, as I say, you think well, all these boardrooms are very staid, traditional, you're not even allowed women in there half the time – and all these guys you know, in their fifties, sixties, businessmen – you don't know do you? You can never tell people's hidden agenda can you? . . . it's deep seated, it's power, you're talking a different realm now, you're talking power now, you're talking influence . . .
>
> Coaching, you actually coaching players – it's not a real, not a real power situation – manager that's still the manager . . . er whereas a coach would put in ideas, you're just coaching, you know, it's not there, not there where the real power is. Not where the real influence is. (Interview, 3 September 1997)

Ruud Gullit's management of Chelsea and Newcastle seems to have been something of an exception, both because of his status within the game, which several of our informants suggested almost transcends notions of race, but also because of his status as a 'foreigner' and the current trend towards appointing overseas managers. As the former Leeds United chairman Leslie Silver remarked on the presence of black managers in England:

> Yes, that is an interesting one. Because he [Ruud Gullit] is a Dutchman, people think of him as a Dutchman rather than as a black man. Yes, that is an interesting one. I haven't even thought of him as black, I thought of him as a Dutchman. (Interview, 20 November, 1996)

Conclusion: The Public Management of 'Race Talk'

Given the ways in which discussions of race within the game have been constructed it seems that it is possible to talk about the absence of racism in professional football but not to talk about its presence. This has the effect of silencing open discussion of the issues and reinforcing the cycle of sensationalism and denial. This was reflected in the refusal of three of our four chosen case study clubs to co-operate with our research. Even where partial access was negotiated one of the things we found in conducting interviews, particularly with players, managers and administrators, was the way in which these encounters were affected by the forms of talk associated with news and sports media coverage. Each of the clubs in question, Everton, Manchester City and Millwall have at one time or another faced sensationalized media exposés highlighting problems with racism at their clubs, which has fuelled the adoption of a cautious approach rather than an open dialogue about the issues involved. Accordingly, we frequently encountered highly managed and defensive patterns of informant response, characterized by bland sound bite statements lacking in analytical content and clearly predicated upon a desire to avoid controversy.

Equally, we observed that football in the community schemes serve an important function as a buffer between clubs, the wider community and the issue of racial equality. In our experience enquiries about the issue of racism are invariably referred to the club's 'football in the community' scheme. This is the area of club administration where black employees are most frequently found and contact with local communities is most heavily developed. The football in the community scheme can therefore be heralded as doing progressive work while the inner workings of the football club remain unchallenged and unchanged.

Nevertheless, even where there is a commitment to want to address the issue, questions of political propriety remain paramount and frame the terms of reference. As a former black player who is now involved in both the administrative and media sides of the game explained:

> I can see areas of the Football Association where there are some quite strong views on racism in football which are never articulated and I'm not entirely sure why that is the case. Since I've retired from professional football I've got into the more political/admin side of the game and I'm meeting people who really, who really do run the game and I'm hearing or identifying people who feel very strongly about racism, [who] don't really know what to do about it. They are caught between a rock and a hard place. Do they come out strongly, say what they feel and risk the danger of being seen, or putting themselves in an untenable position by chairmen, by directors, by managers who think that it's a storm in a teacup or overstating the case? (Interview, 21 May 1997)

In the following chapter we consider in more detail the ways in which attempts to address the question of racism in football have been taken up by the game's institutions as well as by its fans and individual players.

'Let's Kick Racism out of Football': Anti-racism and Multiculturalism in English Football

The Arthur Wait Stand, Selhurst Park, 25 January 1995

Crystal Palace are playing Manchester United in the FA Carling Premiership. It is a nippy evening and under the muffled glow of floodlights, the capacity crowd (limited by building work at the Holmesdale Road End) is keeping warm with a degree of passionate support not always so evident at this ground. Evening fixtures often have this effect at Palace, particularly when the game is a big one and they don't get much bigger than confrontations with the league champions Manchester United and their band of global superstars. Those stars were the target of many of the Palace fans' interventions, with one player receiving more attention than most: the gifted French forward, Eric Cantona who had a reputation for being easily provoked. He was also receiving 'close attention' from the Palace centre back Richard Shaw, so much so that in the fifty-seventh minute of the game Cantona kicked out at the player following a clumsy challenge.

Chants of 'off, off, off' quickly enveloped the stadium, interspersed with individual abuse, one fan beside me shouting 'you dirty French bastard' at Cantona. Almost inevitably the referee produced a red card and the crowd erupted, cheers from Palace fans, cries of disbelief and despair from the Manchester United fans to my left. As Cantona made his way from the field his manager Alex Ferguson avoids eye contact, showing no emotion. Cantona turned towards the tunnel, walking alongside the pitch within ear shot of mocking Palace fans in the main stand. It's hard to take everything in from my position in the Arthur Wait stand on the other side of the pitch, but it's clear that Cantona's getting a hard time from those closest to him, whilst all around the ground people are waving and chanting 'cherio, cherio, cherio'. Sensing a reaction, Ferguson dispatched the kit man to escort his player to the dressing room, but he is too late.

Cantona had launched his boot, kung fu style, at a spectator and then seemed to almost levitate for what seemed an age but was in fact only a fraction of a second as he fell prostrate onto an advertising hoarding before regaining his feet and exchanging punches with his tormentor, Palace fan Mathew Simmons. The whole stadium was in a state of absolute shock and momentary disbelief before anger began to erupt, the volume of abuse increasing and improvised missiles projected in Cantona's direction before he disappeared down the tunnel. Manchester United fans stood almost in silence, many with mouths open, as anticipation of the 'official' reaction led to the realization that the team's talisman might not play for the club again.

As we now know, despite the reaction of the British press, Cantona did play for Manchester United again, after serving a 10-month playing ban and a community service order. More significant for our research though was the contribution that Cantona's response to the xenophobic abuse directed at him by Mathew Simmons made to the debate about racism and anti-racism in football. As John Barnes commented at the time of the launch of the 'Let's kick racism – Respect all fans' initiative later that year:

> To be honest with you in the long run, some good may come out of [Cantona's assault] because that really brought it home that because mostly where [racial abuse] is actually done, black players have not responded to it, so people just make light of it because it can't be that bad because nothing has happened. Now he has actually responded to it they have actually seen how important the issue is because until something like that happens people don't realise how important it is because if someone was to call me a black bastard I will laugh it off and walk off and people would say well it is not that important because he hasn't said anything about it . . . but you have also got to look at the person and the person's personality and his character and Eric is a real volatile character and he responded to it. I have not ever done anything like that but I have felt like doing it, but I have not actually done it, so as I say there is an irony that it has actually taken a white Frenchman. (Interview, 28 September 1995)

Before considering how this course of events began to unravel we want to briefly outline the history of the emergence of anti-racist cultures in English football and the frameworks for understanding racism which were associated with them.

'101 Things to Do with a Nazi Skinhead': 'Fanzines' and the Emergence of Anti-racist Fan Cultures

In the mid 1980s, football in England was felt to be in a state of perpetual decline and crisis. The aggregate Football League attendance had fallen from an all-time high of over 41 million in the 1948–9 season to a total of under 16½ million in the 1985–6 season (although it had recovered to a figure of over 25½ million by the 1999/00 season). A number of famous clubs including Chelsea, Middlesborough and Wolverhampton Wanderers were facing bankruptcy. Perhaps most significantly, the 'moral panic' surrounding the issue of football hooliganism had reached its crescendo in the aftermath of three well publicized 'hooligan' incidents during 1985. These events ultimately led to English clubs being banned from European competition and the British Prime Minister, Margaret Thatcher, suggesting that professional football as a whole might be abandoned (Giulianotti 1994).

The popular image of football supporters at this time was of unruly mobs who needed to be herded to and from grounds using 'special' transport arrangements and police escorts before being, quite literally, caged in to 'pens' used to separate rival fans. At one point the Chairman of Chelsea, Ken Bates, even had 'cattle'- style electrified perimeter fencing installed at the club's Stamford Bridge ground before the Greater London Council ordered its removal. In the eyes of the media the label 'hooligan' came to reference a whole section of the 'terrace subculture' (Whannel 1979). In turn, the symbols associated with this label typically invoked an image of young, white, working-class men who were often represented as neo-fascist sympathizing skinheads, despite the redundancy of this stylized form in the midst of 1980s casual culture (Redhead 1991b).

It was in this context that football fanzines, the Football Supporters' Association (FSA) and other informal fan groupings emerged in an apparent attempt to challenge the image and celebrate an alternative identity within football supporter cultures (Williams et al. 1989; Jary, Horne and Bucke 1991; Redhead 1991b; Haynes 1995; Brown 1998). This 'movement' helped to establish a new discourse which emanated from the fans themselves and which asserted a more humorous and critical stance towards their place within the game. One consequence of this was that football fanzines and the FSA offered a forum for the discussion and representation of football fan culture which was, at least rhetorically, opposed to racism. A whole variety of fanzines of both a general and club specific nature, such as *When Skies are Grey* at Everton and *Eagle Eye* at Palace, dealt with racism in the context of broader discussions of the game. More instrumentally, others began to use the fanzine format as an explicitly anti-racist campaigning tool. This approach was exemplified by Leeds Fans United Against Racism and Fascism (LFUARF) whose *Marching Altogther* fanzine was first published in 1987 in response to the presence of neo-Nazi paper sellers at Leeds' Elland Road ground and commonplace racist chanting at matches.

What was interesting about this campaign, and others that have followed, is the way in which the commitment of fans combined with the political/moral force of anti-racist campaigners. These more activist supporter based campaigns, which emerged as much in response to 'hooliganism' as the racism that had been associated with it (Holland et al. 1995), have been related back to populist responses to racism in the 1970s. As Williams has argued, 'a new popular agenda [was] established by football fans in England which, in some ways, mirror[ed] the anti-racist campaigns around music and football of the late 1970s' (Williams 1992: 24). The misrepresentation of football fans during the 1980s contributed to a tremendous desire on the part of many supporters to 'put the record straight' by presenting an alternative, more 'acceptable' face.

In this context supporter campaigns against racism in football became something of a *cause celebre* during the 1990s with club-specific campaigns emerging at Leicester City, Charlton Athletic, West Ham United, Newcastle United and Manchester United alongside the FSAs national *United Colours of Football* campaign. Football supporters were able to use the medium of the fanzine in co-operation with the organizational experience, numbers and commitment of anti-racist activists. In turn, anti-racists found a public platform through which they could confront neo-fascists and a forum for the promotion of their message which supporter activists could tune to the vernacular forms of the local fan culture. However, in order to mobilize support against a readily recognizable foe and win support from the authorities, LFUARF's publication of the dossier *Terror on our Terraces: The National Front, football violence and Leeds United* (Leeds Trades Council 1988), unconsciously, helped to establish the parameters of debate on this question within the confines of the 'racist-hooligan couplet' discussed earlier in this book.

This trend was epitomized by the regular cartoon feature in *Marching Altogether* entitled '101 things to do with a Nazi Skin'. In each issue of the fanzine a cartoon illustration of a stereotypical skinhead was presented alongside a ridiculing suggestion for what to do with him. These included 'No 26: launch a daring, day-light raid on him using your club's disgusting, dead dog PIES', 'No 42: Practice your heading: Nut the bastard', 'No. 47: Administer a sharp kick in the knackers as part of a re-education programme', 'No 56: Drop heavy things onto him, from the top of the new East Stand'. Whilst these cartoons were presented within a broader fanzine format, which included discussion and jokes about a wide variety of issues affecting Leeds United and football in general, the frame of reference for discussion of racism was very much couched in terms of neo-Nazi, skinhead fan cultures.

There is little doubt that the focus of racist activity at Leeds United during the 1980s did warrant greater attention to the more overt forms of racism than is relevant today. However, this model of working was later taken up by other campaigners, both at a club level and through the Football Supporter's Association's *United Colours of Football* campaign which itself included one of these cartoons. Anti-racist campaigners and other political groupings appeal to these popular stereotypes because fears about this kind of racist 'folk demon' allow them to promote and win support for their activities. We would suggest that this is not necessarily a bad rhetorical strategy and indeed one of us was closely involved in the design of the *United Colours of Football* campaign, which took its lead from the Leeds United initiative for precisely these reasons.

Nevertheless, it is important to ask exactly what kind of populist agenda was being set by such initiatives. One of the lessons of the Rock Against Racism movement of the 1980s was that it collapsed anti-racist politics into an opposition to neo-fascist politics. However, the politics of racism extends far beyond the activities of neo-fascist groupings, whose constituency was and remains relatively small. The lessons from the 1980s suggest that focusing purely on the demonic image of the fascist skinhead blinds the anti-racist agenda to the more banal and very ordinary face of racism within everyday life and British institutions.

Conceptualizing the problem in terms that make popular racism total, monolithic and complete, enables a certain degree of comfort amongst white audiences who are able to satisfy themselves that the campaign is not targeted at 'them'. However, white subjects often harbour complex combinations of racism and anti-racism or non-racism that do not fit neatly into this typology. Somehow it is easier for the racist to be constructed as a 'monster' because when he or she is ordinary and complicated, uncomfortable questions are opened up. The consequence is that while the 'racist' constructs minorities in stigmatized ways, so the 'racist' is constructed in the discourses of anti-racism in similar ways. In short, the political imagination of anti-racism resorts to monolithic and absolute constructions of white racism, which merely reinforce the stereotypical dualism that fuels racist agendas.

This focus, in the midst of overwhelming evidence of a reduction in the more overt forms of politically motivated racist activity also contributed to a fascination with the tactics of such groups. Both in terms of the genre of fanzines, which themselves adopt the comic, pseudo tabloid style of quasi-illegal right wing publications (as pioneered during the Punk Rock era and adopted by the National Front publication *Bulldog* in the 1970s) and the organization of anti-racist 'fighting crews', campaigners have shown a willingness to 'mirror' the tactics of their opponents.

A good example of this is *Red Attitude*, a Manchester United football fanzine which adopted an explicitly anti-racist stance and was set up with support from the broader Anti Fascist Action grouping. Issue 4 of this publication from March 1995, shortly after Cantona's assault at Selhurst Park, has a cover picture showing the image of Cantona kicking Mathew Simmons, as shocked fans look on, above the headline 'Alive and Kicking'. Simmons himself is depicted on the back cover of the same publication in a parody of the Nike advertisement which places Manchester United's French star Eric Cantona in front of a Cross of St George and the words '66 was a great year for English football – Eric was born'. In *Red Attitude*'s version, a menacing picture of Mathew Simmons is depicted in front of a swastika with the words '1974 was a terrible year for English football – Simmons was born'.

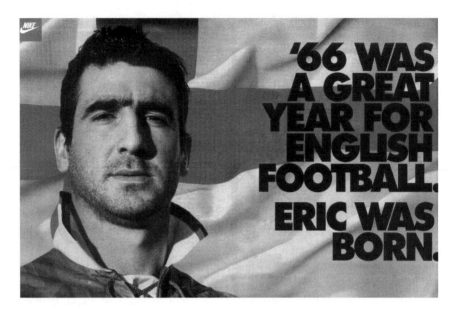

Figure 7.1 Nike's Eric Cantona advertisement.

Figure 7.2 Parody image of Nike advertisement in Manchester United's *Red Attitude* Fanzine.

The intention here is to promote a very particular image of Simmons as a racist football thug. The fanzine's editorial argued that:

> Mathew Simmons . . . undoubtedly deserved what he got. Racist thugs will get no sympathy from this fanzine. Simmons is well-known to anti-fascist activists in London, and has a history of racism and violence. (*Red Attitude*, 1995: 2)

The extent of Simmons' actual current involvement in such activity and Cantona's own knowledge of these associations is not as important as his presentation as a version of the racist-hooligan archetype, which, in turn, allows Cantona's assault to be legitimised as an attack upon a racist thug. Later in the publication the same image of Cantona kicking out is invoked again, in an advert for Anti-Fascist Action (AFA), with the legend 'Beating the Fascists AFA Style'. Elsewhere a cartoon caricature of Cantona depicts the player kicking and smashing a swastika symbol. Another image is offered of a Manchester City supporter lying on the ground clutching a Cross of St George flag, with the caption, 'Man United Anti-Fascists In Action – City BNP Supporter meets Man United Anti-Fascists 28-1-95'. The image of the racist football fan as a thug and a far right activist is thus reinforced, whilst Cantona's attack upon Simmons is presented as a legitimate attack upon racism.

The advantage of representing racism in this way ultimately becomes a constraint. This has implications with regard to the issues of fan ownership and campaigns like 'Let's Kick Racism Out of Football'. For those on the militant left, like Red Action and Anti-Fascist Action, the racist hooligan is a necessary fiction because it can provide justification for their activities and a strange kind of political comfort. The real danger here is that these paramilitary forms of anti-racism do little more than ape their professed foe like an equal mirror opposite. Indeed individuals involved in football violence have been recruited to such groups partly as a result of their ability to provide a forum for confrontation.

This ability was illustrated on the 7 January 1995 when Manchester City supporters drinking in the Clarence pub on Wilmslow Road near City's Maine Road ground were attacked as they attempted to disrupt an Irish Republican march passing by outside. Such tactics are justified on the basis that for those who enjoy violence it is better to use that violence to positive effect. However, this focus on physical confrontation with 'violent racists' can have the effect of further conflating the notion of football violence with organized racist activity and, by extension, opposition to it. The point we want to stress is that anti-racist movements from different points on the political spectrum have remained faithful to the racist-hooligan couplet because of political self-interest. In short, this discourse is useful because it provides a caricature of racism against which practically everyone within the game can rally. In turn, the more banal, casual and ritualized forms of racial abuse, even where challenged, are marginalized from public view and debate, because the more dramatic forms and opposition to them attract attention and the fuel of publicity.

'Fair Play': Institutionalizing the Response to Racism

This point was well illustrated in 1993 when the Commission for Racial Equality (CRE) and the Professional Footballers' Association (PFA) came together to launch the Let's Kick Racism Out of Football campaign. The campaign emerged out of PFA concerns about racial abuse directed at their members and a desire to widen their influence within the game, alongside the CRE's recognition of a high-profile issue around which to highlight a new campaigning approach and more youthful orientation. As the campaign organizer explained:

> The first campaign we did was a football campaign, *Let's Kick Racism Out of Football*, because we looked at the whole area of young people and how to get to them, what medium we could use which would hold a message against racism and for equal opportunity and would also speak very clearly and directly to all people. (Interview with CRE Campaigns Unit, quoted in Carver, Garland and Rowe 1995: 19)

Football then was seen as a medium for changing attitudes in the wider society rather than particularly a problem in itself. In the context of a popular mobilization, the campaign clearly invoked a mode of address that was directed at the fans and general public rather than a call to the football industry to look in on itself. The success or popularity of such a campaign was also dependent upon its ability to secure broad support against a universally identifiable folk demon, the already familiar racist football hooligan. This was made explicit in the CRE's press release that accompanied the campaign launch on 12 August 1993, which declared that:

> Recent press reports reveal that a new generation of football hooligans are around, using the game as a front for a mixture of serious crime and far-right politics. This can obviously involve leafleting racist materials at matches and spreading racial hatred. (CRE 1993)

The result was a publicity-driven campaign, focusing almost exclusively on the racial abuse of players by fans, which further reinforced the image of racism in football as being the product of demonic racist thugs. The effectiveness of this approach as a populist strategy should not be underestimated. The campaign, through national and regional launches and now with its own dedicated campaign team, attracted enormous media interest and support. Indeed the very fact that the Advisory Group Against Racism and Intimidation (AGARI), which emerged out of the CRE-PFA campaign, ever existed is testimony to this success. It was the focus of the campaign around the common opposition to a universally identifiable pariah 'out-group' that helped to bring football's various interests together in such unprecedented fashion. Eventually all of football's governing and representative bodies became involved in the campaign whilst all bar one of the 92 professional clubs in England signed up in support. Similarly, the relaunch of the campaign in 1995 achieved high levels of media coverage and public awareness (Back, Crabbe and Solomos 1996). Perhaps more significantly, as our research has revealed, the expression of overt racism in football grounds has remained at relatively low levels.

There is however also a need to recognise that there was still widespread resistance within the game to the idea that a campaign was needed. In the last chapter we illustrated how 'denial' is a consistent theme within the football industry when it comes to discussion of the presence of racism, which has been reinforced by the PR implications of recognizing a problem and an ingrained hostility towards influences from outside football in general. Whilst making its opposition to racism clear in a general sense, until recently, the FA has not sought to define the problem or to take a proactive stance towards challenging its manifestations within the game. From its inception the FA gave its tacit approval to the CRE-PFA Let's Kick Racism Out of Football campaign, but this support initially had little substance and seemed to be driven by a rather defensive public relations imperative rather than any understanding of or commitment to the issues at stake. The question of racism in the game appeared to be regarded as something of a non-issue or secondary and external issue. However, the situation shifted as a result of a number of developments that helped to shape the FA's response from 1995 onwards.

Significantly, at the annual launch of the campaign at the start of the 1994–5 season, the FA's newly appointed Director of Public Relations, David Davies, was present, and when asked about the organization's commitment to the initiative gave an indication that he would be seeking to strengthen the FA's involvement. Over the course of the following season two incidents occurred that encouraged the FA to get behind Davies' assurances. The first of these was Cantona's assault on Matthew Simmons whilst the second came later that year when a friendly international match between the Republic of Ireland and England at Lansdowne Road, Dublin was aborted after 30 minutes following crowd disturbances apparently instigated by England supporters.

In each of these cases, unprecedented and near hysterical media coverage quickly focused on relationships between the supporters involved and the activities of the far right. Matthew Simmons was portrayed as a thug with convictions for assault and an association with the British National Party, whilst the disturbances in Dublin were widely attributed to agitation by the far-right activist grouping Combat 18, the *Daily Mirror* declaring 'Football Fuhrers-Combat 18 Nazi army plotted war' (17 February 1995). The validity of these assertions is not what is at stake here. Rather what is important is that in the aftermath of these incidents the

FA moved quickly to occupy a much more central position in the campaign against racism in football and became instrumental in the establishment of the football wide Advisory Group Against Racism and Intimidation (AGARI).

The FA's concern with the issue became driven by a more fundamental desire to prevent forms of fan behaviour that were seen as highly media sensitive and damaging to the game's public image. The consequence of this was that the FA's agenda was driven by an interpretation of racism as a product of fan cultures and, more particularly, 'hooligan' or unruly neo-Nazi fans. This was reflected in the AGARI's own focus on 'racism and intimidation', which implicitly defined the problem in terms of 'anti-social' fan behaviour.

In this context, racism in the game becomes understood in very narrow terms that do not readily allow for an analysis of or challenge to racism within the institutional structures of the game. Furthermore, the definition of racism in these terms provides an additional incentive to avoid such an analysis, because to accept the notion that racism plays a part within the administrative structures of the game would be to draw parallels with the behaviour of the racist-hooligan fan pariahs. It is interesting in this context that the more recent recognition of the validity of these issues has been associated with a lowering of the profile of the campaign and the creation of a quasi autonomous campaign unit under the banner Kick it Out, which we discuss further below.

We should point out that it is not our intention to dismiss the achievements of the campaign; rather, we wish to help move the debate beyond the all too easy archetypes, be they images of racist thugs or the assumptions made about the 'culture' of south Asian communities as a means of explaining their absence from the game. One of the most difficult things about the current terms of reference within football institutions is a kind of 'out-thereism'. Racist thugs are 'out there', merely attaching themselves to the game whilst south Asian young men don't get interested in football because of the cultural aspirations and expectations that are 'out there' in those communities. We want to try to think critically about these conceptions and the issues this raises in relation to establishing and maintaining policy alliances.

'Sit Down and Shut Up': The Limitations of the Moral Approach to Anti-racism

Under the auspices of the AGARI, the campaign was increasingly driven by PR concerns that did not always fit with the needs of the situation. The problem of racism was now identified alongside broader concerns with intimidatory behaviour under the campaign banners Respect All Fans and Let's Kick Racism which were launched at a high-profile, well-attended press conference involving all of the AGARI representatives at Wembley Stadium on 28 September 1995.

As David Davies stated, the existence of the AGARI and the presence of AGARI members at the campaign launch marked a unique moment in the development of football in that all of the interested parties within the game were brought together under one banner. The breadth of the campaign was also illustrated by the extraordinary degree of support from highly prominent players and personalities, including Ruud Gullit, Tony Adams, John Barnes and Gary Lineker. Some of these people were speaking out for the first time on the issue of racism and their presence clearly added weight and a high profile to the campaign that was illustrated in the press coverage that followed.

However, whilst the launch attracted much publicity and raised awareness of the campaign, its impact may well have been weakened by the combination of, on the one hand, a strong message of anti-racist intent with, on the other, a whole series of comments from players and officials that there had been an improvement in the experience of black players and a general lowering in the level and intensity of racist activity. An onlooker could be left wondering why a campaign is necessary if this is true.

Whilst, on the ground, our observational work conducted as part of an evaluation of the campaign (Back, Crabbe and Solomos 1996) highlighted the football-wide support for the initiative and sympathy for its message amongst large sections of fans, it also revealed that anti-racist messages from the campaign were not always clearly communicated to supporters. One example that emerged in the context of a regional launch of the campaign at a Football League club on match day illustrates the point well.

Prior to the players taking to the field the campaign was announced on the stadium's public address system. Two stewards wearing white coats brought the campaign banner onto the pitch and displayed it to each of the four stands. The stewards then paraded the banner around the ground in front of the supporters' seating areas. As the stewards passed the areas where the home supporters were sitting applause was audible. However, when the banner reached the away supporters' areas the fans sang a loud chorus of 'You can stick your fucking banner up your arse.' There was also isolated use of racial epithets and monkey chanting.

For some of the away fans the campaign launch allowed a context to counter its anti-racist ethos and to indulge their racism. For others it seemed that their rejection of the campaign was bound up in a more general opposition to the home club and its supporters. In this groups' minds it was 'their' banner and not to do with 'us'. One supporter summed this up by shouting 'Who the fuck do you think you are telling us what to think.' The away fans felt in large part that they were being singled out. Few had any understanding that this was a national initiative. The result was that the campaign launch created an atmosphere of resentment amongst the away supporters leading some to further indulge in the harassment of black players in the home team. The lesson of this incident is that it is important to appreciate the culture of football supporters. Here the issue is about ownership. In the aftermath of the match the incident was discussed with a high ranking police officer with long experience of the away fans in question. He replied:

> If the home team is seen to take any banner 'round the ground then the [away] fans are going to give them stick. They should have seen this coming. If you'd have presented this scenario to me I could have told you exactly what the response would have been. What they should have done was get both teams – the players – to take the banner around. This would have said to everyone in the ground that this is about and for 'US'. Supporters aren't going to boo their own players before a game – they might well after ninety minutes. But seriously, you need to be aware of what is going on between groups of opposing fans in situations like this. (Interview, 5 February 1996)

In order for the campaign's message to be embraced it is important to anticipate the relationships and ritual antagonisms that exist between football supporters in the context of football grounds. Here, overtly racist supporters were given license to practice further racism precisely because the launch of the campaign was rejected by the away fans collectively. Had the players of the away team been seen subscribing to the campaign then it is likely that the ensuing racist activity would have been pre-empted.

Part of the problem here was the campaign's focus on a broader range of 'intimidatory' supporter behaviour. The scope of the campaign's agenda was outlined in a press release at the national launch:

> The campaign under the joint themes of 'Respect ALL Fans' and 'Let's Kick Racism' – brings together players, managers, supporters, the football authorities and all those who care about the game in an effort to make our football stadia more welcoming places for whatever age, sex, colour or creed . . . It recognises that, nine months before Euro 96, when the eyes of the football world will be watching our game with ever increasing intensity, anti-social behaviour, not least racism, cannot be tolerated. Nor can foul language that too often intimidates others and spoils the enjoyment of the vast majority of supporters. (AGARI Press Release 1995)

This process was related to the campaign's need to secure across-the-board support from the football establishment in a context where there was in fact deep scepticism from a number of quarters. Players are understandably wary of discussing or raising objections to the behaviour of other professionals and in an era of growing media and commercial sensitivities find it easier to address the issues in terms of general supporter behaviour. For individual clubs the issue of racism has similarly been dealt with as a problem that remains largely beyond their control in the fan cultures which surround them. On the whole attempts to address the issue are separated from the mainstream organization and taken up by Football in the Community Schemes which often act as a kind of buffer between the clubs' top brass and concern with social issues. In this context a club can be seen to be making the 'right kind of noises' about a politically sensitive issue whilst racial stereotypes and assumptions continue to be pervasive within the inner workings of the club.

The Football League was particularly hostile, as was indicated by the fact that the York City Chairman, Douglas Craig, a highly prominent critic of the campaign, was sent as their representative to an AGARI meeting discussing its future direction. The League's interpretation of racism as an extension of 'anti-social' and 'intimidatory' fan behaviour meant that their involvement was dependent upon the campaign having a broader focus which, in turn, rooted the understanding of racism in the game even more strongly in the context of unruly fan behaviour. This reading was made even more explicit by Barry Norman, a senior officer with the Metropolitan Police who suggested at a meeting of the AGARI in October 1995 that whilst 'we've taken the fan out of the terrace, now we've got to take the terrace out of the fan' (Fieldnotes, 16 October 1995). Essentially racism was seen as an element of 'old-style' terrace culture and whilst the move to all-seater stadiums in the wake of the Hillsborough disaster had made grounds easier to control, the fans that used to inhabit them were seen to carry with them vestiges of stereotypical fan behaviour from the 1980s. The racist fan was seen merely as an exemplar of a more generalized notion of 'terrace thuggery'.

This perspective was not formally expressed by the FA or football's Premiership power brokers, for an increasingly commodified football industry these assumptions were supportive of their own project to generate new officially sanctioned, generalized and less transgressive patterns of supporter behaviour. Just as McDonalds was established as the Premiership's 'official match day restaurant' the rationalization process associated with Ritzer's notion of McDonaldization (Ritzer 1998) could be seen all too clearly inside the nation's football stadia. Efforts have been made to ensure that supporters are more orderly and remain in their seats, experiments have been made with separate 'singing ends' and official 'club bands' and drummers have been introduced to 'lead songs'. Powerful, loud PA systems have been incorporated into new stadium designs which drown out the efforts of fans to build up their own more unpredictable atmosphere in competition with rival supporters. Choreographed card displays have replaced the spontaneous raising of club banners and scarves. Whilst Disney-style club mascots parade the pitch, armies of stewards patrol the stands, guided by Panopticon CCTV in a sophisticated surveillance operation. The ejection of supporters involved in racial abuse is enabled by ground regulations that often locate the problem within a broader set of prescribed behaviour, such that typically 'obscene, abusive or racial language, gestures or behaviour is strictly prohibited'.

These rules enable the club to remove people from the ground, often with the assistance of the police, although in such cases the police are acting as agents of the club and have less protection in law. Accordingly, this task is increasingly allocated to stewards whose authority may well be less respected by the fans being ejected and may well incite opposition from other fans. In some instances this 'packaging' of the campaign message has resulted in its rejection on the basis of its association with attempts to redefine the nature of football fan culture, which has been resisted by a broad spectrum of supporters. The strength of these sentiments was illustrated by one of our informants, an Asian Bolton supporter, Mohammed Atcha, who grew up watching football in the 1970s and 1980s and was subjected to a series of racial insults and attacks during his attendance at matches. Despite these incidents and his own personal involvement in campaigns against racism in football Mohammed indicated that he would prefer to watch football in the charged atmosphere of that era along with the racial abuse than in the more sanitized environment of the 1990s (Interview, 8 May 1997).

Where concerns about the sanitization of stadia and regulation of fans' behaviour are prevalent, attempts to impose further external controls on fan racism can all too easily be read as part of a perceived strategy to change the match day atmosphere. Where supporters are being ejected for a number of reasons it is often not possible for neighbouring fans to assess the legitimacy of one case from another and a siege mentality can emerge where fans will defend their collective right to support their team as they see fit. Indeed one fans' group *Libero!* sees legislative restrictions on racist fan behaviour as 'a justification for eroding the civil liberties of football fans' (Brick and Allirajah 1997: 10). Perversely, whilst many fans sharing this position may be opposed to racial abuse it is precisely in these circumstances that a renewed licence can be given to engage in such behaviour. As a 'controlled' activity, racial abuse becomes another means of testing the authorities' capacity to control the fan collective, whilst the fan's own siege mentality protects those engaging in racial abuse from the informal controls of their peers. This is particularly the case where those fans involved in racial abuse do not fit with the 'racist-fan' identikit and are regarded by their peers as 'ordinary fans' or 'good blokes'.

The chief limitation of this type of approach is that it simply reduces all the issues of racial injustice within sport to an examination of the moral rectitude of the game's loyal fans. The definition of racism as a problem which sits outside the mainstream of the game and which 'everyone opposes', allows the more banal forms of racism and prejudice to be brushed under the carpet and ignored. Those fans who engage in expressive, ritualized forms of behaviour involving racial abuse and more casual, racialized comments are able to define themselves as being *against* racism in football. 'I'm not racist, I'm only winding him up. It's just the same if he's got a bald head or he's fat' or 'Well he *is* black isn't he, if a player's fat I'll call him a fat bastard, if he's black I'll call him a black bastard.' These kinds of rationalizations can be justified, because the 'racist fan' is seen as a fully paid up member of a neo-Nazi organization with skinhead and 'bovver' boots. This point was illustrated by the *Express* newspaper 'Kick Out the Scum' campaign in 1997, which included a series of articles about racism in football presented alongside the image of a threatening skinhead who was photographed during the disturbances at Lansdowne Road in 1995.

While the Let's Kick Racism Out of Football campaign raised some issues with regard to racism in the game it excluded others to the extent that the nature of the public debate about racism in football became part of the problem itself. Perhaps this is why so much energy has been generated against fan racism in a period where those forms of abuse seem to be in dramatic decline, since it is easier to continue worshipping our footballing heroes through vilification of the 'racist football thug' than to examine the complex forms of institutional inequality and patterns of response that exist inside the game itself.

'Banners and Petitions': Pressure Groups, Politics and the PR Imperative

One product of the attention that the Let's Kick Racism Out of Football initiative brought to this topic was the proliferation of work within organizations operating at a grassroots level, superficially free from the constraints of the football institutions. A mixture of community initiatives, supporter groups, left-wing campaigners and arts groups have taken up the issue to pursue a variety of ends. However, whilst these campaigns have often adopted a more sophisticated approach and greater continuity in their work they have also largely relied upon narrow definitions and avoided the question of institutional racism both as a consequence of funding requirements and the uniform representation of the problem by commentators.

The dilemma facing those who wish to organize campaigns is how to play down the extent of the problem, for fear of generating a sensational backlash or alienating sponsors, whilst conceding the presence of racism in order to justify the activity and receive positive PR. One of the most active independent organizations working in this field is the ARC Theatre Ensemble who have produced a trilogy of anti-racist educational theatre productions based on narratives dealing with the issue of racism in football (see Back, Crabbe and Solomos 1996, 2001). Despite the success of these plays, the sponsorship of Midland Bank/HSBC and the flexibility of the producers, the FA would not support the plan to take the play on the road to France during the 1998 World Cup because it was felt that ARC were not presenting the best image of English football. In the context of the FA's heavy investment in the effort to bring the 2006 World Cup to England it was public image rather than the need to address a social problem that took precedence. Similarly, the world governing body, FIFA, has only addressed the issue as an extension of its 'Fair Play' initiative, which is again concerned with the full range of intimidatory and 'unsporting' behaviour. As one FIFA official told us, the organization is 'scared of the 'R' word' (Fieldnotes, 3 September 1997) for fear of alienating potential sponsors and drawing attention to sensitive issues.

This difficulty is further complicated by the attentions of publicity-conscious political machinery that is attracted by the media's interest in football. Politicians seeking to associate themselves with the game require a political hook on which to hang their banner, which the issue of racism can provide. Whilst politicians cannot go too far in terms of interfering with the running of the game, they can declare their opposition to a perceived straightforward 'social ill'. The Football Task Force, a succession of photo opportunities, legislation, alliances between the FA and the National Union of Teachers and the 'Tackling Racism in Football Across Europe' conference, organised by the European Parliamentary Labour Party, are all testament to the political interest in this theme.

One consequence of this political interest is that the boundaries of debate can be further restricted. Within a PR driven framework political capital might only be perceived to be available where politicians are seen to be reflecting in the glamour of a harmonious association with football and its stars. To ask difficult questions and point the finger at those self same sporting icons would run the risk of alienating the football supporting electorate that politicians are attempting to court. Consequently, until now, political interventions around this issue have tended to remain largely at the level of cliché and generality, whilst football clubs themselves continue to play down the problem and maintain a carefully managed public opposition to popular notions of racism in the game.

Following a manifesto commitment, in July 1997 the government established a Football Task Force (FTF) under the Chairmanship of David Mellor, in order to address 'a series of key issues and make practical and balanced recommendations to the Government' (FTF 1998: 6). The Task Force brought together once again the various 'stakeholders' within English football, including administrators, supporters, players, academics and other interested parties. Amongst other things, the terms of reference laid out by the Secretary of State specifically stated that the Task Force should 'consider, and make recommendations on, appropriate measures to: eliminate racism in football and encourage wider participation by ethnic minorities, both in playing and spectating' (FTF 1998: 49).

With a brief that also included issues as wide ranging as disabled access, supporter involvement in the running of clubs, ticketing and merchandising policies, players' behaviour and the consequences of stock market flotations it was interesting that racism was chosen as the first area of enquiry. David Mellor explained this to us by arguing that:

We're gonna' start on racism because it is important and also it will allow the task force to work together. No one's in favour of racism, most people want to do something about it. It's also an area where we can show that we have an ability not just to deal with sound bites but to get into the substance of it. (Interview, 2 September 1997)

This was seen to be in contrast to the other issues where there was a perception that vested interests would create more insurmountable conflicts. Whilst this may have, to some extent, been an accurate assessment (see Brown 1999) it was clear that any such agreement would necessarily dictate a continuing narrow and uncomplicated definition of the nature of racism in football, which did not ask too many questions about the institutional problems discussed in the previous chapter.

David Mellor was undoubtedly genuine in his desire to tackle the issue but whilst the investigation that followed did not take the issue lightly, consulting across the spectrum of elite to grassroots football, players and fans representatives, security firms, anti-racist groups, community schemes, local authorities, academics (including ourselves) and schools, there was still a clear perception that the problem was in some way, 'out there'. In our representations to the Football Task Force there was an almost open hostility from some quarters towards the notion of broadening the conceptualization of racism in football.

The final report to the Minister for Sport does state that 'Racism in football extends beyond the terraces. The commitment to tackle it must cover parks, pitches, clubhouses and committee rooms all over the country and the boot-rooms and boardrooms of professional clubs' (FTF 1998: 13). However, the report's recommendations do not reflect the balance of this statement. Whilst proposed initiatives do move beyond an exclusive focus on the behaviour of supporters, the 'new racists' are primarily identified as being amongst football players, particularly those playing at the grassroots level who are by implication also the professional game's fans.

The recommendations aimed at football's institutions have the feel, in the context of our observations, of rhetorical gestures. Mirroring elements of the Let's Kick Racism Out of Football campaign's 10 point plan, there is a call for a 'comprehensive written equal opportunities policy to cover the recruitment and treatment of all staff' and a statement that the FA should 'ensure that the FA Council – and county FA councils – are more representative of the game and of the communities they serve' (FTF 1998: 5). Whilst laudable these recommendations do not carry the degree of specificity associated with other aspects of the report and have little meaning in a context where football's institutions do not recognize the exclusive practices prevalent within them. The report ignores the ways in which the cultural and structural forms of football's institutions create a world in which whiteness is 'normalized' whereas a variety of forms of 'otherness' retain a problematized quality. Within this framework racism continues to be defined in monolithic terms in line with previous political interventions.

'Into the Mouth of the Lion': Police, the Law and the Demonisation of the Racist

It was in the period of transition following the publication of Lord Justice Taylor's report into the Hillsborough stadium disaster that specific legislation on the question of racism in football was first placed on the statute book. The inclusion of a specific offence of racial chanting in the 1991 Football Offences Act seemed to reflect a general political desire to 'clean up the game' and to be seen to be doing something positive. Whilst the football institutions were charged with the task of addressing the question of stadia construction and management, racism was placed alongside 'hooliganism' as a supporter problem to be dealt with through arrests and conviction. In a context where racism in football was defined in such a narrow fashion it was inevitable that legislative interventions would be similarly constructed.

Section 3 of the Football Offences Act originally stated that 'It is an offence to take part at a designated football match in chanting of an indecent or racialist nature' where 'chanting' means the repeated uttering of any words or sounds in concert with one or more others. This legislation was drawn up on a model of racism in football which was more applicable in the 1970s and 1980s. It is now extremely rare to find supporters engaging in group racialised chanting of the type that was common in that period. Chants such as 'Zigger, zigger, zigger shoot that nigger' and widespread monkey chanting have largely disappeared from the stands (at least in England). Furthermore, such is the complexity of the situation that many of today's chants sung in adulation of black players can embrace similar vocal sounds, such as 'Kan-u, Kan-u, Kan-u', 'Who let the Goat out? Ooh, ooh ooh ooh' or, when chanted, 'Bruce, Bruce, Bruce Dyer' as the monkey chant. Indeed the CPS threw out a proposed prosecution of Millwall supporters alleged to have been involved in monkey chanting since they felt that there was little point in proceeding given that 'any solicitor worth his salt would show that this was a non discursive form of racial abuse' which could equally represent a positive show of support. The legal framework simply isn't subtle enough to be able to interpret this particular style of racism.

The legislation has recently been amended and now enables prosecution of fans engaging in individual insults although it is interesting that this change was introduced and presented as an element of a package of measures designed to provide the police with even greater powers for dealing with football related violence. The framing of legislative interventions towards the issue around questions of public order and the wording of the Football Offences Act ensures then that police responses will also inevitably be targeted at fan communities.

Police concerns with football have historically been associated with questions of public order. Accordingly, the generation of sophisticated intelligence gathering systems in order to challenge 'football hooliganism' have contributed to an emphasis on 'racist-hooligans' and neo-Nazi activity in relation to the question of racism in the game. In the absence of a reappraisal of policing priorities and strategies at football matches it is these forms of activity that the police are best equipped to counter. Since the problem has also been constructed in the public imagination in this way it is inevitable that the police will seek to respond to the more dramatic forms of racial practice. Media scare stories about the prospect of neo-Nazi inspired disturbances amongst rival fans during Euro 96 were commonplace in both the tabloid and broadsheet press and, despite the inaccuracy of these claims, in this context there is political pressure on the police to be seen to be doing something.

Equally there is a degree of self interest to be protected in terms of the need to justify the maintenance of the sophisticated surveillance apparatus established in response to concerns about 'football hooliganism'. The targeting of a universally identifiable public menace of this type, however thin on the ground, will also be seen as a legitimate response to the problem whilst the arrest of Peter Schmeichel on suspicion of racially abusing Ian Wright would be seen as inflammatory, highly inappropriate and even beyond the police's jurisdiction. One Football Intelligence Officer told us that whilst a young racially abusive and aggressive fan might be arrested or at least ejected he would probably just have a warning word in the ear of an older fan making racist remarks. At one level this might seem like common sense policing but in the context of dealing with racism in football it is clear that such a strategy involves the invocation of a broader set of assumptions about who is the more acceptable football fan. The individual becomes more important that the deed.

The difficulties associated with this approach might be illustrated by reference to the case of Kevin Ryan first discussed in Chapter 4. Ryan was captured on video tape exhibiting extreme forms of racist abuse. At the time of his trial he was 40 years old and a committed Millwall fan. He was arrested on 26 April 1997 under section 3 (1) of the Football Offences Act for chanting of an indecent or racist nature. He was given a five-year ban, a £150 fine and £30 costs although, he never served the full length of his ban. The arrest was secured through sophisticated video surveillance of Millwall fans with an officer sitting in the crowd acting as a human microphone. It was the culmination of a season long initiative conducted by Lewisham police using technology previously applied to anti-terrorist work. We had been involved in discussions with the police regarding this initiative from its very beginning as part of our wider commitment to make inputs from our research into the policy sphere.

Ryan was caught on camera abusing Iffy Onuora after he'd scored Gillingham's second goal in a match at the New Den and done 'press ups' in front of the South Stand as an after goal celebration. At the trial the evidence was read out by the prosecution:

During a fixture between Millwall and Gillingham on 26 April 1997 he was recorded using racial abuse . . . during a fifteen minute period the accused was recorded on video equipment shouting *'nigger nigger nigger'* and, against the opposing fans, shouting *'gippos and pykes'*, and during one period of the game the defendant was also recorded singing to the tune 'There is only one Tony Witter', the black Millwall footballer, *'There is only one Tony Nigger, there is only one Tony Nigger, there is only one Tony Nigger'*. This again was being directed at one of Milwall's own players, the black player Tony Witter. Also, later on in the game, the defendant was recorded shouting at an opposition Gillingham player *'you black cunt, you black cunt, you black cunt'*. (Fieldnotes, 3 June 1997)

Ryan produced a mitigating statement. However, the Magistrate was unambiguous, declaring that 'I must say to you that I am not in the slightest bit impressed by this statement – you are not fit to attend any football club or any football game, even at Millwall'. Ryan then interrupted the Magistrate and said 'I don't know what you mean by *even* Millwall'. Magistrate Phillips then raised his voice and became very angry stating 'I am the Magistrate who has the misfortune of seeing many people like you, so called football fans from Millwall, I also know what goes on at Millwar.' Then correcting himself Magistrate Phillips said 'Millwall – I know exactly what happens in that club, in the ground and what happens in the streets outside the football ground – I am sick and tired of seeing people like you come in front of me' – his voice had now been raised to almost a shout – 'If I had the power to send you to prison I would, and I would have absolutely no qualms about doing so. I am afraid until society gives me that power I have to settle for what in my view is a very lenient penalty and I shall be banning you from seeing any football games – I am going to ban you for five years and fine you £150. Because of your unemployed status this fine is the maximum that I can give but let me tell you if you ignore this ban then you will go straight to prison and if you come in front of me and this court again, you will not be leaving out of the front door, you will be leaving out of the back door into the prison cells. I hope you never have to suffer the abuse that you have perpetrated against black people, and I say again, if I had the power to send you to prison I would. It is only in my view a pity that I don't', to which Ryan said 'I know I have done wrong and it won't happen again' (Fieldnotes, 3 June 1997).

Whilst Ryan's behaviour, caught vividly by the audio-visual equipment, was indeed shocking, he is more complex than just a 'racist thug'. As we showed in Chapter 4 he has a close black friend and pictures of Tony Witter, one of the players he was caught abusing, adorn the wall of his front room. This seems to suggest that there is something about the ritual setting of football at particular places and times that provides the launch pad for particular styles of racism. What concerns us is that these nuances are missed by political movements against racism, which have to construct an opponent and an image of what a racist looks like. The consequence is that in the eyes of the public and certainly the legislative and judicial authorities, the racist looks like Ryan who can be demonized as a 'so called football fan from Millwall'. As Ryan himself remarked, within this framework other forms of racism can escape such outrage:

> I was colour prejudiced against him because he scored against us. I don't know him personally, so I can't say he was a nice man or a nasty bit of work. You know, I don't know him. But it's all right for Peter Schmeichel to call Ian Wright a black cunt. That's allowed 'cos he's a professional footballer. He's allowed to do that. He doesn't get banned. He didn't even get nicked, let alone get banned. Wasn't in the public interest or whatever, you know, the Public Prosecutor didn't want to do it. But they nick a paying fan who you know, is just showing emotion basically. Slaughtered me, a five year ban. I can't believe it. (Interview, 23 June 1997)

We are not suggesting that people involved in such cases are in any way victims of the criminal justice system, but clearly the zeal with which this form of fan racism is pursued needs also to be applied to other forms of racism. It is telling that no action was ever mooted with regard to the evident racial abuse occurring on the pitch, to which Ryan refers. One wonders what would have happened if Peter Schmeichel had been standing in the New Den's South Stand when he vented his anger at Ian Wright.

A consequence of the surveillance campaign at Millwall is that it is now widely believed amongst the fans that the stands are 'bugged.' The origin of this rumour was an article that appeared in London's *Evening Standard* newspaper. Beneath the headline 'High-tech Watch on Soccer's Racists' it reported: officers at Millwall decide which fans to target before matches and then place tiny microphones near their seats to record everything they say. They also film them on video cameras' (*Evening Standard*, 6 October 1997). In a classic echo of Foucault's interpretation of panoptical surveillance mechanisms (Foucault 1977) the police have been happy for this urban myth to proliferate as they say it contributes to an atmosphere of caution and restraint. But there remain questions if this is the best way to foster an atmosphere of inclusiveness, there are many who feel resentful of what they see as police spying.

Yet, in terms of arrests and prosecutions, this operation has been the most successful law enforcement operation to be conducted in football. There is a 100 per cent prosecution rate and in the three years following the first prosecution there were twenty one arrests for racist abuse. These figures are particularly striking when one remembers that in 1991 just six prosecutions and five convictions for racist chanting occurred in the whole of England and Wales. In addition to Ryan's prosecution, five Millwall fans were prosecuted for racist chanting at a fixture against Manchester City on 29 September 1998 and were given nine-month exclusion orders and fines of £200 each. Since the amendment of the Football

Offences Act, which now makes individual racist chanting an offence, there have been thirteen further cases.

'The Cult of Doing it': Corporate Multiculturalism and Football

Away from the interventions of the law and more formal campaigning groups, increasingly, corporate sponsors of the game have sought to raise the issue of racism as part of their marketing strategies, in the context of their recognition of a 'multi-cultural reality'. Whilst these associations have adopted a number of forms ranging from Snickers sponsorship of the FIFA Fair Play initiative to Nike's more provocative invocation of the 'Cantona incident' in a television commercial, interestingly it is also these interventions whose message has most readily been synthesized into football fan culture and mobilized the support of players.

What is interesting is that it was at the very time when municipal anti-racism began to lose its nerve in the wake of critiques offered by Paul Gilroy (1987), which questioned the degree to which such initiatives operated within spurious notions of absolute cultural difference, that corporate global service industries embraced versions of multiculturalism as exemplified by Coca Cola and Benetton (see Back and Quaade 1993). Today internationalism and the breaching of national borders seems to be one of the unifying motifs of the capitalist imagination and with sport perhaps representing the biggest contemporary form of global popular culture, sports manufacturers have fully embraced this development. In this context the brand name and its associations becomes everything: 'Mechandising is as much about symbols as about goods and sells not life's necessities but *life's styles*' (Barber 1996: 60).

One such brand name, which has sought to locate questions about race and nation within its global marketing strategies, both at the level of the corporate imagination and the funding of interventions, is Nike. Nike's success has been an extraordinary one. It was only founded in 1972 and has gone from an obscure Oregon-based shoe company dependent on the aerobics market to a global corporate power that captured a $4 billion share of the American market. Nike has really achieved its success not by selling shoes but by cultivating a trademark brand quality that depends on lifestyle choices and the images associated with them. Sport, not shoes, is the key to success. The trick here is to make those who watch football believe that in wearing Nikes they are players too, even if they never get out of their arm chair or at the very least pull on the Nikes for a friendly game of five-a-side. The crucial factor is the ways in which companies like Nike attempt to attach an emotional tie between their customers and the product through its association with sporting icons. Donald Katz who has written a superb history of Nike comments: 'People don't concentrate their emotional energies on products in the way fans abandon themselves to the heroes of their games' (Katz 1994: 6).

The point was emphasized during the 1998 World Cup finals where the football tournament appeared to be played out alongside a corporate battle between Nike and Adidas as represented through the images of Brazil's Ronaldo and France's Zinedine Zidane. The national heroes of yesteryear, personified through emblematic figures like John Bull and Andy Capp, are thus replaced with an international legion of superhuman sporting figures.

The dependence on this notion of heroism is compelling within Nike advertising and, in the context of our research, particularly in relation to representations of Eric Cantona. In many ways the emergence of Cantona in the 1990s was emblematic of a key shift in the English game. Cantona himself seemed in some senses to almost personify the revitalization of the game in England. Nike, the player's sponsor, were keen to cash in on this. Reflecting on the launch of an advertisement that depicted Cantona in front of an English Cross of St George flag with the legend – '66 was a great year for English football – Eric was born' shown on page 190, the company's UK Advertising Manager at the time, Tony Hill recalled that:

Two seasons prior to [Eric Cantona coming to Leeds] people were in despair with the Premier League basically, crowds were down, the football was poor, we weren't doing well internationally, you know everybody was saying 'What are we going to do?' Eric Cantona basically set the torch going a bit at Leeds but then when he moved to Manchester United the playing opportunity of that team had basically ignited the spark and other teams had followed on, I mean Newcastle, Liverpool have improved and basically that resulted in a general lift, so he had in many respects, improved the English game. The English game's highest point is still the '66 World Cup, Eric was born then so why not sort of have a little bit of a jibe – that it's taken a Frenchman to improve the lot of the English game. (Interview, 3 May 1995)

Similarly, in the US, Nike's fortunes had in many ways been mirrored by the ascendancy of Michael Jordan, whilst the company also signed a plethora of athletes to endorse its products who are 'of both sexes; black and white, from several nations, and represent 'the good', 'the bad' and 'the ugly' (McKay 1995: 195). In the context of English football Nike had focused particularly on controversial figures such as Cantona and Ian Wright. However, on 25 January 1995 Cantona surpassed all his and others' previous episodes of sporting controversy when he jumped into the crowd and assaulted Mathew Simmons at Selhurst Park. However, despite initial public condemnation of the player there was a high degree of moral ambiguity surrounding the incident. He had struck out at an abusive fan and many of the black players we have interviewed reported that on hearing of the incident they had secretly admired him for doing so. Ironically, a white Frenchmen had put the issue of xenophobia and racial abuse on the public agenda.

Furthermore, in the aftermath of this incident the imagery used in Nike's advertisement was assimilated and carnivalized within the context of the fan cultures themselves. Crystal Palace supporters, in the fanzine *Palace Echo* (1995) replaced the legend in the Nike advertisement to '95 was a great year for English football. Eric was banned', and changed the Nike brand logo to 'Nicked'. Whilst, as we have already highlighted, in a further twist, supporters of Manchester United, turned the imagery completely on its head, replacing the flag, personnel and language in order to challenge the perceived fascistic affiliations of Cantona's assailant. The point that we want to stress here is the degree of interplay between the symbols and styles of the corporate imagination and fanzines and 'alternative' forms of public text. These forms of representation are not static, they can be played with and subverted and, in the context of the problems that anti-racism campaigns have had communicating their messages this may be significant.

However, whilst such forms of communication may resonate within the popular imagination and supporter cultures there are limitations to this approach. One of the overarching messages of corporate multiculturalism is an insistence that boundaries should be breached, that colour doesn't matter, nationalism is passé, in short, that ideologies don't matter, what matters is not to name differences – *Just do it*! But what is seductive about this is to insist on being beyond the ideologies of race and nation is a kind of ideology in itself. In some ways it is a highly individualistic form of liberalism.

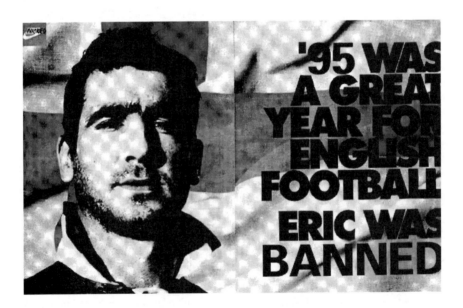

Figure 7.3 Fanzine subversion taken from the Crystal Palace fanzine *Palace Echo*.

It is no surprise then that Nike ended up being one of the key players in the CRE-PFA Lets' Kick Racism Out of Football campaign. The company donated £20,000 and had one of its advertisements on the back of the campaign magazines. This advertisement was itself the product of a fascinating television commercial that was produced on the back of the Cantona affair and turned the controversy in to a moral statement about abusive fans.

The advertisement features Eric Cantona and the black English striker Les Ferdinand. Initially, Ian Wright, another Nike sponsored player, was going to be in the advert but his club at the time, Arsenal, pressured him to pull out because of the supposed controversy. The advertisements were shown in England and France where Ferdinand was replaced by the black French player and Cantona's personal friend Basil Boli.

According to Nike's advertising manager the idea for the film came out of the conversations the company had with their players. Just as a number of players have reported to us, Cantona and others claimed that they usually shrugged off the abuse they received and got on with the game. In many ways this represents an accommodative strategy for survival – not to confront racism but just to keep your head down and carry on. One black player told us that 'if you fought everything, every time a racial comment was made you'd be fighting every day.' It is precisely this strand that Nike picked up on because it fitted perfectly with their '*Just do it*' version of voluntarism. Within this framework anti-racism is only a matter of personal choice as if no conception of society exists at all.

The advertisement elides the notion of dialogue and monologue. Cantona and Ferdinand talk to the camera with the speech intercut to form one seamless piece of dialogue, as though it could be one man speaking:

Table 7.1. Cantona/Ferdinand Nike TV Advert

Visual	*Audio*
Cantona	What do you see?
Ferdinand	A black man?
Cantona	A Frenchman?
Ferdinand	Or . . .
Cantona	A footballer?
Ferdinand	Is it OK to shout racial abuse at me?
Cantona	Just because I'm on a football pitch?
Ferdinand	Some people say we have to accept abuse as part of the game.
Both	Why
Ferdinand	argue about differences?
Cantona	I'd rather play football
Just do it	

The mode of address in the film is to the fan – the YOU of the advertisement. The film presents the problem as the fans who try to bring down these heroes through racism, xenophobia and abuse. The answer is just to play. Why argue about differences? *Just do it*! Once again, ultimately this continues to organize the problem of racism amongst abusive supporters in the stands and away from the institutions of football. As McKay has argued:

> Nike and Reebok advertisements are . . . silent about the extensive racial inequalities in American [and British] professional sport . . . Also missing from the advertisements is the global exploitation of labour that underpins the production and consumption of the sporting goods industry. (McKay 1995: 195)

In some ways the advertisement invites outrage against those who would violate football's heroes. While Nike is selling sports shoes on the back of footballing idols it is also selling a rejection of racism through the same means because it is easier to cheer for Eric Cantona than an obscure unnamed black player being abused in the second division of the Nationwide League.

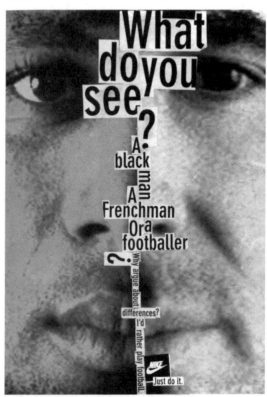

Figure 7.4 'I'd Rather Play Football' Nike's Eric Cantona and Les Ferdinand Advertisement.

However, football clubs, for all their changing qualities, are still a powerful means to mobilize distinctly local forms of identity and consciousness. The Manchester City fanzine *Electric Blue* illustrated this point well with their lampooning of a further Nike advertisement that focused on Cantona's history of confrontations with the game's authorities. Rejecting the sentiment of the advert whilst mirroring the corporate confessional style, the fanzine presented their own version titled 'ZE LAST WORD', again altering the wording of the Nike brand logo to 'Nite' with the addition of 'Mare'.

'Ze Last Word'

I'VE BEEN PUNISHED
For striking a goalkeeper . . .
For spitting at a supporter . . .
For throwing my shirt at ze referee . . .
For calling my manager 'A bag of shit' . . .
Then I called ze jury who punished me 'A bunch of idiots' . . .
Called another referee a cheat . . .
Got sent off many times . . .
Attacked a World Cup official and finally . . .
I attacked a supporter.
OUI, OUI . . . I'M A BIT OF A BASTARD REALLY! (*Electric Blue*,
1995: 28)

'Global' icons do not always work within the context of club based fan cultures, which are often based on fiercely protected local identities and traditions, which can produce greatly contrasting responses to corporate and institutional inter- ventions. Indeed it may be that as football becomes more and more the property of global corporate capital that racism and xenophobia against high profile black and foreign players will become the ultimate expression of contempt for the changing nature of the sport. Certainly the most intense fixtures are often those where small clubs play large ones. Accordingly, we need to understand racism and anti-racism in the wider context of the quiet and sometimes not so quiet revolution that has taken place in our national game over the last ten years.

Conclusion: A New Anti-Racist Agenda

The campaign against racism in football emerged at precisely the time when the orthodoxy of moral approaches to anti-racism was being questioned within other areas of British life. Such an approach is doomed to limited success because it relies on a moralism that does little to understand the social configurations of racism. Yet the starting point for any effective attempt to deal with racism must tackle the issues of silencing and denial that are widespread within the institutions of football. The crude labelling of racists as 'moral degenerates' does little to identify and tackle the forms of banal and ritualized racism within football's institutions and amongst its devoted fans. However, whilst such narrow images of racism continue to dominate public perceptions there may now be a platform for the generation of more sophisticated peer-group activity at the local level and structured development plans at the institutional level.

Recently, a new wave of media, activist and political interest in the game has led to the emergence of a broader agenda concerned with the under representation of black and Asian supporters, the absence of Asian professional players, the continuing presence of overt racism within grassroots football and the identification of discrimination within the institutions of the game. The sheer intensity of interest in the game and pressure brought to bear by Jas Bains' study into Asian participation in football (Bains and Patel 1996) a variety of local interventions (see Powar and Tegg 1998), media, political and supporter activity is making it harder and harder for football to avoid this issue.

We think the whole issue of anti-racist campaigning in football is at a key moment. We have already alluded to the problem of 'political will' and the difficulty of maintaining alliances in a situation where the agenda is widening. These issues are now coming more starkly into focus because:

1 The campaign has performed its PR function, raising the profile of the CRE, PFA and FA whilst associating them with opposition to a universally understood social pariah.
2 The falling incidents of racism amongst fans give the impression of success.
3 Football's institutions are far more powerful than fans and better equipped to stave off accusations of racism.
4 Because of the restricted terms of reference the campaign will appear to have exhausted its own, albeit limited, agenda.

A new political agenda needs to open up these questions and point to the very ordinary, casual and everyday nature of racism in football. We are proposing a broadening of the agenda that attempts to connect responses to manifestations of racism within the sport. This might mean abandoning some of anti-racism's 'others' and facing the complex and respectable face of racism inside the game itself. This will entail focusing on racist *actions*, the time when people enact racism rather than the uniformity of the doers commitment to racism as an ideology.

We are stressing the importance of contextualized and localized strategies. The problem with this is that, almost by definition, it will not attract the kind of high-profile interest that the campaign has secured since its launch in 1993. However, one of the problems with the ways in which this issue has been discussed publicly is the sensationalized nature of media coverage and accusations of racism. As a result the institutions of football and the clubs themselves have become increasingly defensive and closed to open discussion of the issues. In this climate it is hard for black players, coaches and even directors inside the game to speak out for fear of being the focus of the next sensation. In this respect we need to work towards a desensationalization of the public agenda and a focus on acts of racism rather than caricatures of football 'racists' in order to generate a more open, frank and wide ranging debate that transcends the preoccupation with what is going on in the stands. There are two principles that guide such an approach:

1 Targeting the nature of the problem.
2 Grounding responses in locally developed strategies.

Table 7.2 indicates the spheres of the game where racialization takes place.

Whilst some organizations such as Show Racism the Red Card continue to remain committed to a very public, launch-led and moral approach, an openness to more sophisticated techniques is now emerging in other areas of anti-racist activity. The staff of the Kick It Out campaign have for some time now been quietly implementing a lower key, broader but more targeted approach, working with individual clubs and communities and emphasising the positive aspects of action rather than organizing high-profile launches with their attendant media management tensions. As the campaign co-ordinator Piara Powar explained when reflecting on their current priorities:

Well essentially I suppose we kind of classify those as continuing the work that had been done in professional football and taking that further. Secondly was to sort of branch the campaign's message down into the grass roots and identifying the key issues there and what action could be taken. And then coming on top of that we identified – although its part of the work with professional football – we identified the need for football to be working with black communities, with centres for African Caribbean and Asian communities. And that's often integrated now into the work that we do with the clubs, but it is a key kind of separate area for us. Another was this issue of sort of the lack of an Asian player and getting clubs to start thinking about that. And we also talked quite a lot about the need to sort of work through education and working to educate young people through the opportunities the football provides. And then finally we wanted to try to sort of start cracking the European stuff. Not exactly sort of flying England as a model of good practice but certainly highlighting some of the work that's beginning to go on here . . . but essentially I suppose, you know, the focus has been on moving away from that symbolic stuff and really getting some of the key players in British football to try to understand the issues and then to start implementing some action. So with professional clubs we wanted to make sure that they take responsibility for problems

Table 7.2. Racialization in Football: A Framework for Policy Intervention

Arena	Context	Forms of Racialisation	Policy Response
Institutional	Administration, ruling bodies and decision making Players organizations Club ownership and boardroom control	Racial inequality in terms of access to decision-making forums Racial discourses of exclusion	Opening up questions of access and representation of black people within the administrative and ruling bodies of the sport Challenging the normalized nature of whiteness in football environments and the economics of ownership. Challenging the cultures of silencing and denial
Occupational	Scouting and patterns of recruitment Players' occupational culture Transfer market Agents Management and coaching Administration and marketing	Connection between racialised attributes, sporting capacity and professional competence Racialized rumours and decision making Racist abuse within the playing/coaching arena Conceptions of the market and internal culture of football clubs	Awareness within football of racial stereotyping Building a consensus against racialized common sense Tighter adherence to codes of practice for players and coaches caught racially abusing Priority to developing black coaches and scouting Opening up representative roles to black players The economics of the transfer market Structure for working within a multicultural market/exploiting new markets
Culture industry	Advertising and marketing Sponsorship Print media and journalism Electronic media	Imaging racial difference Racialised patterns of commercial endorsement Elite racist discources concerning race and nation	Regulation of the media Encouraging black and Asian journalists Use of advertising/media forms to disseminate non elite discourses
Fan culture	Club, region and identity Geography of support and patronage Player symbols History and club rivalries Expressive rituals of support Under-representation of black and Asian fans Race and nation within the context of the national side	The racialisation of entitlement and belonging Rationalisation of the National body politic Racialised hierarchies and 'neighbourhood nationalism' Positioning of Black players and the club collective identity Racialised forms of abuse The relationship between right-wing politics and fan cultures	Legal interventions where possible Building non racist consensus, white ownership Addressing the 'Monolithic' whiteness of football environments Where appropriate, action against politically motivated racist activity Targetted initiatives at increasing minority respresentation

that are there and obvious for all to see, and that's sort of problems that continue with sort of abuse and chanting inside stadiums, but also wider issues ... you know, the clubs looking at themselves, looking at the make-up of their employees, looking at their playing staff, the whole shebang really. Not just sort of symbolic saying yeah, we're against racism, we agree with the broader message of the campaign, we've got to get, we've got to address racism that's inherent, historically has been inherent within our fan base. (Interview, 26 September 2000)

A series of localized and club-specific campaigns involving partnerships between supporters, local authorities, football clubs, the police and others have emerged throughout the country with the support of Kick It Out, partly as a consequence of this new approach. In 1996 Kick It Out was instrumental in developing a localized initiative in South London that brought together Millwall, Charlton Athletic and Crystal Palace to pool resources and work in partnership with local authorities, the police and black community organizations like the Martin Shaw King Trust. Millwall Football Club has had an active anti-racist committee since 1994. The Charlton Athletic Race Equality Partnership (CARE) was also established and running a variety of educational and equality of access programmes. The South London Kicking Racism Out of Football initiative was launched in February 1998 and managed to use these resources to organize a series of projects and galvanize action. Similarly in the Midlands the 'Foxes Against Racism' initiative based at Leicester City is another example of an attempt at developing strategies to counter racism that are localized.

Football Unites Racism Divides (FURD) was initially launched by a group of Sheffield United fans and youth workers concerned by racist incidents in and around United's Bramall Lane ground. FURD is now engaged in a range of initiatives that aim to reduce racism within the context of a broader based set of community interventions that are only loosely related to Sheffield's professional clubs. Their aim is to increase the numbers of people from ethnic minority groups involved in football as players, supporters and employees throughout the region. The activities include 'Streetkick' mobile football events, the recruitment of Asian women onto an FA Junior Team Managers Course, sponsorship of FA coaching qualifications, anti-racist work in local youth clubs, schools and colleges, a local information and library resource, and a range of other community based interventions that use the skills of charismatic culturally attuned local people.

Drawing on the inspiration of Britain's first black professional footballer, Arthur Wharton (see Vasili 1999), who played for Sheffield United, FURD has also organized a mobile exhibition celebrating the history of black footballers in Britain. This has itself been adapted to reflect the specific local history of black players in the other locations where the exhibition has been staged. The exhibition attempted to encourage this by offering clubs that played host to it the opportunity to construct their own display which reflected the local history of black footballers at their

Figure 7.5 United Colours of Football 2. Published with permission of FURD and Kick It Out.

particular club. In late March and early April 2001 FURD in combination with Kick It Out launched *The United Colours of Football 2* magazine. This publication marked an important shift in the way anti-racist materials had been produced. The editorial team had thought through how to reach adult largely white football fans. It included provocative articles by popular novelist Irvine Welsh, Manchester United manager Alex Ferguson and a piece reflecting the experience of black and Asian football fans. This initiative was important because it transcended the 'moral anti-racism' that haunted the early stages of the campaign. This resulted in anti-racist content 'with edge' that was more likely to be read by its target audience. It was presented in the fan's own cultural terms of reference thus raising the likelihood that its message would get through to them.

FURD is also significant because as an organization it has always reflected the ethnic diversity found within the local neighbourhood. Real alliances have been built between white anti-racist activists and ethnic minority communities. This is evident in their Millennium Volunteer scheme. Of the 171 young people involved in the initiative 58 per cent are drawn from ethnic minority backgrounds. The success of FURD is largely due to its movement beyond the conventional circles of English football culture. Yet, at the same time, FURD has shown a commitment to addressing white football fans in ways that are neither condescending or moralistic. Such localized strategies point to more grounded forms of intervention.

While organizations like FURD are an exception, it is broadly true that ethnic minority involvement in local anti-racist campaigns has remained at a low level. This should not be surprising given that these political interventions emerge from within football culture itself. The paradox here is that, while committed to change, anti-racist politics at club level remains predominantly composed of white activists. As a result the link between grass-roots football where minority involvement is high and the professional clubs and their supporters remains weak.

In the current political climate the shape of contemporary racism is also shifting. This too has important implications with regard to the politics of anti-racism in football. This was brought into sharp focus in 2000 when Millwall Football Club's anti-racism committee organized an exhibition of black footballers put together by FURD to be installed at the New Den. The club produced a booklet to highlight the contribution black players have made to the teams effort and a 'Millwall board' was added to the exhibition. Close to 2,000 local children saw the exhibition and the event passed off without complaint or resistance from amongst the fans. The two-week exhibition also coincided with the first team fixture which provides an annual focus for the clubs anti-racism work. As part of the commitment to opening access the club had offered members of local minority communities free tickets. These tickets were distributed through a variety of means including the Metropolitan Police.

In a spirit of good will the police offered twenty-five tickets to a group of football-loving Kosovan refugees living in a hostel in the Elephant and Castle. The *South London Press* newspaper found out about the offer and published a story about the Kosovans imminent trip to Millwall (*South London Press*, 10 March 2000). In a climate of hostility and xenophobia in Britain surrounding the new immigration in the form of asylum seekers and refugees – in large part produced by the press – the incident created a storm of national publicity. The *Sun* editorial entitled 'The Lions Den' summed up the mood: 'We had to look twice to make sure it wasn't April Fools Day. But it isn't. And the story's true. Hooligan Kosovan asylum seekers are being shown how to behave – by attending a Millwall match.

What will they do next for refugees . . . Give Romanian beggars a day trip to the Royal Mint?' (*Sun*, 11 March 2000). The adverse publicity was translated into a torrent of telephone calls to the club complaining about the Kosovans. Such was the ferociousness of the response in the media and amongst the fans that the offer was withdrawn.

What is significant about this incident is the degree to which domestic or local cultural politics of race and belonging are seen as distinct to what Stephen Dobson calls the 'border questions' relating to refugees and asylum seekers (Dobson 1999). In this kind of climate an anti-racist exhibition demonstrating the multi-racial history of a football club, even one with the reputation of Millwall, passes without incident and is deemed simply not newsworthy. Equally, it is possible for the club to give away hundreds of tickets to established ethnic minority communities. Yet, just twenty-five tickets given to a group of young men from Kosovo unleashed a venomous public outcry in a context where asylum seekers were living below the poverty line, surviving on vouchers that can only be traded for goods and subject to a dispersal policy that is aimed to inhibit them settling in particular areas together. Meanwhile, newspaper editors who professed liberal credentials and Labour politicians tried to justify these draconian measures and the public outcry against the refugees as being 'fair' and 'understandable'. What is striking is that these things can be published and said without any fear of the accusation of racism. Yet, the image of the 'Kosovan hooligan' and 'Romanian beggar' results in a mutating form of racism that combines anti-gypsy and anti-semitic elements to produce a new and distinct variant. Meanwhile, asylum seekers are experiencing harassment and racism, and many are fearful to report it to the police because of their experiences of torture and persecution in the lands from which they have fled. Clearly, anti-racist initiatives in this kind of climate need to anticipate the position in which refugee communities find themselves. The protean nature of racism creates new social pariahs as it makes accommodations with old ones.

In the final part of the book we want to shift emphasis by examining the ways in which issues of belonging, identity and exclusion work at the national level, beginning with an examination of the nature of support for the English national team. In this context we want to apply some of the perspectives developed in the previous chapters and attempt to unpick the relation between race and nation.

Part 3
Race, Nation and Diaspora

'Keep St George in My Heart': England Fans, Race, Nation and Identity

The Globe, Lisson Grove, Marylebone, 6:00pm, Saturday 7 October 2000

The rain is still pouring down outside. It has been pouring all day long. In fact it's been raining for so long and so hard it is a wonder that the game was not called off. But that was never on the agenda, as the game in question was England's last to be played at Wembley stadium – a World Cup qualifier against Germany who England had famously beaten at this ground some 34 years previously to win their one and only World Cup final. Accordingly, this clash between the two teams had been turned into something of a media circus, a party to which the great and good had been invited, complete with singing from the populist English tenor Russell Watson, choreographed crowds and due to culminate with a firework display as the curtain came down on the 'venue of Legends'.

In actuality, despite the hype, for most England fans the day was something of a damp squib. The confidence injected by victory over Germany during Euro 2000 wiped away by a dreary 1–0 defeat, the fireworks swamped by the rain as the crowd turned its back on the stadium that had long since lost the last droplets of glamour that the FA's marketing people had sought to squeeze out one last time. In the pub it was a familiar scene, packed with loyal England supporters who had seen it all before: almost exclusively white men, mostly in their thirties, lamenting the passing of another false dawn as the realization of the manager Kevin Keegan's tactical ineptitude becomes overwhelming. News of a crisis meeting between players, manager and the FA chief executive Adam Crozier in the England dressing room is being stoically analysed over pints and cigarettes as phones start ringing and the words 'he's gone' leave the speculation redundant.

As the news spreads and Keegan comes on the television to publicly announce his decision to resign, there is no rejoicing. The side is managerless with another important World Cup qualifier to play in Finland in four days' time, having got off to a losing start against the group favourites and with their best player David Beckham injured . . . and it's still raining outside. Despite the gloomy introspection which accompanies such moments, the pub discussions had inevitably turned to the choice of successor. Many names were mooted and even the possibility of a foreign coach was raised before being universally dismissed, for there was only one choice, Terry Venables, the cockney wide boy who had previously led the team to the Euro 96 semi-finals. As if to confirm the point, it was Venables himself who gazed out from the television screen as he was asked by Des Lynam to provide the first expert reaction to Keegan's decision.

It didn't really seem to matter that much though, as for these fans the malaise within English football seemed to run far deeper than anything a change of manager could alter. For decades their hopes had been dashed as the England team failed to compete with the best in the world. These fans have long since abandoned any assumptions of victory because following England has become something that lies beyond football results; it is framed by a discourse characterized by notions of pride, passion, loyalty and a set of normative codes and assumptions that go with 'being English'.

* * *

In a context where notions of nationhood and place extend to fast food outlets as diverse as your local Pizza*land* or Kebab*land,* whilst Premiership football teams take to the field without a single British player, national sports teams often provide a means to sustain the fantasies and myths around which nations are constructed (Hall 1998, Jarvie 1994). As the collection of essays contained in *The Ingerland Factor* (Perryman 1999) attests, for England, where the country's decline as a footballing power in some respects reflects the decline in the nation's broader symbolic and geographic political authority, this conflation of sport with nation may be more heartfelt. After all, international football had, to some extent originally grown out of the modernist, 'rationalized' sports project associated with the British Empire of the nineteenth century (Holt 1989, Birley 1993).

As such, it was no surprise that no one mentioned the name of the Italian club Lazio's Swedish coach, Sven Goran Eriksson, in relation to the England manager's job that day. Nevertheless it was his appointment that was to be announced three weeks later on Tuesday 31 October. During the intervening period a debate raged within the game over the implications of appointing a non-English manager, the idea of which attracted condemnation from across the game led by the FA's own ambassador and World Cup winner Bobby Charlton. In the face of Eriksson's eventual appointment it was left to the *Daily Mail*'s Jeff Powell to cancel the usual honeymoon period afforded to new managers with a devastating attack upon the FAs decision. Under the banner headline 'We've sold our birthright down the fjord to a nation of seven million skiers and hammer throwers who spend half their lives in darkness' Powell lamented:

> So the mother country of football, birthplace of the greatest game, has finally gone from the cradle to the shame. England's humiliation knows no end . . . As they preened

themselves over yesterday's installation of Sven Goran Eriksson, did they begin to realise how gleefully the rest of the world would be laughing at us? Welcome to third world Britain. One rainstorm and south-east England resembles Bangladesh, trains halted in a country which once refused to stop for the Blitz. One more week and we shall be stockpiling petrol and hoarding food. And now, to cap it all, we have a Swede managing our national team. (*Daily Mail*, 1 November 2000: 93)

Powell's frustrations, like those of the administrators and managers (including Venables) who joined in the criticism of the appointment, reflect some of the broader concerns about England's loss of status in the football world, but for many fans of the team this sense of alienation is complicated by the hypocrisy of such commentators. For over the last two decades there has been a widespread tendency for England fans to be castigated in equally damning fashion by the full spectrum of media vehicles, including Jeff Powell's column, as the embodiment of precisely this kind of unrepentant nationalistic 'Englishness'.

Through middle class snobbery they have been negatively associated with aggressive masculinity, drunkenness, open displays of nationalism, xenophobia and racism. As Mike Ticher put it in *When Saturday Comes* 'England's style of patriotism is defined by our man slumped in the Rome fountain with the tatty Union Jack (Slough Town) and the 'Do it for Princess Di' T-shirt' (December 1997).

The questions we wish to pose here require us to adopt a more sympathetic outlook and a reversal of that gaze in order to reveal a glimpse of the world as it is experienced and seen by those fans. In this way we hope to gain some degree of understanding of the ways in which support for the England national team intersects with notions of race and nation, the patterns of behaviour which flow from them and the tensions created by the forces of globalization and commercialism within the game. We begin with this account of the circumstances surrounding England's selection of Eriksson as their new manager precisely because it marks a pivotal moment in the history of the game, the significance of which is intimately related to the complex tensions which surround these issues.

England Away: The Media, Football Violence and Social Pariahs

The full force of this media gaze was revealed during the 1998 World Cup finals staged in France and the Euro 2000 tournament staged in Holland and Belgium, and most particularly following the disturbances in Marseilles before and after England's opening World Cup group game against Tunisia on 15 June 1998. The fact that those involved in the disturbances in Marseilles represented only a small minority of England's estimated 30,000 supporters was acknowledged, but the overriding image being presented of English football fans was a familiar one, confirmed by one headline in the *Sun* that proclaimed 'Shame Old Story'(15 June 1998: 2–3). The *Evening Standard* went further, drawing a broader connection with historically grounded English cultural values, declaring that 'bottles and plates flew to the moronic tune of *Vindaloo* [a pop single recorded for the World Cup by the group *Fat Les*, formed specifically to record the track and consisting of the comedian Keith Allen, artist Damien Hirst and Alex James from the pop group *Blur*]. The English were playing the same old game . . . This is our style – the pointless playground bravado, the inane parody of stiff-upper-lipped heroes' (15 June 1998: 3), a perspective which was reinforced, albeit in more measured tones, by the *European* in a lead article entitled 'Mad Dogs – The new face of English nationalism' (22–28 June 1998: 1).

Claims of provocation and local hostility towards England supporters are often presented as a lame excuse by the popular press in such circumstances. However, the fact is that such treatment is nothing new to those who have followed England abroad for some time. The myth and reality of England supporters' reputation is such that upon arriving on foreign soil they are often treated with suspicion and intolerance, which has occasionally been whipped up by local media scare stories, as we witnessed on a number of occasions on trips abroad during the 1998 World Cup and Euro 2000 tournaments. At Tbilisi airport, sleepy supporters arriving at dawn for the match with Georgia were met by a cordon of rifle-brandishing soldiers and led to their coaches; in Katowice, following a game against Poland, the police routinely beat England fans around the legs with truncheons as they made their way back into town; in Rome supporters were indiscriminately attacked by the Italian police inside and outside the stadium, whilst in Belgium hundreds of England fans were systematically arrested and deported before charges could be brought. Neither is this a development uniquely associated with the recent past as Williams et al. (1989: 89–90) noted in their exploration of English hooliganism abroad in the 1980s.

Greigsie, a much-travelled England fan from Greater Manchester, explained that England supporters' reputation can lead them into trouble regardless of their desire to be involved:

> Oh yeah, it's England fans, because of their reputation they're gonna get it, it don't matter where they come from, whether they're good or bad. You've got to answer for it . . . I mean a lot of our lads got turned over in Greece when I was there, because of that reputation. Back home all the fans sit there with their England shirts, glasses on and that, and you take all the shit, you get turned over by a load of Greeks. (Interview, 20 September 1996)

Without wishing to get drawn into a full exploration of the causes of football violence in any great detail here it is worth considering how fan-based hostility in such contexts intersects with football related violence and notions of national resentment and xenophobia. In Marseilles, as in Katowice and Rome in 1997 and again in Brussels in 2000, there were large numbers of local youths who were more than willing to challenge the England fans' reputation for violence. The status that England supporters have as the architects and champions of 'football hooliganism' within the collective imagination of world football has made them an attraction in their own right. They are commonly feared and loathed, but for some young men, football matches against the 'English' also provide a platform upon which their own credentials for toughness and invulnerability can be promoted.

Accordingly, this potential for confrontation and hostility from the authorities coupled with the social conventions of domestic football culture leads many England supporters when abroad to seek collective security and camaraderie in the bars found in the central or 'tourist' areas of cities hosting England games. On the day of a game or those immediately before, a presence is normally established early in the day, which then becomes a focal point for other fans as they arrive in town. Over the course of the day alcohol is consumed in varying quantities, ranging from those fans drinking themselves into oblivion (in Tbilisi one schnapps-drinking Hull City supporter had collapsed on the floor by 9:30 in the morning!) to those maintaining a stoic determination to keep their wits about them.

For all those present, the bars form an important conduit through which tales can be told, incidents reported and reworked and friendships made or renewed. Groups of largely male fans in their late teens, twenties and thirties, numbering anything from two to thirty, provide the core population in these settings. These groups have generally travelled together as units and are usually tied by longstanding friendships rooted in locality and domestic, club-based, football allegiances. However, in the context of an England away game they do not form exclusive 'communities'. Cross group and cross club contact is made between supporters who have met on previous trips, through the general sociable atmosphere and by individual fans who make it their business to talk to others about inter-club conflicts and experiences. Over a period of time the interaction between groups, anticipation of the game and the alcohol-induced removal of inhibitions help to generate a more collective experience, typically characterized by the singing of mutually recognized 'England' anthems such as *Keep St George in My Heart*, *Rule Britannia*, *God Save the Queen* and *En-ger-land*.

It is worth describing the form and content of these songs before moving on. 'Keep St George in My Heart' is a relatively new England song with the chorus:

> Keep St George in my heart keep me English,
> Keep St George in my heart I pray,
> Keep St George in my heart keep me English,
> Keep me English to my dying day.

ending with the punctuating slogan : 'No surrender, no surrender, no surrender to the IRA, scum'.

The choruses of the patriotic anthems *Rule Britannia* and *God Save the Queen* are sung in their traditional format, although the words 'no surrender' are often added before the words 'Send her victorious' in the final verse of the National Anthem, while, *En-ger-land*, pronounced 'In-ger-lund', involves a more traditional football chant sung to the tune of John Phillip Sousa's *Marching through Georgia*. Other songs are sung by England supporters but these are the most popular and enduring, because songs such as *The Great Escape, Three Lions* and *Vindaloo* have only emerged in the context of interventions that are external to the England fan collective itself during specific tournaments or in the context of specific national rivalries such as *Singing Die, Die Turkey Fucking Die* and *I'd rather be a Paki than a Turk*. We will return to this issue later in the chapter.

Whilst largely celebratory, these more collective forms of expression are often underpinned by shared perceptions of local animosity and an associated inward looking apprehension which can fuel outward hostility. Wherever England play, the fans' reputation, prominent occupation of city-centre bars, exuberant singing and exhibition of national flags (displaying names as disparate and far flung as Newcastle and Yeovil) has the potential to affront the local population, and particularly young men. There is nothing inevitable about this outcome and where there is no obvious hostile reaction to the presence of England supporters, as in Moldova, Toulouse, before England's defeat by Romania in the World Cup and Eindhoven where England played Portugal during Euro 2000, disturbances are rare. It is when there is an awareness of a likely challenge to the English presence that the atmosphere becomes more unstable, swinging between a celebratory collective mood and assertive agitation.

'If it Wasn't for the English you'd be Krauts': Working-class Masculinities, National Stereotypes, Racism and Xenophobia

In Marseilles the potential for a challenge to the English presence was only too clear. Marseilles is a tough industrial city, which is characterized by deep racial divisions, urban strife, strong support for the far-right Front National and regular violence between local youths and the police. In this context the matching of Tunisia against England created a rallying point for local youths of North African extraction who were interested in trouble and the assertion of their own masculine and ethnic identities.

In an atmosphere where the celebration of national identity is accompanied by such potential for conflict, confrontations can take on forms which are underscored by notions of racial or national superiority and a whole series of associated stereotypes. In the bars and streets of Marseilles such perspectives were organised around the England fans definition of, and opposition to, the dual national/racial categories of the 'French' and 'Arabs'.

A popular chant sung by English supporters in France when faced by rival fans, the police or other locals was *If it Wasn't for the English you'd be Krauts*. The song plays on the idea that the French had relied upon the English to liberate them from German occupation during the Second World War. It has been sung by fans of English club sides playing against French opposition before. In these contexts the 'targets' have been fans who were regarded as unambiguously 'French' supporters of French club sides where the song has been mobilized in order to 'wind them up' by playing with internal insecurities about their own country's national history. In Marseilles however, the song was occasionally rendered alongside another chant declaring that 'It's [Marseilles] just a town full of Arabs', and targeted at local youths who were predominantly of North African heritage.

On the one hand then, there was an awareness of the significance of the racial tensions that characterize the city and a willingness to invoke these tensions by defining the, implicitly non Arab, English supporters against a racially defined image of Marseilles. However, at the same time, the 'If it wasn't for the English . . .' chant was directed at a broader, and presumably racially inclusive, image of the French nation. Not only were the 'white' French population being ridiculed for their country's role in the Second World War but so were the 'Arab' fans, now resident in France.

In this situation, rather than being a *mutually* recognized and stigmatized group, lying outside normative perspectives of who football supporters are and what they look like, the racial group being referred to were in fact the 'opposition'. They were the very fans that were confronting the England supporters. The peculiarity here is the way in which the racial characteristics of the opposition and the city could be highlighted in order to distinguish them from the English, and then suspended in the context of the broader ridicule of France which was hosting the match and the tournament. In these very specific circumstances the opposition could be vilified not just as 'Arabs', but as French 'Arabs' without the ironic 'play' meanings invoked in the domestic context.

The important point is that such 'wind ups' and abuse are not devalued through their ambiguity because they are not invested with great meaning by those who engage in them. The abuse, which is often spontaneous in form, represents part of the ritualized tapestry of football-related, conflictual 'talk'. Rather than being situated within an ideologically driven, racialized framework for viewing the world, football-related conflict presents a space in which racial and national stereotypes can be 'played' with and mobilized as a resource to be used against a commonly defined 'footballing' enemy. Indeed, with an opposition that speaks another language, the chanting may be more significant in terms of its impact on England fans, unifying those supporters through the articulation of internally understood terrace humour and normative preferences, in collective ridicule of the opposition.

Rather than being instrumental in its celebration of any formal notion of English nationalism, the performance of such rituals emerges out of a more loosely defined defence of the 'English' reputation. Those England supporters who are typically characterized as seeking an involvement in football-related violence and associated racist or xenophobic behaviour can be better understood in terms of their determination to eschew deferential codes of conduct and their refusal to back down in the face of aggression. The attitude is in many ways more defensive than it is assertive.

In an atmosphere where all supporters are regarded as potential 'hooligans' there is a tendency towards inward-looking attitudes amongst those who have been so labelled. Even more so, given that in contrast to the depiction of English football fans in the media and open hostility on the part of foreign authorities, there is a general openness and camaraderie amongst the fans themselves. It is commonly accepted that the majority of England fans, particularly when away from home, are instantly recognizable to one another and it is customary for them to acknowledge and talk with their compatriots when paths meet. This manner, itself related to the hostile conditions in which fans often find themselves, is so engrained that on a trip to Poland one of us was able to establish contact, arrange to spend the evening, travel from Warsaw to Katowice on the overnight train and then share a room with three other fans, having met them only a few minutes earlier, purely on account of a common status as England supporters.

This commonality also relates to conformity amongst certain sections of support with a broader cultural style, or normative mode of dress and behaviour. Many of those England supporters who followed the side away prior to (and a good number since) the qualifying fixture in Rome in 1997 can be characterized in terms of their lineage from the highly masculinized 'casual' culture of the 1980s which was closely tied to the patterns of football-related violence found in that era (Redhead 1993). Whilst not compulsory, casual designer sportswear, particularly Ralph Lauren, Burberry and Hackett shirts and baseball/golf caps, Stone Island and Henri Lloyd jumpers, jackets and anoraks worn with Paul Smith, Armani or other designer jeans are *de rigueur*. In line with Robson's (2000) application of Bourdieu in his interpretation of Millwall fans' embodied practices, this dress code is accompanied by a class-inflected, performative style. A style that is non intellectual, stoic and understated but that finds resonance in such traditional, working-class, masculine values as uncompromising toughness, directness, a lack of pretentiousness and deprecating humour.

In this context the broader social and discursive framework constructed around supporting England is associated with sociability and story telling, alcohol consumption (and, to a lesser extent than other popular youth cultures, illicit recreational drug use), fashion and music, violence and sexual relations within the overall context of football. It is concerned with avoiding mundane restrictions and control, 'lording it' or dominating someone else's 'manor' or patch and being 'sussed' enough to get away with it. Whilst they remain highly masculinized, there are a small number of women who also adhere to the defining principles of these cultural forms, being prepared to endure the hardships associated with following England away and even to run with the crowd into a confrontation. This is not to say that such formations are necessarily unproblematic because, as Armstrong argues, the achievement of these ideals is often accompanied by clearly marked insider-outsider relations:

> With modern-day consumer lifestyles increasingly lacking any sense of danger or ordeal, the issue becomes one of transcending monotony. Consequently, many urban dwellers seek to escape drudgery by creative self-expression in spontaneous group association or partisan spectating. Such activities when manifested around football create a comradeship of fellow fans, but it is double-headed; for in-group friendship is linked to hostility to others. Who gets drawn into this association or the circumstances under which they meet – like the precise role of 'enemy' – can vary considerably. (Armstrong 1999: 54–5)

However, the implied sense of superiority inherent in the social outlook of these 'hardcore' England fans is not so much grounded in nationalistic or racialized values, as class based notions of self-respect and honour. A perspective that, whilst often consumerist, outwardly rejects the dominant commercial and intellectual values of society as well as the instrumental politically motivated activity of both the far right and the far left. As John King's character 'Gary' dramatically and accurately illustrates in the novel *England Away* (1998) in an ironic aside at those in the media that label fans to sensationalist effect:

> There was another journalist trying to get English skinheads to do sieg-heils and there was this trendy wanker from a radio station who asked us to make some threats in his microphone . . . They're a bunch of wankers desperate for a story. They've got no souls. They weren't offering to pay either. I'd have done a sieg-heil for twenty quid, if the cunt had asked nicely. Would've sung the Red Flag for forty. (King 1998: 257)

This is not to say that there is not some sympathy with notions of national superiority and racial demonology amongst sections of England supporters. However, rather than *participation* in violence, intimidatory behaviour or racial abuse it is the acceptance of the legitimacy, accommodation or non interference with these actions and their place within the discursive framework of England fans which characterizes the hardcore of the fan collective. Discussion of violence or the threat of it and the use of national/racial stereotypes often forms part of an accommodative code, or 'assumed knowledge', even amongst those fans who declare that they are simply present to watch the football and have a good time.

The trip from Warsaw to Katowice to see England play Poland was shared with three other white fans from Milton Keynes who had been met at a currency exchange booth at Warsaw airport. Two of the supporters, both called Lee and aged 19 and 23, follow Tottenham whilst the other, Andy, who was in his mid-twenties, follows Chelsea. None of these fans regard themselves as 'football hooligans' and when we talked about England fans and violence, Andy, who has been to see England play away from home approximately ten times, was particularly keen to stress that 'we are not really here for all that'. Nevertheless the significance and inevitable potential for trouble was not lost on the youngest of the fans who was on his first trip to see England play away:

> My Uncle, who was a bit of a thug in his time and followed England about, he said the Polish were the maddest fans that he's ever come across. He said they love the trouble and the police are completely nuts out here. He said it's definitely one of the scariest places he's ever been to with England. Me Mum was getting all worked up about it and worried but I just told her 'well I'm big enough and ugly enough to look after myself now. (Fieldnotes, 30 May 1997)

Furthermore, throughout the evening, on the overnight train and during the day of the game in Katowice itself, the subject of football violence was a feature, whether in relation to previous accounts of trouble, the identification of particular known 'faces' or 'firms', or the threat posed by Polish fans and the police. However, for these fans much of the discussion was framed within a perspective that constructed Polish supporters, and by extension the Polish people, as the principle threat or stigmatized 'out group'. This was done both in terms of the potential for violence from Polish fans, particularly on the train to Katowice when 'we' were heavily outnumbered, and in terms of the potential for being 'ripped off' or manipulated by locals.

These supporters had arrived in Poland with a preconceived notion of the Polish as a hostile nation of people who would be out to 'mug' them, whether physically or through some ill-defined foreign trickery which would be facilitated by their own ignorance of the language and official animosity to the English. However, this perspective was not just blindly adopted it was, to a certain extent, 'learned' and grounded in experience. Not only had Lee's uncle painted an intimidating picture of the country, but Andy and a group of Chelsea fans had been 'ambushed' as they arrived in Katowice at dawn after travelling on the overnight train from Prague the last time England had played in Poland in 1993. Whilst prepared for a fight, the Chelsea supporters had been surprised by the willingness of the Poles to attack them at that hour of the day and were reluctant to engage with them so early in the morning.

The antipathy shown towards the Poles extended beyond the fear of physical assault to a general negative view of the country and the motives of those locals with whom contact was made. A string of negative remarks were made in relation to the general conditions, the quality of train services and the familiarity of the food and drink on offer. Furthermore, judgement of such facilities was generally caged in Anglocentric terms, in comparison with what would be found in England, rather than on the merits of the facilities themselves. This was reflected in, amongst other things, the choice of globally standardized McDonalds meals rather than local cuisine on three separate occasions during the day spent in Katowice, not just by this group but by a continual stream of other England supporters.

It is not our suggestion here that the negative associations being made in relation to Poland come out of any ideological objection to foreign countries or nationalistic sentiment. Rather than reflecting any 'real' sense of national supremacy there was in fact a profound internal lack of confidence in relation to engagement with what was perceived as an alien and hostile country. At the simplest of levels, through their own defensive, class-related, inhibitions and understated manner these supporters were very unwilling to seek out information from or engage with the Polish people. Indeed their approach was far removed from the inquisitiveness associated with Urry's notion of the 'tourist gaze' (Urry 1990) or demanding businessmen who might approach local service providers without hesitation and expect English-speaking Western standards of service. It was still further from the almost colonial image of aspirant 'stiff-upper-lipped heroes' suggested by Alex Renton in the *Evening Standard* (15 June 1998: 3).

What is more concerning is the ways in which these insecurities and fears intersected with everyday racialized notions of 'outsiders'. On the train to Katowice there was continual and exaggerated apprehension about the activity of Polish fans on the train and the possibility that we might come under attack at any moment. In the midst of these concerns the younger of the two Tottenham fans remarked that 'they [the Poles] are like coons this lot aren't they – it's like going up town – the way they all stick together'. He went on to describe an incident to illustrate his notion of black collective solidarity in conflict situations:

> I remember once when I was up town and one of these [black] cunts was flicking bits of paper at me, so I turned around and said 'I'll knock your fucking teeth out if you keep flicking bits of paper at me', at which point he went away and came back with about 30 of his mates and then you have just got to walk away haven't you. (Fieldnotes, 30 May 1997)

It was through this notion, developed in the domestic context, that perceptions of the Polish supporters were now being constructed. The idea was being articulated that the threat from the Poles was intensified because they would 'all stick together'.

A kind of bestial imagery was being presented through which the Polish fans would form themselves into packs in order to launch an attack that was itself constructed through a direct association with overtly racialized readings of the behaviour of black people in England. Interestingly here there was no comparison with the ways in which England supporters behave, rather a stigmatized 'out group' was being constructed, external to implicitly white English values of 'fair play', which was itself related to a domestic equivalent, namely, young black men.

The peculiarity of these perspectives can be found not in the contrast between the England supporters and the two stigmatized 'out groups', but in the degree of fit between the ways in which each of these groups is constructed in different circumstances. At matches such as the 1997 World Cup qualifier in Poland, where there was a heightened perception of the potential for disturbances, there is little doubt that a narrower base of England's support tends to be present. Whilst there were in the region of 2000 England fans in Katowice, it was clear that a large proportion of those supporters could be characterized in terms of their adherence to the defining features of the football 'casual'.

Sizeable groups or 'firms' of up to forty or fifty supporters were 'on show' and prepared to demonstrate both the strength of presence from their own clubs and their commitment to the loose principles that characterize much of England's away support and 'casual' culture more generally. An unfettered celebration of non-deferential working-class cultural values; the freedom to go where you want and do as you please; a sense of self-respect and honour grounded in unflinching commitment, a determination not to run in the face of aggression and a willingness to come together with domestic enemies against mutual opponents. There is no 'army', codified rules, generals or battle plans – just lots of groups of young men who enjoy each other's company and the freedom, respect and excitement that comes with being associated with England on an away trip.

Where England fans were talking in contexts where such cultural confidence and physical invulnerability was in evidence, the 'gameness' of the Poles, again often presented through the use of bestial or 'alien' images of 'snapping dogs' and 'arcade game characters', was almost ridiculed. Any recognition of and respect for their willingness to fight was situated within a broader perspective that to 'have a go' at the English was almost infantile and could only realistically end in one outcome. Furthermore, the apparent lack of unity amongst the Poles, which saw fans from rival clubs such as Katowice, Ruch Chorzow and Legia Warsaw fighting amongst themselves inside and around the stadium, was met with equally bemused reactions.

Where the 'English' become a unified group then, perspectives can be altered. It is they that are now constructed as the feared 'predators' whilst the 'outsiders' are ridiculed for their *lack* of unity and their naive willingness to engage in confrontation. This, despite the fact that the later disturbances between England

and Poland fans were far from one sided, with Polish fans chanting 'you run' in English outside the stadium shortly before the game. Furthermore, some of the main 'faces' in the Aston Villa and West Ham contingents had earlier had their own confrontation shortly before making their way up to the ground, a clash which then led to further internal wrangling and a fist fight amongst the Villa supporters themselves.

For some fans then, the insecurities which can be laid bare when England supporters are located in vulnerable surroundings generate added impetus to the kinds of confrontation that underpin the collective codes and ritual responses associated with England fans collectively. This seems to be particularly so for younger fans who may be attracted by the invulnerable image of England fans, but it is through other, longer standing supporters that it may be possible to draw a connection between support for the England team and broader more ideological notions of nationhood. It is to this issue that we will now turn.

'English, White and Proud of it': Racial Exclusion, Nationhood and the Far Right

Greigsie, as we previously described in Chapter 4, is a Manchester-City-supporting England fan in his thirties from a town in Greater Manchester. A former servant in the British Army, he has been following England for over twenty years and by the time of the 1998 World Cup had attended around eighty England games. He started following the side as a boy and still remembers his first match with great precision and pride, 'Portugal '74, Wembley, 0-0, European Championship qualifier – still got me ticket, £1.20, standing.'

For Greigsie, whom one of us accompanied to the 1998 World Cup qualifier in Georgia and during evenings out in his home town, in addition to several casual meetings at domestic and international matches, the most respected feature of an England fan's biography is his demonstration of loyalty and commitment to the team and country. Interestingly for our inquiry, an emphasis is often similarly placed on the perceived commitment of players who appear for the national team, with interpretations of that commitment often being racialized. There is a profound tendency amongst some sections of England supporters to oppose the inclusion of black players within the side. The strength of this sentiment has at times been illustrated by the reluctance of some supporters to even acknowledge goals that have been scored by black players. Most famously this scenario was played out following John Barnes' remarkable solo dribble and goal scored in the Maracana in 1984 when the player was later subjected to racial abuse from supporters travelling back on the same plane as the first team squad.

Greigsie has indicated his own support for this position:

Well, I don't deny it, but when [Barnes] scored for England I never moved. A prime example of that is against Holland in the 2–2, the one before World Cup ['94] . . . and we refused to acknowledge it – I hate him that much . . . not because of his colour, because of his commitment. He was just out there playing just another football match as far as he was concerned . . . Born in Jamaica, not a bona fide Englishman, just got no passion for it as far as I'm concerned. No love for it, just disappearing in and out of games, but he was also a lot of managers' favourites. That's why he's resented. It's because of his colour as well, I'm not going to argue, but in my view he is a cunt. He's just cheated, cheated a lot of players out of a lot of caps. (Interview, 20 September 1996)

Furthermore, having been reminded that all of the goals in England's 8-1 victory over San Marino in the same qualifying tournament had been scored by black players he went on to argue that:

Yeah, well, San Marino won 1–0 didn't they? [laughter] . . . I know what I'm saying. I'm happy to remember that, yeah, 1–0 to San Marino. That was [Graham] Taylor with his head stuck up his arse again. (Interview, 20 September 1996)

Yet, such a perspective does not itself exclude the possibility of some black players taking on, at least temporarily, the status of national identity symbols. During the decisive World Cup match between England and Argentina in St Etienne on 30 June, Ian Wright (having been left out of the final squad due to injury) stood in the open air on the commentators podium at the Argentina end of the stadium draped in a Cross of St George flag. He was later captured on television, when Michael Owen scored to put England ahead, celebrating in completely unreserved fashion.

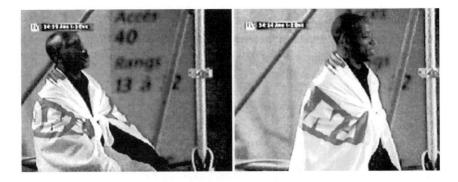

Figure 8.1 Ian Wright at the World Cup Fixture between England and Argentina, St Etienne, France 30th June 1998.

Just as some black players may be able to transcend the parameters of inclusion constructed by white supporters through conformity with established 'markers' of commitment to the national side, similar processes can work in relation to the place of black supporters. Black and Asian fans are pretty thin on the ground at England matches, particularly away from home, but there is a small and growing contingent. At least seven black fans were observed during the course of the trip to Poland and, from a much larger sample, almost thirty black and Asian supporters at the England World Cup matches in Marseilles and Toulouse. What was interesting about a significant number of these fans though was their proximity to some of the violent disturbances that took place in these locations, which are typically characterized as the product of an essentially 'white' English subculture.

In one incident in Katowice, after a minor confrontation with the Polish police had been headed off through a retreat into a bar at the bottom of the main street, several fans attempted to encourage a movement back outside in order to 'save face'. The most prominent of these supporters was a tall black fan, probably in his mid to late twenties who was pushing his way to the front shouting 'well come on let's go back outside . . . what are we doing hiding in here? We are England? Let's get out, let's get at 'em. Why do we stand around? Why do we hide in the pub?' About thirty or forty fans followed his lead and regrouped outside the pub before the main body of England fans reappeared and an elaborate game of 'cat and mouse' took place between Polish and English supporters and the police. Later on in the day, another black supporter who was with the predominantly white West Ham fans was centrally involved in the confrontation with the rival 'firm' of Aston Villa supporters and the running battles with Polish supporters outside the stadium.

Other black fans on the trip were not involved in any of the observed incidents but all of those seen in Poland and the majority of those in France for the World Cup were located within broader groups of white supporters. What these multi-racial alliances seem to indicate, in the context of support for the England team, is the significance of the cultural forms associated with England supporters rather than the racial appearance of those involved. As we have already seen in our discussion of domestic fan cultures the boundaries circumscribing black fans' inclusion within such arenas can be dependent upon their conformity with the 'white' working-class masculine normative structures associated with certain aspects of football culture. It may well be that black fans have to prove their credentials in these contexts by taking leading roles in order to have their inclusion recognized.

Vince, a prominent black Tottenham fan who has made his support for England clear on television and in magazine articles in which he argues the case for black English football fans to support the England national team, commented on the greater numbers of black and Asian fans following England in France. In doing so it is interesting that he made specific reference to these fans' accommodation with the codes of self-presentation typically associated with England's 'hooligan' supporters:

> There were a lot more black England fans in France. It was still pathetic given that we are supposed to be a multi racial country, but there was a lot more black faces than I've ever seen before. I saw maybe 20 or 30 black fans and they were all boys ['hooligans'] man. They were all boys. They were all labelled up. All in their Stone Island and all up for it [confrontation]. I couldn't believe it. I even saw Asian fans. That's the first time I've seen Asian fans supporting England away from Wembley and they were all boys, they all wanted some, I'm telling you. (Interview, 22 July 1998)

The reference here to 'even Asian' is significant. In one sense it is a response to the perceived lack of Asian football fans more generally, although the depth of commitment to football support is often vastly underestimated. But equally it also points to the ways in which such acceptance is based largely on a conventional notion of masculinity that Asian men are supposed to lack. So the 'even' here is as much about the surprise in their display of aggressive masculinity as to their 'race.'

Similarly the recognition by white England fans that black and Asian supporters of the national side might be associated with football violence reveals some of the small-scale, place specific renegotiations occurring around issues of race, nation and belonging within this context. Recalling a series of incidents he experienced during the Euro 96 tournament 'Vince' described the atmosphere outside *The Globe* pub, opposite Baker St underground station in London, prior to the England versus Scotland game on 15 June 1996. This pub is a common rallying point for England fans on their way to Wembley and it seemed if all the serious 'hooligan firms' had turned out for the game. Dotted amongst these groups were perhaps three or four black England fans, all with white friends.

Vince described the acceptance with which these black fans were greeted and the ways in which it was caged within the quasi criminal language and assumed knowledge of 'football hooligans'. This integration even went to the point where total strangers who supported variously West Ham and Wolves approached 'Vince' and offered him support such as 'you get any trouble here today, we're going down with you.' and 'You all right – it must be a bit hard here being a black guy – well fuck it, any problems here, we're with you mate – fucking hell. Fucking black? Well it don't matter, ain't it, supporting England, ain't it?' The open recognition by some of the white England fans of the issue of racism and how it might affect Vince is striking given the wider prevalence of racism within the subculture.

However, the presence of black fans during the tournament forced a grudging acknowledgement even from some politically committed right wing fans. Vince recounts here the moment when the police led a group of C18 supporting football fans away from *The Globe*. C18 are a violent neo-Nazi group established in the 1980s to defend organized neo-fascist political interest. The name stands for C = Combat; 1 = A (first letter of the alphabet); 8 = H (eighth letter of the alphabet) i.e. Combat Adolf Hitler. Vince picks up the story:

> I'm right on the kerb – this is mad – I'm right on the kerb [outside the *Globe Pub*] and C18 are walking past. I'm with my mates and all that, and then they just walked past me. But one guy stopped and clocked me, it was the weirdest thing – total skinhead as well, it was really weird, and he just looked at me and like he nods – I've got a little rose, red rose lapel on and he looked at me, looked at my badge and just nods . . . and goes: 'Yeah, right.' And I just held my own, it was just like eye contact and like: 'Today we're on the same team, yeah, England. Any other day it'd be different, but today it's about the fucking Jocks' . . . He just looked at me and like well I'm their geezer, you know – fucking England . . . and then the Police moved him on and everyone's just like looking around and I was like fuck, and it was so frightening! It was an acknowledgement, it was just all in the eyes though, it was brilliant, it was, in a weird way, in a perverse way it was brilliant. We had a conversation with the eyes in like two seconds and I sort of said: 'Well listen, I know you're a racist cunt, but nothing's gonna happen today, is it, 'cause it's about Scotland?' (Interview, 30 October 1996)

Beyond this embracing of conformity and the working class masculine values associated with sections of England's support there is some evidence that these forms of behaviour may even intersect with the broader use of racialized and xenophobic language by black fans themselves. This was most dramatically illustrated in Marseilles when a group of England fans in the age range 28 to 35, which included two black members, became involved in a violent confrontation with local youths. Following the match against Tunisia a group of around a dozen Huddersfield fans including two black members, one dressed in designer casual clothes and one in an England shirt, were in a side street with a group of a similar number of Leeds fans. In the domestic context these supporters have a long history of confrontation and would normally be fierce rivals. However, in this instance they had apparently just been involved in a violent confrontation with a gang of local youths and were now faced by three groups of Tunisian supporters and local youths, mostly of North African appearance.

The England fans who were by now receiving some element of police protection whilst being assaulted with bricks and bottles, were essentially cornered but were operating as a united unit, punching any rivals who ventured through the police line and 'fronting' their opponents with performative gestures and insults. The fact that their adversaries appeared to be of North African extraction led to their uniform description as Arabs and the racialization of insults within that framework. The black Huddersfield fans were centrally involved in the confrontation and fully embraced by the broader group of England fans. After up to an hour of this stand off, which had been characterized by a cool, street-wise demeanour amongst the England fans a bus was brought in to evacuate them. However, once on the bus the release of tension appeared to give these supporters a context in which they could perform a whole series of overtly nationalistic and racialized chants at the crowd outside, which were largely constructed around references to the Second World War, Nazi concentration camps and Arabs. We are indebted to our friend and colleague Patrick Slaughter who witnessed these events for this observation.

In this context, the colour of individual England fan's skin appeared to be dissolved into the England shirts and Stone Island clothing that they wore, despite the overtly racialized insults that were being directed at their commonly recognized 'Arab' opponents. Where black fans are supporting England and embody the normative modes of behaviour that are invoked in conflict situations it may be that the 'national', and on occasion racial, characterization of the opposition may allow a movement beyond the dismissal of 'race talk' as 'meaningless play' to direct participation in or complicity with certain forms of racial and xenophobic abuse.

Nevertheless the degree to which black supporters can be fully assimilated by England fans and their own willingness to accommodate racialised constructions of Englishness in less tension filled circumstances remains ambiguous. 'Vince' described an incident that occurred during the half time interval of England's match against Scotland at Wembley during the Euro 96 tournament:

> I'm in the toilet – right – and I've gone in the cubicle and I've locked the door. Then these two white Villa fans come in behind me and they obviously don't know I'm in the cubicle. They go: 'Did you see that fucking cunt from Sky [TV] upstairs, he's a cunt.' Then they just started singing: 'English, white and proud of it, English, white and proud of it.' Then I come out the toilet – right. And they looked and they just looked at me and sort of like stared. It went totally silent 'cause there were loads of people in there, and then I answered them: 'English, black and proud of it, English, black and proud of it.' And they just, and all just laughed ahhhhha! (Interview, 30 October 1996)

This incident could have quite easily had a very different outcome, with Vince being attacked, but it did not. In such lived interactions the meanings of race and nation are prised open, revealed and momentarily transcended. However, they also reveal the temporary and contingent nature of these forms of acknowledgement and racial inclusion. It is entirely plausible that the inclusion of black fans like Vince can occur simultaneously with complexly articulated forms of racist culture that were in evidence on numerous occasions throughout our research.

What seemed particularly interesting in the course of these enquiries was the sense of freedom of expression, which at times sat in contrast with the broader fan collective and the reality or otherwise of players' commitment on the field. This sense of freedom of expression, even in relation to overtly racialized readings of the game, appears to be located within the context of the class-inflected camaraderie and cultural confidence generated by the football match experience and more specifically the ambiguities surrounding the racial inclusiveness of the England national team.

This perspective was illustrated by Greigsie the day after the World Cup qualifier in Georgia on the train back to Manchester from London, where the group had stayed on to attend the Remembrance Day Service and celebrate Greigsies' birthday. After looking at the newspaper match reports he stated that 'I noticed three black players yesterday, not too happy about that, getting back to the old 1980s levels'. Previously he had said he:

> always make[s] a point of noting the all white teams. Greece, five nil, all white team . . . Like in this day, alright, ones alright, two I think you're pushing it, but when I mean your having four and one sub, half the team like, it doesn't get on. Some black players are worthy of a place but you can't saturate the team, in my eyes. Anyone who's intelligent enough to look at it from that perspective will tell you the same thing. (Interview, 20 September 1996)

As we previously reflected, whilst he is resigned to the inevitability of Britain remaining a multi-racial country, Greigsie still feels the need to defend his ideal notion of Englishness through management of the racial composition of the England football team. The parading of Union flags with images of the Red Hand of Ulster at their centre and the photos that the group took of one another posing with straight arm salutes during the trip to Georgia provide further indicators of the ways in which this cultural setting provides opportunities for the expression of pseudo-fascist political perspectives and racially pure notions of Englishness that are rarely publicly articulated elsewhere. These forms of practice are an enduring feature amongst a significant proportion of England's travelling support as Debbie, a Manchester City supporter of dual English – Italian heritage, reflects upon her experience of England fans during the 1990 World Cup in Italy:

> They form a large minority of the England fans. Women going to football is not that large a number anyway, but following England it's tiny, like in Sardinia, the campsite in Sardinia, there were probably two or three women, a massive proportion of men, white, males, 18-30 and we'd hear blokes talking about how they were on international duty. And you'd think, 'What are you talking about, you're watching a football game, you're not on international duty'. But they were defending Queen and country, they saw themselves as representing England, the crown . . . (Interview, 12 January 1996)

Nevertheless there is little evidence to suggest that support for the England side is characterised by anything more than the marginal involvement of organized far right political groups. Indeed such notions are often ridiculed by England fans themselves, particularly in the context of the disturbances in Dublin in February 1995 which were widely attributed in the press to the activities of the neo-Nazi C18 paramilitary group. England fans who were at Lansdowne Road widely dismiss the notion that the trouble was instigated by any particular group or individual whereas others have pointed out that the C18 activists who were pinpointed were also reported to have been travelling to Bruge for a Chelsea European Cup Winners Cup tie the same week. Even Greigsie who does acknowledge that there is some far-right influence within England fan cultures, having previously told us of some activity at a game in Norway, was keen to play down the role of C18 in the instigation of the trouble in Dublin:

> I've gotta say that a minority of it were Combat 18, in inverted commas, but I don't think it was particularly wanting to cause trouble. I wouldn't have said it were premeditated, I mean the majority of the fans who went wouldn't have thought it would be premeditated. It was just a few on the piss all day joined in with it. A lot of people do the Nazi salute, so what? They're not necessarily in the National Front or BNP. It's just cos a lot of people do it, they'll do it. (Interview, 20 September 1996)

Nevertheless the prevalence of and sympathy for racist rhetoric within some sections of England support is without question.

Equally there are fans who have made visits to the Second World War Nazi concentration camp at Auschwitz whilst in Poland or other parts of Eastern Europe for England away fixtures. At least some of these fans went in order to mark their sympathy with the Nazi regime as Greigsie reflects on a visit to Auschwitz in 1993 on which he missed out:

> I must admit I'm gutted I didn't go. I mean they all had their pictures taken there Zeig Heiling and all that . . . some of them mean it without a doubt. Some of them went there for a laugh, some of them mean it. I'm sure they wouldn't have gone there unless they wanted to do that. I mean my mate's done it coming back from Yugoslavia and on the way back from the Nuremberg rally, pictures of him Zeig Heiling, Herr Hitler and stuff like that. (Interview, 20 September 1996)

On our trip to Poland, however, visits to Auschwitz by England fans appeared to represent a way of broadening the trip beyond simply seeing the rather depressing industrial town of Katowice and a football match. When the idea of making the visit was raised within our group, Andy recounted how on his last visit to see England play Poland in 1993 he had gone with a group of Chelsea supporters and he recalled how 'there were a few nutters that went down there last time but I just found it interesting. It's not everyday you get the chance to go to Auschwitz'. Similarly other England fans we met during the day in Katowice who had taken the twenty-minute taxi ride to the concentration camp and its museums seemed genuinely compelled by the experience and how well-preserved it was rather than any desire to want to demonstrate some form of allegiance with the political significance of the site.

Similarly the chanting of 'no surrender to the IRA' has become little more than a ritual amongst many England fans, largely predicated upon the need for an easily identified and vilifiable collective footballing enemy and the importance of belonging within an emotive football crowd. However, a minority of fans have shown a clear interconnection in their accounts of English nationalism, Ulster Unionism and popular racism. A survey of the Union Jacks and Crosses of St George that adorn the barriers at any England away match will reveal a significant number carrying loyalist insignia, whilst the passion with which some supporters sing 'no surrender' during the national anthem seems to illustrate some degree of fit between culturally driven behaviour and political perspectives on nationhood.

In the Municipal Stadium in Toulouse during the World Cup match against Romania a group of white England supporters stood behind the goal, who did not have individual seat allocations but had somehow managed to get into this part of the stadium. In the build up to kick off the group sang with varying degrees of commitment, but one member, who was heavily built with closely cropped blond hair and probably in his early to mid thirties, sang every patriotic song, *Rule Britannia*, *God Save the Queen* and *Keep St George in my Heart* with absolute fervour. He also lay particular emphasis on the chanting of 'no surrender to the IRA, scum' at the appropriate moments in each song. When the crowd sang 'English and proud of it' he appeared to be in a state of total joy and wonderment, adding the word 'white' after English to the chorus line and turning to look at the banks of thousands of almost exclusively white, predominantly male, England fans with a broad smile, brimming with pride. At half time I had a discussion with him about the crowd and the patriotic singing and he told me 'this [watching England] is the last place where you can be a white, Anglo-Saxon man and not have to worry what anybody else thinks about it.'

It is clear that the England national team does attract young men who have a passion for an implicitly, if not exclusively, white working-class English culture.

'And we All Like Vindaloo': Embourgeoisment, 'New' England Fans and Resistance to the Manipulation of English Football Culture

The 1990s have witnessed some remarkable shifts in the popularity and representation of English football, both domestically and in the international arena. Ever since England reached the semi-finals of the World Cup during Italia 90 and Gazza's tears covered the television screens and the front pages of the English press, a love affair with football has endured. Furthermore, this phenomenon has not been restricted to any particular section of society, but has been characterized by growing levels of interest in the game across the social spectrum, whether considered in terms of class, income, gender, age or racial background.

However, although these increased levels of interest were reflected in the launch of the FA Premiership in 1992 and expanding live and television audiences for domestic matches, England's failure to qualify for the 1994 World Cup meant that the first test of the public's interest in the fortunes of the national side did not arrive until England hosted the Euro 96 football championships.

Even then, whilst the organisers of Euro 96 billed the tournament through the slogan 'Football's coming home', the build up to Euro 96 in the British press was characterized by speculation that we were about to witness a festival of violence rather than football. The terminology of both broadsheet and tabloid newspapers at times suggested that fans from across Europe were set to stage a re-enactment of the Second World War, typified by *The Times* declaration on the 12th May 1996 that the 'Police Fear 'Third World War' on Terraces of Euro 96'.

The reality was in fact quite different. Indeed Euro 96 generated a further acceleration of interest in the national game and successive record viewing figures for England's quarter final and semi final fixtures against Spain and Germany. As the tournament progressed and England looked ever more capable of winning it, the nation was increasingly gripped. Capacity crowds turned out at Wembley to see England play, which had taken on a more feminized and heterogeneous look than normally associated with support for the national side, partly because of the unique advance marketing of the event. These crowds also seemed to embody a greater sense of occasion than had previously been the case at England games, which has been acknowledged by seasoned, long-standing fans such as Greigsie:

> Oh yeah, it was the noisiest crowd for a long, long time. It's very rarely they [normally] get off their arse. Because a lot of people had to buy their tickets a couple of years in advance and all that, so you really got a lot of people who'd not been to a Wembley game before, and they had all the face paint and the shirtsleeves, the re-emergence of the George Cross at a game for a start, you know it really was a rollercoaster. (Interview, 20 September 1996)

The interest in England's performances extended well beyond attendance at the games themselves though, with the official England song *Three Lions*, recorded by the *Lightning Seeds* and the comedians David Badiel and Frank Skinner, reaching number one in the charts and millions crowding around television and video screens in houses, pubs and clubs throughout the country. The breadth of interest in England's performances during the tournament seemed to mark the emergence of a new sense of national patriotism, which took several forms.

On the one hand there was a concerted attempt to whip up jingoism by the tabloid press, which increased in intensity as the tournament progressed (see the *Daily Mirror* 25 and 26 June 1996). At the same time there was a real attempt to assert a more benign patriotism, with the abiding image of Euro 96 being the thousands of male and female England fans painted with the red cross of St George. Nevertheless, the racial composition of those taking part in the national celebrations was not lost on the racist right in Britain. John Tyndall, then leader of the British National Party, wrote in the aftermath of the tournament that '. . . What was noticeable in the demonstrations of crowd patriotism . . . was the overwhelming whiteness of those taking part' (Tyndall 1996: 7).

Tyndall went on to lament reports that during the dramatic semi-final against Germany, which ultimately resulted in England's defeat by a penalty 'shoot out', more than half of a poll of Afro-Caribbean football enthusiasts were cheering for Germany. Indeed these issues became a subject of debate, from different perspectives, amongst black English football supporters in the build up to the 1998 World Cup in the context of widespread support for Jamaica, who were making their first ever World Cup finals appearance (see McKenzie 1998). The popularity of the Jamaican team in Britain's cities is discussed in full in the next chapter. However, it is interesting to reflect upon the fact that this debate took place within a context in which support for the England national team was broadening far beyond those supporters traditionally associated with notions of racial nationalism.

In fact the new more benign forms of English nationalism displayed at Wembley stadium, to which Tyndall refers, sat alongside the contingent inclusion of black fans within the England team's fan cultures, which we have already noted. Perhaps more significantly, the disturbances which took place in central London after England's game against Scotland – vividly captured in Christopher Terrill's programme 'High Noon' for the 'Soho Stories' BBC series (Terrill 1996) – also marked the emergence of new demarcation lines within the ranks of England's fans not noticed in mainstream reports.

For long standing fans such as Greigsie the appreciation of larger attendances at Wembley, greater passion and displays of patriotism are countered by the unwanted and potentially divisive pressure to moderate behaviour in a more family orientated and feminized environment:

Yeah well you always get your schoolboys there, you know, your coachloads down at the games, down here in the tunnel end sort of thing, you know you're always gonna get that . . . but I do object to a lot of women being at football, I don't like to be told, 'stop swearing' or 'watch your language. That's why I prefer to stand. I mean you buy a seat and you're up and down these days. I like standing anyway but obviously in this day and age you've gotta sit, but if I want a seat and I'm having to bob up and down every five minutes when someone's getting out or saying they can't see it pisses me off. [But] football these days is catering for them. (Interview, 20 September 1996)

These tensions have now begun to shift into new areas of England's fan culture as a result of the increased interest in travelling away to support the team. Prior to the World Cup qualifying fixture against Italy in Rome in 1997, England supporters who rejected the cultural norms established by the broader fan collective had tended to remain rather isolated and to keep their support at a distance. As Debbie, who was involved in the organization of the Football Supporters' Association Fan Embassy during Italia 90 recalls:

> We [would] have people coming into the Embassy – I mean not a lot – but a fair few would come in and they'd be saying they wanted somewhere to stay but not where the England fans were. And these *were* England fans themselves, but they didn't want to be on a campsite where 'that lot' were. (Interview, 12 January 1996)

However, the enormous significance of the 1997 match in Rome, as a result of which either country could qualify for the World Cup finals, along with the romance associated with a trip to the ancient Italian capital, attracted unprecedented interest. In the event approximately 10,000 fans made the trip who were roughly divided between those who had obtained tickets through the FA's England Members Club, and those who had got tickets through corporate hospitality and privately organized packages.

The shifting nature of the supporter base was noticeable not just in the numbers of fans present at the game but in the reaction to the Italian police's treatment of them (The Football Association, 1997). The disturbances in the Stadio Olimpico, which ten years previously would in all likelihood have been reported as an England fan riot, were on this occasion depicted as the gross mistreatment of innocent football fans. This representation was undoubtedly related to the presence of many thousands of fans, who had largely travelled on corporate and private packages totally unused to and unprepared for the hostile reception from the authorities and willing to articulate their concerns to the press and English FA. In turn these authorities were prepared to take the complaints more seriously in the context of England's qualification for France, the FAs own bid to stage the 2006 World Cup and the presence of 'respectable' fans willing to conduct interviews with the media.

Despite the disturbances in Rome, the growing levels of interest and the location of the much hyped 1998 World Cup in neighbouring France ensured that England's support during the finals themselves would be even broader. In spite of the best efforts of the English authorities to deter ticketless fans from travelling to France, at the opening group games in the World Cup against Tunisia, Romania and Colombia, upwards of 30,000 fans were present. Having bought whatever spare tickets were available for prices of up to £250, England fans almost completely took over the stadiums for the matches staged in Toulouse and Lens and were possibly the largest single contingent of supporters from outside France.

The euphoria and optimism surrounding English football seemed to have been carried forward from Euro 96 as fans from a wide variety of backgrounds descended on France. It is not possible to classify these supporters in simplistic terms, such was their diversity, but what can be argued is that new forms of English fandom became recognizable and commonplace in the context of the large numbers attending the World Cup. However, these new forms need to be understood in terms of the specific importance of time and place as well as their relationship with the individual preferences of travelling supporters and the interventions made by the football authorities.

Many of those fans who travelled to France had followed the domestic game for years, but being amongst England fans abroad and even going to a football match abroad was a new experience. This was the case for four of a group of six white male fans in their early thirties, which included two Liverpool, one Leicester City and three Crystal Palace supporters, who travelled to the south of France by car to see England play in the opening stages of the tournament as well as taking in other games of interest. For all but one of the group this was the first time they had followed England abroad and the issues relating to and relative merits of aspects of England fan culture were a subject of debate throughout the two week trip.

They were in St Etienne on the night before England's opening match against Tunisia, having just attended the Yugoslavia v Iran match in that city before planning to head down to Marseilles the following morning. When news was received of the disturbances involving England fans there was an initial general reaction of anger and despair. Nigel, one of the Crystal Palace fans, was so unsettled by the reports of the trouble that he decided he did not want to go to Marseilles. For him, an easy association was made with aggressive nationalistic behaviour by England fans which was reinforced by news of racist abuse in the French press. He was thoroughly depressed and without having witnessed the trouble declared that it had 'ruined it [the trip] for me'. Two of the others who did not have tickets also decided not to go to Marseilles in light of the reported tension in the city but the rest of the group travelled in for the game and then left immediately afterwards.

From that point the group sought to keep away from the centres where England fans would be staying, spending much of the time in Montpellier in the south of France and using that location as a base for travelling to games on the days they were played. Equally, there was a certain amount of apprehension about even socializing with other England supporters, for fear of the potential for getting drawn into confrontational situations.

The potential for similar moments of uneasiness appears to have been a feature for many fans in France as characterized by the rapid dispersal of supporters after the game in Marseilles. Whilst there were upwards of 30,000 England fans in the city for the opening game on Monday 15 June there did not appear to be any further significant concentrations of England fans in one location until the weekend prior to the game against Romania in Toulouse the following Monday. Several supporters that we met on the beach and in bars and clubs around Montpellier indicated that they were simply travelling in on the day of games so as to avoid both the potential for trouble and the restrictions on drinking and socializing imposed by the authorities wherever England played. Equally, for some of those who might have been more willing to become involved in disturbances, there was an imperative to avoid the intense surveillance that would accompany any major gathering of supporters.

In the main though, this desire to be away from large concentrations of England fans did not preclude the open celebration of English footballing identities, or even broader football-related cultural exchange. Throughout our time in Montpellier, the 'English' pub on the city's main square was occupied in the evenings by English football fans. As the evenings progressed, and particularly after any World Cup matches had finished, a group of up to forty or fifty fans, often including a number of women, would sing outside the bar from a wide repertoire of domestic and national football songs. These would range from the England anthems *Keep St George in My Heart*, *No Surrender to the IRA* and *Rule Britannia* to individual fans' own club songs. Equally, where non-English football fans made themselves heard they were often encouraged to do so, with England fans joining in the chanting of other countries names such as 'Norwesh' and 'Italia'. At other times rival fans would chant at, rather than with, one another, but this was always done within the context of a carnivalesque spirit and usually acted as a precursor to friendly socializing amongst the various nationalities represented.

This trend was taken further on the night of France's 4–0 victory over Saudi Arabia when up to a dozen England fans joined French supporters in the upstairs section of one of the many Montpellier bars and sang the *Marseillaise*, '*Zizou*' (*Zinedine Zidane*) , *Allez La France* and other French national songs. After a while the French supporters began singing English football songs as individuals took it in turns to lead renditions of club and national anthems. This was a very specific moment, which at times became quite tense as the realities of footballing allegiances and rivalries were played out. However, through the spontaneity and shared passion for football and its traditions, a form of cultural exchange was generated that eventually resulted in the football languages of the different supporters present merging into one, both metaphorically and linguistically, with the celebratory singing of 'Si tout le monde deteste les Allemangnes [if you all hate Germany] clap your hands'.

These forms of interaction were in stark contrast to the experience of England fans during Italia 90 when large numbers of supporters were concentrated together on camp sites in Sardinia. Within this environment the boundaries of expressive behaviour were much more strictly guarded and internalized. Mark, a Manchester City supporter who followed England through the tournament as well as working at the FSA's Fan Embassy recalls the ways in which this would impact upon notions of racial inclusiveness amongst England fans and broader associations with other supporters:

> We were on this campsite and we're watching a game . . . and there was this Villa fan and a United fan started singing 'Ooh, aah, Paul McGrath [a black Irish footballer who played for Manchester United in the mid to late 1980s before moving to Aston Villa], I said ooh ah Paul McGrath,' and this lad. I've never seen hatred like it. His eyes were popping, he was literally frothing at the mouth, spitting out, he's going 'How can you say that about Paul McGrath? He's a fucking nigger!' . . . You see racism and you see lots of people that are like sheep and that, you know, 'You black bastard, you black bastard', giving lots of stick, but this lad was just so angry, and so violent, because somebody had sung a song about a nigger that must have played for a couple of teams in England and he was an Irish player. And all these Irish fans were packing up the tents the next day and there were fights all the time, wherever we went. There was no room for misunderstandings. Any Italians that tried to ingratiate themselves with the English or just be friendly, they were given loads of abuse and told to fuck off, and if it carried on there was violence. (Interview, 12 January 1996)

However, what is interesting about the new forms of interaction described previously was their construction around the notion of distinct national cultures rather than any sense of cultural hybridity. In some ways they provided a new context for the celebration and re-affirmation of previously defined versions of national identity and 'ethnic absolutism' (Gilroy 1987 and 1993). What was significant was the mutual recognition of supporters' different nationalities, their different histories and different rivalries. Equally the shared celebration of these notions of distinct national identities were policed by internally defined boundaries, reflected in the refusal of several England fans to sing the Scottish anthem *Flower of Scotland*. The collective of nationalities present was then only reunited through the signification of a mutual 'national enemy' and uniform vilification of the Germans.

Furthermore, these modest and partial redefinitions of England fan culture were taking place throughout France during the World Cup, mainly as a result of the influx of a vast new contingent of supporters. As we saw in our discussion of supporter confrontations in Marseilles, rivalries and hostility constructed around notions of nationhood have in other contexts intersected with racialized perspectives of belonging and entitlement. There are clear similarities here with the forms of contingent involvement achieved by ethnic minority fans within local and regional contexts that we discussed in Chapter 3. As in the domestic context 'race' always stands on the sidelines within the armoury of football supporters. This point was illustrated following the murder of two Leeds United supporters before a UEFA Cup semi-final against Galatasaray in April 2000 when reaction amongst English football fans was quickly extended to Turkish football supporters and Turkey in general. By the time of the Euro 2000 finals in Holland and Belgium in June the song *I'd rather be a Paki than a Turk* had become firmly enshrined within the England fan collective's repertoire as a series of reprisals ensued. In the context of the widely apparent racial stereotypes and prejudices applied to the Turkish and north African Diaspora in northern Europe, characterized by notions of knife-carrying, untrustworthy, arrogant, lazy immigrants with alien ways, the domestic configurations of this song discussed in Chapter 2 were disrupted. Rather than playfully advocating a preference for the identity of a mutually stigmatized racial outgroup, the song works within the frames of reference of the England fan collective itself to locate 'Turks' as the principal outsider.

This point was well illustrated on the day of the England v Germany game in Charleroi in 'De Royal Nord' pub on the main street leading up to the stadium, where scores of England fans ritually sang *I'd rather be a Paki than a Turk* and *Die, die Turkey Fucking Die* to the tune of *She'll Be Coming Round the Mountains* despite the fact that the pub was exclusively occupied by England fans. In this context the song does not invoke a mutually recognized outgroup in order to humiliate a footballing rival since the rival is not present. The song performs the function of re-ordering established categories of racial animosity amongst the England fans themselves.

However, what is particularly interesting about England fans rivalry with the Turkish is the extent to which those fans are demonstratively seen to embody unfettered working-class, masculine football-fan cultures that reject the commercialism and sanitisation associated with football in the twenty-first century. Through participation in sport and the sporting rituals associated with their performances at football matches Turks have been seen to embody and celebrate a national culture of machismo enshrined in the notion of being 'as strong as a Turk' (Stokes 1996). As such, whilst England's new 'respectable fans' or 'muppets' who don't 'know the score' and comply with the authorities' attempts to control their behaviour often become the subject of derision and scorn, the loathing of Turkish fans may be entwined with an unwillingness to acknowledge their status as football's new 'bad boys'.

For in the context of contemporary globally marketed football tournaments, characterized by rampant commercialism and glorified media representations, sections of England's support have demonstrated a determination to defend their own displays of passion and loyalty. Given the strength of many supporters' identification with the England team and the fan cultures that surround it, there is a deep suspicion of attempts to interfere with the traditional values of those supporters. The introduction of the England supporters' band provides a good example of the ways in which such interference can promote rather than suppress hostility. The band, which plays a collection of brass instruments and drums, has over the last few seasons become a regular feature at Sheffield Wednesday games, playing the tunes to favoured football anthems in an effort to encourage greater enthusiasm amongst the crowd. Before the World Cup they were invited by the English FA to become the England Team's official supporters' band during the tournament and provided with much valued tickets for all of England's games in the middle of the 'England section'.

Initially, both in Marseilles and in Toulouse, the band was received with considerable enthusiasm by England fans as it beat out the national anthem, *Rule Britannia* and its own tournament recording, the tune to *The Great Escape*. The choice of tunes with such patriotic resonance clearly encouraged supporters, and particularly the newer fans, to accommodate their presence and join in. However, as England's football matches unfolded their natural drama encouraged more traditional crowd reactions and incident-specific chanting. The band's incessant repetition of the same tunes, which was drowning out the crowd's own spontaneous singing, became an irritant for many supporters. In Toulouse and Lens murmurs of discontent began to meet each rendition of *The Great Escape*. This was to some extent ameliorated by a kind of patriotic duty amongst some of those supporters who felt compelled to sing along when *Rule Britannia* was played. However in Toulouse, by the middle of the second half, chants of 'You can stick your fucking band up your arse' were emanating from at least one group of more traditional England fans in defiant contrast with those who sat singing alongside them.

In less formal but more sophisticated fashion the efforts of the band *Fat Les* to influence the broad spectrum of England's support through the pop record *Vindaloo* which have been celebrated in some quarters (see Perryman, 1999) were also only partially embraced. Alex James of the pop group *Blur* and a partner in the project explained in a promotional interview that the song, which hangs around the chorus line 'Vindaloo, Vindaloo, and we all like Vindaloo', is a 'post-modern tribute to multiculturalism'. Keith Allen developed the point:

> That's exactly what it is, but, at the same time it's gonna get the 'erberts at it. All the beer-bellies and the 'erberts, they're gonna have to really bite their tongues and, you know . . . VIN-DA-LOO!! (Sampson 1998b: 12)

The song was undoubtedly popular amongst many football fans, holding the number two spot in the charts for several weeks and only topped by the re-released *Three Lions*, but the degree to which it encouraged active England supporters and Allen's "erberts' to reflect upon notions of national identity is suspect. In fact, if anything it was the traditional football vernacular of the song that was embraced, with the words and meanings themselves being altered by those fans who sang 'In-ger-lund, In-ger-lund and we all love In-ger-lund', thus divorcing the song from its interpretation of a multicultural England.

This clinging to traditional notions of England fan culture was most dramatically illustrated in Lens where the stadium was almost completely taken over by the broad spectrum of England supporters. Throughout the tournament, commercialized carnivalesque notions of football fandom were being promoted through a succession of television images of the colour and choreography found amongst fans, particularly of Brazil, Jamaica and Holland. These images were most uniformly represented through supporters' participation in the 'Mexican Wave'. This involves supporters rising out of and returning to their seats in a wave like motion around the stadium. The term was coined after it became popular amongst football fans during the 1986 World Cup finals but the phenomenon actually developed at American College football games. However, whilst successive attempts were made to begin such a display by some sections of supporters during the game between England and Colombia in Lens, the main body of England fans resolutely refused to join in.

This has been an England fan ritual for many years with fans often responding to the arrival of a 'wave' at their section by collectively raising two fingers in a truly carnivalesque gesture of defiance. In this big match context the point was being made by the hard core fans that the 'Mexican Wave' has nothing to do with England fan culture and that the supporters are there to watch the game and sing in support of their side, not to participate in what are perceived as 'poncey', choreographed displays for the benefit of television and corporate audiences. Their refusal to participate was finally enshrined in the chant of 'You can stick your fucking wave up your arse'. Yet as Jim White was forced to acknowledge in the *Guardian* (30 June 1998):

> The atmosphere inside Stade Felix Bollaert was considerably better than anything else encountered in the tournament so far. Granted it was not as colourful or as good-natured and the Mexican waves were weak, insipid things. But there was a rawness, an excitement, a drive that had not been matched elsewhere. Never can there have been such an active crowd at a football match. Everyone joined in the chanting, right up to the occupants of the Royal Box.

There is in this sense a degree of contestation about who and what should be associated with support for the England national team. Whilst the side has become a focus for the display of a variety of forms of English patriotism, for a significant proportion of fans the national team represents a means through which to associate with historically grounded notions of a particular white, working-class English identity. However, for many of those supporters this has more to do with an appreciation of the normative behaviour and cultural styles associated with football supporter traditions than ideologically motivated notions of England as a nation, or even the racial exclusiveness of those styles.

Nevertheless, Carrington has argued that 'the uncritical acceptance of New Lad/ 'geezer' culture as somehow being an organic expression of working-class life allows for reactionary expressions to emerge, and then be defended as being in some way an expression of authentic English nationalism' (1999: 84). We would argue that whilst the England national football team does indeed represent a site through which notions of England and the English can be interpreted, the relationships between them remain deeply complex and non-uniform. This is reflected in both the degree to which the cultures surrounding the England football team are shifting to become more racially inclusive and less insular and the enduring nature of many of the class, gender and racially influenced principles that underpin accommodation within English football cultures generally. The enduring images of the disturbances in Marseilles, Ian Wright draped in a Cross of St George, the singing of *You'll Never Take the Falklands* and the raw passion of the crowds at England's games during the 1998 World Cup finals, perhaps point the way to a more accurate understanding of the myriad forms of identity which are located around the defining principles of what it means to be an English football fan.

In the next chapter we want to contrast this experience with the ways in which football also provides a means for black and ethnic minority communities in Britain to identify with a sense of home from within a migrant heritage and an experience of being within a disapora.

–9–

Gringos, Reggae Gyals and 'Le Francais de la Souche Recente': Diaspora, Identity and Cosmopolitanism

Casablanca, Wednesday 27 May 1998

Preparation for England's 1998 World Cup campaign reached a crucial stage as the team walked out for its 'warm up' match against Morocco in Casablanca. The fixture proved to be historic in ways that were not immediately apparent. The starting line-up included four black English players, which itself symbolized the profoundly multi-racial nature of the English professional game. It was also to mark the passing, although no one knew at the time, of a symbol of boozy English masculinity: it was to be Paul Gascoigne's last outing in an England shirt. With the teams lined up on the pitch the stadium manager lost the tape with the recording of the English national anthem. A moment of silent chaos ensued. Quickly, the players led by Ian Wright and captain Paul Ince sang 'God Save the Queen' at the top of their voices and the travelling England fans – almost all of whom were white – joined in. The following day the *Sun* newspaper showed a picture of three black players including Ince, Wright and Campbell with Paul Gascoigne as national heroes singing their hearts out (*Sun,* 28 May 1998). The presence of black players in the England side has been an enduring feature of the national game since 1978 when Viv Anderson made his debut against Czechoslovakia. However, what has been striking recently is the number of black internationals playing the game at the highest level. But despite the negotiations around the involvement of black England fans discussed in Chapter 8, by comparison there are few black fans who seem to actively support the national side.

There are different things at stake when black and white people lay claim to icons of Englishness (see Cohen 1998: 301), or add their voice to the song of national stirring in sport. Paul Gilroy, perhaps more than anyone else, has pointed to the difference made when black people identify with Englishness and/or Britishness and in so doing establish new possible vectors of contingent racial inclusion (Gilroy 1993). This is a phenomenon of European states that have colonial histories signalled at the very beginning of this book. Citizens from the colonial margin migrated to the English metropolis along pre-established imperial networks

Figure 9.1 England players sing 'God Save the Queen' unaccompanied in Casablanca 27 May 1998. Published with permission of the *Sun*.

and routeways and in doing so laid claim to the identities of imperial nationalism. As we pointed out previously, there is a tension between, on the one hand, the way football provides a means to define Englishness within a pageant of white nationalism; while on the other hand, the involvement of a minority of black England fans points to the possibility of decoupling Englishness from a seemingly compulsory whiteness.

* * *

This is the context in which struggles over the possibility of 'black' and 'English/ British' being repositioned in a relationship of inclusive mutuality takes on a political resonance. The situation in the US is very different because these struggles over national belonging took on a very different form, where white supremacy has endured in a situation where people of colour are awarded the status of being 'American' without ambiguity (Hoberman 1997). The issue we want to raise in this chapter is the way sport provides a context in which images of national identity can be expressed and debated. Equally, we want to raise the issue of whether, for minority communities in Europe, such forms of contingent admission within the boundaries of the nation are necessarily an advance.

As has been pointed out in the context of recent debates black and minority identifications with Englishness are not necessarily viewed as transformative. This is where the elisions between notions of Englishness and Britishness become most acutely significant (Parekh 2000). During the game between England and Argentina that resulted in England's exit from the tournament (by the inevitable penalty shoot out), Ian Wright, who missed the finals because of injury, was pictured on television wrapped in a Cross of St George flag. Lez Henry – a black fan, musician and sociologist – commented in the aftermath of the game: 'I looked at him [Wright] on the screen and I thought "What the fuck is he doing – has he lost his mind completely!" I mean the St George Cross! That's the worst thing for a black person because according to them people you can't be black and English. Maybe Britishness would be something else because you can be "black British" but English? Never' (personal communication, 10 July 1998). The notion 'British' is widely held to be less racially or culturally exclusive and it is sometimes argued such identification can be sustained within the diaspora communities who reside in the UK alongside associations with the Caribbean, Africa, south Asia, Cyrpus and a whole range of other migrant heritages.

The relationship between these identity registers was brought into sharp focus through the Jamaican national team debut at the World Cup finals in France in 1998. Indeed, there was a significant debate in the black and minority press over whether black Britons should support England or Jamaica. Writer and ardent football fan, Paul McKenzie was the most articulate voice that proposed that black communities should throw their support behind England. He points out in what follows the moment when he was confronted by this question prior to the beginning of the tournament.

It all started down at my local barber's shop [Hackney, London]. The shop was humming as usual when we started talking about the World Cup and, in particular, how well Jamaica will do. Well, I just had to laugh when they started saying things like, 'they might reach the semifinals'. Some dreadlocked guy even thought they might win the damn thing. Then, I unveiled my newly painted St George's flag with the words Hackney emblazoned across it. The place went very silent. You could have heard a pin drop in Kingston. 'Why England?' they quizzed. 'Why?' 'Because I'm English,' I replied. 'But you're black', they informed me.

At this point I should say that I am a black man born and bred in the East End of London. Some people who saw this article in its early stages suggested I should mention this at the top of the piece. But I say to them, as I say to the guys in the barber's shop, it's not important. The 'Do you support Jamaica or England?' argument has rapidly spread and divided the English black community. I find it silly and annoying and, now that some white folks have jumped on board, I can't get away from it. (McKenzie 1998: 8–9)

Paul concluded 'It's dangerous and churlish to assume black fans are bound to support Jamaica' (McKenzie 1998: 9).

What is fascinating about this controversy is that it brought into focus two very clear cultural and political impulses within sections of the black communities in Britain. On one side, there were those – like Paul – who committed themselves to opening up Englishness for those born and bred here to include black people. On the other, there were those – like Lez Henry – who vacated (Back 1996) and distanced themselves from Englishness in favour of making connections between Jamaica and those in the African diaspora more broadly. What is so striking here is that these identifications reveal very different emphases and commitments. It is also true to say that for some it was possible for both views to be held in combination albeit with different degrees of emphasis.

In this chapter we want to begin by looking at the significance of the qualif-ication of the Jamaican national team for the 1998 World Cup and the experience of Jamaican fans – many of whom were born in Britain – and the forms of inclusion and identification embodied around the Jamaican team. The reason why we have focused on the Reggae Boyz is that something unprecedented occurred around these events which stood in sharp contrast to the nature of English football and its associated supporter cultures discussed in previous chapters. Here we want to look at the ways in which football provided a means through which nation and belonging was registered both 'at home' in the Caribbean and within the diaspora. In the concluding part of the chapter we want to explore the question of how this experience compared to the triumphant French national side during the 1998 World Cup who itself seemed to embody a more 'racially diverse' representation of French nationhood. First, we want to plot the rise of the Jamaican team and its support.

'Reggae Boyz, Reggae Boyz, Reggae Boyz!' Blackness, Diaspora and the Jamaican National Team

No one really knows how the Jamaican team came to be named the 'Reggae Boyz'. The Jamaican Football Federation acted quickly and in March 1998 they registered the 'Reggae Boyz' as a trademark in 11 countries. The official story is that the Zambians coined the name during a Jamaican national team tour in 1995 (Mailey and Muller 1998: 56), but in large part the name has stuck because of the pre-match concerts that fused football and dance-hall culture where reggae stars like Dennis Brown and Jimmy Cliff performed. The road to the 1998 World Cup finals for Jamaica was followed keenly within the diaspora. This was made possible by global communications technology often associated with reinforcing predominance of the West (see Massey 1991). In one area of south London a small pub called ironically *The Union Tavern* was the place where on 16 November 1997 a packed house of black fans saw their team draw 0–0 with Mexico and earn their trip to Europe. These events in Kingston, Jamaica had a distinctly local resonance given that this part of the metropolis has such a long standing Afro-Caribbean and specifically Jamaican community.

Elsewhere in London black fans watched the game on Sky Sports amid a carnival atmosphere. Alister Morgan, writing in the *Independent* newspaper, told of the scenes at York Hall in East London where the game was watched by 2,000 people of Jamaican origin. One of the revellers told him:

> It's not just a question of that round ball and 22 men. We're talking about the position of Jamaica and the efforts of a poor people. It's beyond football - in this country we live four and a half thousand miles from home and have been suffering for 40 years. Now Jamaica have qualified all Jamaicans will be uplifted. (*Independent*, 18 November 1997: 31)

This event provided a means for people within the diaspora to identify with Jamaica but also it offered black football fans a possibility to participate in football on their own terms. Equally, in Jamaica, the Reggae Boyz's qualification for France 1998 generated something of a partial process of national healing. Black music journalist John Masouri summed this up:

> Everyone I've spoken to remarks upon how a new sense of togetherness has swept the country since the team qualified for France . . . the Reggae Boyz success has helped heal a fractured nation by instilling hope for a better future amongst their supporters. Crime rates have dropped and patriotism is back on the agenda, with the black, green and gold flag of Jamaica now to be seen fluttering everywhere. Even many Rastas are beginning to glow with a little nationalistic pride these days . . . (Masouri 1998: 12)

Football seemed to provide both a means for domestic renewal and to reanimate connections with the widely dispersed Jamaican diaspora.

The Jamaican team – coached by the Brazilian Rene Simoes – itself featured 'English' black players like Deon Burton of Derby County, Wimbledon's Robbie Earle and Paul Hall and Fitzroy Simpson, both of Portsmouth. The inclusion of players 'from foreign' caused some initial disquiet in Jamaica, where the *Daily Observer* ran an article on 17 March 1998 with the headline – 'No, we won't cheer for a team of British rejects.' Despite some controversy in the Jamaican press, Horace Burrell, head of the Jamaican Football Association was keen to assert the rights of any member of the diaspora to claim Jamaican heritage. In response to questions about the 'English contingent', he told a journalist:

> Well, first of all let me correct you. It's not English players. They are Jamaican players whose parents came here [England] or they were born here, but we still regard them as Jamaicans. Our aim is to parade on the playing field in France the best 11 Jamaican players. That is our aim, and whether they live in England, Italy, the United States or

Jamaica, if they've been able to parade the skills in the way Rene Simoes wants, then certainly they will be a member of the team.

For Burrell an inclusive sensibility made perfect footballing and commercial sense.

As part of their pre-tournament preparation the Reggae Boyz played a series of friendly games in England. The first was a testimonial for the journeyman white player Simon Barker at Queen's Park Rangers on Sunday 22 of March. Unprecedented numbers of black people attended the game. Of the 17,000 fans packed into the stadium on that sunny afternoon probably all but a few hundred were drawn from black communities. Paul Eubanks, a journalist for the Caribbean newspaper *The Gleaner*, wrote:

> Never . . . had I seen so many black people inside one [football] ground. Generations of Jamaicans had come to watch the game. The most emotional moment for me was witnessing grandmothers at a site they would have never dreamed of entering, but they were getting ready to support their beloved team. The weather was consistent with its surroundings of Jamaicans: steel band and reggae music blaring out of the PA system, Jamaican patties on sale and even the odd 'FUNNY' cigarette being passively smoked. (*The Gleaner,* 1–7 April 1998: 30)

The significance of this event is hard to overstate. It marked not only the emergence of unprecedented numbers of black fans actively going to watch live football but also a shift in the nature of supporter culture. What this event revealed was the ethnocentrism of English football and its class-inflected and gendered nature.

One of the striking things about the culture of Jamaican support was the transposition of the rituals associated with Jamaican musical cultures to the footballing context. There should be no surprise in this given the level of fanaticism about football both in the Caribbean and in London's black communities. English Premier League football is followed closely in Jamaica, given the prominence of figures like John Barnes during his career at Liverpool and also Ian Wright at Arsenal. Football matters are debated each Saturday over the counter at virtually every black music record shop in Britain where there are plenty of football fans inside the Reggae music business itself. Earl Bailey and Nazma Muller commenting on the long association between football and music in Jamaica, particularly in relation to Bob Marley, conclude:

> Every DJ worth his salt knows how to kick a ball . . . Given the chance to marry both Jamaican loves, many entertainers turned up at the National Stadium and away matches to rally fans behind the Reggae Boyz. From Beenie Man to Bounty Killer, Yellowman to Jimmy Cliff, they came out to support the national team. (Bailey and Muller, 1998: 88)

In the aftermath of qualification the reggae music industry set about the task of creating a theme tune for the Reggae Boyz. The first Reggae Boyz tune was recorded by the London reggae band The Black Astronauts, although this record was not widely distributed (John Masouri, personal communication 15 September, 1998). In practice Jamaica Unlimited's *Rise Up,* featuring Toots Hibbert, Diana King, Ziggy Marley and Maxi Priest amongst others, became the official Reggae Boyz anthem. One of the best tunes was actually recorded by members of the team. It was called *Kick It* and was released under the name Reggae Boyz. *Kick It* featured Djing from Donald Stewart – himself a musician – and vocals from Paul Hall and Fitzroy Simpson over the Willie Williams' Studio One classic rhythm *Armagideon Time.* The tune has the distinction of being perhaps the only truly plausible pop record ever to be recorded by footballers. A flood of releases followed and singers and DJs gave lyrical tributes at live shows between November and the World Cup finals be it at high-profile concerts or sound-systems strung up in Kingston, New York or Birmingham.

The fusion of music and football garnered around the Jamaican team meant that the experience of going to games was quite unlike anything encountered in Britain before. John Masouri reflected in the black music magazine *Echoes* on the carnival atmosphere and sense of togetherness found in the English grounds where Jamaica played: 'Many of us had never experienced such warm, friendly vibes at football matches before' he wrote (Masouri 1998: 12). Football was also being opened publicly to black women in ways that were – in Britain at least – unprecedented. Plenty of black women had followed football privately and from afar but here they were watching football live. Marlene, a young woman born in London of Jamaican parentage, commented on her visit to Loftus Road:

> It was good to go to football. I've never been to a game before but it wasn't really like the football you see on the TV, it was *just like going to a dance with the music and everything.* It was funny because I think the QPR players were a bit confused when they came out and saw all us black people and so few white faces in the crowd. [our emphasis] (Fieldnotes, 26 March 1998)

The participation of black women in football showed parallels with some of the broader patterns of female expression in Jamaican popular culture. In the context of the reggae dance-hall women have used music to engender female power through dancing and the 'extravagant display of flashy jewellery, expensive clothes, elaborate hairstyles' (Cooper 1993: 155). Carolyn Cooper has argued, these performances embody complex gender politics in which women's power lies in the control over their own bodies and sexuality. It has been argued that through dance-hall culture women have achieved high levels of autonomy and self-affirmation (Miller 1991). Equally, their presence within football grounds raised

Figure 9.2 'Reggae Gyals'.

parallel issues with regard to those discussed previously in connection with the construction of black men within white masculinities in football. Here, black men can be respected through shared masculine codes but also viewed as the bearers of racialized projections around issues of violence and sexuality (see Chapter 3). The range of representations of black femininity within football poses similar questions and we will address these in what follows. It was clear, however, that traces of dance-hall culture are present amongst Jamaican football fans both in terms of their style and the significant numbers of young women in attendance at games.

The second game arranged for Jamaica in the UK was at Ninian Park against the Welsh national team on 26 March 1998. Paul, a black South London entrepreneur, brought 1,000 tickets and organized a fleet of 11 coaches to ferry the London-based Reggae Boyz and Reggae Gyals to the match from the capital. 'I want to give people a whole experience. You can get a coach to the game and then stay in Cardiff for an "after-party" reggae dance' he told us (Fieldnotes, 24 March 1998). Midday outside Brixton Town Hall was an extraordinary sight as hundreds of black people assembled to make the long trip to Cardiff under the grey London

Figure 9.3 Jamaican fan at Maine Road, Manchester. Photograph by Tim Crabbe.

skies. One man was dressed head to foot in black, green and gold like a walking Jamaican flag. Another was draped in a flag with the picture of Bob Marley in the centre; beneath it was embroidered the word 'Freedom.' Two young black women boarded the coach dressed in full Reggae Gyal style. One wore a green wig with a Jamaican team shirt and yellow pants. Her friend had a Jamaican flag coloured into her hair, wore a Jamaica scarf around her neck and a yellow and green leisure suit. For us, as white researchers, it was an unprecedented experience because this was the first time we experienced a football fan culture in England that was centred around black cultural forms and hosted by black people.

A young woman called Pam – aged 17 – had come to the game on her own, something that would be unthinkable under any other circumstances. A night game at Ninian Park – home of Cardiff City – is a daunting place to visit even for the most seasoned football fan. Pam – who lives in Brixton – said:

> Well, I knew that I'd feel safe because I am travelling with all Jamaican people. It might be very different if it was another match. I like football but the first time that I have been to a game was when Jamaica played at Queens Park Rangers. I really liked it

so here I am, and I get to go to a dance as well and I don't have to go to work tomorrow-do you know what I mean! (Fieldnotes, 24 March 1998)

The whole experience of travelling with the Jamaican fans was so different from the usual football excursions to away games. Buju Banton and Beenie Man was played over and over on the sound system, fried chicken and bun was served as we sped down the motorway. But this contrast was more profound than just the quality of the music and the food on offer. The whole social basis of Jamaican fandom was much less tightly scripted than its English counterpart. Older women and men travelled with young people, fans travelled alone safe in the knowledge that they would be amongst 'their own'. Black people who would not ordinarily step inside a football ground attended with the confidence of veterans.

The reality of the game against Wales was dismal in footballing and supporting terms. By the time that the coaches arrived the rain was pelting down. The game was an uneventful 0-0 draw. The largest section of Jamaican support was located in the away stand, which had no roof. The Jamaican performance was poor to say the least but there was something inspiring in the fact that there were over 5,000 black fans braving the wind and rain to watch their team. A black man in his sixties shouted in desperation 'Come on, Reggae Boyz.' The ball ricocheted off Ricardo 'Bibi' Gardener's shin, going out of play ending another aimless run at the Welsh defence. He said, in a voice of muted complaint: 'The man play like cabbage.' This was a turn of phrase perhaps never heard inside a British football ground before but somehow it captured the moment perfectly. On the one hand this small comment registered a new presence, black people coming to football on their own terms with their own unique way of voicing the generic frustrations with which all football fans are familiar. On the other, it was the all to familiar *crie de coeur* of a disappointed fan, a phenomenon universal to people who share a passion for the game the world over.

Events in London and Cardiff highlighted a phenomenon that has been ignored in much of the literature about football culture – namely the participation of black supporters. Much of the discussion has hinged on the apparent, or more correctly the assumed, unwillingness of black fans to attend English football matches (see Football Task Force 1998: 28). The reasons suggested for this vary from the out-and-out racist to claims about 'extenuating cultural and economic factors'. 'Black people don't watch football they follow basketball.' 'They don't like to have to stand out in the cold.' 'They can't afford to pay the high ticket prices.' Looking out on the legion of Jamaican fans that night in Cardiff, draped in black, gold and green with the rain trickling down their necks it became all too clear. The reason why they were here in these terrible conditions was because they felt this to be *their* team and *their* game. As the mass of black fans looked out onto Ninian Park and the Jamaican team, on this cold wet night they saw themselves. This is not to say that there is only one possible choice for black supporters. As we noted at the beginning of this chapter the questions over affiliations to the English team remained open throughout this period. Yet, for the majority of black spectators and ethnic minority fans more broadly it is the experience of English racism and the racially debarred nature of British spectator sports that is the key factor that limits an equal commitment and emotional bind being established between them and the England team and local clubs. This is true despite the fact that black players are playing at all levels of English football. One of the biggest cheers of the night was at half time when it was announced that England was losing 1-0 at Wembley.

'Gringos and Dance Hall Queens': Parc Des Princes, 21 June 1998

Three months later at a sun drenched Parc des Princes the setting was altogether different at Jamaica's second fixture of the1998 World Cup finals against Argentina. The stadium was a patchwork of Jamaican gold shirts alongside the pale blue and white stripes of Argentina. The atmosphere was heavy with anticipation. Jamaican fans of all ages and of both sexes were alongside pockets of Argentinian fans. Two young female Jamaican fans dressed in 'dancehall queen style' held court for the cameramen at the front of the stand. Later after the match the two women said that they had grown up in America: 'But we're Jamaican! Our parents came to New York from the Caribbean' said Debbie, who had her hair bleached and styled up in a kind of bouffant on top of her head. She wore a green leather top with green and yellow hot pants and big platform boots and one of her eyebrows was pieced with a silver ring. Her friend – Paula – was equally striking in her dance-hall style, her hair was permed and ironed so that it was straight up with red sunglasses resting on the top. 'It's been incredible coming to Europe to see the football. We've met so many Jamaicans in Paris and before that we stayed in London but here we are thousands of miles from Jamaica and it's like a big family reunion' she commented after the game.

These two female fans were probably the most photographed women in Paris that day. Relentless waves of Argentinean and later Jamaican men had their photographs taken with them. One portly Argentinian wearing a national team shirt, a false moustache and a kind of wide brimmed gringo hat, posed with Debbie and Paula to the delight of the hordes of paparazzi. On the pitch there must have been 100 photographers in an arc around this spectacle. An important question here is the degree to which these gendered performances are being reinscribed as the pack of press photographers focused their lens. Or, equally how are these women being viewed by the male football fans who flocked to have their pictures taken with them? Sexual carnivalesque is part of the transgressive power of these styles of black femininity and the football stadium provided a new arena for their exposition. But part of Paula's and Debbie's allure – so evident amongst the

Figure 9.4 Paula (left) and Debbie (right) in the Parc Du Prince. Photography by Les Back.

Argentinian and other European men – may have been informed by dubious ideas relating to black women's sexuality and racial biology. Here, the transgressive potential of the dance-hall queen performance, may in turn be reinscribed by a male footballing audience that reduces these women and their agency to sex objects. The balance between these two outcomes is near impossible to calculate but we want to suggest that attraction and desires of male fans here are variegated and may feasibly include dubious elements. The other danger of focusing too much on the dance-hall queens is that the substantial numbers of black women of all ages in the stadium were eclipsed because they followed the Jamaican team in a less stylized way.

The journey to the Parc des Princes started that day at 7.00 a.m. in Peckham, South London. Getting hold of tickets became something of a social achievement throughout the tournament. Our ticket had been acquired through a friend who had bought a ticket from Alvan, a middle-aged black man and stalwart of local football in South London's black community, who had arranged a block of tickets and distributed them locally. Alvan had booked places on the coach from another firm offering a World Cup service. A company of white entreprenuers from Essex had set up the coach and offered a package including transport to Paris and a ticket. The company employed a young black guy called Noel to act as the MC for the day.

With the coach underway Alvan explained that the distribution of the world cup tickets had fallen into the hands of unscrupulous people who operated in semi-corrupt ways. He criticized the white hostess – called Tuesday – and her organization for making quite a lot of money out of this whole enterprise. Bought from the Essex firm a ticket, along with travel, for the game was £189. Alvan had provided tickets and travel at the much lower price of £55. He also said that there had been some highly dubious practices going on in terms of the allocation of tickets to corporate bodies, and in his view the West Indian Football Federation had not dealt with this very well.

The coach was plush, with a TV, a sound system and refreshments. Yet there was a definite tension between, on the one hand, the black entrepreneurs like Alvan and the white working-class entrepreneurs, who were using the World Cup as a business opportunity. As Tuesday walked up and down the aisle to welcome everybody, and offer drinks two worlds rubbed uneasily together as the white working-class entreprenuers from Essex served a predominantly black inner-city working-class clientele going to see the Jamaica game. At the beginning of the book we suggested that for a white ethnographer in such situations these tensions are felt keenly. Yet, these ambivalences only partially coloured the air of anticipation and joy that surrounded the occasion.

The coach full of expectant Jamaican fans wasn't completely drawn from London's black communities. In fact there were a number of white people who were going to the game. Two white women in their thirties and forties, both from Newcastle, sat towards the back of the bus. A white woman and her black husband attended to their child. Another couple, a young South Asian man and his white partner, were going to the game. Having said this, most of this microcosm of Jamaica's support was drawn from black communities, not all of which had family connections and origins with Jamaica.

The coach was like a microcosm of the Reggae Boyz support. There was a significant number of black women travelling, both with groups and also on their own. A woman called Jennifer, in her thirties, was making her first trip to see a football match. Beyond that there was a Jamaican woman in her late fifties, who most people referred to as 'Mama' in the coach, and at least another five or six black women going to the game, some of whom were very young. There were probably four or five young children, but probably the majority of those people travelling were men between the ages of eighteen and fifty. There were approximately sixteen black men on the trip.

The party atmosphere on the outward trip had all the cultural traces of a Caribbean carnival. Noel – the MC – ran competitions to liven spirits by giving away t-shirts which had flags and logos and various Caribbean islands on them and music CDs. The first of these was a challenge to come down and tell a joke, and the audience in turn had to decide whether or not the joke was good enough for a prize to be awarded. There was a lot of laughter and a great atmosphere on the coach on the way to Paris. The Jamaican fans showed an openness to those who were not of Caribbean descent as well as an inclusiveness towards those from the 'small islands' of the West Indies. Alvan sat with his bottle of Rémy Martin, and several cans of Coke, dishing out Rémy Martin and Coke to practically all comers – and food as well. There was Jamaican snappers being shared and fried chicken. Noel played a tape of the black British DJ Macka B's single called *Reggae Boys Allez*, a tune especially tailored for the World Cup. The tune included passages in which Macka B toasted in French.

Then there was Jennifer, a young black woman, who was determined to try and win a prize, but couldn't tell jokes. She tried over and over but she couldn't actually tell a joke with any kind of conviction. Despite her failure she was completely at home in the company of strangers. It was the first time she'd ever attended a football match. Jennifer reflected on how she came to be here after another failed attempt to win a shirt.

Jennifer had gone to a middle-class school in Sydenham in South London and afterwards started a career in the civil service. Now she was working as a civil servant around issues of housing and equality of access. This was her first experience of going to football. 'I just thought to myself, "Why shouldn't I go?" and I decided in my life recently that I am just going to do things on my own if I need to, so I thought Why not? Why the hell not? Why not come and do something like this, to go to a football match?' she said. 'I wouldn't go to football under any other circumstances, but I like football and what with the World Cup and everything, I decided that I would come on this trip and I suppose it is very different coming to football when you know there is going to be a big black presence on the coach, and so as a black woman it is easy for me to come on trips like this in ways that it wouldn't be in any other circumstance' (Fieldnotes, 21 June 1998).

Jennifer had arrived at a point in her life where she was tired of being defined by other people's expectations. We told her that we were sociologists writing a book about football. 'Really?' she replied. 'I don't like sociology it puts people into boxes, black/white, men, women, class . . .' She was interested in less scripted ideas about individuals and was fascinated by psychology, massage and aromatherapy. She talked about the phobia that she developed of taking exams and how it haunted her throughout her life. She said: 'I know that it all goes back to a time when I was taking my O levels and I failed one of the mock exams, and the white teacher called me up in front of class and it was really humiliating, and after then I have not been able to take exams, and it has really hurt me, it just shows you that one reckless act by a white teacher can really do damage to black kids' (Fieldnotes, 21 June 1998).

Jennifer talked about the stereotypes she encountered in the court service: 'There was one time when a judge pulled me to one side after I had worked with him during a particular trial. He came over to me and he asked me "where were you educated?" I told him that I was educated in South London at a grammar school, and he said "they did a very good job on you", and it was really weird, it was as if he didn't expect a black person to be able to speak the Queen's English, and it was really strange.' She also talked about how hurtful it had been for her that she received criticisms from within her own community for the fact that she worked in the civil service. She had often been very defensive about talking openly about what she did for a living because the only black people that she encountered in the criminal justice system were those being prosecuted. 'I expect you have heard the phrase coconut' she said. 'Well I have had people from within my own community try and pull me back because I can speak nicely, or I can speak well, and that really hurts, it really hurts to have some people from your own community putting other obstacles in your way as if there weren't enough. There are plenty of judges who think in the way that that guy I just spoke about does and there are plenty of people who are going to stop you getting where you want to be, and it is hurtful to hear it from your own kind. You don't speak black enough or you are too white, that kind of thing, and I have decided now that I am at a point in my life where I am going to do what I want to do and say what I want to' (Fieldnotes, 21 June 1998). So, for Jennifer, coming to this fixture by herself was another gesture of self-determination that challenged other people's expectations of her. And, in the end, she did win a much-coveted t-shirt. She held it up and emblazoned across the front was 'Barbados', the island from which her parents had come.

Amidst the group of travelling fans there was a minor controversy over what common symbols, songs and forms of collective expression should be sought. While the mock disagreements might seem trivial they revealed a larger issue that centred around the degree to which elements of English football culture should be imported. Jennifer suggested that their rallying cry should be Macka B's tune 'Reggae Boys Allez.' Some of the men from the back of the bus resisted the idea. A group of men who had attended the Croatia game wanted to sing an ersatz version of Steam's pop hit *Na Na Hey Hey Kiss and Goodbye*. The song followed the melody of the original inserting the Jamaican team's nickname at the end i.e. *Na Na Na Na, Hey Hey, Reggae Boys*. One of the fans shouted at Jennifer from the back of the coach: 'Where were you last week when Jamaica was playing Croatia?' However, the questioner's attempt to sort out the true fans from the fair-weather travellers backfired. His neighbour replied 'Peckham, I watched the game on Sky on a wide screen TV.'

A kind of pantomime of football authenticity ensued. Jennifer stood at the front of the bus and said 'Now come on, you can sing this song, and all the men can sing the reggae boys bit and the women can sing allez.' Paul replied 'No, you don't want to do any of that, we have got our own song . . . I have been coming to football and no one is going to tell me what to say – I support Arsenal, Arsenal is my team. Alvan immediately stood up and said 'Well, I support Tottenham.' The pair then played out the ancient North London rivalry in a mock confrontation. Tony, turned round and said over the seat in front well 'I support Man United'. All these men arguing about which teams they supported were laying claim to the rituals associated with football culture in England. It is important to point out that the cultures and rhetoric of English and Jamaican are not completely distinct and hermetically sealed. In many ways what the lads at the back of the bus were doing was assimilating or deploying some of the features of English football fan culture whereas Jennifer was at the front of the bus saying this is all just naff and terrible, and suggested that they take their lyrical queues from a black British reggae MC. Finally, the lads at the back of the bus won out and Macka B and *Reggae Boys Allez* was left on the sidelines. Arriving in Paris the busload of expectant fans joined the footballing throng making their way into the Parc De Princes.

The period before kick off was charged with anticipation. This reached a kind of fever pitch about 10 minutes before the start of the game when the guitar lick from the opening bars of Bob Marley's *Could This Be Love* struck up on the stadium sound system. The whole place erupted with Argentinian and Jamaican fans alike singing and dancing. In an attempt to find a suitably 'Latin' equivalent to Bob Marley the French stadium manager immediately followed the reggae rhythm with *La Bamba*. The choice of Los Lobos' version was somewhat ironic given this tune is a Mexican folk song, made famous in the 1950s by the Mexican American rock'n'roll singer Richie Valens! Regardless, the packed stadium swayed, danced and sung together with equal intensity.

The game itself became almost a side issue as Jamaica fell to a 5–0 defeat. Martin Thorpe wrote in the *Guardian* the following day of the Jamaican side 'for all the infectious joy of their singing and dancing fans, the team simply could not match the high standards demanded on the global stage' (Thorpe 1998: 3). The players in the Jamaican team were certainly treated like second-class citizens in the lead up to this fixture. Robbie Earle recounted the shoddy treatment that they received from the FIFA officials, the team's pre-game warm up on the pitch was shortened to suit the Argentinians and they were ushered away despite Simoes's objection so that the ground could be prepared for the corporate spectacle.

> Incidents like these highlight the fact that we are not yet looked upon as equal. FIFA have based much of their promotion on fair play – it is time that they applied it across the board. Is it not the mentality of a bully to identify its weaker targets and pick on them? We have enough work to do on our own to climb the soccer ladder without any obstructions from the game's administrators. (Earle 1998: 5)

Off the pitch FIFA treated the Jamaican team as a footballing 'poor relation.' Put simply, teams like Argentina, France and Brazil held sway in terms of the corporate sponsorship and financial interests invested in them.

Maybe the Jamaican team were out of their depth on the field, but something significant happened within the stadium itself. The Parc des Princes is the home ground for Paris St Germain, a team with a reputation for a racist following amongst its fans. A black friend who had lived in Paris told of an experience watching Liverpool FC there in 1996: 'It was an incredible atmosphere and the racism was very open. It was funny in a way because we were standing with the Paris St Germain fans and one of the skinheads came up to me and advised me to go and stand somewhere else for my own safety!' (Personal Communication, 15 July 1997).

At half time a long line of Argentinian and Jamaican fans made for the toilets. Descending down a long staircase, bordered by grim grey concrete walls, this throng of Jamaican and Argentinian fans was confronted with the inscriptions of hate that laid claim to the ground and registered its history. Racist graffiti was plastered over virtually every surface of the toilet's area. Above the sinks where a black man was washing his son's hands, read the inscription 'SKINHEADS' alongside scribbled Celtic crosses and swastikas. Elsewhere, FN stickers with a flame coloured red, white and blue were plastered on the cubicles, SS and swastikas scratched into the surface of the metal doors. The fans seemed to ignore these graphic racist outpourings. As the little boy's hands were being washed, the Jamaican motto was revealed on the back of his gold and green shirt: 'Out of many, one goal!' Here a multi-cultural footballing reality was confronted with the subterranean traces of racist football culture. On the door of the exit was daubed in English the slogan 'WHITE POWER.' Ascending the stairs this image provided a stark warning that the transformations manifest around this fixture and the considerable numbers of black fans present was both a temporary and conditional phenomenon.

Jamaican support during the World Cup in 1998 provided a pretext for people of Jamaican heritage to gather in one place. What was striking was that people of Jamaican descent had converged on Paris from a range of itinerant homes be they in New York, London, Manchester or Birmingham. They came from a range of backgrounds in terms of age group, gender and class. But importantly these events showed very clearly the level of interest in football within Britain's black communities, which made the general absence of black fans in English football – at both club and international level – even more stark.

'Noir, Blanc et Bleu?': France 98, Nationalism and the Return of Roland Barthes

In an increasingly globalized world, sporting spectacles like the World Cup offer one of the last vestiges in which nationalism can be expressed ritually and celebrated. The sportswear companies, media corporations and the merchandising moguls set out their wares too, all vying for a piece of this festival of corporate multiculturalism. It seemed apt that the 1998 final, itself between Brazil and France, also staged a confrontation between the finalists' respective sponsors, sportswear moguls Nike and Adidas. Before a ball was kicked Nike edged its superiority in the product placement stakes. Nike overtook Adidas in the *Financial Times* World Cup sponsors index, which measured brand exposure through the teams wearing the various companies' kits. Both Nike and Adidas passed the 1,000 point mark with their closest rivals Umbro at 313 and on the eve of the final Nike were ahead with 1150.4 points while Adidas trailed with 1083.8 (*Financial Times* 11 July 1998).

In this way the World Cup tournament provided the ultimate stage for corporate interests to be played out. But something else beyond business fortunes was also at stake that merits serious attention. What makes football interesting is that it provides one of the few spheres in which ideas about identity, ethnicity and race can be expressed, embodied and performed. It offers the possibility for nationhood to be represented through either a grotesque pageant of fixed archetypes or as a carnival in which the circumscriptions of the national body politic – particularly in terms of race – can be breached, even partially dissolved giving life to new possibilities.

The potential of national sport to possess a recombinant potential was particularly relevant in the aftermath of the French victory. Two years prior to *La Coupe Du Monde,* National Front leader, Jean Marie Le Pen famously rebuked the French team – particularly those whose family origins lay outside of France – for their lack of zeal when singing the *Marseillaise*. Arguing against such multiethnic presences, he said: 'It's unnecessary to bring players in from abroad and baptise them as the French team' (quoted in Fraser 1998: 2). The French national team displayed an incredible diversity and many of its stars were born outside of metropolitan France, including Marcel Desailly (Accra, Ghana), Christian Karambeu (New Caledonia), Patrick Viera (Dakar, Senegal) and Lilian Thuram

(Pointe à Pitre, Guadeloupe). Still others would qualify as what Le Pen would call 'Francais de souche recente' meaning that such players were not 'real Frenchmen' because their parents were too recent migrants. This list included Alain Boghossian (Armenia), Vincent Candela (Italy), Bernard Diomende (Guadeloupe), Youri Djorkaeff (from the former Yugoslavia), Thierry Henry (Guadeloupe) and the goal-scoring hero of the victory over Brazil, Zinedine Zidane (Algeria).

The victory itself seemed immediately to be a triumph over Le Pen's version of racially exclusive nationalism. Philippe Jérôme, correspondent for the French Communist Party paper *l'Humanité*, wrote:

> The two goals of Zidane in the world cup final did more for the equal rights of citizens than a thousand speeches from the left denouncing racism and the policies of Jean-Marie Le Pen's National Front. (Jérôme 1998: 3)

Jérôme was not alone in claiming the victory marked the arrival of a multi-racial French nation. A host of people from the pantheon of French cultural and academic celebrities lauded the triumph as a moment of imminent togetherness. This included people as diverse as film stars and musicians like Catherine Deneuve, Gerard Depardieu and Johnny Hallyday to the likes of Isabelle Huppert and Jacques Chirac. Nick Fraser wrote of an incident he overheard near the Hôtel de Ville in which an elderly white French woman said gratefully to two Arab girls: 'If we win it will be because of you . . . we should have had blacks and Arabs in the team earlier. If we had done we would have won more matches' (Fraser 1998: 2). Equally, it would be wrong to dismiss the presence of Arabs and black citizens among the celebrating crowds, given that the French had suburbanized urban poverty and confined its immigrant populations to the desolate *banlieue* ring of Paris. The visual presence on the Champs Elysées of these otherwise urban-outcasts was significant in that it registered their presence in the national imagination in a less pathological way. These scenes were viewed by some as analogous to historic moments like the Liberation of France in 1944 and the street protests in May 1968.

In the aftermath of the French victory one could almost sense the excitement of cultural critics on the Left as the pages of the liberal press turned and quivered each morning in Paris and London. However, such new found enthusiasm shown in both Britain and France runs perilously close to a kind of trite Zeitgeist hermeneutics, a syndrome that cultural studies – especially that inspired by literary criticism – has sometimes been guilty. One detail quickly dismissed was Le Pen's response. 'I claim this victory for the National Front who designed its framework' he said. Le Pen's apparent change of tack was thought by many to be evidence of a deceitful and fickle opportunism. But perhaps this apparent change of heart is not as complete as it might seem, and Le Pen's views need not be necessarily in direct opposition to the nascent celebration of French diversity in sport. Le Pen

The Guardian Monday July 13 1998

France 98: the final reckoning

Figure 9.5 'Black, Brown or Beige': France's World Cup Triumph. Published with permission of *The Guardian* and Richard Williams.

argued that France could be 'composed of different races and religions' so long as they were French first and foremost. Such a discussion recalls the observations of another famous Frenchman, Roland Barthes.

In *Mythologies*, Barthes' classic study in semiology, he recounts being handed a copy of Paris Match in a barber shop:

> On the cover, a young Negro in a French uniform is saluting, with his eyes uplifted, probably fixed on a fold of the tricolour. All this is the meaning of the picture. But, whether naively or not, I see very well what it signifies to me: that France is a great empire, that all her sons, without colour discrimination, faithfully serve under her flag, and that there is no better answer to the detractors of an alleged colonialism than the zeal shown by this Negro in serving his so-called oppressors. (Barthes 1973: 116)

The connection here between the black French soldier and black athletes recalls Norbert Elias' famous discussion of the 'civilizing process' and the key role that sport has played in what he referred to as the internal pacification of Western societies (Elias and Dunning 1969). But here sport might play a significant role in transition from colonial to postcolonial government. In fact, one might read the fervour generated over the multi-racial French national team as the return – albeit in a neo-colonial form – of a Barthian myth.

For Barthes, a mythical concept derives its power not from didacticism or propaganda, but rather from its ability to naturalise what is essentially an ideological relation. It is through such an embodied implicitness that its mythic definitions work. So, the picture of the Negro soldier saluting the tricolour conjures the concept of French imperiality without naming it, or announcing its arrival. Rather, it is presented as a natural state, 'as if the signifier *gave foundation* to the signified' (Barthes 1973: 130). Similarly we might think of the spectacle of a multi-racial French team as the embodiment of a mythical concept. 'For no man or woman really believed in a multi-cultural France,' wrote Nick Fraser. 'They left what they considered to be a grotesque illusion to Americans, British and Dutch . . . French people probably merely wanted foreigners to be *more like themselves*' [emphasis added] (Fraser 1998: 3). The French version of diversity amounted to little more than an assimilationist nationalism that insists on a sovereign French identity above all else. It is perhaps not surprising that its new hero, the slightly balding Zinedine 'Zizou' Zidane is of Algerian origin from the Berber region. Zidane's father had been a soldier – a 'harkis' – who came to France after fighting alongside the colonialists *in opposition* to Algerian independence. Multi-racial France – as a mythical concept – embodies within the theatre of national sport, the complex combinations of national transcendence and neo-colonial accommodation.

In the aftermath of the victory Olivier Poivre D'Arvor, Cultural Counsellor to the French Embassy, wrote in London:

> Living abroad for ten years, trying to give my host cultures an open and enlightened image of my country, always hanging to old certainties ('the country of the Rights of Man', the Enlightenment, 'French culture is made up of borrowings from abroad'), I had felt ashamed. Ashamed at every national, regional and local election. Ashamed that this image of a racist country was being popularised beyond our frontiers. The night of the 12th July [1998], for the first time in a long while, I could breathe more easily. No, it's not true, this is not the France we love. Le Pen is just a very bad dream.
>
> The summer has come and gone. The phenomenon is still with us. Something lasting, I think I can safely say. But at the same time, a doubt crosses my mind. What if France had not qualified for the quarter-and semi-finals? What if Desailly had scored an own goal? What if Zidane had got injured? That is a lot of 'ifs'. Alas, only one thing is certain: France has won a World Cup, but Le Pen has not been eliminated. (Poivre D'Arvor 1999: x)

What comes through so strongly in this account is the contingency in any shift made in the cultural politics of sport.

The victory had helped Le Pen's opponents to 'breathe more easily' but the paradox remains that French racism can comfortably co-exist with a more cosmopolitan image of French nationalism on the field of play. Hugh Dancey and Geoff Hare conclude in their review of the impact of France 98 that France's 'multi-racial' team, under the direction of ex-school teacher Aimé Jacquet, came to re-symbolize old themes within popular French self image albeit wrapped in a new skin. They suggest that the whole picture is only complete when one sees how the national coach is the cipher around which his team is organized. 'Jaquet was presented as incarnating the three integrative forces of old: not only the primary school teacher (method and hard work), but also the provincial priest (community) and finally Saint-Etienne factory work (solidarity and *cohésion*). If the Republic is once again threatened in its cohesion, in its fraternity, in its *banlieue* and elsewhere, much of the French press saw Jacquet's traditional values and self-belief as the answer' (Dauncey and Hare 1999: 220). Reflecting on the historic victory there remains an uncertainty about the meaning of those mixed congreg-ations gathered on the Champs Elysées and whether the victory has left something lasting. It is perhaps best to see such events as culminating in partial and unevenly developed shifts. For example, the participation of France in Euro 2000 was not followed by a radical reconfiguration and opening up of the social constituency of French football fans. Rather, France's migrant and minority communities stayed in the *banlieue* only communing with the team's image of French diverisity via their television sets. Unlike a contradiction that can be resolved, the paradox of postcolonial nationalism in Europe is that it combines shifts towards cultural diversity with a proliferation of new racisms as it reproduces old bigotries.

Conclusion

In this chapter we have explored the relationship between nation and race in contrasting European contexts and showed that postcolonial expressions of English and French nationalism are best seen as undergoing incomplete and partial shifts in the direction of cultural inclusion. Jamaican fans used a rhetoric of nationhood that confounded any simple notion of the limits of its borders. Its nascent and permeable boundaries allowed it to be embraced by a diverse group of people that included those whose heritage is linked to the West Indies and other affinities and associations. This provided a stark contrast to assimilating European nationalisms for whom passports to entry for black citizens are issued with specific terms and conditions. Returning to the question that we posed at the beginning of this chapter, we want to argue that it is important to keep open the possibility of the emergence of a more racially inclusive notion of Englishness. For, as black football fans like Paul McKenzie insist, there is some 'black in the Union Jack'. It is equally, crucial to be aware of the limits that are placed on the degree to which the relationship between race and nation can be redefined.

The support garnered by the Jamaican national team from black metropolitan communities showed the vital and animate Jamaican belonging in Europe. This is not to suggest that all people of Jamaican origin should identify with the Jamaican team as some form of primordial ethnicity. Some black fans avoid having to make these kinds of absolute preferences because they reflect an underlying 'either/or' logic that means a choice between erasing their Jamaican heritage or the experience of growing up in England. We want to suggest that something profound was captured in the groundswell of support for the Jamaican national team in the run up to the 1998 World Cup that not only reinvigorated connections with the Island for those of Jamaican heritage. It also revealed that fifty years after mass migration from the Caribbean, a significant number of the children of those postwar migrants see the option of being identified with England and Englishness remote and implausible. At the same time there remains the strong current to broaden the spectrum of Englishness and the colours of belonging. Picking up on the coverage of Ian Wright's tearful celebrations after England's 0-0 draw in Rome that secured England's passage to the World Cup, Ben Carrington concludes:

> Nevertheless, the costs for this inclusion may be too high if it means we are unable to engage with (re)defining what constitutes the borders of such an identity beyond its more populist nationalist appeals. An expansive and inherently protean sense of black Englishness that could include the positionings adopted by [Ian] Wright *and* [John] Barnes, and even [Frank] Bruno, is one to be preferred to a situation where only those willing to cry for their country are accepted (Carrington 2001: 118).

The World Cup showed that a 'protean sense of black Englishness' is emergent alongside the disavowal of that identity.

As one of the hostesses said as the bus drove through Brixton in the early hours of the morning returning from Cardiff: 'We're all Jamaicans, ain't we?' The itinerant belonging to England – often challenged by popular racism both in football and outside – coexisted with a strong commitment to the vibrant registers of Jamaican football. Uniquely, it fused the dance hall and the football stadium engendering a supporter culture that was open and more inclusive in terms of gender, age, class or even colour. No doubt the Jamaican Football Federation made the best of the situation financially through sponsorship, paid appearances and friendly games. But equally, football momentarily gave a glimpse of unity to this fractured Caribbean nation, best expressed in the utopian tones of reggae music. Tony Rebel chants these telling lines in Jamaica Unlimited's *Rise Up*:

> Because of you.
> Progress.
> I have seen oneness and difference in this country.
> Don't be intimidated, even when tested.
> Small axe can fell a big tree.

Corporate football has little room for 'small acts' like the Jamaican national team, who may never be able to fell name-brand sponsored footballing giants like Brazil (Nike) or France (Adidas), but the significance of football as a form of popular culture is in the identifications and imaginations it allows to be articulated and defined ritually. This is expressed in a space that lay between the fan collective and their team's iconic status. It is in this encounter that the micro-politics of race, nation and belonging are lived.

The World Cup brought black people into places like *Ninian Park* and the *Parc Des Princes,* and for many of these fans they were entering the formerly exclusive white spaces for the very first time. However, with the tournament over and Jamaica's fans back in their Caribbean or diasporic homes, the public spheres of football reverted to their previous owners. Little connection has been made between the large numbers of black spectators that came to watch Jamaica in England during 1998 and the local and national fan cultures that call these grounds their home. Rather, black football fans returned to their own spheres of public life to talk about what might have been and their love of the 'beautiful game'.

Conclusion: The Changing Face of Football

The Hawthorns is the home of West Bromwich Albion, and the symbolic starting point of this project. The scenes in the ground on 27 July 2000 were altogether different from the expressions of racism we had witnessed at the fixture between Crystal Palace and the Baggies in the winter of 1993. The game was a summer pre-season friendly between West Bromwich and the Indian national side. It was the first time the Indian national team had toured and this was the second in a series of three games. The first had been against Fulham in London and the final match was set to take place in Leicester, to be played against Bangladesh. Like the Reggae Boyz before them, the Indian national team brought an unprecedented number of minority football fans together in the ground of a professional football club.

Piara Powar, coordinator of the national Kick It Out campaign, attended all three of the fixtures, and he remembers the occasion at West Bromwich like this:

> I went to all three, that was the one where I think, you know, everything clicked sort of perfectly. And there were like 12,000 people there to see India, and India are, you know, what are they, if they were playing in professional football they'd be a sort of second division side or something, you know, if that. I'd say it was sort of 95% Asian. There were a few West Brom season ticket holders around, and it was amazing, you know, that sort of colour and vibrancy. And it wasn't just the physical presence but it was also the kind of expressions of support. There was literally a dhol [a small drum] on almost every aisle. The one enduring memory is of these old guys passing around little cups of Baccardi to each other. And to get the sort of older kind of retired pensioners out for that game, you know, was quite something. And then outside it was just a complete buzz, you know, and you could see some of the West Brom fans walking around, some of them looking very, very happy and others were just a little bit like 'Wow, is this what it's like,' you know. (Interview, 26 September 2000)

Like the examples cited in Chapter 9 in relation to the Jamaican national team, the ground as a cultural space was transformed, breaching the divide between the multi-ethnic neighbourhoods surrounding the ground and the club's support as the parallel universes of Handsworth, Smethwick and *The Hawthorns* merged. Piara continued:

The sort of cultural expressions that you just don't associate with football being played out in and around the football stadium, it was amazing, it really was. And the local pub, the Hawthorns, the pub that most of the fans go to was overrun with Asians alongside a sort of section of traditional white West Brom fans in the corner, and it was something else. And I think, you know, we were having this discussion in the office a while ago, is that an effective anti-racist intervention? Does that move us on? And again, you know, it does. It does because it's showing people in the game that, you know, these communities have a passion for football. And they can bring something to support within a localised sort of stadium environment. (Interview, 26 September 2000)

Yet, Piara is clearly aware that the gains of such transformative moments can be easily lost. They are exceptional. The emotional pull within the diasporic communities toward the ancestral home becomes the symbolic lure through which the informal segregation that haunts the local environment is breached. But this does not mean that the identifications and commitments evident in support of India or the Reggae Boyz get transferred to the local team when it plays at home. Rather, as in this case, the attraction and symbolic pull follows the Indian team as it returns to the airport. For Powar: 'Those interventions and the gains of those interventions can easily be lost. I think that's one of the problems that we have an issue with, about how do you firm them up, how do you make them long lasting and positive?' (Interview, 26 September 2000).

As we have tried to argue throughout *The Changing Face of Football*, we can only begin to understand situations such as this by contextualizing the role of football clubs in specific environments. As fans pass through the turnstiles they need to possess implicitly the right kind of 'cultural passport'. We have tried to understand this through the normative identity that is embedded within the rituals of football culture. This does not work through explicit forms of crude exclusion, but rather within the realm of what is assumed and the routines and meanings associated with football clubs as symbolic entities. Entering these spaces is then not just about assimilating an identity; it is also about making sacrifices. Piara Powar captures key features of this complexity when he argues: 'You have to lose something of yourself and your history to fit into the space that you're stepping into . . . Whereas in other areas of life you can go somewhere where you know that the scene will reflect your history and your being and your identity' (Interview, 26 September 2000).

The spectacle of football chants being brought to life in bhangra or dancehall rhythms serve as a reminder that there are alternative ways of expressing a passion for football. Yet, their momentary and passing presence inside grounds like *The Hawthorns* and *Ninian Park* provide a reminder of the forces that inhibit change in the English game. The point here is that something subtle is at play, which can't be simply defined as racism in either popular or institutional forms. In this sense the forces that inhibit the reflection of the evident diversity in urban multiculture need to be explained by the weight of history that infuses the identities which are expressed through football fandom. These cannot be simply redefined by edict because in large part they are assumed and enshrined within ritual expressions that need not be stated consciously. It is the nature of these implicit mechanisms that we have tried to get to through the idea of a 'cultural passport' that equips and facilitates belonging and identity. This, we feel, explains how even in a situation where overt racism is absent, football grounds can still remain exclusive white preserves, because for black and Asian fans to enter them involves a process analogous to cultural and historical erasure. As we have argued, where black and Asian fans have gained access to English football, they have had to do so on terms not set by them. Rather, the points of contact come through shared experiences of masculinity, neighbourhood and class.

We have tried to argue that these exclusions are not just about money. True, English football, particularly at its highest levels, has become incredibly expensive as the top clubs become global corporate entities. It is undoubtedly the case that this has implications in terms of 'pricing out' the often poor, working class and multi-ethnic communities in which football clubs are located geographically. Yet, the great mistake is to assume that the absence of black and Asian fans can only be explained in financial terms. This is the kind of 'cod sociology' espoused in David Mellor's Football Task Force Report (1998). Rather, it is more accurate to say that for many people in England's minority communities the financial and cultural price is simply not worth paying.

Writer John Masouri has highlighted what he sees as some of the limitations of a purely economic explanation for the absence of black fans in football grounds. John is a music writer and football fan whom we quoted at length in Chapter 9.

> It was their thoughts on the question of why more black supporters don't attend matches that really interested me, but reading between the lines, it seems that they dragged out the same old patronising stereotypes yet again. Personally, I think the numbers will rise as clubs increasingly detach themselves from the local, tribalist affairs and enhance their status as international brand names. Many already have leading black players from around the world representing them, and once it's possible to attend matches without encountering the risk of violence or racism, I can't see high ticket prices proving too much of an obstacle. After all, the cost of Versace or Tommy Hilfinger clothing doesn't prevent large numbers of black people from wearing it, nor even the stigma of certain fashion houses being controlled by gays (!!!). It's the fact that many older black males were beaten up by their own team's supporters or intimidated by racist groups at grounds during the seventies that seems to have made the deepest impression upon the collective, black British soul where football's concerned, and until the sport become less xenophobic (which is difficult, given the state of our tabloid press), I guess it's always going to remain a mere (but hotly contested) talking point, rather than a shared experience. (Personal Communication, 10 July 2000)

The passion of black and Asian fans for football is undoubtedly strong in many cases, as the experiences of teams like Arsenal, Leicester and Bradford has shown, but in general the cultures of support remain discrete and segregated spatially if not temporally. Black and Asian fans may be tuning in to hear the results at 4.45 p.m. every Saturday with equal anticipation. But, this is not the same as saying that the experience, or, the 'structures of feeling', to use Raymond Williams' phrase, are shared.

Masouri's suggestive point that an intensification of globalization and commercialization in English football will enhance multicultural diversity rather than inhibit it amongst fans raises interesting issues for the future. His analysis runs counter to many of the nostalgic and often mournful commentaries about the commercial transformation of English football. It is certainly true to say that the informational age has made new types of fandom possible. The support for the Jamaican national team during the 1998 World Cup is a salutary reminder of this. The fortunes of the team were followed in Europe and North America because Sky TV and other television channels made it possible for the diaspora to tune in. In addition the global nature of the biggest clubs, such as Manchester United, means that they are less dependent on ticket sales for income. In 2000, for example, Manchester United generated £23.6 million in global merchandising sales alone (Warner, 2000: 56). Anthony King has argued that Manchester United fan culture has transcended the nation state and is locked into a European network of clubs and possesses a 'post national' and cosmopolitan quality. Here there is a 'devolution of interests to the level of the local and the urban' (King 2000: 427) so that sections of United's fan base see themselves as representative of their city – and not their country abroad – a kind of traveling band of Mancunian tribunes who look down on atavistic nationalism and the 'parochial hill-billy' sentiments of England's 'hick towns' (King 2000: 435). King doesn't discuss the relationship between this phenomenon and racist practice amongst Manchester United fans. The degree to which such post national football cultures lead to greater cultural inclusiveness in their urban localities is itself a moot point.

It is estimated that internationally Manchester United has something like 20 million fans, and the club's capitalization reached over £1 billion pounds at one stage. In this context it could be argued that 'the stadium' provides little more than cultural flavour. Ticket sales at Old Trafford are no longer the crucible of the club's financial fortunes. While ticket sales may still be the single largest revenue stream, taken in the context of Manchester United's overall financial strategy they may soon become relegated to little more than the equivalent of 'fiscal icing' on the corporate cake. As a money maker, ticket sales will ultimately come second by a long way in terms of financial priorities to the media and informational technologies that enable the club to have a global reach. Indeed, it is for this reason that the club has been teaming up with new media partners that include Vodafone,

BSkyB and Granada. The image of the future is that the 'Global Reds' will be able to see match-highlights, read post game analysis, and pay for mechandise all on Manchester United branded mobile phones. Despite the hostility expressed towards BSkyB's unsuccessful bid to buy Manchester United (see Brown and Walsh 1999), the new informational industries have a symbiotic relationship with the club, precisely because companies like Vodafone aim to use football to break into new markets. Helen Keays, brand and advertising director of Vodafone, told Bernard Warner: 'We are interested in entering some of the same markets that Manchester United is already popular in' (quoted in Warner 2000: 58). In this context the digital cable networks may facilitate the generation of new modes of fandom which come to eclipse the cold and drizzly corporeal realities of stadium spectatorship.

While Manchester United is a special case and by a long way England's largest club, there is something significant here. The digital disembodying of football spectatorship may mean that football culture becomes less sensuous, but at the same time it may provide a safe vantage point for ethnic minority fans to experience the game free from hate and hostility. In our own research we found some evidence to support the idea that the emergence of 'digifans' has broadened the gender and ethnic diversity of football spectators. Ginna, for example, started following Manchester United while she was living in her native Nigeria. She has never been inside a football stadium: 'I watch every game on Sky, my husband hates it. Lot's of people in Nigeria follow Manchester United and I send clippings and things to my family back home now that I live in London' (Interview, 2 January 2001).

Perhaps it is also worth exploring more fully the parallels between the emergence of black sports men and women in Europe and the earlier experience of American sport. There is much reference to the Americanization of football and the future vision of the English game. In popular imagery, and despite its long history of segregation before the 1940s and 1950s, American sport has rarely been plagued by the kinds of popular racist practices witnessed in English football. Yet, many commentators have discussed the profound damage that American sport has done with regard to reproducing ideologies of race (Hoberman 1997) and the obsession many American writers have with the relationship between sporting prowess and racial biology (Entine 2000). Paul Gilroy, among others, has suggested, that the commercial colossus of American sport has thrived financially by marketing and wrapping its games within the skin of the 'superhuman' black body (Gilroy 2000b).

Douglas Hartmann has concluded recently that American sport is best characterized as a contested racialized terrain:

> In many ways, the unparalleled athletic prominence and prowess of African American athletes is one of the most striking and seemingly progressive features of a society otherwise marked by persistent racial inequalities. Yet, at the same time, it is not clear if

success in sport contributes to the advancement of racial justice. Even more problematic are the ways in which this sporting success actually seems to reinforce and reproduce images, ideas, and social practices that are thoroughly racialised, if not simply racist. (Hartmann 2000: 230)

As we have argued the emergence of black sporting figures has been met with a range of mutable racialized responses within the institutions of sport and outside. The legacy of racism in sport is unfinished because it both combines old racism with new variants. In this sense, the recent commercialization of English football may reinvigorate modern ideologies about the supposed difference that 'race' makes to athletic prowess.

The writing of so called 'race realists,' like Jon Entine, make for particularly chilling reading. Entine's fixation with 'race' is nowhere more apparent than when he tried to apply his logic to football. His book *Taboo* is an attempt to make a connection between 'races' and sporting prowess. At the beginning of the book he asks: 'Is it more than just cultural serendipity that Brazilians are time and again the best soccer players . . .' (Entine 2000: 21). In a variety of sporting contexts he attempts to connect the alleged possession of 'fast-twitch muscle fibres' by blacks with West African origins with dominance in power sports. After quoting a passage from a Norwegian physiologist on the explosive power of Brazilian centre-forward Ronaldo, he proclaims with bogus authority: 'As we would expect, there are relatively more blacks – almost all of central West African heritage – in the speed positions in soccer, basketball, and [American] football and relatively fewer in positions in which short-burst activity is less crucial than strength: center in basketball, center and guard in [American] football, and defense in soccer' (Entine 2000: 256–7). Even the most ignorant and racist manager or coach in England would be reluctant to articulate such crude and inaccurate caricatures. If books like *Taboo* are anything to go by, the contemporary fascination with genetics may mean that those who seek to link racial biology and sport are making a comeback.

The image of English football as moving down the road to global corporate transformation is perhaps enticing to some, but the picture on the ground is more messy and complex. Few, if any, English clubs can come close to the opportunities now opening to Manchester United. The growth in 'foreign players' playing in Britain has accelerated in an unprecedented way but the degree to which their presence has transformed the culture of the clubs that have offered them a home is still a moot point. Piara Powar, is one commentator who remains sceptical about the enduring effect of international players on domestic football: 'I think one needs to scratch beneath the surface to see how international is the game in Britain. How multi-ethnic is the game? And I think if one does that then you find that all sorts of problems are emerging.' He argues that while the assimilation of high profile black overseas players challenges our assumptions about white working class fans they do not necessary signal a complete shift:

When Arsenal fans are singing 'we love Patrick Viera, he's from Senegal.' There's something going on there clearly which, you know, one can't ignore in terms of race in football, and hearing a kind of a white working class football fan singing the name of somebody from Senegal and being aware he's from Senegal. For me this kind of flies in the face of world economics and, you know, the things that are usually ascribed to white working-class people. And there's something happening there, unquestionably. But I don't, personally think they're solid enough for them to be enduring. So in two generations' time, a generation's time, we don't know what's going to happen to football. It could be that the likes of Patrick Viera will be forgotten and we're into a kind of a new period of darkness. One looks at the attitudes outside of our kind of major cities and I certainly don't think that that's, you know, improbable. (Interview, 26 September 2000)

In short, the assimilation of international players need not produce an ethos of internationalism. Rather, international players are assimilated within the local identities or regional affiliations. While this may operate through a language of 'the local' it is not necessarily about neighbourhoods and residence. As we have shown, white fans travel great distances to support their team and 'play at home'. Rather, it is a kind of 'nationalism of the stadium' that is celebrated and defined when the team plays. What matters above all – regardless of the national origin of the players in the line up – is that the players 'wear the shirt' with all its charged symbolism, history and rootedness in a particular place.

Indeed, one of the lessons that we draw from the research we have done for this project is that discussions of the politics of racism in England cannot be simply read off from the situation in the largest cities, be they London, Manchester, Liverpool or Birmingham. Looking at football and its pageant of localisms that hang like team colours around each club, provides a stark reminder of how unevenly developed changes in the cultural politics of racism are within the nation as a whole. While there are real and important shifts going on within the main cities, it is equally true that vast areas have been virtually untouched by the muting of overt expressions of racism. For this reason, we would argue for a radically contextualized understanding of the place of popular racism within football that calls for an anti-racist strategy that is localized and sensitive to the variegated, contradictory and ambivalent presence of racism in football.

This begs the question of what is to be done. One road, as we discuss in some detail, has been law enforcement, what one police officer referred to as the imperative to 'let's get these people nicked'. The use of video surveillance has been in some ways incredibly effective, as we show in relation to Millwall in Chapter 7. In fact, the tape of Millwall supporter Kevin Ryan venting his racism has been shown in a variety of contexts, including the Race and Violent Crimes Unit directed by John Grieve at Scotland Yard. The image of Ryan's hateful outpourings being projected onto a wide screen and loud sound system is certainly arresting. One police officer put it to us: 'What are we going to do about the Kevin Ryans of this world?' The kind of response which emerges from the account we have outlined suggests that demonizing people as unambiguously racist, and rotten to the core, is not necessarily the most productive route. Rather than making people who 'do racism' deviant pariahs it would be more challenging to see the ordinariness and in many cases respectability of racism. This might be summed up as concentrating on the deeds and actions, rather than being preoccupied with racism as a category of being.

What is telling is that the suggestion to move away from uniform and homogenous notions of 'the racist' is that it is so often resisted. For the police, there is something uncomfortable about the suggestion that racists can conduct themselves unspectacularly in everyday life. As we have argued throughout this volume, however, people who 'do racism' don't have to be, and are often not monsters. This does not in any way make them less culpable for their acts. In fact, focusing on the acts themselves deepens the culpability in that it focuses on making people responsible for their conduct. If racism is defined in deeds, then there can be no appeal to a damaged self, background or identity that can mitigate responsibility. The racist doer can so often invoke a self-exculpating fiction – 'it was my culture that made me like this' or 'everyone is racist around here' – as a cipher to explain his or her conduct.

From this point of view, one might ask what kind of moral act is at work when 'racists' are projected on screen and witnessed by a disapproving audience? Those in the aisles can feel shocked and repulsed. Yet, such images of the picaresque are comforting because they picture racism as something remote to the viewers' experience, up there on screen, sounds and faces that have been brought back from a distant and grotesque world. Such moves organize racism into particular social locations, namely those of the white male working-class. At the same time, racism is ushered out of the respectable spheres in which whiteness remains as an invisible normative centre (Dyer 1997). In opposition to such a simplified perspective we want to suggest that it is important to develop an ethical position that has two central elements. First, a commitment to identify and judge the ways in which racism features in fan cultures as specific acts. Second, a commitment to remaining critical of the ideological processes which organise simultaneously racism into the bodies of 'deviant' white working-class men and out of the middle class professional spheres where racism and racial inequality possess more genteel manners.

In Part Two we tried to show in a nuanced manner the ways in which the boundaries of institutional inclusion and exclusion work through informal and embodied cultural processes. Here we want to suggest that something more subtle is at play than what is usually referred to as 'institutional racism'. The Macpherson report into the death of Stephen Lawrence defined institutional racism as:

Conclusion

> The collective failure of an organisation to provide an appropriate and professional service to people because of their colour, culture, or ethnic origin. It can be seen or detected in processes, attitudes and behaviour which amounts to discrimination through unwitting prejudice, ignorance, throughtlessness and racist stereotyping which disadvantage minority ethnic people. (Macpherson 1999: 28)

This is not the place to engage in a detailed discussion of the veracity of this definition, but we do want to raise some questions about the adequacy of applying this definition to the types of inclusions and exclusions that operate within the context of football culture.

Macpherson may be right to point to the implicit processes that result in the forms of institutional exclusion, but the problem with focusing on a formulaic identification of institutional racism is that it can result in a blanket definition of racism that does not give us a language to identify racism in process. Rather, we want to suggest that it is possible to name and stipulate the ways in which inclusion and exclusion is policed through the issuing or revoking of the cultural passports that define how to be a player, a coach, a manager or an executive. We want to suggest that it is only possible to apprehend how these complicated exclusions operate inside the game if a new language emerges that can identify these processes and how they are performed and embodied.

Unlike the spaces occupied by football fans the board room, football field, training pitch and dressing room do not usually facilitate the expression of crude and explicit forms of racism. However, this does not necessarily lead to the conclusion that professional cultures of football offer a model of social integration. Rather, we would argue, the forms of racial understanding within these spheres often operate in ways that normalize particular cultural formations at the expense of others. What is prevalent within the English game is a reliance on the notion that 'others,' whether black, foreign or Asian, should assimilate within the normative – white coded – working class, masculine traits that form the cultural centre of English football.

These implicit forms of exclusion are however disguised or rendered invisible in 'white eyes' by their very normalcy. In contrast to the occasional explosion of overt forms of racist expression amongst fans, the non-articulated racialized practices within the institutional cultures of the game do not reveal themselves or figure as priorities inside the institutions and the organizational bodies and within the public debate about racism in football. In turn this enables football to discard the notion that racism exists inside its professional structures whilst stating its public opposition to overt forms of racism found amongst the fans and individual players.

* * *

We want to end by posing a question that we often reflected on in the course of our research. If black players can pull on the England shirt, is it possible that one day there could be a black manager of England? Since 1995 – when we began the research for this book – there have been four England managers. Most recently and controversially, the job has been given for the first time to an overseas coach, namely the Swede Sven Goran Erikson. The reverberations about this appointment have been reviewed in Chapter 8. Interestingly enough, objections to this appointment have been expressed widely, including from some well-known black professionals inside the game. For example Ian Wright complained on national television that the new manager wasn't an Englishman, not 'one of our own'. Such vociferous statements highlight the ways in which the position of England manager is still talked about as a symbolic role that represents the hopes and aspirations of 'the nation'.

Whatever the merits of appointing a foreign manager to manage England, it is an intriguing thought to imagine the possibility of a black Englishman taking up this challenge? We put this question to a range of people during our research, including Glenn Hoddle while he was England manager. Asked if he could imagine a black successor, he replied:

> See in my eyes, that day is round the corner, that can happen – and you will see it happen. Again, it is whatever the talents are – if they are talented and they do enough in football that they feel that they could become good managers then that warrants it – it is nothing to do with what colour of skin they have, or where their backgrounds have come from - it is about the ability to do a job. (Interview, 21 October 1996)

Here Hoddle reproduces the commonly held assumption that football is a meritocracy, that talent wins out in the end, and that in sport it is ultimately about ability. Increasingly, managerial jobs are viewed as a matter of 'personality appointments.' But being a football manager is also about being viewed as a safe bet, someone who can cope with the dressing room and command respect. Inside, the game there linger stereotypes and images about the capacities of black players to make the transition into management. These ambivalences are often expressed through rumours that are laced with racial stereotypes that range from some black players being viewed as having 'difficult personalities' to concerns about alleged 'sexual indescretion' and scandal. One white manager put this crudely. He claimed that the managerial aspirations of a former black professional would be scotched because 'he can't keep his dick in his trousers'. In this context 'personality appointments' refer to particular types of racialized personality.

On the same day that this question was put to Glenn Hoddle we also asked Ian Wright if he ever saw a day when there could be a black England manager? His response was immediate and unequivocal:

> No, simple as that, I can't see it. I don't think there will be, for whatever reason. It is a very tricky little area there you are going into, so I would like there to be one [a black

England manager], but honestly in your heart of hearts can you see it? (Interview, 21 October 1996)

This echoes Stuart Hall's observation that while black sports personalities like Ian Wright have come to represent the very essence of the English game on the pitch there remains little prospect of this being carried through into the boardrooms, executive boxes and dug outs (Hall 1998).

Some of the faces have changed in English football. Yet, this has not produced much of a shift towards a more multicultural game. Piara Powar identified the key issue when he concludes: 'There are very few places where . . . this game of football is not an affirmation of whiteness, it's not an affirmation of the sort of white working-class identity' (Interview, 26 September 2000). Here he identifies an all-pervasive, yet unspoken, whiteness that lies at the centre of English football both inside the institutions and in its stadia. Stan Collymore told journalist Simon Hattenstone that his early retirement from the game was because he fell foul of a 'white, middle-aged, hard core football mentality'. He simply didn't fit within the unspoken norms of English football. Collymore liked to read the broadsheet newspapers and keep up with current affairs but was also prone to depression and infamously struck his then girlfriend Ulrika Jonsson in a nightclub. Collymore concluded that the palpable consequences of his depression are simply incomprehensible to those inside the game:

> Ninety nine percent of football managers are white, working-class blokes. They grew up with football and alcohol. You can be an alcoholic and get sent to prison and be welcomed back for your strength of character in English football. But if you suffer from an illness that millions suffer from, one of the only illnesses in which people take their own lives, you get called spineless and weak. (Cited in Hattenstone 2001: 4)

In Collymore's case his depression was taken as evidence of an effete and flawed character. Through such forms of dismissiveness white managers can situate players like Collymore outside of the values and preferences that define English football culture. The emergence of black and overseas players may have changed the face of the game, yet amongst its white fans and those inside the sport these changes have been met by an ambivalent mixture of acknowledgment and ridicule that can flip in turn between love and loathing, adulation and hatefulness. It is a game where partial acceptance and racism are two faces of the same coin.

Despite the groundswell of interest in football since the early 1990s that has moved its fan base well beyond its conventional class constituency, sport is still viewed largely as trivial by writers, academics and cultural critics. It has yet to make it to the intellectual 'top table' for serious cultural attention. This is a mistake because the true significance of sport is in its ability to bring into focus the lines drawn around belonging, collective identity and exclusion. Part of the drama unfolding in football stadia is the ambiguous contours of racial exclusion and cultural integration in England. Here we can find not only the bearing of cultural shifts but also the enduring racisms that dress racial biology or absolute ideas about 'foreign cultures' in a new uniform. This is not to say that we can read society through the cipher of sport. As Mike Marqusee has written, while sport reflects important cultural shifts, it is in fact a 'distorting mirror' (Marqusee 1999: 295). The emergence and success of black and minority athletes may belie, or mask, the deepening of marginalization and exclusion in the communities from which they emerged. The rising prominence of black footballers points to a real shift within English culture but at the same time there are limits in the degree to which the English game is becoming more culturally inclusive. In the end the result is a partial and incomplete assimilation, in which black players are playing a game on terms defined by white power brokers and the core values of English football culture. This not only tells us something about the diagnosis of our present predicament but it also provides insight into the kind of multicultural future, with all its paradoxes, that lies ahead.

Bibliography

Advisory Group Against Racism and Intimidation (1995) *Press Release: Football Unites Against Racism and Intimidation Campaign Launch for 1995/96 Season*, 28 September 1995, London: AGARI.

Allan, J. (1989) *Bloody Casuals: Diary of a football hooligan*, Aberdeen: Famedram.

Allison, L. (1997) 'Biology, ideology and sport' in Allison, L. (ed.) *Taking Sport Seriously*, Aachen: Meyer & Meyer Sport.

Appadurai, A. (1995) 'The production of locality' in Fardon, R. (ed) *Counterworks: Managing the Diversity of Knowledge* London: Routledge.

Armstrong, G. (1993) 'Like that Desmond Morris?' in Hobbs, D. and May, T. (eds) *Interpreting the Field: Accounts of ethnography*, Oxford: Clarendon Press.

—— (1994) 'False Leeds: The construction of hooligan confrontations' in Giulianotti, R. and Williams, J. (eds) *Game Without Frontiers: Football, identity and modernity*, Aldershot: Arena.

—— (1998) *Football Hooligans: Knowing the score*, Berg: Oxford.

—— (1999) 'Kicking Off with the Wannabe Warriors' in Perryman, M. (ed.) (1999) *The Ingerland Factor: Home truths from football*, Edinburgh: Mainstream.

Armstrong, G. and Giulianotti, R. (eds) (1997) *Entering the Field: New perspectives on world football*, Oxford and New York: Berg.

Armstrong, G. and Harris, R. (1991) 'Football hooligans: theory and evidence', *Sociological Review* 39, 3: 427–58.

Back, L. (1991) 'Social Context and Racist Name Calling: An Ethnographic Perspective on Racist Talk within a South London Adolescent Community', *European Journal of Intercultural Studies* 1, 3: 19–39.

—— (1996) *New Ethnicities and Urban Culture: Racisms and multiculture in young lives*, London: UCL Press.

Back, L. and Chapman, K. (2000) *Black Lions: A history of black Millwall players*, London: Millwall Football Club.

Back, L., Crabbe, T. and Solomos, J. (2001) *Ooh Ah Showab Khan: Evaluation*, ARC Theatre Ensemble.

Back, L., Crabbe, T. and Solomos, J. (1996) *Alive and Still Kicking*, London: Advisory Group Against Racism and Intimidation.

—— (1998) 'Racism in Football: Patterns of Continuity and Change' in Brown, A. (ed.) *Fanatics! Power, identity and fandom in football*, London: Routledge.

Back, L. and Quaade, V. (1993) 'Dream Utopias, Nightmare Realities: Imaging Race and Culture with the World of Benetton Advertising', *Third Text*, 22: 65–80.

Back, L. and Solomos, J. (eds) (2000) *Theories of Race and Racism: A reader*, Routledge: London.

Bailey, E. and Muller, N (1998) *Jamaica's Reggae Boys: World Cup 1998*, Kingston: Ian Randle Publishers and Creative Communications Inc.

Bains, J. and Johal, S. (1998) *Corner Flags and Corner Shops: The Asian football experience*, London: Phoenix.

Bains, J. and Patel, R. (1996) *Asians Can't Play Football*, Birmingham: D-zine.

Bale, J. (1994) *Landscapes of Modern Sport*, Leicester: Leicester University Press.

Barber, B. R. (1996) *Jihad vs. McWorld: How globalism and tribalism are reshaping the World*, New York: Ballantine Books.

Barnes, J. (1999) *John Barnes: The autobiography*, London: Headline.

Barthes, R. (1973) *Mythologies*, London: Paladin Books.

Bateson, G. (1978) 'A Theory of Play and Fantasy' in Bateson, G. *Steps to an Ecology of Mind*, London: Paladin Books.

Bauman, Z. (1988) 'Exit visas and entry tickets: the paradoxes of Jewish assimilation', *Telos*, 77: 45–77.

Benjamin, W. (1992) 'Theses on the Philosophy of History' in Benjamin, W. *Illuminations*, London: Fontana Press.

Benson, R. and Raphael, A. (1993) 'Football vs. Racism', *The Face*, 54: 54–60.

Berger, J. (1991) *And Our Faces, My Heart, Brief as Photos*, New York: Vintage Books.

——— (1995) *Face To Face with Jeremy Isaacs*, London: British Broadcasting Association.

Bloch, M. (1974) 'Symbols, Song, Dance and Features of Articulation, or is Religion an Extrene Form of Traditional Authority', *Archives Europennes de Sociologie*, XV, 1: 55–81.

Bourdieu, P. (1986) *Distinction: A Social Critique of Judgement and Taste*, London: Routledge.

——— (1999a) 'The State, Economics and Sport' in H. Dauncey and G. Hare *France and the 1998 World Cup: the National Impact of a World Sporting Event*, London: Frank Cass.

——— (1999b) 'Understanding' in Bourdieu, P. (ed) *The Weight of the World: Social suffering in contemporary society*, Cambridge: Polity Press.

——— (2000) *Pascalian Meditations*, Cambridge: Polity Press.

Bowler, D. and Bains, J. (2000) *Samba in the Smethwick End: Regis, Cunningham, Batson and the football revolution*, Edinburgh and London: Mainstream Publishing.

Brick, C. and Allirajah, D. (1997) 'Racism and the football fan: perceptions of the problem', in *Partnership to Keep Racism out of Football: Conference proceedings*, Reading: Public Impact Communications.

Brimson, D. and Brimson, E. (1996a) *England My England*, London: Headline.

—— (1996b) *Everywhere We Go: Behind the matchday madness*, London: Headline.

—— (1997) *Capital Punishment*, London: Headline.

—— (1998) *Derby Days*, London: Headline.

Bromberger, C. (1993) 'Allez L'O.M., forza Juve': The passion for football in Marseille and Turin' in Redhead, S. (ed.) *Passion and the Fashion: Football fandom in the new Europe*, Aldershot: Avebury.

Bromberger, C. with Hayot, A. and Mariottini, J-M. (1993) 'Fireworks and the Ass' in Redhead, S. (ed.) *Passion and the Fashion: Football fandom in the new Europe,* Aldershot: Avebury.

—— (1994) 'United Colours of Football', *The Big Issue*, North West Supplement 19: 16–17, 23–29 August 1994.

—— (1995) 'Football and Race: "Asian Games", *When Saturday Comes*, February, 96: 14–17.

—— (1997) 'Let's All Have a Disco? Football, Popular Music and Democratization', in Redhead, S. *The Club Cultures Reader: Reading in popular cultural studies*, Oxford: Blackwell.

—— (1998) *Fanatics!*, London: Routledge.

—— (1999) Thinking the unthinkable or playing the game? The Football Taskforce, New Labour and the reform of English football, in Hamil S., Michie J. and Oughton C. (eds), *A Game of Two Halves: The business of football*, Edinburgh: Mainstream.

Brown, A., Crabbe, T., Ennis, G., Thomas, P., Bishop, S. and Galbraith, R. (1994) *United Colours of Football*, Liverpool: Football Supporters Association.

Brown, A. and Walsh, A. (1999) *Not for Sale: Manchester United, Murdoch and the defeat of BSkyB*, Mainstream: Edinburgh.

Buford, W. (1991) *Amongst the Thugs*, London: Secker & Warburg.

Bull, D. (ed.) (1992) *We'll Support You Evermore: Keeping faith in football*, London: Duckworth.

—— (ed.) (1994) *Football and the Commons People*, Sheffield: Juma.

Burns, J. (1999) *Barca: A people's passion*, London: Bloomsbury.

Canter, D., Comber, M., and Uzzel, D. L. (1989) *Football in Its Place: An environmental psychology of football grounds*, London: Routledge.

Carrington, Ben (1997) "I love my people, I'm no Uncle Tom!": race, nation and the sexualisation of the black male sporting body', Paper Presented to the North American Society for the Sociology of Sport Annual Conference: Border Crossings: Sport, Bodies and the Third Millennium, 5–8 November, University of Toronto.

—— (1998) 'Football's coming home but whose home? And do we want it? Nation, football and the politics of exclusion', in Brown, A. (ed.) *Fanatics! Power, identity and fandom in football*, London: Routledge.

—— (1999) 'Too Many St George Crosses to Bear', in Perryman, M. (ed.) *The Ingerland Factor: Home truths from football*, Edinburgh: Mainstream.

—— (2001) 'Postmodern blackness and the celebrity sports star: Ian Wright, "race" and English identity' in Andrews, D. and Jackson, S. (eds) *Sports Stars: the politics of sport celebrities*, London: Routledge.

Carrington, Bruce (1986) 'Social Mobility and Sport', *British Journal of Sociology of Education*, 7, 1: 3–18.

Carver, M., Garland, J., and Rowe, M. (1995) *Racism, Xenophobia and Football: A preliminary investigation*, Research Paper 3, Centre for the Study of Public Order, University of Leicester.

Casella, P. and Gilman, P. (1993) 'Millwall's problem? Football's problem? Society's problem?', *The Lion Roars*, (Millwall) 47: 16–17.

Cashmore, E. (1982) *Black Sportsmen*, London: Routledge & Kegan Paul.

—— (1983) 'The Champions of Failure: Black Sportsmen', *Ethnic and Racial Studies* 6, 1: 90–102.

Chaudhary, V. (2000) 'Indian Summer Kicks Off At the Cottage', *The Guardian*, July 22, p. 6.

Centre for Contemporary Studies (1981) *Football and the Fascists*, London: CCS.

Clarke, J. (1973) *Football and the Skinheads*, Occasional Paper, Centre for Contemporary Cultural Studies, University of Birmingham.

—— (1978) 'Football and Working Class Fans: Tradition and Change', in Ingham, R. (ed.) *Football Hooliganism: The wider context*, London: Inter-Action.

Cohen, P. (1972) 'Subcultural Conflict and Working Class Community', *Working Papers in Cultural Studies 2*, Birmingham: CCCS.

—— (1988) 'The Perversion of Inheritance', in Cohen, P. and Bains, H. (eds) *Multi-Racist Britain*, Basingstoke: Macmillan.

—— (1998) 'Review Symposium – Routes of Racism: The social basis of racist action,' *Race, Ethnicity and Education*, 1, 2: 296–303.

Cohen, S. (ed.) (1971) *Images of Deviance*, Harmondsworth: Penguin.

Commission for Racial Equality (1991) *Press Release* 12 August 1991, London: Commission for Racial Equality.

—— (1993) *News Release 'Kick Racism Out of Football': Campaign Launched by CRE*, 12 August 1993, London: Commission for Racial Equality.

—— (1994) *Kick It!*, London: Commission for Racial Equality.

—— (1995) *Kick It Again*, London: Commission for Racial Equality.

Conn, D. (1997) *The Football Business: Fair game in the '90s?*, Edinburgh and London: Mainstream Publishing.

Cooper, C. (1993) *Noises in the Blood: Orality, gender and the 'vulgar' body of Jamaican popular culture*, Basingstoke: Macmillan Caribbean.

Critical Eye (1991) *Great Britain United*, 12 September 1991 London: Channel 4.

Critcher, C. (1991) 'Putting on the style: aspects of recent English football' in Williams, J. and Wagg, S. (eds) *British Football and Social Change: Getting into Europe*, Leicester: Leicester University Press.

Dauncey, H. and Hare, G. (1999) 'Conclusion: The impact of France 98', in H. Dauncey and G. Hare, *France and the 1998 World Cup: the national impact of a world sporting event*, London: Frank Cass.

Davidson, S. and King, C. (1998) *Black Fan's Experience at Anti-Racist Focus Matches: Report for the Kick it Out South London Initiative*, London: Martin Shaw King Trust.

Davies, P. (1990) *All Played Out: The full story of Italia '90*, London: Mandarin.

Dobson, S. (1999) *Cultures of Exile: An examination of the construction of 'refugeeness' in contemporary Norwegian society*, dissertation submitted for the degree of Doctor of Philosophy in the Graduate Studies and Research in Humanities, Nottingham Trent University.

Duke, V. (1991) 'The Sociology of Football: A Research Agenda for the 1990s', *Sociological Review* 39, 3: 627–45.

Dunning, E. (1999) *Sport Matters: Sociological studies of sport, violence and civilization*, London: Routledge.

Dunning, E., Murphy, P. and Waddington, P. (1991) 'Anthropological versus sociological approaches to the study of football hooliganism: some critical notes', *Sociological Review*, 39, 3: 459–78.

—— (1992) *Violence in the British Civilising Process*, Discussion Papers in Sociology No S92/2, Department of Sociology Leicester: University of Leicester.

Dunning, E., Murphy, P., and Williams, J. (1986) 'Spectator Violence at Football Matches: Towards a Sociological Explanation', *British Journal of Sociology* XXXVII, 2: 221–44.

(1988) *The Roots of Football Hooliganism: An historical and sociological study*, London: Routledge.

—— (1988) 'White', *Screen*, 29, 4: 44–56.

Dyer, R. (1997) *White*, London: Routledge.

Earle, R (1998) 'Bully boys pick on the small fry', *The Observer*, 28 June, p. 5.

Edwards, H. (1969) *The Revolt of the Black Athlete*, New York: Free Press.

—— (1973) *Sociology of Sport*, Homewood: Dorsey Press.

Electric Blue (1995) *Electric Blue: End of season special*, No. 30.

Elias, N. (1969) *The Quest for Excitement: Sports and leisure in the civilising process*, Oxford: Blackwell.

—— (1978) *The Civilising Process: The history of manners*, Oxford: Basil Blackwell.

—— (1982) *State Formation and Civilisation*, Oxford: Basil Blackwell.

Fleming, S. and Tomlinson, A. (1995) *Football, Xenophobia and Racism – Europe and the old Britain*, Draft Submission to European Union Human Mobility Network, Chelsea School Research Centre, University of Brighton.

Football Association (1997) *Report to FIFA relating to the FIFA World Cup qualifying match: Italy v England, at the Olympic Stadium, Rome*, 11 October 1997, London: Football Association.

Football Task Force (1998) *Eliminating Racism from Football: A report by the football task force submitted to the Minister for Sport*, London: The Football Trust.

Foucault, M. (1977) *Discipline and Punish: The birth of the prison*, Harmondsworth: Penguin.

—— (1979) 'On Governmentality', *Ideology and Consciousness*, 6: 5–23.

Fradley, K. (1983) *Football Hooliganism Demystified: An Examination of Football Crowd Disorder in the West Midlands*, MPhil Dissertation, University of Birmingham.

Francis, M. (1997) *Guvnors*, Bury: Milo.

Fraser, N (1998) 'Cup of Joy' *The Guardian, G2* 15 July, pp. 2–3.

Fynn, A. and Guest, L. (1994) *Out of Time – Why football isn't working*, London: Simon & Schuster.

Garland, J. and Rowe, M. (1996) 'Football, Racism and Xenophobia II: Challenging Racism and Xenophobia', in Merkel, U. and Tokarshi, W. (eds) *Racism and Xenophobia in European Football: Sport, leisure and physical education trends and developments*, Volume 3, Aachen: Meyer & Meyer Verlag.

Geertz, C. (2000) *Available Light: Anthropological reflections on philosophical topics*, Princeton: Princeton University Press.

Gilroy, P. (1987) *There Ain't No Black in the Union Jack: The cultural politics of race and nation*, London: Hutchinson.

—— (1990) 'The End of Anti-Racism' in Ball, W. and Solomos, J. (eds) *Race and Local Politics*, London: Macmillan.

—— (1993) *Small Acts: Thoughts on the politics of black cultures*, London: Serpent's Tail.

—— (2000a) 'The Dialectics of Diaspora Identification', in Back, L. and Solomos, J. (eds) *Theories of Race and Racism: A reader*, Routledge: London.

—— (2000b) *Between Camps: Race, identity and nationalism at the end of the color line*, London: Allen Lane.

Giulianotti, R. (1993) 'Soccer Casuals as Cultural Intermediaries', in Redhead, S. (ed.) *The Passion and the Fashion: Football fandom in the new Europe*, Aldershot: Avebury.

—— (1994) 'Social identity and public order: political and academic discourses on football violence', in Giulianotti, R., Bonney, N. and Hepworth, M. (eds.) *Football, Violence and Social Identity*, London: Routledge.

—— (1996) *A Sociology of Scottish Fan Culture*, University of Aberdeen, Department of Sociology, Unpublished PhD Thesis.

—— (1999) *Football: A Sociology of the Global Game*, Cambridge: Polity.

Giulianotti, R., Bonney, N., and Hepworth, M. (eds) (1994) *Football, Violence and Social Identity*, London: Routledge.

Giulianotti, R. and Williams, J. (eds) (1994) *Game Without Frontiers: Football identity and modernity*, Aldershot: Arena.

Goldberg, D. T. (1993) *Racist Culture*, Oxford: Blackwell.

Greenfield, S. and Osborn, G. (1996) 'When the whites go marching in? racism and resistance in English football', *Marquette Sports Law Journal* 6, 2: 315–35.

The Guardian (1998a) [Ross, I.] 'Soccer star's fury at racist insult', 5 March, p. 3.

—— (1998b) [Thorpe, M.] 'Orange dreams . . . in black and white', 5 June.

Hall, A. (1998) 'Is NASSS homophobic and racist?', *Sociology of Sport Online*, http: www.brunel.ac.uk/depts/sps/sosol/index.htm.

Hall, S. (1978) 'The Treatment of Football Hooliganism in the Press', in Ingham, R. (ed.) *Football Hooliganism: The wider context*, London: Inter-Action.

—— (1981) 'The Whites of Their Eyes: Racist Ideologies and the Media', in Bridges, G. and Brunt, R. (eds) *Silver Linings: Some strategies for the eighties*, London: Lawrence & Wishart.

—— (1998) 'Aspiration and attitude: reflections on Black Britain in the nineties,' *New Formations*, 33, Spring: 38–46.

Hall, S., Clarke, J., Critcher, C., Jefferson, T., and Roberts, B. (1978) *Policing the Crisis*, London: Macmillan.

Hall, S. and Jefferson, T. (eds) (1976) *Resistance Through Rituals*, London: Hutchinson.

Hamilton, A. (1982) *Black Pearls of Soccer*, London: Harrap.

Hartmann, D. (2000) 'Rethinking the Relationship Between Sport and Race in American Culture: Golden Ghettos and Contested Terrain,' *Sociology of Sport Journal*, 17, 3 : 229–53.

Hattenstone, S. (2001) 'The Monday Interview All Played Out: Stan Collymore', *The Guardian G2*, 16 April, pp. 2–4.

Haynes, R. (1995) *The Football Imagination: The rise of football fanzine culture*, Aldershot: Arena.

Hebdige (1979) *Subculture: The meaning of style*, London: Routledge.

Hewitt, R. (1986) *White Talk, Black Talk: Inter-racial friendship and communication amongst adolescents*, Cambridge: Cambridge University Press.

Hill, D. (1989) *Out of His Skin: The John Barnes phenomenon*, London: Faber & Faber.

Hobbs, D. and Robbins, D. (1991) 'The boy done good: football violence, changes and continuities', *Sociological Review*, 39, 3: 551–79.

Hoberman, J. (1997) *Darwin's Athletes: How sport damaged black America and preserved the myth of race*, Boston: Houghton Mifflin Company.

Hodgson, D. (1985) *The Everton Story*, London: Arthur Baker Limited.

Holland, B. (1992a) 'Burnden's Burden – Summary of Findings from a Survey of Residents Living in Burnden, Bolton, on their experience of Racial Harassment from football fans attending Bolton Wanderers Football Club Matches' Unpublished Working Paper, University of Bradford.

—— (1992b) 'Racial Harassment in Football', in Stirling District Council (1992) *Tackling Back: Racism in Scottish Football*, Report of Conference Proceedings University of Stirling, 30 June 1992 Stirling: Stirling District Council.

—— (1993a) 'Evidence on Racial Attacks and Harassment in and Around Football Grounds – Submission to the House of Commons Home Affairs Committee 1992–93 Session', University of Bradford.

—— (1993b) 'Racial Harassment in and Around Football Grounds: Uses of the Football (Offences) Act 1991 and Other Legal Options' Paper delivered to Seminar on Racial Harassment: The Legal Dimension, York, 24–25 June 1993, Commission for Racial Equality.

—— (1993c) 'Marching Altogether: Resistance to Racism by Leeds United Football Fans: A Case Study', Unpublished Paper.

—— (1995) '"Kicking racism out of football": an assessment of racial harassment in and around football grounds', *New Community*, 21, 4: 567–86.

—— (1997) 'Surviving leisure time racism: the burden of racial harassment on Britain's black footballers', *Leisure Studies*, 16: 261–77.

Holland, B., Jackson, L., Jarvie, G. and Smith, M. (1996) 'Sport and racism in Yorkshire: a case study' in Hill, S. and Williams, J. *Sport and Identity in Northern England*, Keele: Keele University Press.

Holt, R. (1989) *Sport and the British*, Oxford: Oxford University Press.

Home Office (1986) *Committee of Inquiry into Crowd Safety and Control at Sports Grounds: The final report*, (Popplewell Report), London: HMSO.

—— (1990) *The Hillsborough Stadium Disaster – 15th April 1989: Final Report of Inquiry by Lord Justice Taylor*, London: HMSO.

—— (1991) *Policing Football Hooliganism: Second report of the House of Commons Home Affairs Committee Vols I and II*, London: HMSO.

—— (1994) *Racial Attacks and Harassment: Third report of the House of Commons Home Affairs Committee Vol II*, London: HMSO.

Hornby, N. (1992) *Fever Pitch: A fan's life*, London: Victor Gollancz.

—— (1993) *My Favourite Year: A collection of new football writing*, London: H. F. & G. Witherby.

—— (2000) 'Arsenal Man and Boy', *The Observer – Sporting Monthy* 5, 10–15.

Horton, E. (1995) *The Best World Cup Money Can Buy: The World Cup of 1994 and the world of football*, Oxford: Ed Horton.

Houlston, D. (1982) 'The occupational mobility of professional athletes', *International Review of Sport Sociology*, 2, 17: 15–26.

The Independent [Blair, O.] 'They think they've no chance before even kicking a ball', 1 November 1997.

The Independent on Sunday (1995) [Malik, K.] 'Minorities face 'wall' in soccer', 17 September, p. 9.

Ingham, R. (ed.) (1978) *Football Hooliganism: the wider context*, London: Inter Action.

International Review for the Sociology of Sport (1998) 'Review Symposium: Darwin's Athletes', 33, 1: 83–99.

James, C. L. R. [1963] (1994) *Beyond a Boundary*, London: Serpent's Tail.

Jarvie, G. and Maguire, J. (1994) *Sport and Leisure in Social Thought*, London: Routledge.

Jarvie, G. and Reid, I. (1997) 'Race relations, sociology of sport and the new politics of race and racism', *Leisure Studies*, 16, 4: 211–19.

Jary, D., Horne, J., and Bucke, T. (1991) 'Football "fanzines" and football culture: a case of successful "cultural contestation"', *Sociological Review*, 39, 3: 581–97.

Jérôme, P (1998) 'Zizou's two goals did more for the equal rights of citizens than a thousand speeches denouncing racism', *The Guardian G2* 15 July, p. 3.

Katz, D. (1994) *Just Do It: The Nike spirit in the corporate world*, Holbrook: Adams Publishing.

King, A. (2000) 'Football fandom and post-national identity in the New Europe', *British Journal of Sociology*, 51, 3: 419–42.

Keith, M. (2000) 'Identity and the Spaces of Authenticity' in Back, L. and Solomos, J. (eds) *Theories of Race and Racism: A reader*, Routledge: London.

King, C. (2000) *Play the White Man*, Critical Urban Studies – Occasional Papers, London: Centre for Urban and Community Research, Goldsmiths College.

King, J. (1996) *The Football Factory*, London: Jonathan Cape.

—— (1998) *England Away*, London: Jonathan Cape.

Kuper, S. (1994) *Football Against the Enemy*, London: Orion.

Lansdown, H. and Spillius, A. (eds) (1990) *Saturday's Boys: The football experience*, London: Collins Willow.

Leeds Trades Council (1988) *Terror on our Terraces: NF, football violence and Leeds United*, Leeds: LTC.

Levi, P. (1987) *Moments of Reprieve*, London: Abacus.

Lindsey, E. (1999) 'Di France Ting' in Mora Y Arauio, M. and Kuper, S. *Perfect Pitch: 4. Dirt*, London: Headline.

Long, J., Tongue, N. and Spracklen, K. (1996) *What's the Difference: A study of the nature and extent of racism in Rugby League*, Leeds: The Rugby Football League.

Macdonald, I, Bhavnani, T. Khan, L, and John, G. (1989) *Murder in the Playground: The report of the Macdonald Inquiry in to racism and racial violence in Manchester schools*, London: Longsight Press.

Macpherson, Sir W. (1999) *The Stephen Lawrence Inquiry: Report of an inquiry by Sir William Macpherson of Cluny*, London: HMSO.

Maguire, J. (1991) 'Sport, Racism and British Society: A Sociological Study of England's Elite Male Afro/Caribbean Soccer and Rugby Union Players' in Jarvie G. (ed.) *Sport, Racism and Ethnicity*, London: Falmer Press.

Marcus, G. E. (1994) 'After the Critique of Ethnography: Faith, Hope and Charity, but the Greatest of these is Charity' in Borofsky, R. (ed.) *Assessing Cultural Anthropology*, New York: McGraw-Hill Inc.

Marks, J. (1999) 'The French National Team and National Identity: 'Cette France d'un "bleu métis"', in H. Dauncey and G. Hare *France and the 1998 World Cup: The national impact of a world sporting event*, London: Frank Cass.

Marqusee, M. (1999) *Redemption Song: Muhammad Ali and the spirit of the sixties*, London: Verso.

Massey, D (1991) 'A Global Sense of Place', *Marxism Today*, June: 25–26.

Masouri, J (1998) 'Funkin for Jamaica', *Echoes* 13 June, p. 12.

McKay, J. (1995) 'Just Do It': corporate sports slogans and the political economy of 'enlightened racism', *Discourse: Studies in the cultural politics of education*, 16, 2: 191–201.

McKenzie, P. (1998) 'Whose side are you on?', *The Big Issue*, May 25–31, pp. 8–9.

Melnick, M. (1988) 'Racial Segregation by Playing Position in the English Football League: Some Preliminary Observations', *Journal of Sport and Social Issues*, 12, 2: 122–30.

Mercer, K. (1994) *Welcome to the Jungle: New positions in black cultural studies*, New York and London: Routledge.

Miles, R. (1989) *Racism*, London: Routledge.

Miller, D (1991) 'Absolute Freedom in Trinidad', *Man* 26: 323–41.

Mills, C. Wright (1959) *The Sociological Imagination*, Oxford: Oxford University Press.

Moorhouse, H. F. (1991) 'Football hooligans: old bottle, new whines?', *Sociological Review* 39, 3: 489–502.

Mundt, S. (ed.) (2000) *Cultural Studies and the Working Class: Subject to change*, New York and London: Cassell.

Murphy, P., Williams, J. and Dunning, E. (1990) *Football on Trial: Spectator violence and development in the football world*, London: Routledge.

Murray, B. (1984) *The Old Firm: Sectarianism, sport and society in Scotland*, Edinburgh: John Donald.

Nawrat, C. and Hutchings, S. (1995) *The Sunday Times Illustrated History of Football*, London: Reed International Books.

The Observer (1999) 'Not in front of the Queen', 12 September, p. 16.

O'Connor, J. (1993) Translator's Introduction to Christian Bromberger 'Allez l'O.M., forza Juve': The passion for football in Marseille and Turin', in Redhead, S. (ed.) *Passion and the Fashion: Football fandom in the New Europe*, Aldershot: Avebury.

O'Donnell, H. (1994) 'Mapping the mythical: a geopolitics of national sporting stereotypes', *Discourse and Society*, 5, 3: 345–80.

Orakwue, S. (1998) *Pitch Invaders: The modern black football revolution*, London: Victor Gollancz.

Palace Echo (1995) *Palace Echo*, Issue 2, March 1995, back page.

Parekh, B. (2000) *The Future of Multi-Ethnic Britain: Report of the Commission on the Future of Multi-Ethnic Britain*, London: Profile Books.

Parkinson on Sport (1994) *Racism in Football*, Radio 5 Live, 12 August 1994.

Perryman, M. (ed) (1999) *The Ingerland Factor: Home truths from football*, Edinburgh: Mainstream.

Poivre D'Arvor (1999) 'Foreword' in Dauncey. H. and Hare, G. *France and the 1998 World Cup: The national impact of a world sporting event*, London: Frank Cass.

Porter, G. (1992) *The English Occupational Song*, Uppsala: Swedish Science Press.

Powar, P. and Tegg, B. (1998) *Kick it Out: Annual Report 1997–98*, London: Kick it Out.

Red Attitude (1995) 'RA Editorial', *Red Attitude*, 4 March 1995.

Redhead, S. (1991a) *Football with Attitude*, Manchester: Wordsmith.

—— (1991b) 'The era of the end or the end of an era: Football and youth culture in Britain', in Williams, J. and Wagg, S. (eds) (1991) *British Football and Social Change: Getting into Europe*, Leicester: Leicester University Press.

—— (ed.) (1993) *The Passion and the Fashion: Football fandom in the New Europe*, Aldershot: Avebury.

—— (1997) *Post-Fandom and the Millennial Blues*, London: Routledge.

Redhead, S. and McLaughlin, E. (1985) 'Soccer's Style Wars', *New Society*, 16 August.

Renton, A. (1998) 'Oafish bravado of le style anglais', *Evening Standard*, 15 June, p. 3.

Ritzer (1998) *The McDonalisation Thesis*, Thousand Oaks: Pine Forge Press.

Robins, D. (1984) *We Hate Humans*, Harmondsworth: Penguin.

Robson, G. (2000) *'No One Likes Us, we don't care': The myth and reality of Millwall fandom*, Oxford: Berg.

Robson, G. (1999) 'Millwall Football Club: Masculinity, Race and Belonging', in S. Mundt (ed) *Cultural Studies and the Working Class*, New York: Cassell.

Rosaldo, R. (1989) *Culture and Truth: The remaking of social analysis*, London: Routledge.

Ross, I. (1998) 'Soccer star's fury at racist insult', *The Guardian*, 5 March, p. 3.

Rowlands, A. (1990) *Trautmann*, Derby: Breedon Books.

Rushdie, S. (1991) *Imaginary Homelands*, London: Granta Books.

Russell, D. (1997) *Football and the English: A social history of association football in England, 1863–1995*, Preston: Carnegie.

Sampson, K. (1998a) *Awaydays*, London: Jonathan Cape.

—— (1998b) 'Fat of the land', *Guardian Weekend* 6 June, pp. 10–16.

Silverman, D. (1993) *Interpreting Qualitative Data: Methods for analysing talk, text and interaction*, London: Routledge.

Sir Norman Chester Centre for Football Research (1996) *FA Premiere League Fan Survey 1995/6*, Leicester: Sir Norman Chester Centre for Football Research, University of Leicester.

Sociological Review (1991) 'Special Football Issue', 39: 3.

Solomos, J. and Back, L. (1995) *Race, Politics and Social Change*, London: Routledge.

—— (1996) *Racism and Society*, Basingstoke: Macmillan.

Stirling District Council (1992) *Tackling Back: Racism in Scottish Football*, Report of Conference Proceedings University of Stirling, 30 June 1992, Stirling: Stirling District Council.

Stokes, M. (1996) '"Strong as a Turk": Power, Performance and Representation in Turkish Wrestling' in MacClancy, J. (ed.) *Sport, Identity and Ethnicity*, Oxford: Berg.

Stubbs, D. (1997) 'The Drinking Man's Game', *Goal*, February 17: 50–5.

Sugden, J. and Tomlinson, A. (1994) *Hosts and Champions*, Aldershot: Arena.

The Sunday Mirror (1995) [Silver, N.] 'Boss in Race Storm', 29 January, p. 60.

Suttles, G. (1968) *The Social Order of the Slum: Ethnicity and territory in the inner city*, Chicago: University of Chicago Press.

Szymanski, S. (1997) 'Beaten in the race for the ball', *New Economy*, pp. 212–17.

—— (1999) 'The market for soccer players in England after Bosman: Winners and losers', in Kesenne, S, and Jeanrenaud, C. (eds) *Player market regulation in professional team sports*, Antwerp: Standaard Uitgeverij.

—— (2000) 'A Market Test for Discrimination in the English Professional Soccer Leagues', *Journal of Political Economy*, 108, 3, 590–603.

Taylor, I. (1971) 'Soccer Consciousness and Soccer Hooliganism', in Cohen, S. (ed.) *Images of Deviance*, Harmondsworth: Penguin.

—— (1982) 'On the Sports Violence Question: Soccer Hooliganism Revisited', in Hargreaves, J. (ed.) (1982) *Sport, Culture and Ideology*, London: Routledge.

—— (1987) 'Putting the Boot into a Working-Class Sport: British Soccer after Bradford and Brussels', *Sociology of Sport Journal*, 4: 171–91.

Taylor, R. (1992) *Football and its Fans: Supporters and their relations with the game 1885–1985*, Leicester: Leicester University Press.

Taylor, R., Ward, A., and Newburn, T. (eds) (1995) *The Day of the Hillsborough Disaster: A narrative account*, Liverpool: Liverpool University Press.

Terrill, C. (1996) 'High Noon', *Soho Stories,* BBC: London.

Thorpe, M. (1998a) 'Batistuta dances around bewildered Reggae Boyz', *The Guardian*, 22 June, p. 3.

—— (1998b) 'Orange dreams . . . in black and white', *The Guardian*, 5th June.

Thrill, A. (1998) *You're Not Singing Anymore: A riotous celebration of football chants and the culture that spawned them*, London: Ebury Press.

Thurgood, J. (1998) 'Ungoodthink: Race busy bodies in big flap', *Spearhead*, 347, January, p. 17.

Ticher, M. (1997) 'When in Rome', *When Saturday Comes*, No. 130, December, pp. 14–16.

Tuan, Yi-Fu (1974) *Topophilia*, Englewood Cliffs NJ: Prentice-Hall.

—— (1976) 'Geopiety' in Lowenthall, D. and Bowden, M. J. *Geographies of the Mind: Essays in historical geography*, New York: Oxford University Press.

Turner, R. (1990) *In Your Blood: Football culture in the late 1980s and early 1990s*, London: Working Press.

Tyndall, J. (1996) 'Euro 96: Faces of Nationalism', *Spearhead*, No. 330, p. 7.

Urry, J. (1990) *The Tourist Gaze*, London: Sage.

Vasili, P. (1994) 'The Right Kind of Fellows: Nigerian Football Tourists as Agents of Europeanization', *The International Journal of the History of Sport*, 11, 2: 191–211.

—— (1998) *The First Black Footballer, Arthur Wharton 1865–1930: An absence of memory*, London: Frank Cass.

—— (2000) *Colouring Over the White Line: The history of black footballers in Britain*, Edinburgh: Mainstream Publishing.

Wagg, S. (1984) *The Football World: A contemporary social history*, Brighton: Harvester.

Walsh, N. (1977) *Dixie Dean: The story of a goal scoring legend*, London: Pan Books.

Walvin, J. (1975) *The People's Game: A social history of British football*, Newton Abbot: Readers Union.

Ward, C. (1989) *Steaming In: Journal of a football fan*, London: Simon & Schuster.

—— (1996) *All Quiet on the Hooligan Front*, Edinburgh and London: Mainstream Publishing.

Warner, B. (2000) 'Net Strategy with Balls', *The Industry Standard Europe*, 2 November: 54–61.

Waters, C. (1988) *Racial Chanting and the Ultra Right at Football Matches*, BA Dissertation Leeds Polytechnic.

Webster, O. (1998) 'United they Stand', *The Guardian*, 14 July, p. 3.

West Midlands Sports Council (1991) *Sport, Race and Racism* , Birmingham: West Midlands Sports Council.

Whannel, (1979) Football, crowd behaviour and the press, *Media, Culture and Society*, 1, 327–42.

When Saturday Comes (1993a) 'Racism in Football', Feature incorporating 'Colour Field', 'Winter's Tale', 'Leeds by Example' and 'Black and Blues' 72 [February]: 16–19.

—— (1993b) 'Football and Race', 80 [October]: 8–10.

White, J. (1998) 'Unwelcome guests ready to party on their own', *The Guardian*, 30 June.

Wickham, G. (1992) 'Sport, Manners, Persons, Government: Sport, Elias, Mauss, Foucault', *Cultural Studies*, 6, 2: 219–31.

Williams, J. (1986) 'White Riots: the English football fan abroad', in Tomlinson, A. and Whannel, G. (eds) *Off the Ball*, London: Pluto.

—— (1991) 'Having an away day: English football spectators and the hooligan debate', in Williams, J. and Wagg, S. (eds) (1991) *British Football and Social Change: Getting into Europe*, Leicester: Leicester University Press.

—— (1992) *Lick My Boots – Racism in English football*, Leicester: Department of Sociology, University of Leicester.

—— (1994) '"Rangers is a Black Club": "Race", Identity and Local Football in England', in Giulianotti, R. and Williams, J. (eds) *Game Without Frontiers*, Aldershot: Avebury.

Williams, J. , Bucke, T., Dunning, E. & Murphy, P. (1989) *Football and Football Spectators After Hillsborough: A national survey of members of the Football Supporters' Association*, Sir Norman Chester Centre for Football Research, University of Leicester.

Williams, J., Dunning, E., and Murphy, P. (1989) *Hooligans Abroad: The behaviour and control of England fans in Continental Europe*, Second Edition, London: Routledge.

Williams, J. and Wagg, S. (eds) (1991) *British Football and Social Change: Getting into Europe*, Leicester: Leicester University Press.

Williams, J. Long, C. and Hopkins, S. (2000) *Passing Rhythms: Football, music and popular culture in Liverpool*, Oxford: Berg Publishers.

Willis, P. (1977) *Learning to Labour*, London: Saxon Press.

Willis, P. and Trondman, M. (2000) 'Manifesto for Ethnography', *Ethnography*, 1, 1: 5–16.

Wolf, B. [1947/8] (1993) 'Ecstatic in Blackface: the Negro as a Song-and-Dance Man' in Mezzrow, M. and Wolf, B. *Really the Blues*, London: Flamingo.

Woolnough, B. (1983) *Black Magic: England's black footballers*, London: Pelham.

Wright, I. (1996) *Mr Wright: The explosive autobiography of Ian Wright*, London: Collins Willow.

Index

Adams, Tony, 130, 159, 195
Adidas, 207, 270
Advisory Group Against Racism and
    Intimidation (AGARI), 12, 95, 192–3, 194–7
alcohol, association with football, 139–41
Alexander, Keith, 181
Allen, Keith, 249–50
American sport, and racism, 281–2
Amokachi, Daniel, 52, 112–13
Anderson, Ijah, 116
Anderson, Viv, 182
Anelka, Nicolas, 156, 177
Anti-Fascist Action (AFA), 191
anti-racism
    campaigns, 192–7, 211–18
    corporate multiculturalism, 206–11
    fan culture, 187–92
    institutional responses, 193–4, 197, 199–200
    legislation, 202–6
    political interests, 199–201
    see also racism
ARC Theatre Ensemble, 12, 199
Arendt, Hannah, 30
Armstrong, G., 229
Asian fans, 31, 236, 277–80
Asian players, lack of, 177–9
asylum seekers, racism against, 217–18
Atcha, Mohammed, 198
Auschwitz, 14, 240–1

Bailey, Earl, 258
Bains, Jas, 31, 177–9, 212
Bale, John, 41, 47
Barker, Simon, 258
Barlow, Colin, 174
Barnes, John, 52–5, 142–3, 181, 186, 195,
    233–4
Barnsley, racist fans, 121–3
Barrett, Earl, 113
Barthes, Roland, 272–3

Bates, Ken, 187
Bateson, G., 58
Batson, Brendon, 106, 151
Baumann, Zygmunt, 77–8
Beckford, Darren, 146
Berger, John, 9, 73, 74
Berkovich, Eyal, 146
Birmingham City
    black fans, 87, 88
    violence by fans, 98–9
black fans
    abuse of, 87–8
    England supporters, 235–9
    and 'Englishness', 255–6, 275
    hooliganism by, 86–7, 236
    inclusion of, 85–95, 101–2
    Jamaica supporters, 13, 255–63, 265–70, 275
black players
    acceptance of, 78–85
    and England supporters, 233–5
    England team, 173, 253–4
    friendship groups, 150–4
    imperial legacy, 3–4
    Jamaican team, 257–8
    as managers, 180–2
    numbers of, 22–3, 31
    racial abuse by fans, 1–2, 21, 49–50, 52–5,
        127–32
    racial abuse by players, 146–50
    sporting prowess of, 281–2
    wages, 175
    see also foreign players
Blake, Nathan, 23, 171–2
Blake, Noel, 182
Blanchflower, Danny, 47
Blissett, Luther, 181
Bloch, Maurice, 73–4
Boli, Basil, 209
Bourdieu, Pierre, 13, 95, 143
Bowry, Bobby, 83–5

Bowyer, Lee, 144–5
Brentford, v Millwall, 116
Bright, Mark, 96, 145–6, 152, 175
British National Party, 15, 106, 193, 243
Britishness, and 'Englishness', 255
Bromberger, Christian, 7–9, 42
Brown, Adam, 70
Bruno, Frank, 143
Burrell, Horace, 257
Burton, Deon, 257

Campbell, Nicky, 168–9
Cannoville, Paul, 1–2
Canter, David, 26–7
Cantona, Eric, 21, 156, 185–6, 189–91, 207–11
Carbone, Benito, 177
Carling No.1 Panel, 161–2
Carrington, Ben, 153, 251, 275
Cass, Bob, 162
chants *see* football songs
Charlton, Jack, 146
Charlton Athletic, 41
Charlton Athletic Race Equality Partnership
    (CARE), 215
Chelsea
    electric fencing, 187
    foreign players, 1–2, 154
Cohen, Phil, 30
Collymore, Stan, 146, 148, 177, 287
Combat 18, 21–2, 193, 237, 240
commercialism, sponsorship, 4–5, 206–11
Commission for the Future of Multi Ethnic
    Britain, 5–6
Commission for Racial Equality (CRE), 28–9,
    192
Cool Cats, 86
Cooper, Carolyn, 259
Coppell, Steve, 161, 162–3
corporate multiculturalism, 206–11, 270
Craig, Douglas, 197
Crichter, Chas, 32
Cripps, Harry, 78
Croatians, stereotypes, 35–6
Crooks, Garth, 50
Crystal Palace
    black fans, 99, 102
    black players, 96–8, 143, 175
    case-study research, 10

class composition of fans, 46–7
fan culture and racism, 96–102
fanzines, 208
goal celebrations, 154
and Millwall, 84
songs of fans, 44, 46
Cuff, Will Charles, 48
Cunningham, Laurie, 106, 151, 152

Dalglish, Kenny, 181
Dancey, Hugh, 274
Davidson, Sharon, 91
Davies, David, 193
Dean, William Ralph ('Dixie'), 50–1, 141
Desailly, Marcel, 155–6
Di Matteo, Roberto, 2
Dobson, Stephen, 218
dress code, England supporters, 228
Duberry, Michael, 144–5
Dyer, Richard, 142

Earle, Robbie, 257, 268–9
Edwards, H., 180
Elias, Norbert, 272
Emerson, 1, 177
England supporters
    behaviour abroad, 223–33, 242–51
    black fans, 235–9
    and black players, 233–5
    culture of, 228–9, 232, 251
    increase in, 242–4
    in Marseille, 223–4, 226–7, 237–8
    and Mexican Wave, 250
    nationalism, 233–42
    in Poland, 14, 224, 230–3, 235, 240–1
    in Rome, 244–5
    and Turks, 248–9
    World Cup 1998 (France), 245–51
England team
    black players, 173, 253–4
    manager of, 221–3, 286–7
    v Germany (Wembley, 2000), 221–2
    v Ireland (Dublin, 1995), 21–2, 193, 240
    v Italy (Rome, 1997), 244
'Englishness'
    and black fans, 255–6, 275
    meaning of, 223
    of supporters, 71–2

support for, 123–6
whiteness of, 254
Ennis, Graham, 53–4
Entine, Jon, 282
'entry ticket' metaphor, 9, 77–8, 278–9
Eriksson, Sven Goran, 222–3, 286
Eubanks, Paul, 258
Euro 96, English patriotism, 242–3
Everton
  abuse of David Ginola, 114–15
  abuse of Ruud Gullit, 127–30, 131–2
  black players, 112–13
  case-study research, 10
  founding of club, 48
  insults by Millwall, 59–62
  Liverpool comparison, 51–2
  Liverpool derby matches (1987), 52–5
  racist reputation, 7, 50–1, 52–5, 65–6, 113

fan culture
  anti-racist, 187–92
  England supporters, 228–9, 232, 251
  inclusiveness, 9, 95
  Jamaica team supporters, 259–61
  and locality, 42–7
  normative structure, 9
  and racism, 96–102
  sounds of, 47–55
  structure of antipathy, 127–32
fanzines, anti-racism, 187–92
Farrer, Donald, 86–7
Fashanu, John, 80–1, 143
Ferdinand, Les, 209–10
Ferguson, Alex, 36, 185, 216
FIFA, and racism, 200
Fleming, S., 32
Football Association
  and anti-racism campaigns, 193–4, 199–200
  'white' culture of, 167
Football in the Community Schemes, 197
football culture
  racism, 7–9
  see also fan culture
Football League, and anti-racism campaigns, 197
Football (Offences) Act (1991), 27, 55, 202
football songs
  Crystal Palace, 44, 46

England supporters, 225–6, 227, 246–7
  group identity of, 72–4
  legislation against, 202
  Liverpool, 48–50
  Manchester City, 68–70
  Millwall, 44–6, 55–66, 74
  racism of, 43–6, 49
  sequences of, 59–66
Football Supporters' Association (FSA), 187, 188
Fan Embassy (Italia 90), 244, 247
Football Task Force (FTF), 200–1
Football Unites Racism Divides (FURD), Sheffield, 215–17
foreign players
  image of, 8–9
  racial abuse of, 113–15, 127–32
  reactions to, 154–8
  see also black players
Foxes Against Racism, 215
France
  multiculturalism, 270–4
  see also Marseille; World Cup 1998 (France)
Francis, Mickey, 86
Fraser, Nick, 271, 273

Gascoigne, Paul, 253
Gilroy, Paul, 4, 15, 152, 177, 206, 253, 281
Ginola, David, 114–15
Gordon, Dean, 47
Gould, Bobby, 23, 171–2
Gray, Andy, 47, 84–5, 96, 175
'Greigsie', 123–6, 224, 233–5, 239–41, 242–3
Grieve, John, 283
group identity, football songs, 72–4
Gullit, Ruud
  Let's Kick Racism campaign, 195
  as manager, 1, 182
  media perceptions of, 35
  racial abuse of, 114, 127–30, 131–2

Hall, Paul, 257
Hall, Stuart, 3, 149, 287
Hare, Geoff, 274
Harkness, Steve, 148
Hartmann, Douglas, 281–2
Hearn, Barry, 167–9
Hegazi, Hussein, 78

Henry, Lez, 255–6
heroism, and advertising, 207
Hill, David, 142–3
Hill, Jimmy, 54, 163–4
Hill, Tony, 207
Hillaire, Vince, 47, 49
Hillsborough stadium disaster, Taylor report,
    27
Hoberman, John, 33, 35, 143, 149, 153, 156,
    175
Hoddle, Glenn, 286
Holt, R., 23
home, notion of, 40, 74
hooliganism
    and black fans, 86–7, 236
    and England supporters, 223–6
    impact of, 186–7
    and racism, 23–9, 106–7, 191, 193–4
humour, role in racism, 111–13

imperialism legacy
    black sportsmen, 3–5
    Liverpool, 48, 50
Ince, Paul, 253
Indian team, English supporters, 277–8
inflatable bananas, at Manchester City, 68
institutional racism
    definition, 284–5
    denial of, 164–6, 183, 193
    'normalization' of, 166–73
    racial stereotyping, 173–9
Ireland, Republic of v England (Dublin, 1995),
    21–2, 193, 240
Italia 90, 244, 247
Italy, England supporters, 244–5

Jackson, Paul, 103–5
Jacquet, Aimé, 274
Jamaican team
    black English fans, 13, 255–63, 265–70, 275
    black English players, 257–8
    music of, 259
    women supporters, 259–62, 263–4, 266–7
    World Cup 1998 (France), 255–6, 268–9
James, Alex, 249
James, C. L. R., 3–4
James, David, 52
Jérôme, Philippe, 271

Jewish identity, Tottenham Hotspur, 109–10
Johal, Sanjiev, 31
Johnson, Michael, 121–3
Jordan, Michael, 207
Juninho, 1

Kamara, Chris, 179, 181
Katz, Donald, 206
Keane, Roy, 159
Keays, Helen, 281
Keegan, Kevin, 221–2
Keith, Michael, 149
Kelly, David, 142
Kelly, Graham, 161
Kendall, Howard, 70
Kicking Out, 12, 174
Kicking Racism Out of Football, 215
Kick It Out campaign, 33, 213, 215
Kick Out the Scum campaign, 199
King, Anthony, 280
King, Colin, 91, 159
King, John, 229
Koeman, Ronald, 114
Kosovan refugees, tickets to Millwall, 217–18

Lawrence, Junior, 147–8
Leboeuf, Frank, 2, 156, 158
Lee, Trevor, 78, 89
Leeds Fans United Against Racism and Facism
    (LFUARF), 187, 188
Leeds United, racism, 30
legislation, anti-racism, 202–6
Leicester City, Foxes Against Racism, 215
Leicester University
    research on football violence, 25–6
    survey on racism, 65–6
Le Pen, Jean Marie, 270–2
Let's Kick Racism Out of Football campaign,
    12, 28–9, 95, 192–4, 199, 209
Let's Kick Racism/Respect All Fans campaign,
    12, 95, 186, 194–6
Leyton Orient, 167–8
Libero!, 198
Lineker, Gary, 195
Liverpool F.C.
    Everton comparison, 51–2
    Everton derby matches (1987), 52–5
    the Kop, 48

songs of fans, 48–50
see also Merseyside
locality, and football culture, 42–7
Long, Catherine, 48

Macpherson report, 14, 163, 284–5
Maguire, J., 175
managers, black, 180–2, 286–7
Manchester City
  black fans, 86–7
  case-study research, 10
  'Englishness' of supporters, 71–2
  fanzines, 211
  inflatable bananas, 68
  institutional racism, 174
  and local community, 39–41, 43, 71–2
  racism of fans, 106
  reasons for supporting, 66–8
  songs of fans, 68–70
Manchester United
  British players, 158
  globalisation, 280–1
  and Manchester City, 70
  Red Attitude fanzine, 189–91
Manning, Bernard, 170
Marqusee, Mike, 288
Marseille
  England supporters, 223–4, 225, 226–7, 237–8
  immigrants, 8, 227
Martin Shaw King Trust, 215
Masouri, John, 257, 259, 279–80
Mauge, Ronnie, 146
McCormick, Peter, 145
McDonaldization of stadia, 197–8
McKay, J., 210
McKenzie, Paul, 255–6, 274
Mellor, David, 200–1, 279
Melnick, M., 175
Mercer, Kobena, 76
Merseyside
  imperialism legacy, 48, 50
  Liverpool/Everton comparison, 51–2
Mexican Wave, 250
Middlesborough, foreign players, 1, 177
Mihajlovic, Sinisa, 157
Millwall
  anti-racism, 203–5, 215, 217–18

black fans, 87–94
black players, 76–85
  case-study research, 10
  and Crystal Palace, 84
  fan culture, 44–5, 47–8, 75–6, 89
  Kosovan refugees, 217–18
  racism of fans, 118–21, 133–4
  racist reputation, 7, 81
  songs of fans, 44–6, 55–66, 74
  stadium move, 41
  surveillance of racists, 205–6
'monkey noises', 50, 81, 202
Montgomery, Alex, 162
Moran, Richie, 149–50
Morgan, Alister, 257
Morley, Paul, 68
Muller, Nazma, 258
multiculturalism, 206–11
  France, 270–4

Najeib, Sarfraz, 144
National Front, 21, 86
nationalism
  England supporters, 233–42
  and racism, 123–6
'neighbourhood nationalism', 37, 46
neo-Nazi supporters, 14, 193–4, 237, 240–1
Nevin, Pat, 1–2
Newcastle United, 114–15
Newton, Eddie, 2
Nigerian players, 175–6
Nike, 4, 206–11, 270
Noades, Ron, 174–5, 181
Norman, Barry, 197

O'Donnell, Hugh, 35, 158
O'Leary, David, 144
L'Olympique de Marseille, 8
Onuora, Iffy, 203
Other, songs aimed at, 63–4

Paphitis, Theo, 80, 133–4
Parry, Rick, 161
Patel, Raj, 31, 177–9
Pearce, Jonathon, 162
Perkins, Sean, 65
Peterson, Frank, 78
Petit, Emmanuel, 156, 177

players *see* black players; foreign players;
  white players
Poivre D'Arvor, Olivier, 273
Poland, England supporters, 14, 224, 230–3,
  235, 240–1
political groups, right-wing, 106–7, 237, 240
political interests, anti-racism, 199–201
Popplewell inquiry, 26–7
Powar, Piara, 179, 213–15, 277–8, 282–3, 287
Powell, Jeff, 222–3
Professional Footballers' Association (PFA),
  192

racial abuse
  age of perpetrators, 116–17
  anti-Semitic, 109–10
  control of, 197–9
  and humour, 111–13
  by players, 146–50
  of players, 1–2, 21, 49–50, 113–15, 127–32
  structure of antipathy, 127–32
  types of, 107–17
  and violence, 115–16
  see also racism
racial biology, 281–2
racialization, 33–8
  framework for intervention, 214
  identity structure, 55–66, 93–4
  sporting prowess, 281–2
racism
  control of, 283–4
  convictions for, 103–5, 117–23
  and fan culture, 6, 96–102
  and hooliganism, 23–9, 106–7, 191, 193–4
  institutional, 163–6, 193, 284–5
  media reporting of, 65–6
  and nationalism, 123–6, 233–42
  nature of, 29–32, 105–7
  normalization of, 117, 133–4
  perpetrators of, 117–26
  research agendas, 32–8
  stereotyping, 173–9, 267
  unwitting, 163
  see also anti-racism; racial abuse
racists, fans, 117–26
Ranieri, Claudio, 158
Ravenelli, Fabrizio, 1, 177
Redhead, Steve, 69

Redknapp, Harry, 157
Reggae Boyz *see* Jamaican team
regionalism, football songs, 55–66
Regis, Cyrille, 32, 105–6, 151, 152
Regis, Dave, 146
religion, comparison with football, 41
Renton, Alex, 231
research methods, 9–15
Respect All Fans *see* Let's Kick Racism
Robson, Bryan, 181
Robson, Garry, 41, 43, 44–5, 60, 61, 84
Rock Against Racism, 189
Ronaldo, 4–5, 207, 282
Ruddock, Neil, 156–7
Rushdie, Salman, 6
Ryan, Kevin, 117–21, 203–5, 283–4

Salako, John, 47, 96
sanitization of stadia, 197–8
Schmeichel, Peter, 147–8, 149, 203, 205
Shearer, Alan, 159
Sheffield United, Football Unites Racism
  Divides (FURD), 215–17
Show Racism the Red Card campaign, 142,
  213
Silver, Leslie, 182
Simmons, Mathew, 21, 185–6, 189–91, 193,
  207–8
Simoes, Rene, 257
Simpson, Fitzroy, 257
Simpson, O.J., 111–12
Sinclair, Frank, 2
Slaughter, Patrick, 238
Smith, Alan, 176
songs *see* football songs
Southwell, Ken, 103–5
stadia
  sanitization of, 197–8
  as symbolic home, 41, 43
stereotyping, racial, 173–9, 267
structure of antipathy, fan culture, 127–32
Sunderland, v Millwall, 116–17
surveillance of racists, Millwall, 205–6, 283–4
Szymanski, Stefan, 175

Taylor, Gordon, 161
Taylor, Ian, 24–5
Terrill, Christopher, 243

Thomas, Michael, 52
Thorpe, Martin, 268
Thrills, Adrian, 48
Ticher, Mike, 223
Tomlinson, A., 32
Tottenham Hotspur, Jewish identity, 109–10
Turks, and England supporters, 248–9
Turner, Richard, 28
Tyndall, John, 243

Ulster Unionism, 106, 241
United Colours of Football campaign, 188
United Colours of Football 2 magazine, 216–17
Urry, J., 231

Van Hooijdonk, Pierre, 177
Vasili, Phil, 22–3
Venables, Terry, 35, 161, 222
Vialli, 'Luca', 154, 158
Vieira, Patrick, 146, 156–7, 283
Vindaloo, 249–50
Vodafone, 280–1

Wakeling, Vic, 161
Walcott, Derek, 3
Walker, Phil, 78, 89
Walsh, Nick, 50
Walters, Mark, 52
Watson, Russell, 221
Welsh, Irvine, 216
Wembley stadium, last game at, 221
West Bromwich Albion, 277
Wharton, Arthur, 215
White, Jim, 250–1
whiteness
  and Englishness, 254

normalization, 141–6, 163
white players
  banter, 141–3
  racial abuse by, 146–50
Whylie, Gary, 81
Williams, John, 30, 31, 142, 165, 187
Williams, Raymond, 280
Wimbledon, black players, 143
Wise, Denis, 1
Witter, Tony, 76, 81–3, 84–5, 116–17, 119
women
  Jamaica team supporters, 259–62, 263–4, 266–7
  racist behaviour, 116–17
  supporters, 244
Woodgate, Jonathon, 144–5
World Cup 1998 (France)
  England supporters, 245–51
  French team, 270–4
  Jamaican team, 255–6, 268–9
  Jamaica supporters, 263–70, 275–6
  official band, 249
Wright, Ian
  abuse by Millwall, 81–3
  abuse by players, 146
  at Crystal Palace, 47, 97, 175, 176
  on England manager, 286–7
  nationalism of, 152–3, 234–5, 253, 255, 275
  and Nike, 209
  respect for, 126
  and Schmeichel, Peter, 147–8, 149, 205

Yeboah, Tony, 155
Young, Eric, 175

Zidane, Zinedine, 207, 273
Zola, Gianfranco, 2